Seven Sacred Sites

Magical Journeys That Will Change Your Life

Serene Conneeley

SEVEN SACRED SITES: Magical Journeys That Will Change Your Life

First edition US copyright © 2010 Serene Conneeley

National Library of Australia Cataloguing-in-Publication Data:

Conneeley, Serene
Seven Sacred Sites: Magical Journeys That Will Change Your Life
1st edition 2009
ISBN: 978-0-9805487-0-9
        203.5

1. Voyages and travel.
2. Spirituality.
3. Sacred space.
4. Magic.
5. Nature – religious aspects.

Published by Blessed Bee
PO Box 449, Newtown, NSW 2042 Australia
Website: www.SereneConneeley.com
Email: SevenSacredSites@yahoo.com.au

Cover: Daniella Spinetti
Photos: Serene Conneeley
Illustrations and author photo: Justin Sayers

To see the colour photo gallery that appeared in the Australian edition,
visit www.SereneConneeley.com/gallery.html

"Twenty years from now you will be
more disappointed by the things that you
didn't do than by the ones you did do.
So throw off the bowlines.
Sail away from the safe harbour.
Catch the trade winds in your sails.
Explore. Dream. Discover."

Mark Twain, 19th century American author

"The journey not the arrival matters."

TS Eliot, American poet

Praise for Seven Sacred Sites

"Sometimes, if you're lucky enough, you'll come across a book with an energy so great it moves beyond its pages. This is such a book. Brilliantly written and stunningly produced, it will inspire you to dream, to travel and to ponder your own place on our wonderful planet."   *Kylie Matthews, Manly Daily*

"This book is a rich and lovely, very wise and tender companion, with lovely insights and lots to share and inspire you in your travels, be they physical or imaginary. Serene is a beautiful writer, and captures the mythos and history of each place in bright, delicious ways."   *Lucy Cavendish, author*

"This spiritual, historical and geographical journey will help you discover not only about our wondrous surroundings but, perhaps more importantly, yourself as well. A must-read book." *Andrea Black, travel editor, New Idea*

Praise for A Magical Journey

"Serene has released another gem for the adventurers amongst us. This is about recording the inner journey, whether you're on the road to Timbuktu or on the sofa contemplating your navel. The first section explains the benefits of journalling, with exercises to express your deepest desires and tools to release emotional blockages and unleash your authentic self. The journal itself, peppered with inspiring quotations, forms the second part. What distinguishes it from the pack is Serene's emphasis on enchanting the writing process. She includes full information on the Wheel of the Year, and lots of ideas on how to bring the festivals, feast days and seasonal cycles alive in the exploration of your inner world."   *Joanne Lock, Spheres magazine*

"A beautiful journal to plan and record your spiritual journey to a sacred place or on the inner planes. It joins her first book on my essential reading list for sacred journeys to Egypt."   *Elisabeth Jensen, Isis Mystery School*

"This helped me connect back to self. I am so much more at peace and aware of my behaviours – good and not so good! I venture forth with boldness and a renewed sense of self, and I thank Serene from the depths of my heart and soul for this opportunity to grow." *Marissa Clarkson, bereavement counsellor*

Praise for The Book of Faery Magic

"This is a delightful guide that blends traditional faery lore with modern magical practices like guided meditation, setting up a faery altar and creating a wand, planting a faery garden and recipes and craft projects to deepen your relationship with the fae and discover your own inner wild self (not to mention have fun along the way!). There is a vast amount of information and a strong environmental message."   *Bryony, Fae Nation*

"This is the ultimate guide to all things faery, and is entertaining, informative and enthralling. If you believe in faeries or are just curious, there is much to learn in this book, from history and legends, magical gifts and sites, to unique beings from around the world."   *Larissa Chapman, Good Reads*

Thank you...

Love and gratitude to Nigel Bartlett, Elisabeth Knowles and Justin Sayers for reading this book as it took shape and offering compliments, criticism and encouragement through the long and winding journey, to Fiona Horne, who first suggested that I write a book when she read my emails from Peru, to Daniella Spinetti for making my cover vision so real and so beautiful, to Mum and Lily for testing the recipes, and to Karen Pierce, who held me safe in the jungles of Peru.

A special thank you to the wonderfully inspiring Cassandra Eason, Lucy Cavendish, Doreen Virtue, Colette Baron-Reid, Jude Currivan, Alberto Villoldo, Elisabeth Jensen and Shirley MacLaine, for sharing their stories of their favourite corners of the world.

Love and blessings to...

My sweet husband and precious beloved Justin, for making me tea as I wrote, listening as I nutted out each chapter, motivating me when I was too tired to keep going, drawing the gorgeous illustrations, being on my side through all the battles, sharing my favourite places – and showing me that home can be just as magical as any sacred site.

My wonderful parents, Di and Rob, who believe in me and love me no matter what, who trusted my choices (even when it meant moving far away) and offered support and advice as I worked to manifest my dreams, and who always encouraged me to follow my heart.

My gorgeous sister Amber and her blessed little family, Lily, Grace and Stevie. And Margie and Pete, my "other mum and dad", for loving, helping and supporting me throughout my life and my travels.

All of my beautiful friends, and all those who are working to preserve the earth, from the wisdom keepers of all cultures and environmental groups such as Greenpeace, WWF and Care2 to the individuals who plant a tree, protest about logging, write about global warming, sail pirate ships on the high seas to save the whales, campaign to protect their local area or do any of the million other little things that make such a difference... thank you for making the world a better place.

"We travel, some of us forever,
to seek other states, other lives, other souls."

Anais Nin, French-Cuban author

"We live in a wonderful world that is
full of beauty, charm and adventure.
There is no end to the adventures we can have
if only we seek them with our eyes open."

Jawaharlal Nehru,
activist and first prime minister of India

"Travel is more than the seeing of sights;
It is a change that goes on, deep and permanent,
in the ideas of living."

Miriam Beard, American author and historian

Contents

The magic of the earth

Since ancient times, sacred sites have had a powerful effect on people. Their vibrational essence, beauty, tranquillity and history, along with the magnetic power infused in each one by centuries of pilgrims steeping it with love and energy, can heal people physically, activate them spiritually and open the soul to its divine purpose.

Some are intricate manmade structures, such as the old Inka city of Machu Picchu in Peru and the Pyramids of Egypt, while others are ancient paths of energy like the Camino, a pilgrimage across the north of Spain. Some are elaborately engineered stone circles such as Britain's Stonehenge, and others are natural formations like the Tor, the sacred hill in Glastonbury, England; Uluru, the ancient rock in Central Australia; and the volcanoes, mountains and waterfalls of Hawaii.

There are many more. Each country has several sites that are recognised as sacred, as do all religions and cultures throughout history. Every civilisation has had places permeated with meaning and power, and many of these have survived the ravages of time, conquest and tourism to provide insight into those who lived long ago. Sometimes the original purpose of a site has been lost over the years, yet today the energy can still be felt, even if we don't understand why.

Sacred sites are spiritually significant places that inspire the imagination and activate change and healing in those who spend time there. Visiting any one of them will be both a literal and a symbolic adventure, a journey to one of the most beautiful places on the planet as well as to the deepest, most sacred parts of your self. Interacting with the energies at the site and feeling the power invested there will open you up to the magic of the universe, within and without.

These locations are imbued with a sense of the spiritual, the divine essence some people call God and others call nature, the universe or the supernatural. Yet you don't have to be religious to feel their power or experience the immense peace and emotional growth they inspire, because their impact goes beyond any individual belief system or culture. These areas have a physical energy that is absorbed by everyone who goes there, whether they are consciously aware of it or not.

So what makes a place sacred? I believe every part of this amazing planet is sacred, and that it's the meaning we give a site that provides it with its special power. Areas of nature have a magic to them and create a sense of peace and wellbeing in those who visit, yet cities can weave their own enchantment, fuelling people with strength, ambition and belief in themselves, and inspiring them to move forward in their life.

Different sites are special to different people and for different reasons, yet on a universal level there are some that resonate with everyone, regardless of culture or beliefs. Often these places have been considered sacred for centuries, and countless rituals have been performed, prayers recited and personal power soaked into the earth there which can still be felt today. In other cases it's believed that people from thousands of years ago imprinted their knowledge in the stones or crystals of an area, and this can now be accessed for personal growth. The pyramids and megalithic circles are just some of the sites thought to be repositories of this ancient wisdom.

The weight of the ages also adds significance. In Egypt it's hard not to be moved by the monuments, heat-baked desert and mighty Nile River, which have been central to human history, myth and legend for millennia, and have more recently inspired numerous Hollywood tales.

Most sacred sites are located on leylines, invisible pathways in the earth through which currents of magnetic energy run, similar to the acupuncture meridians of the human body. Our meridians carry chi, life force, while the world's leylines channel the life force of the universe.

Also known as earth currents, holy lines and telluric tracks, leys have been described as the nervous system of the planet. They are routes of spiritual energy that have an intense, measurable power that activates growth and healing, and many people believe it's this powerful earth energy that makes sacred sites so transformational.

Being on or near a leyline increases vitality, heightens awareness and amplifies spirituality and inner wisdom, because their energy is absorbed when you interact with them, either by walking along the lines or spending time at the sites they run beneath. This boosts physical health, increases psychic abilities and connects you to the life force of the planet. Plants grow better along leylines, animals thrive and the air itself sparkles with vivid energy and possibility.

The ancients were aware of leylines, and understood their purpose and how to attune themselves to and work with the energies. The druids and shamans of indigenous cultures utilised this potent earth power by building stone circles and other monuments along the leys. In much the same way that acupuncturists regulate the chi flowing through the human body with the use of tiny needles and heat, the people of old activated and restored the energy of the land by puncturing it with stones and lighting huge bonfires on hills along the alignments.

This also enabled them to tap in to the vibration of the earth and draw it upwards. Power would flow from within the land in to the circles of stones and other sacred places, which people would absorb, harness, amplify and direct through healing rituals and ceremonies. Early Christian monks felt the power of the leylines on some level too, and built churches and temples over existing pagan sites, often using the sacred stones in their construction. And today people are becoming aware again, beginning to sense the magic of the earth energy that has always existed and that can be interacted with at any time.

While the existence of leylines is disputed by some because they can't be seen, they are a universal concept, recognised by cultures that span the globe. Native Americans call them the spirit path, while the Australian Aboriginals have songlines and serpent tracks that link their sacred places. The Inkas of South America had a system of energy grids called ceques, and the art of geomancy known as feng shui is based on the Chinese belief in lung mei, dragon paths, the lines of energy that flow through the earth and influence the fate of those who live along them, and thus the location of towns, the placement of buildings and even the arrangement of furniture.

In Peru a line dubbed Wiracocha's Route links the holy cities and archaeological centres of the Inka Empire in a northwest alignment. In England two intertwining leys, the Michael and Mary lines, run directly from the southwest tip, at Saint Michael's Mount in Cornwall, to Norfolk, the most easterly point, passing through the country's most sacred places – including Boscawen-un stone circle, Glastonbury and Avebury – on the way. Another set, the Apollo and Athena lines, snake around each other in a similar way but run southeast from the bottom of Ireland, intersecting with the Michael and Mary lines at Saint Michael's Mount then flowing through the ocean to Mont Saint Michel in France and through Italy and Greece to the Holy Land.

Dowsers can identify these geomagnetic energies with divining rods, which I experienced within the inner circle of Stonehenge. As a leyline is crossed the rods swing dramatically, before stilling again once it's passed. Some people see this energy clairvoyantly, while others sense it as a physical sensation within the body or as a purely emotional recognition. In Britain in particular a new category of earth science is developing, which recognises and explores the power of leylines.

Spending time at sacred sites, at these mystical places where the physical world becomes the spiritual, lets you experience something greater, something outside of the ordinary. And while some people go on holiday simply to relax, to party in an exotic location or to soak up the sun at a tropical resort, increasingly people are searching for meaning and identity when they travel. They yearn for a sense of spiritual connection or a transformative experience.

A true magical journey will change you in some way. You will be touched by the place you visit, and be inspired to do more, see more and be more when you return to the little corner of the earth that you call home. It will stir the longing in your heart to achieve your dreams, follow your heart and live the connection your soul feels to this great universe, even when you're back in your daily routine. Spending time at any sacred site will allow you to go within, and will open up your heart and transform you and the way you see and experience life.

There will be places in the world you're drawn to, where you'll feel a sense of belonging, a deep knowing that you're home. Maybe you have a heart connection to a people or place, a deep fascination with an ancient culture, a taste for a certain cuisine, a yearning to go somewhere you've never seen. My mum experiences it in the temples and villages of Bali, my aunty feels it in the countryside of France, and my dad is the luckiest of all, for his sacred place is the little corner of Western Australia that he and Mum have made their home for the past 30 years.

No one really knows why people are drawn to certain sites. Perhaps it's reincarnation, and a life lived there long ago. Perhaps it's a genetic memory passed down from distant ancestors – although that hardly explains Mum's Balinese passion. Perhaps it's a sense of peace and familiarity with the type of earth energy that runs through the land.

Whatever it is, journeying to the sacred place that calls to your heart will allow your soul to soar. Sitting by Chalice Well in Glastonbury, you can tap in to the wisdom of the priestesses who used its magical waters for healing. Visiting Uluru in Central Australia will connect you to the primal essence of the earth and attune you to the spirit of nature and the elements. Walking the Camino in Spain, merging your own energy with the planet's leylines, will provide you with profound insights into your past, your present and your future. Performing rituals in the Amazon jungle will help you understand yourself and the fears that are holding you back from achieving your dreams.

These seven sites are some of the places that affected me most deeply as I journeyed around the world, and this is the book I was searching for but never found before I set out on my adventures. It's not so much a guidebook, because there are lots of those available. Instead I wanted to know the spiritual power of each place, its magical history, the way the energies of the earth felt there and how it would open me up to the world and activate change within me.

And so I visited enchanted places as the seasons shifted, took part in ancient rituals to celebrate life and nature, spent time with witches, shamans and healers, and interviewed inspirational spiritual teachers and travellers including Shirley MacLaine, Paulo Coelho and Doreen Virtue. And I discovered that you don't have to be initiated into certain wisdom traditions or be able to clairvoyantly see the spirits of a place to submerge yourself in the energies of these sacred sites.

I'm not a professional psychic, a specially trained priestess or a geologist. I don't channel aliens or dolphins or believe in ascension to another level. I'm just a normal girl who wanted to see the world and experience the magic of it, who followed her intuition and wound up in some of the most incredible, life-changing places on earth.

My wish for you is that, whether you travel overseas or connect to the energy of a foreign place from home, you will start to see the world with new eyes, allow the beauty and magic of this enchanted planet to open you up to your own truths, and most importantly that you will discover the sacredness of your own self.

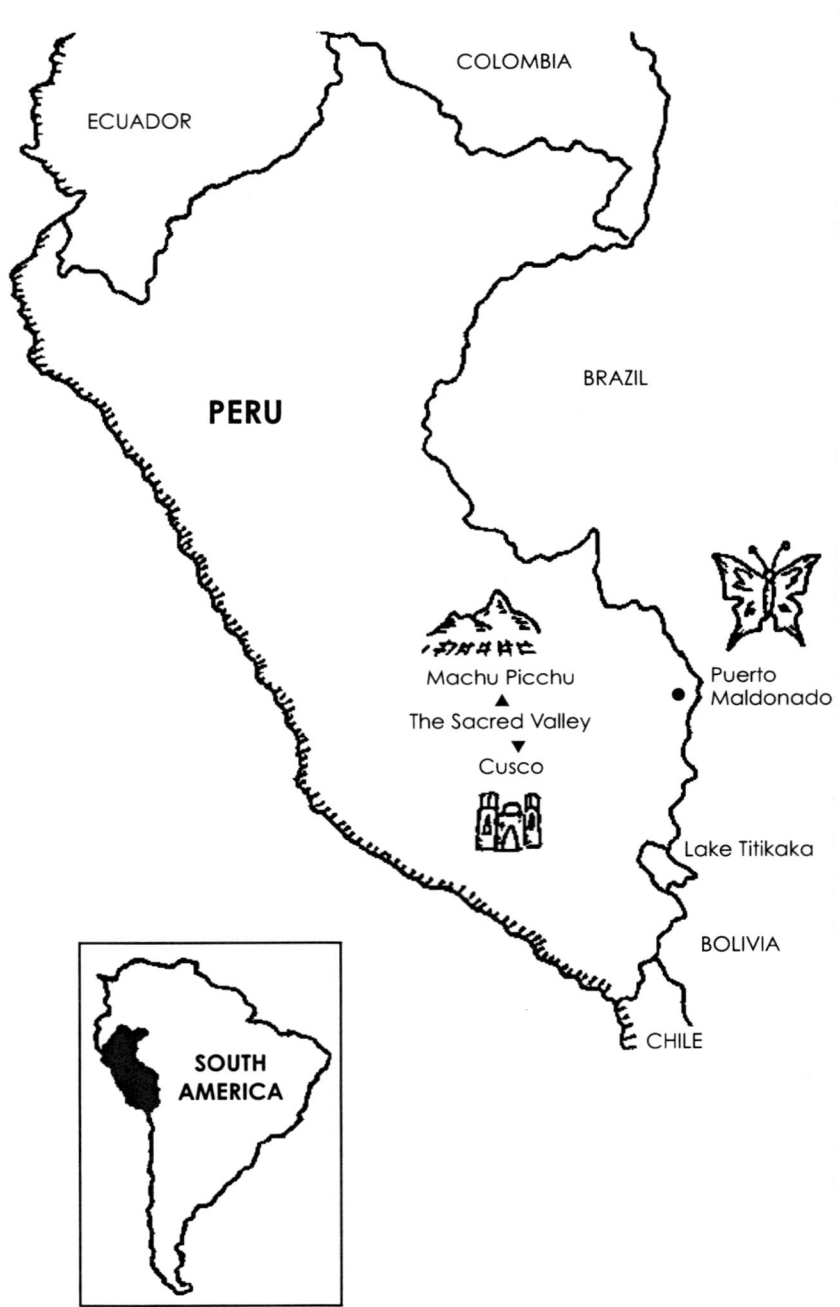

ECUADOR

COLOMBIA

PERU

BRAZIL

Machu Picchu
▲
The Sacred Valley
▼
Cusco

Puerto
Maldonado

Lake Titikaka

BOLIVIA

CHILE

SOUTH
AMERICA

Cast off your old self
and be reborn

Machu Picchu and the Amazon jungle
Peru, South America

Journey deep into the lush Amazon jungle and take part in ancient rituals that cause the death of your old self and lead to spiritual rebirth, then climb the sacred peaks of the Andes to the breathtaking ruins of Machu Picchu and feel your spirit soar above the world, reborn and renewed.

The place

"Each of us used Peru to grow internally. We felt the vividness of our waking hours as intensely as our sleeping hours, each of us experiencing strong dreams that had powerful impact. It was as though we were centred in an energy power point that amplified what ordinarily would have been a more low-key experience."
Shirley MacLaine, American actor and spiritual author

South America, with its wild jungles, powerful rivers and smiling people, has long captured the imagination of people in the west, who are fascinated by the tribal cultures, the lush greenness, the vividly coloured and vibrant wildlife and the almost savage magic that envelops the land and its inhabitants.

It has inspired and intrigued millions of travellers from around the globe, from the backpackers who take off to the jungles, beaches or party towns for months at a time, to the spiritual seekers determined to find divine truths hidden within the ancient ruins, the traditional shamanic practices and the sacred landscape of the continent.

Peru, on the central west coast, is regarded by many as the most spiritual of the South American countries. Its location has made it a melting pot of cultures and traditions, while its geography – tropical beaches and coastline, jungle wilderness, sweeping desert plains and the stunning snowcapped mountains of the Andes – has shaped a diverse nation. It also has the largest indigenous population in the Americas, so the Old Ways have been well preserved and passed on.

The capital, Lima, is a modern city of learning and technology, yet in remote villages, on Andean hilltops and deep in the Amazon jungle, a way of life continues that has endured for millennia. Woolly llamas wander the mountain passes, laughing children in brightly coloured clothes play with homemade dolls, medicine men practise ancient healing methods, traditionally dressed musicians play their haunting flutes, and the hard-working indigenous people eke out a living in often harsh conditions. It's a place where Inka Cola rather than Coke is the biggest-selling soft drink, a country proud of its traditions and sometimes reluctant to share its secrets.

Along with Egypt, Peru is one of the most popular destinations for pilgrims in search of enlightenment. The mix of sacred earth energies and leylines, nature-based religious beliefs, old ruins and local shamans revealing their magic to visitors draws people to the country. Inspired by Shirley MacLaine's book *Out On a Limb*, about the inner search travelling there sparked in her, and the stories of adventure and transformation in James Redfield's *The Celestine Prophecy*, many people have booked a ticket to Peru in their own quest to find themselves and to connect with the mysticism and spirituality of this land.

The jewel of the region is Machu Picchu, the fabled Lost City of the Inkas, which floats, mist-shrouded and obscured by clouds, high in the mountains. The Inkas were a brilliant civilisation that expanded to unite many diverse cultures from the early 1200s until the 1530s, when the Spanish invaded the continent. This weathered citadel is a testament to their advanced building techniques, and also provides insight into their religious beliefs, lifestyle and type of worship.

It was dedicated to the sun god Inti, and made up of more than a hundred buildings, including temples, sanctuaries, homes and storehouses, as well as parks, fountains and agricultural terraces.

The site's power comes from its location, at the place where one of the most sacred mountain peaks meets the headwaters of the mighty Amazon River, but it is also overlaid with the etheric footprint of a civilisation that used it as a holy place – an energy that was protected and magnified when the city was lost to the world after the Spanish conquest. While the rest of the country's temples and sacred places were destroyed, Machu Picchu remained hidden until its rediscovery in the early 20th century, so its secrets and power still exist today.

It is Peru's main tourist attraction, with hundreds of thousands of people travelling from all corners of the globe every year to feel its energies, take part in ancient rituals and experience the breathtaking power of nature, history and the divine coming together in one sacred place. It was voted one of the New Seven Wonders of the World in 2007, is a favourite ceremonial site of North American shamans and their students, and is renowned by some as the planet's heart centre. It is a marvel even to those unaware of its spiritual significance, while for those drawn to its earth energy and power, standing in the shadows of its walls is a deeply transformative experience.

Machu Picchu is visited by spiritual pilgrims and adventure seekers alike. The arduous four-day trek along the historic Inka Trail to the citadel is a physical challenge embraced by serious hikers, while Aguas Calientes, the quaint little village at the base of the mountain, is filled with those who have come to witness the splendour of the ruins and seek there the secrets of the universe, of a lost civilisation, and of their own inner wisdom and enlightenment.

Another attraction of Peru is its culture and ancient spiritual practices. Many westerners go there to study with shamans, the traditional healers who have combined the roles of doctor, priest and counsellor for thousands of years. Long before the Inkas ruled the land, smaller tribes lived in the jungles and mountains, in touch with the power and energy of the earth, worshipping the sun and moon and a host of deities, and revering the cycles of the seasons.

Today, in a world that seems to have lost touch with nature in its striving for technological advancement and progress, many people are increasingly inspired by the simple values and natural magic of indigenous belief systems. Thousands of westerners, particularly in North America, have begun studying shamanism in a quest to bring balance to their lives, heal themselves physically and emotionally and reconnect with the energy of the earth.

As a result, some Peruvian wisdom teachers and healers are now based in the US, conducting simplified but ongoing apprenticeships in their native traditions, or commute there to present seminars and teach classes. Others open their tiny homes, high in the Andean mountains or deep in the Amazon jungle, to students who travel to their ancient land to learn the ways of old.

There are also many spiritual tours of Peru, led by indigenous shamans, western healers and authors, which you can be part of. Some people sign up for these to learn about shamanism and take part in mind-expanding plant medicine rituals in a safe environment, while others do so in order to visit the sacred sites not on the itinerary of more conventional travel companies. Others make their own way around the country and find their own teachers, or simply absorb the powerful healing vibrations of nature and this sacred earth.

Wherever, however and why ever you are drawn to spend time in this mystical and magical land, you will find your heart opening to the beauty and power of nature, the wonder of the past and the magic of the people who live there today.

The present

"Machu Picchu is the City of Light for initiates, an ancient site fed by grids of powerful natural energies patterned by surrounding mountains and extensive underground tunnels. Throughout the ages, such geophysically conducive atmospheres were used for initiatory centres, ritual and mind-altering experiences."
James Arevalo Merejildo (Mallku), Andean shaman and author

Peru is immense and varied in its spiritual impact, from the mystery of the Amazon jungles to the magic of the northern plains, the sacred mountain peaks where the guardian spirits reside, and the enigmatic Nazca Lines near the coast. The pretty town of Cusco, once the imperial capital of the Inkas, is the gateway to the Sacred Valley, which is re-emerging as a centre of spirituality and the Old Ways, while further south is Titikaka, a sacred, magical lake that is one of the largest in the world, and considered by some to be the birthplace of civilisation.

For many people Peru is the first "spiritual" place they visit, and so it was for me when I set out with my backpack, a Spanish dictionary and youthful enthusiasm to walk the ancient landscape and engage with a culture so different to my own. There is a sense of otherness about Peru that really makes you think about your self, your life and your beliefs. Touching the walls of the old stone temples, learning the bloody history of the country and witnessing the wisdom of the past contrasts with your safe world and forces you to look within, challenging your views and helping you see things in a different way.

I had experiences there that were so frightening, transformative and ultimately healing that by the time I left the country I felt like a new person, my eyes opened to the world, my heart a little wiser, my past a little further left behind. This is a place where people go to change, to grow, to die – figuratively speaking – and to be reborn.

Most visitors are drawn first to the archaeological wonder and spiritual power of Machu Picchu. The mysterious city was only built in the 15th century, but the site had been sacred to the medicine men and women of the Andes for more than ten thousand years. This place had been the location of initiations for millennia, and today locals still go there to take part in ceremonies far older than the stone ruins.

It's known to shamans as the Sacred City and the City of Light, because of the knowledge they believe is encoded there and its power to initiate you into new levels of spirituality and wisdom. Some claim it was once a university where young people learned spiritual sciences, and that the caves beneath some of the buildings have been used for thousands of years for rituals of purification, protection and psychic insight. Many cultures lived, prayed, learned and built there, drawing on the grid of earth energies and the power of the mountains and rivers to access healing and other dimensions.

This deep magic comes from its location, on a ridge between the Machu and Wayna Mountains, with the Urubamba River, a headwater of the Amazon, rushing along 450 metres below. It is a place where the elements of water, air and earth meet and where the sun, representing the element of fire, was worshipped – with the combination of these four elements resulting in access to the spiritual and celestial realms.

The people of the Andes have long revered the mountains as sacred because they recognised the electromagnetic power within them. They also believed that the apus, the gods, lived on the peaks. Many Inka temples were built in such places to pay homage to the spirits of the mountains, thank them for their protection and communicate with the divine. Today the Quechuas, the descendants of the Inkas, still perform regular ceremonies to worship the mountains and pay tribute to the power of nature.

The incredible beauty of the area touches the heart and opens the senses to the realms between the worlds and the energy that connects all things. The area is also crisscrossed with leylines, the magnetic earth energies that activate spiritual growth and inner truth. It's been described as a magnetic focal point, and the power and vibrations of the place can really be felt. Thousands of people travel across the world to tap in to these unique energy fields, get in touch with past lives and heal present issues both physical and emotional.

Machu Picchu itself also has an intense healing power. When I first stood in the entrance gateway and saw the buildings spread out before me, I was overcome with a sense of awe and an immense feeling of homecoming. It is so beautiful, with a magnetic, mystical force I could feel as a physical sensation in my body. As I moved through the grounds the energy shifted, just like the light and shadow at the site did as clouds floated across the sun.

Strangely I had none of my usual fear of heights as I leaped around the grounds, perched on precipices, ran up and down the stairs, stood on the very edge of the mountain and felt my spirit soar. I sensed somehow, deep within me, that I had been here before, and flown around between the surrounding peaks. Later a Quechua guide told me there were once priestesses who flew out of their bodies and across the air between the mountains for rituals, communicating with others and bringing back knowledge. Whether I had a past life here or just dreamed it, and whether I was flying, astral travelling or simply imagining it, I don't know. Whatever it was, I felt a deep sense of belonging.

Machu Picchu was an engineering marvel and the ultimate expression of the archaeoastronomical knowledge of the Inkas, with temples, palaces, houses, royal tombs, ceremonial baths, open squares and agricultural terraces perfectly harmonised with the sacred landscape. Some buildings were hewn out of the existing rock, while others were constructed from huge stones and perch on the edge of a sheer cliff, with the views out over the river valley and of the surrounding mountain peaks a significant part of the planning.

While the Inka civilisation's culture and their sun worship was masculine-centred, this city has a deeply feminine vibration, and a sense of gentle yet intense power. Being here and absorbing this beautiful energy opens you up to your inner strength and the depth of your own feminine power, regardless of your gender. To meditate at this site, on the edge of the mountain with the ruins laid out before you, is to draw into yourself the power of the whole universe.

Machu Picchu means old peak in Quechua, the language of the Inkas, which is still spoken by a third of Peru's population of thirty million. It is the name of both the mountain the settlement is built on and the city itself, which lies in the shadow of Wayna Picchu, the young peak. This is the lush mountain that provides the backdrop to Machu Picchu in all the photos, and I could feel its spirit like a physical presence as I wandered through the ruins.

Today some people leave offerings at the base of this peak, in the manner of old, while others climb its scarily steep path to the top in order to commune with the gods thought to live on the summit. To the Inkas it was an important element of the citadel and of their religious procedures and rituals, and it still has significance to locals too.

All the surrounding mountains, including Putucusi, the sacred peak across the river, were a part of their astronomical observatories, providing sight lines for calculating the days of the seasonal year and enabling them to study the stars and celestial bodies. The Inkas believed that mountains were axis points of the world, dividing time and space. They also thought that everything, not just people, had a spirit, so this was the perfect place to commune with the essence of the mountains, earth, air, rivers, stones and trees.

While the area had long been revered by local tribes, construction of Machu Picchu didn't begin until the 1400s, making it much less ancient than many people assume. It was built at the height of the Inka Empire under the legendary ruler Pachakuti, who reigned from 1438 to 1471, and was continued by his successors.

Experts now believe that in addition to being an astronomical observatory and a place of worship it was also a royal retreat, with access limited to high priests and nobles and a specially chosen worker class who lived nearby and serviced the city.

Exquisite stonework constructions and stunning temples were built, and water was carefully irrigated to reach 16 sacred fountains throughout the complex. For more than a hundred years it was an integral part of the empire, but it was abruptly abandoned in 1572, still not quite finished, after the Spanish conquest of the country.

Fortunately the invaders never found Machu Picchu, and the mysterious city was covered up by nature like the castle in Sleeping Beauty. Partly due to its remote location atop the mountain and the thick jungle that grew over it, it lay hidden from the world for centuries, its sacred ground untouched by the conquistadors.

Perhaps there was also magic in its ability to slip behind the mists and avoid the fate that befell the rest of the country, for the invaders destroyed everything they found, tearing down temples and using the holy stones to build their own churches on the same site.

Yet the people who lived in the hillside and valley communities surrounding Machu Picchu always knew it was there and understood its importance, treating it with reverence and respect, as a sacred place watched over by guardian spirits. Once it was abandoned they farmed on the terraces, but they never lived within the walls, because it was a place of such deep and ancient power.

The beautiful city remained undisturbed and lost to the world until 1911, when US archaeologist and history professor Hiram Bingham was led to it by locals. He was searching for Vilcabamba, the legendary last stronghold of the Inkas, but instead found Machu Picchu. He spent three years camped there, pruning back the jungle, excavating, documenting and uncovering the secrets of the place. His photos and articles in *National Geographic* magazine and his book *Machu Picchu: A Citadel of the Inkas* brought the site to the world's attention, and in 2011 it celebrates its centenary of rediscovery.

The Peruvian Government eventually recognised its value, and in 1981 the Historic Sanctuary of Machu Picchu was created, which preserves not just the many archaeological sites but also the unique flora, fauna, geography and culture of the region.

Two years later its historical significance and ongoing spiritual importance led UNESCO, the United Nations Educational, Scientific and Cultural Organisation, to declare it a World Heritage Site, chosen because it represents a masterpiece of human creative genius and bears unique testimony to a civilisation which has now disappeared.

And in 2007 Machu Picchu became one of the New Seven Wonders of the World, alongside the Great Wall of China, Petra in Jordan, Brazil's Christ the Redeemer statue, Mexico's Chichen Itza Pyramid, the Colosseum in Rome and India's Taj Mahal. The list was voted for by 100 million people worldwide as an update of the Seven Wonders of the Ancient World, of which only the Pyramids of Egypt remain.

"Machu Picchu is a trip to the serenity of the soul, to eternal fusion with the cosmos. There we feel our own fragility. It is one of the greatest marvels of South America, a resting place of butterflies at the epicentre of the great circle of life. Another miracle."
Pablo Neruda, Chilean poet and politician

Machu Picchu is situated in the upper Amazon basin on the eastern slopes of the magical Andes mountain range, 2450 metres above sea level. While much of the impact of the place comes from the enigmatic mountains, the old city is also full of important temples and ceremonial sites, and has a power and influence all its own. It was divided into two sections, an agricultural area made up of cultivation terraces where they grew food and bred livestock, and an urban area that included the civil section where people lived as well as the religious part where the temples and royal houses were located.

The most significant was the Temple of the Sun, which was dedicated to Inti and mirrored the shape of the empire's chief temple, the Koricancha in Cusco. It was built to calculate the most important day of the year – Inti Raymi, the winter solstice. This semicircular construction encloses a natural rock formation that acts as an altar, which was specially carved so the sun's rays on solstice morning would come through the window and illuminate it. Here astronomers made their observations to calculate the dates of the seasonal turning points, offerings were made and rituals were performed.

Attached to this temple is the high priest's enclosure, and opposite are the remains of the royal palace, signifying the close relationship of the empire's ruler – called the Inka – with the divine, and his belief in his own importance and god-like status. While the permanent population of Machu Picchu was around three hundred, this swelled to a thousand when the royal family and its extensive retinue arrived.

Beneath the Temple of the Sun is a cave with beautifully carved rocks and niches for offerings. It was used as a royal mausoleum, where mummified nobles were laid out and cared for. Ancestor worship was an important part of the Inka belief system, and they treated the dead with respect and reverence, clothing, feeding and communicating with them as though they were simply in another realm of existence.

Caves had immense significance to the Inkan people as they were considered entranceways to the sacred mountains for the gods who resided there, and one of the borders between the physical world and the spiritual. They also represented the lower world, the uju pacha, one of the three levels of existence in Andean cosmology.

One of the most intriguing sites at Machu Picchu is the Intiwatana Stone, the Hitching Post of the Sun, which served as an altar in major religious ceremonies. It's at the summit of a pyramid-shaped hill that was artificially flattened on top to create a sacred area, and is reached by climbing a series of stone stairs cut in the side. The Intiwatana is a huge block of stone cleverly sculpted with different levels and a pillar rising upwards from the centre, created from the actual tip of the hill with the surrounding area carved away.

As well as being a ceremonial site, the Intiwatana Stone marked the spring and autumn equinoxes, the two times of the year when the sun is directly above the equator and night and day are of equal length. On these two days the sun stands directly above the stone at midday and casts no shadow, and in this way the priests could calculate the passing of the year and know the cycles of the seasons, crucial to any agricultural community and also vital for their sun worship.

Intiwatana is thought to mean hitching post of the sun, and it was named for the sacred ceremonies that were performed at the stone on the equinoxes in order to tie the sun – and the sun god – to the people. The Inka and the high priest attached a golden disc to the altar to symbolically hitch the sun to the earth and continue the cycle of the seasons. As inti means sun and wata means year, it can also be translated as the place where the solar year is measured.

According to the shamans of Peru, putting your forehead against this sacred stone today can open up your inner vision and a connection to the spirit realm, a belief shared in cultures throughout the world. In the British Isles people touch their forehead to the stones of the megalithic circles in an attempt to access the wisdom held within them, and in Australia the Aboriginal people absorb the energy of the great rock Uluru in secret ceremonies.

Today the Andean people still carry out initiation rituals at this very spot. On the morning of the winter solstice, the Intiwatana becomes the House of the Initiate. A shamanic apprentice stands with their hands on the nearby ceremonial stone, and at the moment the sun crests the mountain horizon their forehead is bathed in sunlight, awakening energy and power within. The sun slowly illuminates the face, throat and heart of the initiate, while on the rock two carved concentric circles are lit up in a triangle of light, a phenomenon that only happens at this time of year, when the sun and stone are specially aligned.

During Inka times Intiwatana Stones were common throughout Peru, but the conquering Spanish destroyed them in an attempt to wipe out the country's culture, because the people of the Andes believed if the sacred stones were broken the gods of the place would die. Machu Picchu, hidden away within the jungle and cradled by the mountain peaks, was protected from this violation so the Intiwatana remains, a vital link to the beliefs and ways of this lost civilisation.

Another important place is the Intimachay, the Cave of the Sun, on Machu Picchu's eastern slope. On the morning of the summer solstice the rays of the rising sun shine through the tunnel-like window and hit a spot within the cave, indicating this date. It is the longest day of the year, and the shortest night, and as solar-worshippers, it was most significant, celebrated with major ritual throughout the land.

These seasonal markers and carefully engineered planetary alignments give credence to the view that the city was an astronomical observatory as well as a place of worship, because to the Inkas the cycles of the seasons, the earth, weather, humans, animals and even the gods were all intertwined, connected in a special and sacred way.

At the heart of the settlement is the Sacred Plaza, a ceremonial area which includes two temples that are still mostly intact, bar the thatched roofs that wore away long ago. The Main Temple was dedicated to Wiracocha, the supreme creator deity, and was the primary place of worship. It includes an altar stone along the back wall, high niches that held ceremonial pieces, and a sacristy room behind it.

The Temple of the Three Windows looks out over the gentle green grass of the plaza as well as the breathtaking mountain range to the east. Within its walls it features a central altar stone as well as a smaller stepped one that appears to have been an echo stone of the surrounding mountain peaks. There's also a stone carved with representations of the three worlds – the lower, the uju pacha; the middle, the kay pacha; and the upper, the hanaq pacha.

Lower down on the eastern hillside lie the remains of the ceremonial baths and fountains, places of residence and many other buildings, including a roofless one that was used as an observatory. There are two bowls carved in the floor, which were filled with water to reflect the stars in the sky and show the priests the future. There are also terraces where food for the settlement was grown, along with maize for chicha, the ceremonial beer, and sacred herbs for healing and ritual.

This area is like a maze, where you can wander for hours into intricate rooms, down laneways, up amazing staircases, between buildings and past fountains and water canals, feeling the pulse of the mysterious city. Also in this section is the Temple of the Condor, which was devoted to worship of Apu Kuntur, the condor god.

It's a dramatic, fascinating place, and another example of the Inka skill at blending their constructions with the natural landscape. The temple is built around a large rock in the floor that was carved into a statue of a condor's head and neck, with a natural rock formation behind it shaped like the wings of the great bird.

The layout of Machu Picchu itself was designed in the pattern of a condor in flight, heading west, while Wayna Picchu was terraced and built on to highlight its puma head shape, with rocks quarried out in the shape of eyes, and the mountain behind it stretching out like the animal's body. And down below, the river snakes around the base of the hill like a serpent, completing the trinity of the three creatures that were the sacred symbols of the Inka rulers.

A cave beneath the Condor Temple and a labyrinth-like section of rooms behind it add to its mysterious feel and sense of worship and holiness. I could feel the power within and breathe in its religious significance as soon as I entered. In daylight there is a tangible shift in the atmosphere here, and at night it's even more intense.

"To live fully is to let go and die with each passing moment, and to be reborn in each new one."
Jack Kornfield, US author, meditation teacher and Buddhist monk

Part of my time in Peru was spent on a spiritual adventure with a shaman and six of his American students, visiting sacred places, taking part in rituals and exchanging healing. We spent three days and nights at Machu Picchu with a Quechua guide who shared the history of his land and its people, and led some of our ceremonies with chants and prayers in the native tongue. It was amazing to hear his stories of the sanctuary, what the different rooms and areas were used for, and the beliefs and customs of the people who built it as well as those who came before and those who live in the region now.

On our second day we spent 12 hours wandering through the grounds, then returned after sunset, re-entering the ruins in darkness for a powerful healing ritual. It was a little spooky having the whole city to ourselves, and only three torches between us, but so beautiful and tranquil. This is how the local medicine people conduct their rituals today, alone and quiet in the dark of night, when the tourists have left for the day and an expectant hush has fallen over the site.

The moon cast ghostly shadows over the complex as we made our way carefully through the gateway and wound our way down to the Temple of the Condor and into the cave beneath it. Calling on the energies of the serpent, symbolic of the lower world, we grounded ourselves within the security of the earth. I felt great strength and safety within the dark cocoon of this ancient land, and sensed the first of my protective layers begin to break away.

As we solemnly stepped back inside the temple and formed a sacred circle around the Condor Rock, the moon shone down, aiding our releasement ceremony. Our guide sang his ancient prayers to the mountain guardians and local deities, and I felt a wave of protective energy pass over me. Our shaman sprayed each of us with flower water, and we blew our intentions into a kintu, a set of three coca leaves that is used in shamanic ceremonies. Then we chanted together beneath the moon, building power and creating a conduit for the condor to take our wishes skyward to the realm of spirit.

After that we went around the circle offering individual prayers of love, healing or forgiveness, releasing whatever it was that had held us back from moving forward on our path. I summoned the courage to speak mine aloud – a big thing for me – and felt the strength of it when a breeze like the swish of wings rippled over me in the inky blackness. Climbing back out afterwards I had a sense of being reborn, of leaving behind insecurities and fears and emerging into a new light.

Later we moved up to the Intiwatana Stone and were led in more Quechua chants and prayers, and each of us saw shimmering, luminescent columns of light surrounding our circle. It's said that the geomagnetic vortexes and leylines of Machu Picchu awaken your luminous body, so I'm not sure whether we were seeing etheric beings or just our own and each other's inner radiance.

This is also renowned as a place to communicate with extraterrestrials, and a few in our group related personal stories of such experiences. Legend has it that the alien beings seen here are from a star called Apu, and have been visiting the area for centuries, offering healing and technological help to the locals and living in the mountains where the altitude is too high for human habitation. Perhaps these were the mountain gods the Inkas called apus.

A few hours after we'd entered the sacred ruins we closed our circle and made our way quietly down the mountain to our cosy hotel in the river valley below, where we each fell into bed for a short, restless sleep. The next morning we rose early and headed back up the 14 dizzying switchbacks of the mountain to perform a magical sunrise ceremony of revitalisation and manifestation. We were all gathered at the Intiwatana Stone at the moment the sun rose, breathing in the solar energy and feeling attuned to the people of long ago who worshipped the sun for its life- and light-giving properties.

After a dawn picnic in a circle of stones we hiked up to Intipunku, the Sun Gate, and spent some time in meditation, absorbing the energy that is so strong in these mountains. The Sun Gate is about an hour back along the Inka Trail, and is the place where hikers on this famous route first spot Machu Picchu. For while most people come by road or train through the Sacred Valley from Cusco, some make it a pilgrimage, spending four days trekking in the footsteps of history.

The Inka Trail was the path the Inka and his family took to reach Machu Picchu – although he had it easy, being carried in a litter much of the way. They would stop at various way stations and shrines along the path, such as Winay Wayna, the place of the fountains, to take part in religious ceremonies, make offerings and spend the night.

Today the 45 kilometre track that winds from Ollantaytambo to Machu Picchu is Peru's most popular hiking route, a high-profile, high-altitude part of the pathway that once linked the whole empire.

Paved with stone, it winds through the beautiful flowers, plants and bird life of the cloud forest and past carved stone settlements, waterfalls and stunning views. It's hard work though, straight up (and straight down!) through steep mountains at incredibly high elevations, with few amenities and often inclement weather.

Serious hikers also climb the sacred mountain of Wayna Picchu, which was an important part of religious life for the Inka people. Their ruler and his priests performed ceremonies at the summit, closer to their gods and the spirits of the mountains, and observed the area and the night skies. On the northern side of the peak is the glorious Temple of the Moon, with its cave, temple and amazing stonework, and there are also shrines, an usnu – a pyramidal platform used as an altar and a throne – and agricultural terraces where tea was grown.

Everyone who visits Machu Picchu feels a connection at a different place, somewhere that the energies and the history particularly touch their heart and become meaningful. One of our group led a personal ritual of forgiveness at the Sacred Rock at the base of Wayna Picchu, but my connection came in a little room low down on the eastern side.

I spent hours there on the first day in a trance-like state, sitting on the lush green grass in a building open to the vivid blue sky, my back to the central stone altar and reality shifting around me. A tour group came in at one point, and their guide explained that it had been a place of sacrifice. I heard them laughing, and someone asking if I was the Inka sacrifice, but I felt apart from them, as though I was in a different dimension. I had a strange sense of belonging and peace in that room, and spent the rest of the day there, time passing in a haze.

That night I discovered our shaman had been searching for me but couldn't find me – despite knowing which room I was in and others telling him I was there. He said every time he'd looked he couldn't see me, even though he'd sensed my presence. I don't know what happened. Was I invisible? Did I not want to be found? Was someone or something protecting my alone time? I'd felt very strongly that I needed to be there, alone and uninterrupted, to soak up the energies and process all that I'd seen, heard and felt on the sacred mountain. And so I was.

Perhaps that is part of the magic of Machu Picchu – its ability to hide what does not want to be found, to protect itself and its people.

"Water, known by the original peoples of the Americas as Life Blood, is more essential to plants and animals than food. Springs flow from the ground of Mother Earth and represent her giving, cleansing and purification. For thousands of years there have been reports of miracles occurring as a result of bathing in or partaking of the waters from these natural springs."

Steven Farmer, American author and shamanic practitioner

At the base of Machu Picchu is the village of Aguas Calientes, named for the natural underground sulphur springs that bubble forth there from within the mountains. Shallow pools have been built over the spring, and the healing power of the warm mineral water works on both physical and emotional levels. It was immersed in a similar hot spring that Shirley MacLaine had many of her most profound spiritual revelations, detailed in her classic book and movie *Out On a Limb*.

Ranging from 38-46°C, these thermal baths are renowned for their therapeutic properties, with claims that the waters are helpful in the treatment of rheumatism, joint pain and kidney disorders, amongst other things. In addition to their healing powers they are pure bliss to soak in, an indulgent reward to soothe body and soul. We spent a night at the baths, luxuriating in the warm water and feeling the tension drain from our muscles. As the bubbles danced against our skin, the warmth seeped into our bodies and we floated in the strangely buoyant water, relaxing and processing all of our experiences.

Aguas Calientes is the base from which most people visit Machu Picchu. It has a variety of accommodation, from backpacker hostels and cheap hotels to high-end places, lots of restaurants, bars and cafes, as well as friendly villagers trying to sell massive jewel-coloured butterflies in glass cases and gigantic, nightmare-inducing spiders.

On top of the hill, right next to Machu Picchu, is a controversial luxury hotel, which was built against the wishes of locals and the scientific community, and highlights some of the issues surrounding the settlement. Peru is a poor country, and the money brought in by tourists visiting this sacred place is important to the nation's economy. Yet increasing numbers of people – half a million travel there each year to marvel at the stunning site – could potentially destroy it, and it's on a few lists of endangered locations.

The pleas of scientists, historians and conservationists are starting to pressure the government into limiting numbers, and international outrage won out over big time developers when plans for a cable car to scale the mountain were finally vetoed over concerns it would damage the citadel and the fragile natural environment. A limit has been set on how many people can enter each day, and the number of hikers on the Inka Trail has also been restricted, with permits required and trekkers having to go through a registered travel company so preservation of the pathway can be more closely monitored.

The gateway to the wonders of Machu Picchu, and the tourist hub of the region, is the gorgeous old town of Cusco. It is breathtakingly beautiful – and will also quite literally take your breath away, being situated at 3600 metres above sea level. The constantly offered coca leaf tea is to help counteract the effects of such high altitude. While the town appears so foreign to westerners, there is a deep feeling of connection and belonging. A surprising number of visitors experience a sensation of homecoming and feel completely at ease here, despite the language barrier and the wildly different culture.

Cusco combines the architecture of the Spanish conquerors with the old temples, natural beauty and sense of spirit of the indigenous people of the land. At night restaurants, nightclubs and pubs sparkle with noise and light, but by day it's the historical buildings, traditional practices and the people that capture the imagination.

An artisans' quarter and colourful market stalls beneath cool stone arches provide insight into the way of life of the locals, and the old cobblestone streets all lead to the Main Square, the Plaza de Armas, which the Inkas called Huacaypata, the Square of the Warrior.

It's filled with green grass, vibrant flowers, park benches and children laughing as they play and pose for tourist cameras, while around it are many of the buildings that make Cusco the archaeological capital of the Americas. The town has been declared a World Heritage Site because of its cultural traditions and the outstanding examples of architecture that illustrate significant stages in human existence, and today it reveals the secrets, history and memories of the cultures of the Inkan, pre-Inkan, colonial and republican peoples who have ruled from this city over the last thousand years.

"Shamans are healers, seers and visionaries who are in communication with the world of gods and spirits. They are not only spiritual leaders but also artists, poets, judges and politicians – and the repositories of the knowledge of the culture's history. They are familiar with the cosmic as well as the physical geography, and are technicians of the sacred and masters of ecstasy."
Joan Halifax, American shaman, author and anthropologist

Today many of the old wisdom keepers and shamans are coming down from the mountains – where for five hundred years the knowledge has been passed down through a lineage of apprentices who kept it hidden from the world – to share their healing methods with a new generation of local trainees as well as foreigners. Cusco is filled with people promising enlightenment, but with the rising interest from westerners there is also an increase in those claiming to be shamans who lack experience and deeper knowledge. If you're seeking a teacher, research the subject, ask for recommendations and follow your intuition.

On our first afternoon in Cusco we went to see a healer who has worked with our shaman for years, and comes from a long tradition of native wisdom keepers. We wandered down the dusty paved streets to his tiny, darkened store, where he sells artefacts and medicine pieces in the front and treats clients out the back.

He saw us each individually, and didn't say a word, just looked within our hearts and opened them up, transferring energy through his hands and eyes. It affected my roommate deeply, and started a deep healing process where she was able to let go of things from the past that had been holding her back and creating fears.

That night we ventured out again, walking through the beautiful city as the sky darkened, the lights came on and exotic cooking scents filled the air. We went down a winding, crooked alley to a small room where we were introduced to a frail old shaman, a master renowned even in the US for his powerful healing work, who was going to facilitate a plant medicine ceremony to introduce us to the country and its ancient spiritual traditions and beliefs.

In the centre of the room was a mesa, a Peruvian healing altar, and we took it in turns to place our sacred objects on it so they would be charged with the energy of the group and our own intentions for the ritual. I had a small goddess statue and a crystal with me, which still sit on my altar today. Throughout my time in Peru they were charged with earth, solar and lunar power at some of the most sacred places on the planet, as well as by the energies of each member of the group, which I was able to draw on after my return home.

After being blessed by the shaman, who came around the circle fanning us with a condor feather and chanting a prayer over each of us, we drank a cup of the plant medicine san pedro, made from a cactus that contains mescaline. It's been used for thousands of years in Peru for its visionary properties, and to open the doorways of perception and create profound healing. A strange tasting tea-like brew, it's specially made by an experienced shaman for the specific needs of each group. He adapts the ingredients and dose then prays over the medicine in a complex ritual, connecting to and communicating with the spirit of the plant and attuning himself to its energy.

We settled down around the room in the gloomy dimness as we waited for it to take effect. We were each handed a kintu of three coca leaves, which we blew our prayers into then chewed and swallowed to integrate our spiritual intention within our physical body.

The coca bush was the divine plant of the Inkas, and shamans have long used the leaves as offerings to Pacha Mama, the earth goddess, receptacles for their prayers, messengers to the gods and as a part of religious ceremonies. They also inhale the smoke to induce a trance state and help them enter the spirit world.

While coca leaves have been corrupted by westerners as a source of cocaine, in the Andes they've been used for five thousand years in sacred rituals and to counteract the effects of altitude sickness, improve circulation and brain oxidation and as a medicinal plant. The Inkas valued them for their nutrients – they're rich in vitamins, protein, calcium, iron and fibre – and because drinking the tea or sucking on the leaves minimised hunger and thirst and increased energy levels and endurance for those who took messages between towns by foot, farmed far from home, lived high in the mountains, were on military campaigns or simply ran short of food. They were also chewed by women in childbirth to ease pain and hasten labour, given as an offering to new family members and guests, and buried with nobles in their tombs.

The cocaine content of the leaves is less than one per cent, and must be heavily processed before it becomes a drug. But while the tea is served in every cafe and recommended in every hotel as an innocent way to combat the debilitating effects of altitude sickness – which I know from experience, having ended up on oxygen one night in Cusco – be aware that while you won't be affected by cocaine in the usual manner, you could test positive for the drug if you're checked at the airport. Bringing even three leaves through customs also contravenes drug trafficking laws, so don't try to take a kintu home with you.

After making our coca leaf prayers we created a despacho, an Andean earth offering, which would be completed on our return to Cusco at the end of the trip. These offerings to the gods are made from natural materials such as seeds, corn, quinoa or leaves, and are imbued with prayers and petitions. Later they are given back to the earth in gratitude for the healing and strength received – they can be burned to take these prayers to the spirit realm, or left as offerings on the ground for Pacha Mama, the earth mother.

As the plant medicine took effect we sang and chanted. I felt my third eye tingling and hot, opening up to what was to come. The shaman said there were light beings with us, and I could feel the magic and power in the room. Part of his talent was to see inside our soul and recognise our life path, challenges and the best way for us to achieve our goals. He surprised one woman by telling her she would work with plants – and could study with him after our trip concluded.

Throughout our journey we each had a deep connection with a different place, healing method or healer. Everything was incredibly individual and personal, which seems to be the magic of Peru – it opens you up and readies you for the experience you need to have, even if you aren't consciously aware of what that is at the time.

That night my roommate and I both dreamed the same dream – we were doing battle with a dark male force, and had to band together to defeat it. It turned out to be a premonition of sorts, and throughout our adventure we energetically held each other safe as we faced a series of emotional and spiritual ordeals that bonded us forever. It was no accident that we had been paired up to share a room, and I was eternally grateful for that synchronicity as we learned and experienced and went through so much at the different sacred places of Peru.

The past

"From 3000BCE the basic foundations of ancient Andean civilisation were laid. By this time most of the domesticated plants and animals that were to be so important to Peruvian societies had appeared, the result of the long and developing relationships between people and the environment in the preceding period."
Nicholas J Saunders, British historian, author and anthropologist

It's intriguing to me that when people speak of Peru's history, they refer to the "ancient" Inka Empire. I had visions of a civilisation at least as old as the pharaohs of Egypt, stretching back thousands of years before the time of Christ. Yet the Inkas were quite recent, flourishing from the 13th century until their brutal demise at the hands of the Spanish conquistadors in the 16th.

There have been tribes in the area now known as Peru for millennia though – the Inkas were simply the last evolutionary stage of a people thousands of years old, a force that united the different cultures in the region into a single empire with one language and one notion of the divine. They were the most advanced and sophisticated civilisation the continent had seen, perfecting the agricultural methods, technological achievements and spiritual worldview of their predecessors.

Scientists estimate that tribes of hunters and gatherers were living in South America twenty thousand years ago, and possibly twice that. Modern agriculture began there in the Lithic Age, which started around 12,000BCE (before common era), and distinct cultures have been recorded dating back to at least 3000BCE. Ancient ceremonial structures uncovered in northern Peru prove that the ritual burning of offerings – plants, sea shells, crystals and guinea pigs – which continues to this day, has been taking place for thousands of years. Because they didn't develop a written language, the histories of many peoples have been lost, but ancient ruins, religious art, metalwork and distinctive pottery have been unearthed that have allowed archaeologists to begin piecing together the fascinating history of the country.

In the beginning small communities lived in relative isolation from each other, separated by large mountain passes and vast coastal plains. Some trade was established, but it wasn't until the 14th century BCE that the Chavin civilisation, located in the northern Andes, began to expand and have influence on further flung tribes. Its capital became a place of pilgrimage, with an oracle where the future was divined, and they developed strong shamanic traditions.

They're characterised by their distinctive pottery, metalwork and stone sculptures, and artwork has been found from this period that features representations of supernatural beings with the bodies of men and the faces of animals such as jaguars, caimans and eagles, reflecting their proximity to the jungle and its influence on them – and echoing the human-animal gods worshipped in Egypt at the same time.

The next recognisable societies to emerge were the Nazca and the Moche. The Nazca people were of the southern coastal plains, and developed some time around 150BCE, maintaining a definable presence for almost a thousand years. They depicted whales, cats and falcons on their ritual objects, and were identified by their burials, which involved the bodies being mummified by the desert heat.

They continued the shamanic beliefs of their predecessors, using hallucinogenic plants to communicate with the spirit realm for healing and advice, and created the ritual pathways and geometric shapes of the famous Nazca Lines, which are only visible from the air.

At the same time, the Moche culture was developing in the north of Peru, later expanding its influence through military conquest of the surrounding lands. They had a strongly segregated society, much like the Inkas, and built impressive palaces for the rulers that became their mausoleum when they died. Royal tombs have been discovered that were filled with precious goods and sacrificed companions or servants. They were also known for their huge mudbrick structures, distinctive style of painted pottery and incredible metalwork, and were the first people to begin uniting the country on a large scale.

The Wari of the central highlands were the next major civilisation to rise, around 400CE, and are renowned for their incredible road building feats, agricultural terracing and the keeping of administrative records – qualities the Inkas later perfected. They had trade ties with the Tiwanaku, who were centred on the shores of Lake Titikaka in the south, had a shamanic culture and built impressive monumental buildings, such as the celebrated Gateway of the Sun.

The Wari were followed by the Sican civilisation, which flourished from 800-1375. Like the Inkas, they were led by rulers who claimed divine descent and clad themselves in gold and other riches. They traded far and wide and broadened their influence throughout the region, becoming known for their metalworking and the alchemical blending of gold with copper and other metals.

Around the same time, further north, the Chimu emerged, who were the last to be added to the Inka Empire. They too had a hierarchical society ruled by god-like kings, and they shared their creation myths with the Sican, who they eventually incorporated into their fold. Unlike previous cultures they're known for the mass production of their artwork rather than the high quality of it, although their ceremonial clothing was elaborate, symbolising the importance of spirituality that was a common thread throughout the history of the Andean people.

The Inkas emerged around 1200 in the Cusco Valley. For some time they were just one of many tribes who lived in the region, with their own beliefs and rituals. They were ruled by the Inka, a hereditary royal figure who's been traced back to Manco Capac, the man revered as the first leader, who reigned from the beginning of the 13th century with his sister-wife Mama Ocllo. Legend states that they were the first two humans, the children of the sun god Inti, born to found a mighty empire and lead the Children of the Sun.

By the mid-1400s, led by the celebrated ninth Inka Pachakuti, they began a campaign of expansion, uniting much of the west coast of South America under their leadership, their gods and their language. At its height the Inka Empire covered most of what is now Peru, Bolivia, Chile, Colombia, Ecuador and Argentina. Later Pachakuti handed the armies to his son Tupaq, who was considered the Alexander the Great of South America, and concentrated on administration and rebuilding.

The Inkas perfected engineering and architectural styles, with many of their works outlasting their conquerors. Theirs is recognised as a spiritual and evolved civilisation, with great importance placed on the relationship between people, nature and the gods. While it was a hierarchical society, with the Inka at the apex followed by the nobility then the local chiefs, merchants, craftspeople, farmers and labourers, everyone was born with rights to land and water. Agriculture was the economic mainstay, and their clever engineering enabled huge productivity in difficult geographical conditions.

There was no money – instead food, clothes and shelter were provided by the state in return for labour, be it in the fields, growing crops for the temples, building roads or as part of the military. There were strict laws and religious observances, and people lived harmoniously in a society free of crime. Even in their expansion phase, the Inkas offered tribes the chance to join the empire peacefully, allowing local chiefs to continue ruling as nobles under the Inka umbrella.

The Inka Empire was the largest of the pre-Columbian cultures, which included the Mayans and the Aztecs, so named because they flourished in the Americas before Christopher Columbus's discovery of the New World in 1492. But after that history changing event, European powers such as Spain and Portugal invaded the continent, claiming the land as their own, plundering the gold, minerals and other riches, and forcibly converting the people to Christianity.

"May the Sun remain a young man and the Moon a young woman. May the world not turn over. Let there be Peace!"

Inka prayer

The Inkas worshipped a pantheon of deities, headed by the creator god Wiracocha, who was said to have moulded people from clay and breathed life into them, echoing creation myths from around the world. He is credited with making the sun, moon and stars to bring light to the world, and giving his people language, songs and agriculture so they could survive. But there were few temples dedicated to him because he was considered to be not of the world, existing above and beyond his people, invisible and unable to be communed with.

Instead the sun god Inti was his representative on earth, the physical manifestation of the divine, and it was he who was worshipped as the primary deity, particularly by the Inka. He was considered the giver of life, light and warmth, the power that made the crops grow and the source of human existence. He ruled over fertility and agriculture, and there was a sun temple dedicated to him in every town.

Just as important to the people of the land was the earth goddess Pacha Mama, which translates as mother universe, who's been revered and honoured since the world began. The Inkas believed that as long as they lived in harmony with the earth, Pacha Mama would provide for them and protect them, and they poured libations and made offerings to her to nourish her in return. They regarded the planet as a living being, infused with spirituality and possessing a soul.

Pacha Mama was a fertility goddess, and incorporated the principle of the divine feminine, representing balance and duality. She ruled mountains, rocks and plains, and was worshipped as the mother of all humans, the giver of life, divine nurturer and great protector goddess. Also significant was the moon goddess Mama Quilla, the sister-consort of Inti. She ruled over and protected women and marriages, and was connected with the passage of time, the calendar and festivals. The precious metal silver was considered a gift of her tears for humanity.

Another influential deity was the weather god Illapa, who ruled over storms, thunder and lightning. He controlled the weather and the seasons, and was also depicted as a god of war. The ocean goddess Mama Cocha, the sea mother, ruled over fishing and was a comforting mother goddess who provided food and nourishment for her people. And the harvest deity Mama Allpa, who oversaw agriculture and fertility, was an earth goddess depicted with many breasts, worshipped by men to increase crop yield and women for their own fertility.

The civilisations that were incorporated into the Inka Empire had to add Inti to their pantheon of deities, but were able to continue worshipping their own gods as well. And they were all fairly similar, being nature-based religions that revered the sun, the earth, the seasons and the celestial bodies. The people believed that the divine spirit, or "god", lived in all things, including the sun, moon, earth, mountains, wind, rocks, trees, oceans and rivers, all of which they held as sacred. Like most indigenous cultures, this made them far more environmentally aware than modern man.

Each of the deities had a priesthood to venerate them, perform ceremonies in their honour and make offerings. There were also temple priestesses who tended crops, grew plants, weaved cloth and brewed chicha, the maize beer that was used as a libation and sacrifice during rituals. The highest priests advised the Inka, while others cured illness or divined the future, as shamans had for millennia.

There were three levels of existence in the Inka world. The first was the lower world, the uju pacha, which was not like the hell of the Christian belief system, but was rather considered another realm of existence, or non-ordinary reality, that existed on top of our physical world. Symbolised by amaru, the snake, this domain represented the subconscious mind, and shamans journeyed there to bring back knowledge from the Otherworld, particularly from animal spirit guides.

Second was the earth plane, the kay pacha, the everyday existence of humans and the conscious realm, represented by choquechinchay, the puma. The third was the upper, celestial, world, the hanaq pacha, symbolised by kuntur, the condor, which was believed to be the place of the gods and the realm of spirit. It was another plane of existence that shamans journeyed to in order to access healing and wisdom and communicate with ancestors, deities, angels and spirit guides.

Ancestor worship was also a strong part of the Inka belief system. They considered their ancestors to be protective spirits who helped them in their day-to-day life. Tombs were sacred objects, especially those of the kings. Even in death the rulers retained their power – their bodies were mummified and looked after by specially trained people who performed rituals for them and displayed them at special events. The spirit was believed to live on in the embalmed body, and the royal mummies sat in state, were consulted for advice by the current king and paraded at festivals so people could make offerings to them. The whole line of Inkas was preserved in death, and one of the first things the Spanish did was destroy these holy relics as a way to convince the people their gods had no power.

Life in Inka society revolved around the cycles of the sun and the seasons. The major celebration was Inti Raymi, the winter solstice, which marks the longest night and the shortest day of the year, and was the festival where everyone paid homage to the sun, the solar god and the imminent return of the light to the land.

Today it is still celebrated throughout the country, and the primary event, held in Cusco, is a colourful ceremony that evokes the old magic. A man representing the Inka is carried in a royal litter from the Temple of the Sun to the main square, where he addresses city officials. He is then taken on to Sacsayhuaman, where a traditional priest-led ritual is performed involving thousands of people. At sunset everyone returns to the town square to continue partying through the night.

Capac Raymi, the summer solstice, the longest day and shortest night, was traditionally celebrated with a royal feast which involved formal ceremonies to initiate young royal males into manhood.

"The city of Cusco is the greatest and the finest ever seen in this country or anywhere in the Indies. We can assure Your Majesty that it is so beautiful and has such fine buildings that it would be remarkable even in Spain."

Francisco Pizarro, 16th century Spanish explorer who "discovered" Peru, to King Charles V of Spain

Cusco was the heart of the Inka world and the geographical centre of the empire. It was the focus of religious, administrative and political power, and the home of the royal family. It was also the location of the Koricancha, the most sacred temple in the Inka Empire. This made Cusco a holy city, as spiritually significant to the people of the Andes as Rome was for the Christians or Mecca for the Muslims.

The Koricancha was considered the navel of the earth. At the centre of the complex was the elaborate Temple of the Sun, dedicated to Inti, and within the grounds there were also smaller temples – the Temple of the Moon, dedicated to the moon goddess Mama Quilla, and others devoted to Venus, Illapa and the rainbow god Cuichu.

The walls of the Temple of the Sun were sheathed in gold, and there was a gold statue of Inti inside, flanked by the mummies of prior Inkas. In the Temple of the Moon the walls were covered in silver, the colour of the moon's face in the sky, and a silver statue of Mama Quilla was surrounded by the mummies of past Inka wives, known as coyas.

Beneath the precious metals the walls were constructed of perfectly cut stone blocks, quarried from sacred mountains to add a further spiritual boost to the place of worship. These blocks fitted together with no need for mortar, another example of the advanced engineering skills of the Inkas. Their buildings were perfectly made to withstand earthquakes, unlike the Spanish churches constructed over the top of them, which came crashing down when the ground shook.

After the Spanish conquest the Church of Santo Domingo was built over the Koricancha complex, but in 1650 a major earthquake hit Cusco, destroying the just-completed church. It was rebuilt, but in 1950 another major earthquake hit the city, toppling it again. The granite walls of the Koricancha – and many other historic buildings – were exposed, and this time locals urged the council to keep them on show. Today the original Inka walls, gates and some of the rooms of the site can be seen, and you can walk inside the original temples.

The Koricancha was also the centre of a series of sacred pathways or spirit lines called ceques, although their original significance is no longer understood. These lines of earth energy radiated outwards from the temple to the mountains, with a series of shrines known as huacas located along each one. The huacas were the physical manifestation of each ceque, and their placement revealed the alignment of each of these lines of power.

The huacas were holy places, and included hills, rocks, caves, springs, pyramids, carved stones and tombs. They were considered the residence of sacred spirits and powers, a part of the Inkan worship of nature. At each of them the veil between the worlds was a little thinner – these places were the border between the physical world and the spirit realm, and communication with the gods, the ancestors and their etheric guides was believed to be easier at these sites.

There were 41 ceques that divided the land into political and military sectors. These invisible lines moved outwards from the central temple and through the city, the valley and then the entire region, connecting the Koricancha to the shrines, holy places and mountains of the extensive empire and sending divine power between them.

Some think the lines followed paths of energy, like the European concept of leylines, others that people's worship at the places along them was what imbued the land with power. Certainly the Andeans considered the earth to be a living entity, similar to the human body in that it was made up of meridians, energetic and electromagnetic centres or vortexes, and positive and negative energy charges. The land had its own power, which they had learned to tune in to.

The ceques were also astronomical indicators, serving as sight lines for celestial observations. Some huacas were hills, and when the sun hit a certain point on them it indicated the time of year and the changing seasons, and that it was the day to plant new crops or harvest them. The ceque system was thus a giant agricultural and astronomical calendar, with one huaca for each day of the year.

It also formed a series of pilgrimage paths. Different families or groups tended each huaca, leaving offerings and performing rituals there to appease the gods and the spirits of the land. On special days they made ceremonial processions along a ceque, saying prayers, chanting and making offerings as they walked.

Cusco was built in the shape of a puma, the symbol of the Inka ruler. Its stomach was the main plaza of the city, its spine was the Tullumayo River and its head was the temple fortress of Sacsayhuaman. On the morning of the winter solstice the first rays of sun hit the head then illuminated the city from the tail upwards, awakening the town and shining rays along special alignments in the temples – another display of their incredible archaeoastronomy skills.

Sacsayhuaman is an elaborate stone ruin that was once a royal temple of the sun. Situated on a hill overlooking Cusco, its size and position led the Spanish to believe it was a fortress, and while it could perform that function, it was in fact one of many places of worship, where Inti was revered along with several other deities.

To the Inkas, prayer and connection to the gods was a central tenet of life, and their intricate temples were flamboyant proof of their dedication to the divine, boasting several smaller houses of worship, their own water supply, housing, terraces and store rooms.

Once richly decorated, Sacsayhuaman's stark ruins remain a fascinating example of Inkan architecture, with amazing views over Cusco and its surrounds. It reportedly took twenty thousand men more than seventy years to build, overseen by several successive rulers. It's believed to have been an astronomical observatory, because of certain alignments in its construction, as well as the place where local priests carried out mysterious rituals and meditations.

At the height of the Inka Empire this was an awe-inspiring, formidable site, built partly as a show of power, but when the Spanish came they carted away some of the massive stones to rebuild Cusco. As a result, today it's intact up to a certain height then left bare by the plunder. Yet the sculpted terraces and the zigzag walls constructed to look like the teeth of the puma's head remain, and the place still holds a deep, ancient and powerful energy, which I could feel as I walked between the stone walls and across the grassy open spaces.

We performed a ceremony of rebirth here, tapping in to the power that had been raised and imbued in the sacred stones centuries ago. Slowly we wove through a pitch black passageway in the ground, relying solely on our hands and our instincts to find our way through the darkness and out into the sunshine at the other end. It was a strange feeling to be walking through the earth, within the womb of the mother goddess, yet somehow comforting and nurturing.

Once we'd emerged into the light we wound our way through a stone formation to the other side of the complex, where we did a deep meditation with the gatekeeper who watches over the site, a man with a gentle, grounding energy. Then we formed a circle around the mesa that held our sacred objects. Earlier our shaman had handed me his condor feather, as this was the day I had to lead the ritual, so I went around to each person, touching their crown chakra with the feather and directing their energy down into the mesa. Then I moved around again, energetically charging the earth with the love, power and healing prayers from their heart and solar plexus chakras.

For a solitary practitioner who has always worked alone in a spiritual sense, it was a challenge to be the focus of the rite, but it was empowering too. Every woman in the group was a lot stronger and knew a lot more than they gave themselves credit for, and I hoped that during this ceremony where their energy was recharging the earth they'd begin to understand their own power and potential, and how much wisdom they have. That they would begin to trust it, and start looking within for answers rather than to external gurus and teachers.

Another sacred place where we performed a ritual was nearby Tambo Machay, the Temple of the Water, which was the major complex of baths and fountains for the Inka nobles. Water, known as unu, was a sacred element, and all the major temples had baths within the grounds so they could worship this element.

This site consists of a system of elaborately carved and tiered platforms that channel the water from a holy spring into three waterfalls, which were used to energetically cleanse and purify the royals. The fountains have been pumping water for centuries, and still work today. Sitting within the niches on the top platform we sensed a deep power, and feeling the water run over our wrists was energising and refreshing both physically and on a deeper level.

The temple and amphitheatre of Qenqo, near the dazzling white statue of Christ that can be seen from Sacsayhuaman, was once the location of religious ceremonies that took place on the solstices and equinoxes. We did a moving ritual here with the traditional Andean musicians who accompanied us for a few days. Qenqo, meaning labyrinth, was a centre for rites honouring Pacha Mama, and although it's now partly ruined, the altars, steps, underground chamber and carvings that make up part of this complex are worth exploring.

The beautiful archaeological site of Pisaq, built on the side of a sacred mountain, is situated in the energy laden Sacred Valley. In Inka times it was both a solar observatory and an important ritual centre, as well as being a strategically located city with defensive capabilities. The impressive stone ruins include temples, baths, an urban sector and terraces that are still farmed today.

We climbed the steep path to the Temple of the Condor, where we performed a beautiful ceremony, drifting away to the sound of the flute and tuning in to the energy of the spirit and celestial realm represented by the sacred bird. Later, around the Intiwatana Stone in the ruins of the Temple of the Sun, a local shaman did coca leaf readings for each of us, startling us with his accuracy and insight.

Above the temple area is a series of burial sites and tombs, which were looted and desecrated by the Spanish. The Inka people believed that after death there was a new life, so they mummified then buried their dead with precious jewels and other treasures, in a similar manner to the Egyptians. And back down in the valley are the Pisaq Markets, famous for their cosy alpaca wool sweaters, vivid ponchos, medicinal herbs and despachos, souvenirs, artwork and fresh produce.

Further along the valley is Ollantaytambo, known as the Sanctuary of the Wind and the House of the Dawn, another significant religious site that lies partly in ruins. It was a spiritual sanctuary as well as a tambo, a town that offered food and lodgings for travellers. The modern-day village is located within the old urban sector, so some of the locals live in buildings that once housed Inka nobles. The main complex on a hill above the town boasts temples, a royal chamber and princess baths, with many fountains and a large altar stone.

At the fountains we invoked the water spirits and did an energy cleansing ceremony, then in the main temple area we called on the power of the wind to bless us. One of our group had an intense past life experience, which is apparently common at this energy vortex, while the rest of us climbed the wide terraced steps and marvelled at the beauty of the stone constructions and the tangible sense of power.

Two other magical Inka sites have just been rediscovered, Choquequirao and Vilcabamba. The first has been dubbed the other Machu Picchu, but while its (so far) unspoiled grandeur makes it a fascinating destination for spiritual pilgrims, it's hard to reach and has few amenities – and locals want to keep it that way to protect its purity and energetic power. In 2006 just six thousand people travelled there, compared to the half a million who visited its more famous sister site.

Choquequirao was built by Pachakuti's successor Tupaq, and served a similar purpose to Machu Picchu, with temples, solar observatories, palace and residential areas and agricultural terraces. The nearest town is Cachora, and from there it's a 32 kilometre hike through steep, unforgiving mountains. It's been described as the hardest trek some frequent climbers have ever done, and takes at least two days each way.

The remote jungle town of Vilcabamba, 130 kilometres west of Cusco, is the real Lost City of the Inkas, where the last of the native rulers and their loyal armies retreated in the years after the Spanish conquest, and the one Hiram Bingham was searching for when he stumbled on Machu Picchu. It's a beautiful place, with the ruins of temples, palaces and other buildings hidden beneath the wild vines that have grown up over the top. But it's a long and strenuous journey to get there, with guided hikes taking three days each way.

All the Inka sites, which are up to eight hundred years old, reveal a deeply spiritual people who were in tune with the earth and ran a society that, while hierarchical, looked after all members. They unified hundreds of disparate cultures with their incredible administration skills, transformed the harsh landscape with terracing and irrigation, and built thirty thousand kilometres of roads through dramatic mountain passes to connect the empire. The poverty that followed the Spanish colonisation was unknown and unimaginable to them. But while this advanced civilisation seemed undefeatable, it was not.

"As for your pope of whom you speak, he must be mad to talk of giving away countries that do not belong to him. As for my faith, I will not change it. Your own god, as you tell me, was put to death by the very men he created. But my god still looks down on his children."

Atahualpa, 16th century Inka chief, on hearing
Pope Alexander VI had declared Peru a possession of Spain

When the Inka ruler Huayna Capac died in 1527, two of his sons squabbled over the vast lands. Refusing to share the reign, they engaged in the bloodthirsty War of the Two Brothers, a five-year battle in which a hundred thousand people died. While Atahualpa eventually triumphed, the civil war left the empire weakened, and when Spanish explorer Francisco Pizarro arrived on their shores in 1532, lured by talk of riches undreamed of, the country was easily conquered.

Francisco founded Piura, the first Spanish settlement in South America. But Atahualpa was unconcerned because his army, even depleted as it was, numbered forty thousand, while the Spanish had less than two hundred men. He was so confident of the might of his empire and his own divine right to rule that he completely misunderstood the extent of the threat. He sent the Spaniard gifts, and at the end of that year Francisco travelled to the town of Cajamarca to meet him.

Atahualpa expected the stranger to pay tribute to him, but instead he tried to convert him to Christianity and submit to the rule of the Spanish king. When the Inka refused to recognise any power greater than his own, he was taken prisoner in a surprise attack. For despite being completely outnumbered, the Spanish had guns and horses, and Atahualpa was surrounded by advisers instead of bodyguards.

The Inka bargained with his captors, offering a roomful of gold and two of silver. Francisco took the treasure, and for a time he used Atahualpa to influence the local people, but eventually he decided the native ruler was too big a threat and had him executed. The conquistador had also taken Atahualpa's daughter by force, and condoned the rape of indigenous women by his soldiers, adding to the betrayal.

With the Inka king dead, the Spanish took over by force of arms, stealing the country's gold, their culture and their lives. Francisco and his soldiers marched to Cusco, the empire's capital, and proclaimed their conquest of the nation. They created a Spanish stronghold, building over the foundations of the imperial city and its temples with palaces and Catholic churches, before later moving the capital to Lima.

For several years Atahualpa's heirs ruled their people from the mountain refuge of Vilcabamba, maintaining their spiritual ties to the land and their gods and occasionally mounting unsuccessful battles against their oppressors. But in 1572 the invaders decided to wipe out the rebels once and for all, and waged war on the survivors. This bloody battle marked the end of the resistance to Spanish rule. Tupaq Amaru, the last of the Inka line, was captured and dragged back to Cusco, accompanied by the golden statue of Inti and the sacred mummies of his predecessors, to be executed along with his generals and most of his family. He was hanged in the main square of the former empire's capital, crying to the people and the gods with his final breath: "Pacha Mama, witness how my enemies shed my blood."

Within forty years the conquest – and the almost total annihilation of the mighty Inka civilisation – was complete. The indigenous people succumbed to the superior weaponry and mysterious horses of the Spanish, as well as to imported diseases such as smallpox, which decimated a population with no immunity to it.

The invaders quickly stripped the country of its immense treasures, destroyed and banned a culture that was rich in history, spirituality and skills, tore apart a well integrated society, forced the surviving population into a slave-like regimen and imposed a new religion and way of seeing the world on this once-proud culture. In its place they left division and poverty, and created an underclass without land, literacy, education or political or religious rights.

There was turmoil on the other side too. The Spanish, who only cared about plundering the nation's resources and converting the natives to Christianity, couldn't even agree among themselves. It's ironic that while Francisco "discovered" Peru and is the most successful of all conquistadors, claiming the most land and treasure for a European power with the smallest army, his desire to lead the country was thwarted when he was murdered by one of his own men.

From his first step on Peruvian soil he cheated his companions out of a share of the Inka spoils, lied to them and refused to let them rule any part of the nation, resulting in civil war between the invaders. Finally, in 1541, he was assassinated by the son of a colleague he had killed. The Spanish royals, sick of the squabbling in their new territory and intent on making money out of it, appointed a viceroy to rule the country, but he too was murdered by warring factions.

Later, the last surviving conquistador wrote in his will of the shame he felt at what he and his fellow adventurers had done, describing the well-governed, hard-working and moral civilisation they had destroyed, a society with no thieves, adulterers or violent criminals, and his embarrassment at the cruelty inflicted by his countrymen. Reports claim that of the Inka population of twelve million just before the invasion, only a million were alive at the conclusion of the conquest.

After the death of Francisco, the Viceroyalty of Peru was pronounced, creating a colonial administrative district with a viceroy ruling on behalf of the Spanish king. It was the largest in South America for a few hundred years, but as Portugal's colony of Brazil expanded and other regions prospered, Peru weakened in power.

In the early 1800s the criollos – locally born people of Spanish descent – began planning their emancipation. Battles were waged against the Spanish army, and in 1821 Jose de San Martin, who was born in what is now Argentina, proclaimed Peru's independence from Spain, becoming the first president of the country. He was aided by Simon Bolivar, who led many independence movements and was at various times president of Peru, Bolivia, Colombia and Venezuela.

Since then Peru has had an at times bloody, dictatorial and corrupt political history, with terrible poverty affecting a huge proportion of the population. Yet the people remain an inspiration, open hearted and giving. The shamans who are starting to teach the traditional wisdom again say now is the time for forgiveness and compassion, not bitterness or revenge, and that all the people of the country must join together to help each other and heal from the bloody past. It can't be changed, but a new future can be created that benefits all Peruvians and continues to inspire people from around the world.

Today around forty-five per cent of the population of Peru are Amerindians, descendants of the indigenous people, and thirty-seven per cent are mestizos, of mixed Amerindian and Spanish ancestry. While Spanish remains the main language, a third of the people speak Quechua, the language of the Inkas, which is undergoing a resurgence in schools. In areas where the native tongue, such as Quechua or Aymara, dominates, it's considered the official language. Peru is the only place in the Americas where there's still a thriving indigenous population, which is why anthropologists find it so fascinating.

After the Spanish conquest, Catholicism was forced on the people, but many blended it with their native beliefs. There was an artistic movement that painted Christ and the Virgin Mary as Inti and Pacha Mama, and the Peruvians still made offerings at their local huacas and said prayers – of apology, loyalty and despair – to their gods. Many of the Christian celebrations were imposed over older days of ceremony, so the ancient rituals continued to be played out, albeit in a new way.

Now Peru is at the beginning of a new era of indigenous power and spirituality. They believe time is divided in cycles of five hundred years. The one beginning at the end of the 15th century, with the discovery of the Americas, was a time of darkness and repression, which followed the enlightened age that had culminated in the Inka Empire.

But the end of the 20th century heralded the beginning of a new cycle, an age of tolerance, harmony and shared spirituality. The wisdom keepers who have lived in the mountains from the time of the Spanish invasion, protecting and passing down their knowledge and traditions, have declared it's time to move forward into the light again.

The purpose

"Shamanism is related to the harmonies of the earth, a subtle and alchemical process designed to transform and elevate the spirit beyond the constructs of the known limits of reality. It teaches how to choreograph the energies of the universe, because all things are alive, and to heal the mind and heart."

Lynn Andrews, American author and spiritual teacher

For thousands of years, the shamans of Peru have performed their craft deep in the jungle, high in the mountains and within the coastal plain villages, and it is their knowledge that draws many people to the country today. Learning the ways of these medicine men and women has become big business, and there are many mystical tour groups that include sessions with a shaman as part of the itinerary, as well as a growing number of indigenous healers willing to share their skills.

Shamanism is a nature-based religious and spiritual path that's been practised around the world since prehistoric times. While different cultures and countries have their own unique blend, all share a deep connection to the earth, incorporate a holistic approach to healing and commune with the gods of the land. Shamans, the priest-like village elders, are known by many names – in Peru they are curanderos, laikas, amautas and sages, while in other places they are medicine men, wise women, druids and witch doctors. They are all highly regarded within their community, a mix of doctor, priest, counsellor, teacher, healer, mystic, psychic, storyteller and adviser.

Peruvian shamans see the universe as interconnected and each person as a tiny part of the greater whole. They honour the gods, the earth, the elements – earth, air, water, fire and spirit – and the directions with offerings and prayers, and believe in different levels and dimensions of existence. They enter trance states and undertake spirit journeys in which they access information from the ancestors, animal spirits and deities to heal physical, emotional and mental issues. They perform shamanic healing and soul retrieval, mediate between the seen and unseen worlds and act as a bridge between their people and the gods.

They believe in a divine source that is both masculine and feminine, a perfect combination of energy and elements. While Inka society and its priests were male-dominated, before that the view was balanced. Both men and women were healers, and they recognised a feminine face of god as well as a male, as evidenced by their reverence for Pacha Mama, the earth goddess who gave them life and nourishment.

Shamans are deeply connected to their personal mesa, a healing altar they use to manifest physical wellbeing and emotional change. This altar is a collection of sacred power objects that have been specially consecrated, a kind of doctor's kit, which serves as a focus for their energies. They create ceremonies to heal people and banish disease, as well as practising other therapeutic methods such as herbalism, chanting, prayer, ceremonial cleansing and exorcism.

They can perform divinatory rituals to learn what neighbouring communities are up to and discover the location of food and water. They possess telepathic and psychic abilities and precognition, can astral travel, and are believed to influence the weather and the agricultural harvests. They have a strong faith in the spirit world, and communicate with divinities, ancestors and spirit animals, who impart information to them and aid their work. Animal spirit guides have become trivialised in western culture, but to the shaman they are powerful allies that work closely with them in the spirit planes, protect them, guide them through other realms and assist their healing efforts.

Today many westerners follow the beliefs and ideology of shamanism, and consider themselves practitioners, yet in traditional cultures a shaman trains their entire life to be their community's healer and sage. It's a lifetime occupation, which you're called to rather than choosing. Often a near-death experience, serious illness or terrifying psychic ordeal in which they access the spirit realm sets them on the path.

Such a person then undergoes a decades-long apprenticeship with a master shaman in which they learn about the plant medicines of their region, the spirits and how to work with them, the balance between people and nature, and the different levels of reality – the lower, middle and upper worlds – and how to move between them.

It's an often lonely, isolated existence, with great hardship endured to learn all the skills and master the journeying between realms and states of consciousness. Fasting, suffering and physical and spirit journeys are often required on the part of the shaman in order to bring about healing, and it can be physically taxing and dangerous work.

Historically the shamans of Peru have closely guarded their secrets, imparting their knowledge only to their individual apprentices, who would spend years studying to learn the ways of the healer. But as younger people moved away from the jungles and villages to the cities and populations were wiped out, the knowledge was being lost, and the shamans have been called on to share their wisdom with others.

They also believe the world is in a time of great change, and that the plundering of natural resources and the greed of western governments need to stop to ensure the survival of the planet and the human race. For this reason they are opening up to strangers, hoping that if more people become aware of the wisdom of the earth and incorporate it into their hearts, they will live more loving, caring lives and help halt the destruction of our world. Increasingly there are centres and lodges in the jungles of Peru, as well as in Cusco and the Sacred Valley, where shamans are teaching students. They also facilitate ceremonies and transformative rituals on spiritual tours.

As well as encouraging the preservation of the planet, the ancient wisdom of the shamans is impacting on health. Not that long ago modern medicine rejected shamanic healing methods as superstitious nonsense, but science is finally realising the value of the plant medicines of Peru. Many conventional pharmaceutical drugs are based on the compounds found naturally in herbs and plants, and the rainforests of the Amazon are now being searched for cures for everything from cancer and high blood pressure to fatigue. There are untold varieties of plants within these rich ecosystems, which shamans have been using to heal people for thousands of years.

In addition to the medicinal properties of plants, shamans also utilise the spirit of many plants for physical, emotional and spiritual healing, believing that they possess a life force and intelligence that can teach them the reasons and remedies for illnesses.

While the idea of communicating with a plant's spirit is hard to fathom, its effectiveness has been documented in communities such as Findhorn in Scotland, where residents discovered how to grow lush gardens with larger than normal vegetables and tropical plants not native to the area, despite cold weather, snow and barren, sandy soil. They discarded common gardening principles and instead asked the plants what they needed, communicating telepathically with their spirit.

The people of Findhorn claim they were told by specific plants how far apart to sow their seeds, when and how to prune them, how often to water and the way to merge their energy with the plant's to improve growth. *The Celestine Prophecy* describes a similar program, and there are a number of communities around the world employing such principles of energy work and interaction with the spirit of plants.

"The most influential journeys I've had have been with ayahuasca, a medicine man's journey drug where you go inside. It's not a social thing, it's an internal experience. I don't do it recreationally, it's inner work. You go right into your psyche and know it more deeply. It's a wealth of information in there. I learned a lot about myself."
Tori Amos, American singer and musician

The shamans of the Amazon have long used a medicine made from the ayahuasca plant for healing, purification, divination, spirit journeys and as a window to the soul. It's a serious and heavily ritualised experience, where the plant medicine is taken in a sacred manner to acquire healing and knowledge. It is considered a holy sacrament, and they are disappointed by the fascination of westerners who misconstrue it as a drug for getting high or tripping out.

Like the ritual use of tobacco in some cultures, this sacred plant medicine is taken in a controlled environment in carefully determined doses for a specific purpose, with a specially trained shaman, an ayahuascero, overseeing the ceremony. It's a therapeutic method that incorporates all levels of healing – physical, mental, emotional and spiritual. It can lead to physical recovery, and also uncover the cause of an illness, dissolve emotional and psychological blocks and provide spiritual insight that can profoundly change your life.

Traditionally ayahuasca was used only by shamans, who would ingest the plant medicine, after fasting and meditating, and go on a spirit journey to seek wisdom, determine future events or challenges for the community, or to uncover the cause of an illness in another person and learn the cure. However it is now becoming increasingly popular to have a personal ayahuasca experience rather than consult an expert on your behalf, and to seek your own healing.

Many of the spiritual travel groups include two or three days of meditation, ritual and ayahuasca ceremonies with a master shaman deep in the Amazon jungle, and ours was no exception – although I had no idea what was involved. One of the women in our group asked me if I was nervous, and I shook my head, puzzled. Why would I be? Ignorance is bliss they say, and my naivety meant I had no preconceptions or anticipatory fears plaguing me.

Later I found out ayahuasca translates as vine of death, so named because it's believed that taking it causes the death of a part of your self. It's about surrender and release, of letting the parts of you that you no longer need be killed off so you can be reborn, whole and healed.

As we floated up the river from Puerto Maldonado in a tiny canoe-like craft beneath a lush canopy of jungle trees, my heart opened up to the immense beauty and intense energy of this wild, still-pristine part of nature. I smiled as the local guide told us that the butterflies dancing around us drink the tears of the turtles along the riverbank, a touching metaphor of pain being transformed into love, of the interdependent and interwoven layers of the natural world.

Later, walking through the tropical rainforest of the wildlife reserve we were staying at, a beautiful butterfly, a symbol of joy, alighted on my shoulder. It whispered in my ear before dancing lightly down my arm and on to my tummy and the butterfly tattoo there, which is a marker of my own desire for transformation and transcendence from prior pain. Perhaps in this lush ancient land I would find it.

After unpacking in the tiny wood cabins that reminded me of my childhood – no electricity, no window panes, no hot water – we paddled out on a crystal clear lake and leaped into the freezing water, ritually cleansing our bodies for the night ahead. The late afternoon sun sent golden light through the trees, bathing us in a warm glow that quickly faded when the guide told us there were piranhas swimming with us.

That night we skipped dinner, as fasting is part of the preparation for the ayahuasca ritual. Then as darkness fell we walked single file down a path lit by torches, a touch of nervousness descending around us as the solemnity of the occasion sank in. We entered the small wooden ritual room, its walls open to the richly scented night air and candles casting pools of light and shadow, and took our places.

The master shaman, an elder from the area who had studied the medicine ways of his people since he was a boy, slowly gazed around at each of us. He spoke no English, but he had no need for words, communicating with us on a heart level. There was a power that flowed through him from the earth itself, flooding him with the wisdom of the Amazon and its plants and creatures. His spirit reached out to touch ours, learning all our secrets, our histories and our pain as he gazed within our souls. I felt stripped bare, but we all had an immense trust in this wise and dignified healer, who was about to accompany each of us on this journey to transcend our conditioning and prior hurts.

Our shaman sat with him, supporting him energetically in the work that was about to begin. He poured each of us a cup of the plant medicine he'd brewed earlier, infused with prayers for our own personal quests, and an assistant passed it to us in turn. When we had all drunk our individually prescribed dose of the potion – thick, bitter, pungent and difficult to swallow – we settled back nervously to wait.

The candles went out and the ayahuascero gently blew the smoke of his mapacho cigar over each of us, purifying us with the spirit of the sacred tobacco. Then he began to chant and pray, a rattle in his hand as he communed with the spirits and raised energy in the room. He sang icaros, the hypnotic, haunting spirit songs taught to him by the plants, which help guide him as he journeys between the realms, and which also communicate with our souls and free them to travel.

I felt the power build, and there was a shift in the atmosphere. The room grew hotter, and time seemed to stretch out then snap back into place. I sensed reality shifting around me, yet each time I seemed about to float away the sound of the rattle would bring me back to earth, grounding me in the room, in the present, in the real world.

The ayahuascero also drank the sacred plant medicine, to bend the rules of time and space so he could be with each of us simultaneously. He was aware of the physical present and how each of us was feeling, yet at the same time he experienced all that we were going through on the inner levels – which some people say is a bit embarrassing!

If one of us seemed anxious or adrift he was instantly by our side, etherically holding our hand and soothing our fears, or physically shaking the rattle over us to lift the energy or shake off a spirit that had swooped too close. Part of me was conscious of time passing, while I also suddenly understood that it is not a linear concept. I saw it drifting around me, bending, circling, returning to a different point. I felt dizzy and a little uncomfortable, as though I was drunk and had to struggle to stay coherent. I sensed the woman next to me stand up and her assistant help her outside, where she was violently ill.

We each had a local guide assigned to us, entrusted with looking after us through the experience. I wasn't aware of mine, but he must have been bored. I sat, leaning against a wooden pole, from start to finish, not moving, not speaking, not sick, not freaking out. Yet others were having a terrible time, running outside to throw up, screaming in pain as they dealt with inner demons, and crying with anguish as they tried to leave the space. Later I discovered that if you don't throw up it can represent a failure to be vulnerable, to let go, and I felt sad that I'd remained so controlled and not given in to the sacred medicine, especially that first night when for some reason I held back.

"It provokes a profound state of altered consciousness that allows you to move beyond defence mechanisms into the depths of the unconscious mind – a unique opportunity that can't be duplicated by non-drug therapy. You come back with images, communications. You reconceptualise prior experiences. Having had a profound psycho-spiritual epiphany, you're not the same as you were."
Dr Charles Grob, US psychiatry professor and ayahuasca researcher

Everyone experiences ayahuasca differently, yet as a group we were also connected, and over the three nights we took part in the ceremonies many relationships and emotions were played out. Since the day we'd met at a US airport to fly to Peru, we'd been aware it was no accident that we were here together. Others had booked but then dropped out or postponed, and at one point the trip was going to be cancelled, except that I, a stranger from Australia, had confirmed my place and paid for my flights, and the American office felt they couldn't back out.

We all felt there were past life connections between us – love, loss, resentment, grief, friendship, jealousy, kin ties – and as the moon turned to full and shone down through the open walls of the cabin, many of them were re-experienced, often painfully, and resolved. At other times we each dealt with personal issues, battling all kinds of things from our pasts, and found our own inner healing.

The first night I thought that I wasn't really affected by the ayahuasca, although I realised later that I was, in different ways to the others. I desperately clung to sobriety and lucidity because I felt for some reason that I had to protect the others. Despite being the youngest, that night I felt like their mother, very protective, and responsible in some way for their health and wellbeing.

And the next morning one of the women told me that she had felt my presence as a Buddha – calm, solid and nurturing – as she had drifted through painful memories and relived terrifying events from her past. They had threatened to drown her, except that each time she was going over the edge she had felt me reach out and bring her gently back, grounding her in love and light.

Perhaps I was her mother in a previous life, or maybe it was simply because I've found myself playing that role in many of my relationships, and it was as much a lesson for me to examine my own actions.

Ayahuasca has hallucinatory properties, and during each ritual I had strong visions. The first night they were all about the power of women, of the healing we can give each other, and the support we are in each other's lives. I felt a power pulsing within me, saw images of goddess archetypes from around the world, and felt an energy flowing into me and back out to the world, connected to everything.

I had a new understanding of my own strength, knowledge and power, and no longer felt intimidated by being the youngest. I realised that each of us had something to offer the others, and that we all, no matter our age, had something we needed to receive. For me that night was all about healing self-esteem issues and beginning to acknowledge my worth, and it was powerful and intense.

The following night I had a lot more visions, and some of them made me laugh out loud. I was flying and swooping on brightly coloured carnival rides, celebrating and nurturing the child within. Then I was sucked into a whale's stomach and shot forth from the hole in the top of its head as the water that nourishes the land, the birds, the people – all of us connected. At one point I had a vision that I was married, and sensed it was reflective of my attempt to integrate both the masculine and the feminine within, a kind of sequel to my images of goddesses and powerful warrior princesses the night before.

Then I was suddenly dropped into a too-real vision of something that had happened years earlier and affected me deeply. My body froze as I felt myself re-experiencing it, so vividly and painfully, step by cruel step. Emotions flooded me, crippling me, but then I heard the sound of the rattle, and felt the comforting hand of the ayahuascero on my shoulder, and the energy spiralled around me, lifting me upwards.

And I saw myself as I was now – older, stronger – enter the vision and change the outcome. It was such a liberating, powerful feeling. A sense of relief washed over me, and also a sense of forgiveness, for both myself and the person involved. And I realised that I am strong enough that people can do anything to me and it will no longer affect me. I can acknowledge my hurt and pain and feeling of betrayal, rather than denying it, but then I can let it go, free of the burden.

On the third night my roommate decided not to take the ayahuasca, as she'd felt during the day that she'd have to look after me at some point. And she spent most of the night tramping through the jungle searching for me, calling my name anxiously, frantic when she couldn't find me. She told me later that she'd thought I'd left the cabin and walked off outside because in my space was a native Peruvian woman with two long black plaits and a red woven shawl.

We can't explain why she saw that – especially as she wasn't having visions – or what it was that she saw when she looked at me, because I hadn't shifted all night. Ironically I had been frozen, physically unable to move and trapped within my body. I'd been sitting in the same spot I'd been every night, unable to move a muscle, in my own little world and oblivious to her search for me.

It was a crazy night all round, and it took us all days to piece together what had happened in that little cabin deep within the jungle, under the silvery light of the full moon. People did die and were reborn, and while it was ultimately healing, it was also deeply harrowing. I was asked to go to the Other Side – by a person not a spirit – which I discovered later would have been a one-way trip. To this day I'm grateful for whatever it was that made me say no.

"I've never had an ego-destroying epiphany, a direct experience of the transcendent, eternal, fathomless mystery at the root of all religious thought. But the ayahuasca brought me close to something fearful and profound and deadly serious. The spectacular visions opened a doorway to another world of frankly cosmic possibilities."
Sting, British singer and musician

As we'd taken our places in the cabin that evening the ayahuascero had beckoned to me and handed me a small egg-shaped crystal. "You must hold this for protection," whispered his interpreter. Before I had time to wonder from what, the ayahuasca hit and I suddenly felt really stoned, like I was tripping. It was far more intense than the previous nights. I felt disconnected and detached, and my sense of time and space was warped – sometimes I thought the shaman was right in front of me, yet when I focused I realised he was on the other side of the room.

I had a series of really terrifying, bizarre visions. A bunch of jungle animals flashed by first, and the tigers came out to say they were watching over me. Then it got really dark in tone, with spiders and huge insects crawling all over me, tearing at my flesh and burrowing into my organs. I clutched the crystal tightly, scared now, as I faced down other visions of hell. A series of freaky images swooped at me, growing bigger and more intense, and then I saw myself dive down into a pit of flames, the archetypal "hell", then plunge a knife into my heart.

While part of me screamed in pain, anger and fear, another part realised this was the metaphorical death we'd heard about – the casting off of our fears, of the things that hold us back, of past events that no longer need to affect us – and the transcendence through the hell we create with our own actions and emotions.

It was at this point that I realised I couldn't move, which frightened me further, and also that something weird was going on around me. Two of the women were outside, making really primal animalistic sounds of pain and fear as they battled something only they could see. They were each exorcising their own demons, purging remnants of the past that had been affecting them, and mourning aspects of themselves that they were letting go with immense difficulty.

People have reported throwing up in a bucket and seeing black snakes and other strange things within it. Whether it's a hallucination, imagination or emotional blocks manifesting in physical form and being purged, it indicates a deep form of release.

Everyone's journey is different. Some people sit calmly, feeling gentle sensations and seeing only pleasant things. Others experience incredible spontaneous physical healings with no emotional impact. Some think nothing has happened, as their healing is a lot more subtle. Others aren't ready to let go and may not undergo any change.

Some people have conversations with dead loved ones and resolve issues or are told things that are later proved true. Some shapeshift into an animal and travel through the jungle seeing things through their eyes, filled with a sense of the unity of all things. Others face an animal and commune with it, terrified at first, yet learning much from the spirit being as it shares its wisdom and medicine with them.

While we were all experiencing our own journey, there were also intense scenarios playing out within the group, which is why such ceremonies should only ever be done with an experienced ayahuascero shaman, who can ensure you are taking the correct dose for where you are at emotionally in that moment, guide you as your spirit journeys to do battle with your neuroses and examine your psyche – which can be an intense, painful process – and bring you safely back.

Like any spiritual or healing experience, you should listen to your own intuition and do some research on the topic. Today there are some people who profess to be ayahuasceros who don't have the experience and wisdom necessary to create the right plant medicine brew or psychically anchor the group and control the situation.

Ayahuasca can also react with some medications and even common foods, and adding the wrong herbs, such as datura instead of chakruna, or the wrong amounts, can change the experience. A high level of trust is required between you and the shaman, and if you feel uncomfortable in any way you shouldn't take it. Ayahuasca is a psychoactive substance that works on very deep levels, and while miraculous healings from all kinds of issues, physical and emotional, have been reported, it must be treated with respect and caution.

Researchers claim ayahuasca has cured cancer, arthritis, drug and alcohol dependence, depression and anxiety disorders. In South America it is legal, and is used to treat psychological illnesses and addiction. North American scientists are battling its illegality there in order to study its curative powers – although they concede it could be as much the shamanic ritual attached to it as the actual medicine that leads to healing. Proponents argue that it's not a hallucinogenic, implying a recreational drug, but an entheogenic, a substance that helps you connect to god or your concept of the divine.

Any kind of healing is about trust and surrender, and happens when the time is right. Being in the jungle and taking part in such sacred ceremonies can help you find perspective, balance and healing, and the courage to leave behind the parts of yourself that you no longer need. Each of us felt a profound change as a result of our experiences in the jungle. We were completely drained and depleted in the following days, but slowly we felt ourselves emerge, like butterflies from a cocoon, a little more vibrant, a little more whole and healed.

"The difference between what we do and what we are capable of doing would suffice to solve most of the world's problems."
Mahatma Gandhi, Indian political and spiritual leader

In addition to all the incredible spiritual experiences that can occur in Peru, spending time there will also open you up to new cultures, languages and belief systems. Travel broadens your mind and exposes you to people, ideas, dreams and ways of life, and makes you more aware of the world and its issues, politics and injustices.

For all its rich culture and incredible sacred history, there is a lot of poverty in Peru, which can be confronting. Land ownership remains weighted against the indigenous population, and the west continues to exploit the country's rainforests and other resources. Health care is almost nonexistent for much of the population, and thousands of children can't afford to go to school. In many communities the water is contaminated, forcing women to walk miles each day to get enough to drink, and they have no money to buy the seeds to grow crops.

In Cusco, tiny, brightly dressed children wander through the main plaza begging for money, asking tourists to buy them cake or desperate to appear in a photo for a fee. Coming from such a relatively wealthy place as Australia, it was shocking and totally heartbreaking to see, a very profound part of my travelling experience. As a result, one of the most inspiring moments I had in Peru was after the spiritual tour, when I stayed on in Cusco to meet Amalic, the young girl I'd been sponsoring through Plan International for the past few years.

I've been sponsoring a child since I was an idealistic 13-year-old inspired by Bob Geldof and Band Aid, but standing next to this little girl in the dusty village she calls home, in the sacred land of the Inkas, opened my heart and touched me in a very profound way. I'd arranged with Plan for the local field officer to take me out to Amalic's community, so early one morning we rattled along a narrow, rock-strewn road on the edge of a mountain, past dusty, infertile fields baked dry by the intense sun, to the small village with its tiny, poorly built huts.

When we got to Amalic's place it was hard to hide my shock as I was greeted by her parents, who are bringing up three children in a tiny home with a garden plot so dry and small it would be hard pressed to feed a single person. But I was also filled with awe and respect for these warm, wonderful people. Her mum was only in her late twenties, but she looked years older, and has lived such a difficult life. Yet she is surviving, raising her children and caring for them as deeply and lovingly as any mother anywhere in the world.

Her son was tied in a rug to her back, so he could hear her heartbeat and be comforted. Being carried like that provides babies with a strong sense of security and love, which is finally being understood and copied in the west, where similarly styled baby carriers are now in vogue. Yet the Peruvians have been doing this for centuries, because they're so in tune with their children, life, growth and nature.

Amalic's mum was really shy, but gracious, warm and giving. She had made me a traditional clay whistle, crafted and painted herself, and two bracelets, which moved me deeply. These people have nothing, they struggle just to survive, yet she had taken time and precious resources to make me a gift. I felt completely humbled by these amazing people, and very mindful of the petty things that often consume my time and attention.

Amalic was waiting for us at school though, so I hugged her parents goodbye and made my way to meet her. She looked terrified at first, which was understandable, because people were pushing and pulling her, making her hug me and hold my hand while she stood there, bewildered. I was the first westerner she – and most of the kids – had ever seen, which also explained her shyness around me.

She and her sister showed me around, then took me to Amalic's classroom, where the children sang a song for me. Then I was led back to the quadrangle, where the whole school had gathered for a ceremony of welcome, because I was the first sponsor to visit the community. The gorgeous children sang songs and the teachers all spoke, with the field officer trying valiantly to translate for me. I was embarrassed, sitting in front of everyone, but it was so touching – I sat there choking back tears, Amalic by my side, as a little boy gave a speech, welcoming me with all of his heart and telling me how grateful they all are. And my eyes welled further when the principal of the school spoke, saying how important my contribution is and what a special person I am.

I felt like a fraud. My contribution is so small, yet for these people who struggle every day for survival, where education is a luxury not a right, it makes a massive difference. The money I send, along with donations from other people from around the world who also sponsor children in the community, enabled them to dig a well to get clean water, which made a huge difference to their health, and carry out other vital projects. Amalic could start going to school, and it now has books, toilets and furniture, with the kids no longer sitting on bricks all day and the teacher allowed the "luxury" of a desk and chair. And the villagers have been able to buy seeds so they can grow crops to survive, and agricultural equipment that will help them become self-sufficient.

It's a sad truth that the price of a coffee in the west can feed a family in a developing nation for days – yet it's amazing too, because it means everyone can make a real difference. For years I'd been told that the money doesn't get there, that it's pointless, that sponsoring a child supports the poverty consciousness of these people – all selfish excuses from people who don't want to open their eyes to the reality of this world. In the 10 years I've now been sponsoring her, Amalic has grown up into a healthy teenager with an education and a little more hope, in a community that is far more self-sufficient than it was.

When the ceremony was over, and Amalic had presented me with flowers and I'd given her presents, her mother arrived at the school and dished up a meal she'd prepared especially for me – guinea pig! I gulped. I've been vegetarian my whole life, and if I was ever going to lapse I'd never dreamed it would be for a tiny guinea pig. But I also knew how much this meant to her and the sacrifice it was to be giving it to me, and thought it would be rude to refuse. I was prepared to eat it if I really had to, because I had no desire to offend these beautiful people.

I asked the field officer, who'd been eyeing the plate covetously, whether I had to have it, trying to explain that I'd never eaten meat before – a lifestyle choice they can't afford – but she said it was alright, she would eat it. It is a delicacy in South America after all!

Whatever you do in Peru, wherever you go and whoever you meet, your eyes will be opened and your life will be changed. Your old self will die, washed away in the sacred waters of the Amazon, blown away by the holy winds over the Andes, burned away by the sun god Inti or buried deep within the sacred earth, and you will emerge renewed, stronger, and more fully and truly yourself.

The psychic connection

Quick tips to immerse yourself in the energy of Peru

1. Explore Andean shamanism by doing a workshop or reading books about it. For thousands of years the people of Peru have lived in harmony with nature and with the philosophy of ayni, sacred reciprocity, which states: "Today for you, tomorrow for me." Shamanism is not so much a religion as a path of personal power and confidence, which also stresses compassion and service to others and the planet.

2. Buy a small piece of Peruvian pyrite and absorb the energies of this crystal and the land it was created in. Its golden colour, which led to it being referred to as fool's gold, associates it with the sun, and it is recognised for being able to strengthen your connection to the earth. Pyrite boosts psychic development and communication with the subconscious, and energises and awakens the body and mind, while physically it increases oxygen supply and circulation and eases digestion, physical burnout, fatigue and lethargy.

3. Save endangered rainforest from your desk by simply clicking on www.therainforestsite.com or www.ecologyfund.com. Advertisers pay each time someone clicks on the sites, and the funds are used by conservation groups to buy and preserve land in Peru, Ecuador and other locations worldwide. It costs you nothing – just a moment of your time every day – and is an easy way to combat deforestation and promote awareness. You can also buy locally made products and art through the sites, with a percentage of sales going to buy more land.

4. Another way to be part of the magic of Peru is to sponsor a child, and correspond with the family as he or she grows up. You can learn a lot about the country and the culture through progress reports, photos and letters, and it's often possible to visit them. Health services are very limited in many areas of the country, with poor sanitation and inadequate access to medical care resulting in high morbidity and mortality rates, and little or no education available.

5. Do your bit to recognise the sacredness of the earth. The people of Peru are ecologically aware, with a deep respect for the planet, and they recycle and reuse not just to save money but also to protect precious resources. Being more aware of your own usage is the first step. You could also organise a clean-up day in your local area or take part in a national one, plant trees, protect a water source or an endangered species in your town or write to council members to push for the addition of a recycling program or some other local issue.

The armchair traveller's guide to Peru

"Preserving what we love at home and beyond has never been a greater challenge. Listening to native people and learning from them has never been more crucial. They've preserved the ancient wisdom that we are part of nature, not separate, and that what happens to nature happens to us. Indigenous communities nurture the values that can sustain us in the future and help keep the earth alive."
Christopher McLeod, American filmmaker

If you can't make your own physical journey to Peru just yet, there are other ways you can connect with the powerful and transformative energies of the country. Much of the magic of Peru is in the land itself, which is imbued with earth energy that affects you when you walk upon it, and in the soaring mountain peaks that the indigenous people of the country consider the residence of the apus, or gods.

This is a concept that crosses cultures and religious beliefs and spans the globe. Mount Olympus was home to the Greek gods, Tibet's Mount Kailash is a holy place to both Hindus, who believe it's Lord Shiva's home, and Buddhists, while Japan's Mount Fuji has been considered sacred since ancient times. Early Christians also believed it was easier to commune with their deity on top of a mountain, and many of their early churches were built high up, from the tiny stone structures of Skellig Michael off the coast of Ireland to the glorious Sacre Coeur in Paris, so they could be closer to God.

Climbing a mountain, or even a hill, can be a sacred way to connect with Peru and get in touch with your own sense of the divine, be that an external deity or the inner part of you. The views from the summit can be breathtaking, especially at sunrise and sunset, and whether you are on a snowcapped peak, a cliff or a grass- or forest-clad mound, you'll gain a new perspective on the world and your self. From a great height everything looks smaller, including your problems.

You could also make offerings to the earth and mountain spirits of your home, as they do in the Andes – anything from a libation of water, a crystal or a prayer to a service like cleaning litter from the area.

The people of Peru have a very close link to nature and the earth, and deep concern about the environment. You may not be able to go to the Amazon jungle right now, but there is probably some kind of rainforest or at least a grove of trees near your home. Visit your nearest forest, or simply sit with your back against a tree trunk, and breathe in the energy and the oxygen. Revel in the biodiversity of the plants and wildlife, marvel at the ancient trees, plants and vines, and sit quietly and listen to the incredible sounds of the birds calling above you, the insects buzzing around you and the wind dancing through the leaves.

Learn about the plant medicine in your area too. Indigenous groups have long known the powerful cures that lie within their forests, mountains and deserts. Being alone in nature also provides a sense of freedom and exhilaration that is often missing in day-to-day life.

You can also get in touch with this powerful energy by fostering a respect for the earth and the way the planet is treated. Plant a tree in your own garden or a park, or join a tree planting group in your area. In Peru, the awful destruction of the Amazon rainforest is a particular concern. The loss of these old-growth trees and their ecosystems has serious ramifications for the entire planet in terms of protecting against ozone depletion and the effects of greenhouse gases. Cutting down this precious jungle is also leading to the extinction of native tribes and many animal species, and the loss of unique plants that could be the basis of cures for a number of diseases.

Greenpeace is one of many organisations that works to protect the Amazon region and lobby South American governments to save their environment. In 2007 the group had a massive victory when it convinced the Brazilian Environmental Agency to close a port in the Amazon because huge quantities of soybeans from deforested areas of these precious habitats were shipped from it. The trees were being cut down to plant soybeans, not to feed the world but simply for fodder for the cattle bred for hamburgers, and the clearing was causing problems. Another victory came in pressuring McDonald's to become aware of the consequences of its actions – the fast food giant has now told suppliers it won't buy produce that contributes to deforestation.

You can join Greenpeace in its work by supporting campaigns financially or becoming a cyber activist who raises awareness and lobbies governments. You can also keep up to date with companies who are helping – or harming – the world at www.greenpeace.org, as well as with the other important issues the organisation works on, including campaigning to save the whales and other wild creatures of the earth, raising awareness about climate change and nuclear use and pressuring politicians to make global change.

Today more than ever people are becoming conscious of the dangers of deforestation and the effects of climate change, and everyone can do their bit. Lobby your government to protect the forests of your own country too – the whole world is in the grip of industrialisation that is destroying the environment, so wherever you are some eco sense is needed! Australia, America and Europe don't have a great record of preserving their old-growth forests and natural habitats either, and acres of jungle in Asia are being chopped down as you read this.

You can also join the mailing list, become a member or just check out the information from the Sacred Sites International Foundation, www.sacred-sites.org. A volunteer organisation, its members advocate and lobby for the preservation of sacred places around the world – including Machu Picchu – as they believe these sites are the key to preserving traditional cultures, maintaining religious freedom and respecting our beautiful earth. They work to protect places of nature including sacred mountains, rivers and rock formations, as well as pilgrimage routes, burial and ceremonial sites, shrines and temples.

The website includes lists of places that need protection, with the contact details of relevant government officials you can write to to urge action, plus other ways you can help. They have information on many different locations, regular newsletters on the most pressing environmental concerns, and members also organise spiritual journeys to different places around the world. There are links to organisations that work specifically for individual sites, resource books and websites, a list of guidelines for visiting sacred sites, and different levels of membership, some of which include a beautiful book on the topic.

The Earth Island Institute's Sacred Land Project also aims to protect the world's sacred places. Its website, www.sacredland.org, includes information on at-risk sites, the political ramifications and conflict going on, the histories of different sacred places, updated information, people to contact to add your voice of support, annual reports, newsletters and lots more. Members also create films to raise awareness about the need to protect these amazing places and the cultural and religious traditions attached to them.

"Shamans act as an intermediary between the human community and the larger ecological field, ensuring there is an appropriate flow of nourishment, not just from the landscape to the human inhabitants, but from the human community back to the earth."
David Abram, American ecologist, anthropologist and author

Studying shamanism, the earth-based spirituality of the Amazon and Andean peoples, can also connect you to the magic of Peru. Its foundation is a belief in the interconnected nature of all things, a sense of the sacred in daily life, communication with the spirits of plants, animals, rocks and the land, the honouring of your ancestors and, for long-time shamans, the ability to journey between the worlds.

Shamanism is about getting in touch with nature and with yourself, respecting the earth and its people, facing your fears and learning about your past in order to become whole and healthy. You can begin by simply shifting your reality and your perception of the world around you. Embrace the beauty of nature and notice the perfect moments in each day, which can lift your spirits and open your heart – a glorious sunset, a crashing lightning storm, the fall of an autumn leaf. Live your life and perform all of your actions in a sacred manner. Look for the beauty and love in all things, and all people. Try to see through personal conflict to the things beneath that you do share.

This doesn't usually involve much effort at all, for it is the intent with which you do everything that is most important. Shamanism is a way of life rather than a religious dogma, and influences the way people relate to the world, themselves and the people around them.

It is a broad term for something that is practised in different forms by many different cultures around the world, from Brazil and Mexico to Siberia and North America. Andean shamanism has its own unique belief system and style, and today there are many great books by indigenous shamans as well as others who have studied the path from an anthropological viewpoint, which instruct on different aspects of the craft. There are also many workshops and courses offered around the world which can connect you to the energy of the Andes.

An important aspect is the ability to journey to non-ordinary reality, to move between the lower, middle and upper worlds and communicate with animal and spirit guides to seek wisdom, knowledge and healing. This takes years of study, meditation and practise to master, but there are ways to learn if the subject intrigues you, even if you can't get to Peru to study with an indigenous healer and teacher.

If you feel drawn to the shamanic concept of spirit animals, and communion with these guides for personal healing, information and divination, begin forging a relationship with them. Shamanism holds that we each have a personal animal spirit guide who is with us to help us through life, much like the concept of a guardian angel.

Some people are already aware of which animal is their guide. If not, pay attention to any that repeatedly try to interact with you, either in the physical realm, in your dreams or through art, symbols or any other means. There are also many CDs that feature guided shamanic journeys during which you can meet your spirit animal. It's like any new friendship though – it takes time to get to know each other, and you must be open, honest, trusting and patient, spending time with them regularly. Don't expect to get the answers to the universe straight away – it will take time to learn how to communicate with this guide and understand the wisdom it can impart to you.

You can connect with your animal spirit through meditation or shamanic journeying, by drawing them, writing to them, visiting them at a zoo or wildlife park or in the wild, reading about them, having pictures or photos of them around you, singing or chanting to them, studying their characteristics and habitat, sitting outside and calling to them or campaigning on their behalf through various wildlife organisations or a specific group that works with your animal.

In addition to your personal spirit guide, all animals have something to teach us. Some may pop in for a while to help with an issue, or you can call on a specific animal to offer wisdom in an area or fill you with specific strengths, such as giraffe for foresight, dolphin for joy and cougar for confidence. Shamans take animal guides very literally, as distinct from other energies, although I believe that whether you call on Bear, Archangel Michael or Mother Earth, you're tapping in to an archetypal energy of strength, power and protection that's available to everyone, and can be accessed no matter what name you call it by.

The snake, puma and condor have always been significant in Peru. The serpent represents wisdom, healing and resurrection, and is related to the lower world in Andean cosmology. The energy of the snake, amaru, can ground and anchor you, and also help you move forward, letting go of past issues or events and emerging with renewed energy and life force. In many ancient cultures serpents represented wisdom and healing, as well as the kundalini energy that snakes up through your spine, awakening you and activating your chakras. The spirit of snake also represents initiation and new knowledge, so it is a powerful energy to connect with – and nothing to be afraid of.

The puma, choquechinchay, represents assertiveness, power and leadership, and is related to the middle world in the Andean worldview – the physical realm, of action and reality. It can help you manifest goals, make things happen and be more present in the moment. Call on the spirit of puma if you're lacking direction or motivation and need assistance to make decisions or be assertive, strong and brave.

The condor, kantur, represents the realm of spirit and your fullest potential. It sees everything, not just the small area you're aware of, so call on the spirit of this majestic bird when you want to soar above a problem or issue in order to see with much greater perspective and find a solution you hadn't considered. It can help you to comprehend the depth of who you truly are and what you can become, and begin to perceive yourself as the powerful, beautiful being that you are. It can also assist you to integrate your blossoming spiritual beliefs and new energetic vibrations into your life and your soul.

Another part of shamanic healing is soul retrieval. Practitioners believe that when trauma occurs you lose a little part of your self – a part of your soul or spirit breaks off as a protective mechanism. It could be your innocence, trust, self-esteem or ability to love or be loved that you lose, and this loss can lead to issues such as addiction, personality disorders, disassociation or behaviours you feel ashamed of.

This splintering off is a way to survive a devastating trauma, and for that part of you to avoid further pain. I can very clearly see images of myself at a few different ages – young, scared, imploring, and angry that I didn't protect her. Once I communicated with one of these young selves, writing a letter to her with my right hand and letting her converse with me through my left. It was a fascinating process, and she had much to teach me about why I act the way I do, and why I no longer need to protect myself in that way. During the ayahuasca ceremonies in the jungle I faced another one of my younger selves, and resolved an issue with her and the part of my self that had been wounded.

Many people can undergo this kind of process and heal this level of pain and trauma through conventional psychology or psychotherapy. Sometimes revisiting the event, discussing it with those involved and understanding it as an adult can help too, because often perspective is a big part of it. It's possible that a small incident, misunderstood, could lead to a child creating a deep sense of abandonment or betrayal, which could be neutralised by understanding the true context.

In shamanism, which holds that the loss of a part of your soul can lead to illness, the process of soul retrieval is used to heal. The shaman journeys on behalf of the patient, seeking the parts that have been lost and calling them back to the person. Beautiful ceremonies are performed to retrieve them and welcome them back, then further healing is done to help integrate the missing parts of your self. There are shamanic practitioners who can facilitate this process, as well as books and courses on the topic if you want to explore it on your own.

You can also set up and use a shamanic mesa, a healing altar. This can be as simple as finding something to represent the four elements – earth (allpa) in the south, representing Pacha Mama, the earth; water (unu) in the west, representing Mama Quilla, the moon; wind (wayra) in the north, representing Wiracocha, the creator; and fire (nina) in the east, representing Inti, the sun – plus something in the centre that represents spirit to you. Arrange your objects on a small flat area that will become your sacred space.

You could have a crystal or rock in the south, a cup of water in the west, a feather in the north and a candle in the east, with a small god and/or goddess statue in the centre, or anything that calls to you on a deep level. A golden piece of pyrite can help you honour the solar energy of Peru and the sun god Inti. Other objects that are meaningful to you and a part of your spiritual journey and unfolding knowledge can also be added when the time is right – just follow your intuition.

When I was in Peru my mesa was begun with a goddess statue from home, a chunk of amethyst and a tiny Inkan artefact from Cusco. Each time we did a ceremony these pieces were put in the central mesa and charged with power and intention, and the energy of the earth.

As I travelled new objects were added – the crystal from the shaman I had clutched so tightly in my hand that night in the jungle, a feather gifted to me, a miniature toy llama from the Pisaq Markets.

Since my time in Peru I've collected new things for my altar – a beautiful wand made by a friend, a tiny cauldron from Prague, crystals, statues and sacred objects that have meaning to me. Your altar is a reflection of you and your beliefs, the physical manifestation of your spirituality. An Andean shamanic mesa is quite structured, and while mine is now more Celtic in arrangement, it still retains a little of my time in Peru, and all the things I learned there.

An altar is the focus of your attention and prayers, a place where you can manifest dreams into reality and make offerings to the gods you believe in or for any cause you feel strongly about. For shamans it is a powerful healing tool developed over years of apprenticeship and initiations, and it grows, changes and becomes more potent as time passes and their wisdom increases. It can be used to channel healing, commune with spirit guides and offer prayers to the universe.

You can also tap in to the energy of Peru by honouring your ancestors, which was very important to the people of the Andes. Include photos of them on your altar and nourish them energetically with your time and attention. Shamans journey the spirit paths to meet with the ancestors and bring back knowledge. You can send prayers of gratitude to yours, and develop your own form of communication to discover more about your family and your history.

It's also important to honour the people in your life now, while they are still in the physical realm, and not wait until they die to recognise their value. Spend time with your loved ones. Ask your parents and grandparents about their lives and what they were like when they were young and full of dreams. Everyone has a fascinating story to tell and lessons to impart. Find out about your family's past and where you are from. Create a family tree, put together a photo album that spans generations or write it all down to preserve your unique history. Unravel the love stories that underpin the relationships of your relatives and celebrate all the love in your life.

Andean philosophy embraces the principles of munay, yachay, llan'kay, kawsay and ayni. Munay is about unconditional love and acceptance, yachay embraces the ideals of learning and sharing knowledge, llan'kay refers to the balance of inner and outer work and life, kawsay incorporates the interconnectedness of all things, and ayni is sacred reciprocity, a kind of compassionate service that they know enriches their own life as much as it does the people they help.

Regardless of religious or spiritual beliefs or allegiances, these concepts are beautiful, timeless methods of living that will fill your life – and the lives of those around you – with love, happiness and contentment.

Postcard from Peru

Cuban-born Alberto Villoldo is a medical anthropologist and psychologist who has studied shamanism and healing in the Andes and the Amazon of Peru for more than two decades.

He is an energy medicine teacher and author of several books that bridge ancient shamanic healing practices, modern medicine and psychology, including *The Four Insights: Wisdom, Power and Grace of the Earthkeepers*, *Shaman, Healer, Sage* and *Courageous Dreaming*. He founded The Sanctuary Project, which provides shelter to indigenous healers as they descend from the Andes and documents their work to preserve their spiritual traditions.

Alberto is the founder of the Four Winds Society and teaches shamanism and energy medicine to students around the world, culminating in an annual journey to Peru, where life-changing initiations take place at sacred sites with the indigenous medicine men and women of the country. Visit www.thefourwinds.com.

Everybody who goes to Peru is touched by the power of the feminine, the earth, the spirit of the land and the people who live there. Everyone, whether they are consciously aware of it or not, is changed by its energies. This is the feminine energy of the mother, of Mother Earth or Pacha Mama. This energy is everywhere we are, but it's especially alive in the Andes. Peru is the only place in the Americas where there's still a thriving indigenous population, so all the traditions are alive, and all of their sacred places are still vibrant.

Machu Picchu is a very powerful place. The veil between the worlds thins there and you have access to the world of spirit very directly. There are seven leylines that intersect at the main temple, the Temple of the Sun, which makes it a place of tremendous power. And the city is in a bowl, like a concave mirror, that focuses all of the energy from the surrounding mountains into it.

It was only built in the 1400s, but Machu Picchu existed as a site for ten thousand years before that, and it is still a place of initiation for the indigenous people of the Andes. There are medicine men and women who go there at night and climb up the back of the mountain to hold their initiation ceremonies. By day it can be overrun by tourists, so try to go in at night, because that's when the city comes alive.

The Inka priests left spiritual guardians to keep anyone from trespassing energetically, so you must bring an offering with you. This can be in the form of a prayer, or a gift you leave for the earth or spirits, and then you're allowed access. They say that the white man always comes empty handed, and in Machu Picchu in particular you have to bring a gift to be able to tune in to the spiritual richness of the place.

It is one of three sacred cities of the Inkas – there are two others of the same scale and power, Choquequirao and Vilcabamba. Many of the indigenous people are now going to these sites for their rites of passage and initiation, in order to avoid the tourists, but it's a two-day hike up and down mountains to get to either of these places. If you want to see them, you should go in the next five years, before they start building roads and turning them into tourist attractions.

There is also a series of ruins in the area of the Sacred Valley, temples comparable to the Egyptian temples, of the same grandeur and stature, built by the Inkas on top of the ruins of earlier peoples.

When I apprenticed with the shamans in Peru I went back to the roots of the Inka civilisation, to the vestiges of a five-thousand-year-old tradition. Scattered through the remnants of the empire were a number of sages who remembered the ancient ways. These shamans had access to extraordinary capabilities of the human brain. They were the scientists, the saints, the sages. They understood that the natural world has a visible and an invisible component to it. They were able to birth and bring forth from the invisible into the visible world, whether it was to heal an individual or to guide the destiny of an empire.

Shamanism offers a direct communion with the divine and the possibility to influence the course of one's own destiny. There are no levels of management between you and spirit, it's you *and* spirit. It's not a religion. There's no Christ, no Buddha, nobody says: "Follow my footsteps." It demands that you take your own steps with courage, compassion and vision, that you learn how to learn from nature. It has direct access to power, but is tempered by compassion and service.

I've worked with ayahuasca shamans as part of my training, and taking this plant medicine can be an extraordinary life-changing experience that opens your vision up, but it can also be extremely hazardous and destabilising if you do not work with a master. It takes you beyond death to face every fear you've ever had. It's not an easy experience, yet it's become so commercial now that you have to be very discerning as to who you work with. In Peru today everyone claims to be an ayahuasca shaman, because they know tourists will pay a hundred dollars to do a session, so interview them very carefully.

The wisdom of Peru is the wisdom of the Americas, it's the same as the Hopi and the Mayans – it's the wisdom of the earth peoples. And the earth peoples' way is the way of the feminine, of honouring the feminine and honouring the earth. Not of raping and looting and pillaging, but of stewardship. And that's the greatest teaching of Peru – the stewardship of the earth, and of each other.

GREAT
BRITAIN

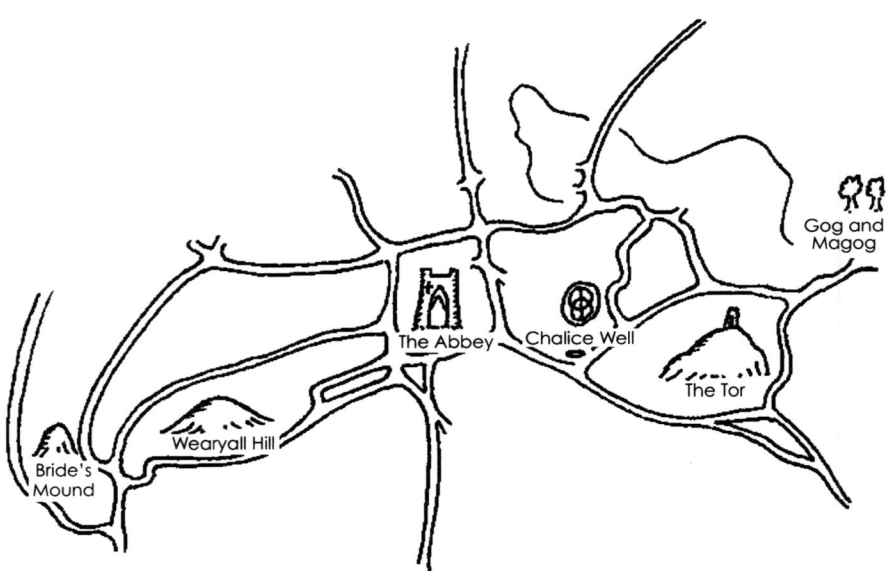

Gog and
Magog

The Abbey   Chalice Well

The Tor

Wearyall Hill

Bride's
Mound

Unlock your inner priest or priestess

The sacred Isle of Avalon
Glastonbury, Somerset, England

Immerse yourself in the ancient magic of the priestesses and druids of the British Isles, attune yourself to the beating heart of the earth and its sacred energies, and hear the whisper of history in this mystical place where the early Christians worshipped, King Arthur lived valiantly, and the wise women made their potions.

The place

"There is on the confines of western Britain a certain royal island, called in the ancient speech Glastonia, marked out by broad boundaries, girt round with waters rich in fish and with still-flowing rivers, fitted for many uses of human indigence, and dedicated to the most sacred of deities."

Saint Augustine of Canterbury,
first Archbishop of Canterbury, seventh century CE

Deep within the swirling mists of the ancient land of Britain is a tiny town of immense spiritual, religious and historical significance. Glastonbury, just a few hours southwest of London, England, has long been acknowledged as the spiritual heart of the country. It is a place of legend and myth that draws people of all faiths to wander the sacred earth and submerge themselves in a landscape that opens everyone up to the truth within their own heart.

Renowned as the mystical Isle of Avalon, it has been a place of magic and spirituality since ancient times. For centuries the priestesses did healing work and followed the goddess there, druids worshipped alongside Christians before religion turned to war, and King Arthur and the chivalrous Knights of the Round Table built Camelot and defended the country from barbarian invaders.

Even today it is a melting pot of cultures, ideas and beliefs. In the last census it had the most residents of any town in the United Kingdom reporting "other religion", and pagans, Christians, Buddhists, Sufis, Hindus, New Age spiritual searchers and atheists all seem to happily co-exist in a community that fosters healing, growth and self-awareness, no matter what your path.

Made famous in Marion Zimmer Bradley's enchanting bestseller *The Mists of Avalon*, which details the pre-Christian goddess worship of the Old Religion and the real-life magic of the priestesses, Glastonbury has touched the hearts of thousands of people from around the world, while somehow retaining the quaint charm of a working farming village in the English countryside.

The town consists of just four main streets arranged in a square amongst tiny winding lanes lined with wild hedgerows, fields of sheep and buttercups, cute little cottages and shops filled with organic produce. Yet it has something for everyone tucked away behind the faded storefronts, within darkened stone churches and at the mystical places of nature for which it has become so popular.

Spiritual pilgrims today are drawn to the powerful energy of Glastonbury Tor, the massive green hill that towers over the town. It's been considered a holy place for millennia, and can be seen from miles away, an instantly recognisable piece of the sacred landscape, and a place where the veil between the worlds is thin.

Visitors climb straight to the top and marvel at the views and the strong, masculine energy of the hill, or weave their way to its centre by threading their way through the ancient seven-level labyrinth, a physical and metaphorical journey within. Believed to have once been crowned with a stone circle, and now holding the ruins of an old church tower on its top, the Tor is variously said to be a faery hill, a pathway to the underworld and Archangel Michael's mount.

Nestled at the base of the Tor is Chalice Well and its beautiful peaceful gardens. This is where the Priestesses of Avalon did their seering, gazing into the sacred wellspring to divine the future, and where they drew the waters to concoct potions for physical and emotional healing. Today people still flock here to drink from the sacred Red and White Springs, which have been credited with miracle healings, or submerge themselves in the pool to absorb the vibrational essences, as pilgrims seeking cures did centuries ago.

Chalice Well is also said to be the place where Jesus's great uncle Joseph of Arimathea took the chalice of the Last Supper, so it has special significance for Christians too.

Nearby, in an enchanted glade, are Gog and Magog, the magical oak trees that are the only two left of the ancient druidic processional avenue that once wound its way up the Tor, which provide a place of powerful, nurturing energy. Across town, on the outskirts heading south, are the gentle slopes of Wearyall Hill where, according to legend, Joseph planted his staff and a sacred thorn tree grew.

And in the centre of town are the ruins of Glastonbury Abbey, which is recorded as the first Christian church in England, and thus holds within its crumbling stones the history and beliefs of this two-thousand-year-old religion. Throughout the beautiful grounds are tumbled down chapels, the exposed foundations of tiny monks' cells, the intact old Abbot's Kitchen, tranquil lakes, apple orchards and the graves of King Arthur and his queen Guinevere, whose story is a vital archetype and part of Britain's soul.

Glastonbury is a place of myth and magic, of history and legends come to life, but it is also a modern village where people live normal lives – farming, running their businesses, selling crystals, herbs, books or hardware, going to school and church, commuting to London or working in one of the many cafes.

Alternative spiritual beliefs flourish alongside more conventional ones – Christians converge on the town on holy days, there's a beautiful Goddess Temple, where the new Priestesses of Avalon undergo their apprenticeships, celebrate pagan festivals and hold open rituals, as well as a number of churches, healing centres and even an ashram that encourages eastern meditation and yoga for those who stay there. Whatever a person's faith, or lack thereof, Glastonbury is a sacred and timeless spiritual sanctuary that awakens the light within everyone who spends time there.

In addition to its significance through the ages and the reverence for the past it instils, which manifests in the form of goddess worship and other religious practices and rituals, Glastonbury also has a very modern effect. Even if its potent history is dismissed, the very land lives and breathes with a beautiful nurturing quality that embraces all who visit, regardless of beliefs or intent.

Walking through the streets of the village, up and down the hills and through the beautiful gardens by the sacred wells and springs, your heart will reawaken because of the power that resides in the very earth here, and you will begin to see the magic within your own self as your inner priest or priestess is activated by your interaction with these incredible energies.

The present

"Avalon is a landscape of the soul, a country of the heart. It's the land the poet and mystic see in visions, where the artist and musician find inspiration, and the soul goes for healing and spiritual refreshment. A timeless land that offers initiation and enlightenment to all those who embark upon the inner voyage."
Mara Freeman, British druid and author

While people travel to the town of Glastonbury, for many it's the mystical dimension of Avalon that they seek. This is not a physical place but rather a state of being, a realm where you can access the inner world and your deepest intuitive self. Long ago, when the town was called Avalon, it was renowned as a centre of druidic initiation and knowledge. Women came from all over Europe to serve the goddess and train as priestesses, and people worshipped the Great Mother, practised the healing arts and communed with the divine on this sacred land.

It was a place of enchantment and deep transformation, but when the new religion of Christ sent the Old Ways into the shadows, the wisdom was hidden away, so that now, reaching this magical realm has evolved into a vision quest of sorts. Not everyone who goes to Glastonbury reaches Avalon, or wants to. It is possible to walk through the town, have tea and scones in a cafe and climb to the top of the Tor without feeling the swirling air of magic and seeing the sparkling enchantment of this other world.

But many people have reported accessing this dimension. They have seen the light change and the atmosphere ripple before them, and felt the mists closing around them. Some experience Avalon descending as they sit in quiet contemplation by the sacred Well, while others stumble upon it as they walk along a wooded path as darkness falls and shadows lengthen. Some have crossed over into Avalon while walking the ancient labyrinth on the Tor, and others have gone there in dreams, bringing back wisdom to integrate into their waking life. Times of change – sunrise, sunset, midnight, as well as the turning points of the seasons – can make this magic easier to access.

Avalon is another dimension, a place between the worlds, but it also has a physical, geographical location, anchored on the slopes of the Tor and in the waters of Chalice Well. It is slightly removed, a kind of parallel universe that touches the seams of the real world yet floats apart, accessible to those with the eyes and heart to see. Avalon is where you can find answers and guidance, recharge your body and spirit and reawaken to the magic that is within you. It opens you up and reminds you there is more to life than the limited part that is seen. You can dare to dream, to live full out, to achieve your goals. You can reconnect to your own heart and soul, rediscover the beauty of the world and the potential you have to create your own perfect reality.

Avalon is a place you can reach no matter where you are in the world, because it is within you, a state of being where everything is possible and you are awash with magic and potential. But the easiest way to get there is by spending time in Glastonbury, visiting its sacred places and allowing yourself to absorb and be absorbed by the mystery and myth that permeates it.

The town lies in the shadow of the Tor, a beautiful grassy hill that mysteriously shapeshifts with distance and the changing light. While its outline can be spotted from other villages, up close it seems to disappear. There are places in town where it and the ruined church tower on its top can't be seen at all, despite its hulking size.

Part of the Tor's mystery also comes from its shape – from some angles it looks like a symmetrical rounded hill, but from others it is completely different, almost rectangular in layout, with a narrow strip of land and a gentle slope from its base near Chalice Well, and an almost sheer drop on the other side. As the hill is climbed, the tower on the top also appears to move, sometimes looming high above then suddenly dropping below the summit, other times appearing to the left then later to the right. In photos it looks like a kid playing a trick, always in a different place, on a different level, yet from the top it's clear that the tower is located at the highest point.

The Tor, named for the Celtic word for hill, has been described as a magic mountain, the grail castle, a centre of goddess rituals, the land of the dead and a gateway to Annwn, the Otherworld, which was ruled over by the faery king Gwyn ap Nudd. It's also said that within the hill there are chambers, a crystal cave, the tomb and resting place of the great King Arthur, or even a hall of records holding ancient wisdom.

Walking up the pathways of the Tor to its summit is a spiritual experience in itself. One, the Pilgrim's Path, winds up the slope closest to town. It's a gentle approach, starting from the bottom of Wellhouse Lane near Chalice Well and climbing up past the place where esoteric author and spiritual teacher Dion Fortune lived and worked in the 1920s and 30s. There is a bench halfway up so climbers can catch their breath and gaze out across the town to Wearyall Hill, then from there the path slopes slowly upwards to the tower at the top, which is approached with a sense of reverence and awe.

Another path rises steeply from the base at the other side. It's a shorter route, and was recently landscaped to better conserve the slopes and prevent erosion from the thousands of eager feet that climb this enchanted hill each year. The Tor is managed by the National Trust, which has taken on the sacred charge of protecting the area while maintaining access for all who wish to visit.

Standing barefoot on top of the hill in the sunshine, gazing out over the beautiful countryside of flowers, patchwork meadows, ancient trees and quietly grazing cows, the power of the place is deeply felt. I've sat for hours on the grass here – in sunshine and rain, at sunrise, noon and sunset, in darkness and light, under the full moon and the dark moon – sensing the energy rise and fall.

I've had epiphanies about my self and my beliefs, realised the reasons for things that have happened in my life, let go of past hurts and embraced the future with a strength and positivity that owes much to the site and the energies it activates within.

Atop this sacred hill I could feel a tangible force, a vibration that quickens the heart, the spirit and the soul. It is the life force of the earth, which pours forth so strongly on the Tor's grassy slopes. Part of this energy is from the impact of the Michael and Mary leylines that run through the hill, two powerful lines of earth energy that race upwards and intersect on the summit in a swirling vortex of power and a melding of masculine and feminine energy.

Leylines amplify feelings, experiences and emotions – love and the quest for enlightenment, but also fear, anger and bitterness – and that can be painful unless you're aware of it and ready to face the things within you, the weaknesses we all have. A local guide who took me to nearby Cadbury Castle, the reputed location of Camelot, said Glastonbury is a hard place to live because it brings up a lot of stuff within, issues from the past and present, and not everybody is ready to deal with that. The worst fights he's ever had have been on the Tor, because it amplifies everything – positive and negative.

Conflicts of the heart and self are played out here, and the mysteries of love, hate, death and rebirth are revealed. Glastonbury itself means Isle of Glass, and residents say that living here is like being in a place where your thoughts and emotions are constantly reflected back to you. And you'd definitely have to be ready for that!

It is up on the Tor that I have most strongly felt Avalon surround me, as I sat watching the legendary mists roll in. As the sun sets and the shadows lengthen, as the cold settles in place over the warmth of the day, a thick, swirling cloud creeps into the hollows of the town, between the hills and over the fields, wreathing its way around houses and through the Abbey ruins, drowning trees, animals and buildings as it rises and spreads out over the land.

Referred to as the Lake of Wonder and the White Lady, this mystical phenomenon covers all the lower ground, and only the grassy hills – the Tor, Wearyall Hill, Bride's Mound – remain above the tide line.

Coloured by the last rays of the sun, and later by the rising moon, the mist is an ethereal, enchanted substance, holding secrets within each molecule. Breathing it in can change you, can transport you, can transform you. People hear whispers in this mist – the voice of the goddess, of the faeries, of your own inner knowing. It speaks to you of things you always knew but had forgotten, putting you back in touch with your soul and opening you up to hear the voice of your heart.

Another way to access the dimension of Avalon is to walk the old labyrinth carved in the side of the Tor. While debate continues over the exact purpose of its construction, whether or not it was intended as a sacred pathway doesn't really matter – it is one today because we have made it so. Spiritual pilgrims from around the world walk the spiral path to the Eggstone, the psychic centre of the labyrinth, and back out as a meditation and a transformational step in their own spiritual development, a modern-day initiatory experience or rite of passage. It is an amazing process, a sacred ritual you can do alone or with a group of people with the same intent.

For various reasons I didn't end up making this pilgrimage until my fifth visit to Glastonbury. Perhaps I wasn't ready until then. But finally I tied a red ribbon around my wrist, symbol of the goddess Ariadne who oversees such journeys, and walked the ancient path that winds around and around the Tor and back in on itself, into the heart of the hill and the other dimension of Avalon. I followed the labyrinth into my heart, my self, my desires, my needs, my limits. I moved through the mists of my mind, and through the veil that separates the real world from the Otherworld that lies over Glastonbury.

It is a beautiful, meditative walk, through apple orchards and a magical wood on the lower slopes, then along the steepest sides at the top, where it's hard to get a foothold and you have to cling to the almost vertical slopes with your hands, fingers clawing into the earth.

Each of the seven levels is linked to an element, an emotion and a chakra, which activate as you walk, opening you up to the universe and your own inner wisdom. You can feel the spiritual footprints of the pilgrims who trod this track before you, and reach out for the lessons and knowledge they accessed, which now lie within the etheric path around the Tor. You'll be touched by the history floating around, and will feel the wisdom of the priestesses, or the saints, or even Arthur and his companions, brush against you as you make your journey.

It takes several hours each way, between four and eight depending on how you walk it and what you need to get out of it. It's suggested that you make your way inwards one day then walk out another, psychically holding yourself within the centre of the labyrinth while you physically return to the base of the Tor down the ordinary path, then going back to the centre another day to wind your way out.

This allows the wisdom you acquire and the realisations that occur to sink deeper into your soul, penetrating all layers of your psyche. You should also pay special attention to your dreams on the nights in between, when your spirit self remains at the centre of the labyrinth, because secrets will unfold and answers will be revealed to you.

And so a few days after I wound my way inwards I walked back outwards – away from my past and towards my future, towards my true self. I felt lighter, transformed, having let go of my fears and the things that had scarred me, the things that no longer matter. Recently engaged, I walked towards my forthcoming marriage, but for everyone it is a personal journey, a way to deal with the past, prepare for the future, answer a question or learn to listen to your inner guidance.

Another aspect of the Tor's powerful impact is the spiritual emanation of thousands of years of worship and ritual that have taken place atop this grassy knoll. Everything seems possible up here, as you feel the heartbeat of the planet and hear the whisper of the spirit. It affects people from all over the world, who follow all kinds of spiritual and religious paths. I've spoken to Christians, pagans and atheists up on the summit, and all felt something uplifting and inspiring them. Some call it God, some goddess, some believe it is nature or science, and others simply soak it up and are grateful for the experience.

"Sacred wells and springs form a centre of healing and ritual, dedicated to the deities or saints of the religion of the dominant culture, but still the waters from the Mother's womb. They have attracted worship and been sacred to many religions because of the powerful earth energies that converged at the spot, making Otherworldly connections easier."
Cassandra Eason, Celtic witch, teacher and author

At the foot of the Tor is Chalice Well and its beautiful gardens and water features. For millennia it's been an important source of healing and spiritual power to all those who have lived in the area, no matter what their beliefs. Pagans saw it as the goddess Ceridwen's cauldron of knowledge and revered its healing powers, while for Christians it became the chalice of the Last Supper, placed there by Joseph. Both interpretations are symbolic of the holy grail and enlightenment, and encapsulate a form of healing that transcends the physical and works on the emotional and spiritual levels as well.

Natural springs and wells have long been revered both for their life-giving water and as a source of spiritual power and magic, places where the veil between the worlds is thin and communication with the gods and goddesses of the nature religions and with other dimensions can be made. They're regarded as gateways to the spirit world, and throughout time they have been used to divine the future, cast spells, send messages and act as a metaphoric mirror to the soul.

Chalice Well is all these things, but most importantly it's a place of healing. In ancient times the local priestesses used the vibrational power of the water to treat the sick, and today it is still renowned for easing pain, curing illness and treating emotional and spiritual malaise. Modern pilgrims have claimed cures for everything from migraines and kidney disorders to chest infections and depression.

Miracles of healing attributed to the waters of Chalice Well have been documented for centuries. In 1582 John Dee, the Elizabethan mathematician and alchemist, claimed to have found the elixir vitae – the elixir of life and immortality – at the Well. And while he did die, it wasn't until he was in his eighties, a grand old age in those days.

In 1750 a man dreamed that if he drank the water every Sunday for seven weeks he would be alleviated of his life-long asthma. He followed his vision and claimed he was cured, as did many of the thousands of people who poured in to the town in the hope of their own healing.

Glastonbury was a famous spa town throughout the 18th century, when people would travel great distances to take the waters, drinking from the spring as well as submerging themselves in the Pilgrim's Bath in the gardens near the Well. A pamphlet of the day, called *The Virtues and Efficacies of the Waters of Glastonbury*, records dramatic healings from rheumatism, deafness, "most difficult and troublesome respiration", ulcers, tuberculosis, paralysis and leprosy.

There was also a Pump House in Magdalene Street, opposite the Abbey, an earlier version of current spa resorts, where people went to bathe in and drink of the water that was pumped there from the Well.

Today many of the healings seem to be on a more subtle but deeper level. The water is full of iron and other minerals, but that's not what causes the healings – a multivitamin could do that. Instead there is a vibratory force that is released and activated when the spring water comes to the surface from deep within the earth, and interacts with the elements of air and light above. This water is also infused with the energy of the leylines that run through Chalice Well Gardens, and the magic of this extraordinary place.

Experiments have found that the water from holy wells is lighter than normal water. And while this effect is not yet understood, pilgrims continue to visit the Well for healing and spiritual transformation, knowing that it works and unconcerned by its cause.

Chalice Well is fed by the Red Spring that pours forth from under Chalice Hill, the gentle mound that rises in the shadow of the Tor. The water is a constant 11°C and has a red tint and a metallic taste due to its high iron content, caused by ferrous oxides oxygenating as the water reaches the surface. Across the lane outside the gardens is the White Spring, which is fed from a source deep within the Tor. Unlike the iron-rich water of the chalybeate Red Spring, this water is calciferous, with a high calcium carbonate content.

The Red Spring is considered to be for physical healing, while the White Spring imparts a spiritual quality, so a mix of the two is recommended to create physical and emotional wellbeing. Only a small amount is required – a few drops of each in tap water imparts benefits, and too much can be a little unsettling on the tummy. The two springs also represent the alchemical melding of male and female energies to create wisdom and life force, with the White Spring representing the masculine and the Red or Blood Spring representing the feminine.

Prehistoric tribes drank from the Red Spring at least five thousand years ago, and the Well has been in constant use since long before the time of Christ. It pumps out a constant 112,000 litres a day, and has never failed or run dry, even when the country was in drought – there have been times when Chalice Well was the town's only water source.

Long ago a stone well shaft was built over the spring. Some date it to around 1200CE, but the remains of a two-thousand-year-old yew tree which was part of a processional way to the Well have been dug up, and Iron Age shards and Roman pottery have been found around it, indicating that it could be far older. Connected to the well shaft is a stone chamber that is illuminated by a beam of light at sunrise on the summer solstice, which also points to ancient origins.

Once the well shaft stood above the ground like a more traditional well, but since then the surrounding area has been built up with earth, and the well head is now at ground level, covered by a beautiful lid bearing the vesica piscis symbol and surrounded by overhanging trees, flowers, stones and steps where people sit to meditate near the source. The vesica piscis is the ancient sacred geometric pattern of two interlocking circles, which symbolises the merging of the conscious and the unconscious, the physical and the spiritual, yin and yang, god and goddess, and the inner and outer worlds.

Today the Well is surrounded by the enchanted realm of Chalice Well Gardens, and a small entry fee is charged to help maintain the beautiful space. In 1912 educational pioneer Alice Buckton bought the Well and the land around it, which at that time was the site of a Catholic monastery, and held it in spiritual trust for the people of the area. She created a college and guest house there, produced mystery plays, wrote visionary poetry, performed rituals with others – Dion Fortune, Frederick Bligh Bond and the famed Avalonians of the early 20th century – and allowed access to the place for spiritual contemplation.

After her death Wellesley Tudor Pole, a spiritualist who instigated the Silent Minute during World War II, formed the Chalice Well Trust and bought the Well and the adjacent house to prevent it being used for industrial purposes. The Trust has managed the gardens and grounds ever since, maintaining the magic and intent of the place and ensuring it will remain a sacred site accessible to the public for all time.

Walking up the cobblestone path under a canopy of flowers to the entrance and stepping through the gateway is like entering another world. You feel a sense of reverence like being in a church, yet this is an outdoor shrine, a place of nature and the goddess. When I first spent time in the gardens I was flooded by a great sense of homecoming. It was as though I had lived here before, and understood the deeper purpose and the subtle vibrations of the place.

Sitting quietly at the Well and gazing into the dark waters under the ancient yew trees, I had a vision of the priestesses in their long robes, gathering water for their healing potions, strewing herbs on the surface as they watched images of the future unfold before their eyes, making blessings and respecting the ancient water element and its power.

The air shimmered and my skin tingled. Had I been here before, with them? Everything felt so familiar, so much a part of my very being. My heart expanded as I felt their energy and intent merge with mine. I sensed their devotion to their healing work, which connected us across the centuries, and an inner peace and tranquillity that I longed to reconnect with. I also felt washed clean by the energy of the place and the sense of gentle nurturing that permeates the air.

Another beautiful place to absorb these vibrations is at the lower pool, near the garden's entrance and shop, which has been built in the shape of the vesica piscis. The pool is fed by a goddess-shaped water feature that has been stained red by the iron-rich waters, which have long been associated with the life-giving blood of the earth mother and the fertility of the planet, the goddess and women.

This feminine aspect of the site was lost for centuries when the Christians claimed it for their own, insisting the waters ran red because Joseph hid the chalice of the Last Supper there, overlaying the old symbolism of the place with their own new meaning. They adopted the vesica piscis as their own, using its sacred geometry when they designed their cathedrals. They also took the shape made by the intersecting circles – the fish shape they called an ichthys – as their symbol, yet again it was appropriated from a nature worship thousands of years older than theirs, as evidenced by the ancient cave paintings and carvings of goddess figures and yoni sculptures in the same form.

On the way up to the Well is the Lion's Head Fountain, where the water can be drunk as it pours forth through the carved mouth. There is a soft green lawn and a sweet-scented, colourful garden surrounding the fountain, so you can sit where the water spills out, meditating in the sunshine, absorbing the warmth and comfort of the dancing sunbeams and drinking deeply of the healing liquid.

Down some stone steps is King Arthur's Courtyard, a shady, walled garden area where the water cascades down in a crystal clear waterfall to fill the Pilgrim's Bath, the place people have come for centuries to submerge themselves in the healing waters. This is where the Michael and Mary leylines intersect again, after previously meeting in the Abbey grounds and then later winding up and around the Tor to connect on the summit, so it is a powerful place of swirling energy.

The first time I walked through the archway into this quiet area it touched my heart in a way I'd never felt before. I sat at the bottom of the waterfall under the shade of a giant tree, being splashed by the sparkling spray of water and gazing at the tiny flickering candles, flowers and ribbons left here as offerings, and cried. They were happy tears, tears that seemed to wash away years of pain and bitterness.

I felt my heart open – a physical sensation, not just a metaphor for an emotion. I was shaking and a little off-balance, moved by the power of the place and mesmerised by the misty spray and the lush, vivid green. I felt linked to the ancient source of healing in a way I couldn't really comprehend, but could deeply feel.

Later the sunshine peeked through the leaves overhead as I sat with my feet and hands in the healing waters of the Pilgrim's Bath and soaked up the peace and mystical air. It's so quiet here – people only speak in hushed tones, and the water spilling down into the pool sounds so tranquil and calming. Suddenly I felt such a jolt of connection and recognition. I don't know whether it was because I'd once lived a life as a Priestess of Avalon, whether it was the energy of the leylines that activated deep emotions within me, or something else altogether, but it doesn't matter. I felt healed, renewed, awakened and somehow lighter, transformed by the beauty and power of this site.

This was also where I met a man from Holland who had come to give thanks for the extraordinary healing he had received from Chalice Well. He'd been in hospital, dying, when a friend showed him photos of the garden and the spring. Somehow the energy of the place healed him, and he had come as soon as he was well enough to experience its power for himself, express his gratitude and drink the waters. Many others have also reported distant healing, showing that you don't even have to visit the place physically to connect with its energies.

There are other magical places in the gardens too. There's a peaceful area near the Well called the Sanctuary, a small courtyard garden where two small springs meet in a tiny pool and statues gaze tranquilly down. The Meadow is a beautiful grassy area overlooking the whole complex, where people picnic and chat, and the Cress Field is the place where the Guardians light the Beltane bonfire, and where I've taken part in a few pagan ceremonies over the years to mark the seasons and the ancient Wheel of the Year.

And rising above it all is Chalice Hill, from where the water emerges. It's a beautiful, gentle mound of grass and sunshine, which is dwarfed in size by the nearby Tor, but has its own power and majesty.

Those who lived and worshipped in this place thousands of years ago would be so happy with the way the Well and the gardens have been protected, maintained and celebrated. There's not a single spiritual cliche here, just respectful and magical guardianship of a place that will hopefully remain preserved in this manner for centuries to come.

The Trust also operates a retreat house within the grounds, with accommodation for Companions. This provides 24-hour access to the Well and the gardens, and is one of the most beautiful experiences in Glastonbury. It's truly magical to drink the water under the silvery light of the full moon, or to wander through the enchanted realm in the pre-dawn mist, hours before the gardens open to the public, watching tiny squirrels scamper along the grass and butterflies float above the healing pools. And sitting alone at the Well when everyone has gone for the day, while the golden light of sunset illuminates the grounds, makes the sense of peace and healing complete – it's truly a balm for the soul.

But even when the grounds are closed there is constant access to the vibrationally charged water from both the Red and White Springs on Wellhouse Lane, near the bottom of the path up to the Tor. On the outside wall of the gardens is an outlet for the Red Spring water, and across the road there's one for the White Spring, trickling out from a semi-abandoned building where locals fill massive containers.

Once there was a pretty wooded valley between the Tor and Chalice Hill, and their two springs emerged side by side from the earth so the energies of the waters could mix freely. Now however a road and a reservoir separate them. There is a conservation group trying to restore the old setting and reawaken old rituals there, but until that happens it is people who continue to create the alchemy of blending the energies from both springs as they imbibe the healing waters. Some drink only one or the other, but most combine the powers of the Red and the White Spring waters to receive the full range of healing.

"People have long gone to sit beneath the mighty oak to gain strength and spiritual renewal. The outside world can be forgotten and the inner world can slip back into perspective. The oak can help you find new understanding and vision, gained from your experiences, and bring strength and courage to face your life. The oak tree's mighty presence helps restore faith in yourself."
Glennie Kindred, English artist, writer and pagan celebrant

Another beautiful, spiritual place to spend time is in the shade of Gog and Magog, the last two remaining oaks of a long-ago processional way that led to the top of the Tor. The druids trod this path two millennia ago, when their ways and their reverence for nature were respected. Gazing at these massive old trees, silent sentinels over so many centuries, I could understand why these ancient people spoke of shifts in perception as they walked beneath the branches. I could picture them moving through the darkness in candlelit procession, the full moon shining down, long robes swishing around their bare feet, the priestesses with blue crescents emblazoned on their foreheads, and overhead the leafy arches of an avenue of sacred oaks.

It's a long, steep walk from the base of the Tor, down a beautiful country lane and across an old-fashioned country stile, to reach these two trees, which are suffering the vagaries of time, sometimes appearing dead or at least in a long sleep. It's been said that they alternate energy, and that usually only one is covered in foliage while the other remains bare, and then they swap, taking it in turns to receive and be nurtured, the way a relationship should be.

Traditionally such avenues of sacred trees consisted of pairs, and each alternated feminine and masculine energies. Thus Gog and Magog are deemed a couple, and attributed with personalities and human characteristics. Perhaps this is why people are so outraged that in 1906 a farmer chopped down the long pathway of ancient oaks to clear the ground for cattle, leaving these two Oaks of Avalon as the only reminder of what once was.

They have been dated to around two thousand years old, and are so wide that it would take several people holding hands to reach around their trunks. One of their now-gone friends was almost four metres in diameter and had more than two thousand rings when it was felled, reinforcing the druidic wisdom that the oak is king of the forest.

Gog and Magog stood alone for a century, but recently the Glastonbury Conservation Society replanted a line of oak trees to commemorate the ancient processional way. This is another thing I love about the town – people respect nature and the past and want to preserve it. The group is involved in many conservation projects in the area, such as improving pathways to prevent erosion and increasing the number of trees – they've planted almost forty thousand in and around the town. They've also nominated Glastonbury for a place on UNESCO's list of World Heritage Sites in order to better preserve the cultural and natural significance of the place.

The countryside of England was once covered in forests of oak trees. They were sacred to the pagan tribes, representing strength, endurance and courage. Druids performed their rituals and ceremonies within a grove of oaks, and wands made from the wood helped magical practitioners get in touch with their inner power and symbolised protection, strength and fertility.

Medicinally, a decoction of oak bark was used to ease congestion, improve muscle tone and heal infections, the leaves were used to stop bleeding and decrease inflammation, and a homeopathic remedy eased stress, aided relaxation and controlled cravings.

Oaks were also associated with the crowning of kings, the preaching of gospels and the meeting places where laws were proclaimed. They marked boundary lines and processional routes, people got married and performed other ceremonies beneath the leafy branches, and it was thought that energy, wisdom and calm could be absorbed from the tree by leaning back against its trunk.

It's certainly very peaceful sitting in the shade of these two oaks, which are entwined with tangled rose bushes and wild berries. It feels like a place of faeries and magic, where time can stretch and your perception can shift. Gog and Magog are hollow in parts, with caverns, nooks and burrows at the roots – possible houses for creatures of all kinds. Offerings hang from the branches and nestle in the cracks, including crystals, ribbons, bells, incense, jewellery and water brought from Chalice Well to nourish their roots.

They're also surrounded by honeysuckle and wild nettles, which sting with a long-lasting, bitter ache. Like many things in nature however, the antidote grows right next to it – the leaves of the dock plant ease the pain of the nettles. The druids and priestesses who worshipped the old oaks understood nature, and believed that the earth always provides a cure to anything toxic that it creates.

On the way back to town I walked up through the field of buttercups where the processional route once ran. There's so much energy on this ancient path – I could really feel it seeping into my body and my being. There is old magic soaked in the ground here, imprinted on the ether, as there is at many of the places in Glastonbury, which have gained power over the centuries through the varied but constant worship of the landscape and the deities that once ruled it.

Another sacred tree is the holy thorn that first grew on Wearyall Hill, another beautiful mound to the southwest of the Tor. Legend has it that when Joseph of Arimathea returned to Glastonbury to found his church he stuck his wooden staff in the top of the hill, where it took root and sprouted into a living hawthorn tree – which was a fairly common event in the lives of the saints.

Whether you believe this legend or not, there is something miraculous about this particular plant and its descendants, which flower twice a year, once in spring, as all hawthorns do, then again in winter, around Christmas, which many perceive as a Christian miracle.

No one has been able to explain how this occurs, but attempts to make it happen to unrelated trees or grow one from seed always fail – it's only the trees grown from a cutting of the original that flower twice a year. There are a few of these holy thorns in the town – the windswept one on Wearyall Hill, as well as those in the grounds of the Abbey, in Chalice Well Gardens, outside Saint John's Church and on Magdalene Street – all grown from cuttings from Joseph's tree.

The original thorn tree was reportedly chopped down and burned by Oliver Cromwell's troops during the English civil war of the 1600s, which was ironic given that the Christians this tree meant so much to had done the same thing to the sacred groves of the druids when they forced their religion on them.

In pre-Christian times the hawthorn was also a sacred tree, the symbol of springtime and fertility, and was believed to have special powers of transformation. Its white flowers were used to boost circulation and improve heart health, its red berries to relieve stress and anxiety, and an infusion to aid kidney health and long life. Magically it was used for good luck and protection, and was connected to the faeries.

"Glastonbury has always been a centre of pilgrimage. Although the Goddess is here in the land, people of all faiths come because this is a spiritual centre for all. There's something very powerful in the energy of the place itself that draws people."
Kathy Jones, Celtic priestess, teacher and author

For all the magic and history of Glastonbury and Avalon, these days it's best known to most people as a three-day music festival, which is actually held on a farm 10 kilometres east, in the village of Pilton. It began in 1970, when Marc Bolan headlined, and throughout the years acts as diverse as David Bowie, The Cure, Boomtown Rats, REM, Hole, White Stripes, Coldplay and Robbie Williams have appeared.

In the hippie spirit of the area the festival is environmentally friendly, with recycling and camping facilities, and millions of dollars have been raised over the years for charities such as Greenpeace and Oxfam. I've never been to it, although I've been in the town while it was on, but each time I plan a trip to Glastonbury I'm asked if that's why I'm going.

For spiritual seekers it is instead the earth energy, the sacred landscape and the transformative powers of the Tor, the Well and the Abbey ruins that make Glastonbury a place of pilgrimage. And unlike many sacred and magical places, it's fairly easy to visit. While crossing the mists to Avalon involves a much deeper quest, it isn't hard to physically reach Glastonbury.

From London you can catch a bus or hire a car to make the 220 kilometre journey. The gentle slopes of the Tor and its crumbling tower can be seen from several towns away, acting as a beacon to draw visitors nearer, teasing as it seems to change direction and shape as the road twists and turns. I still vividly recall the first moment I laid eyes on it, as I travelled there by bus, the sky bright summer blue and the hill a deep green, and the most recent time, trying desperately to arrive in my little car before dark, the tower lit up by the rays of the approaching sunset, melding dramatically with a black storm cloud as autumn turned the whole world golden.

Considering the size of the town, there are a surprising number of places to stay, from camping sites and the friendly hostel in the 16th century coaching inn on Market Place to the luxurious George & Pilgrims Hotel just a few doors up, which was originally built for pilgrims to the Abbey and is reputed to be haunted. There are also many B&Bs to choose from, as well as several self-catering places, an ashram with budget accommodation and the Chalice Well Gardens retreat house, which includes 24-hour access to the Well. To stay here you must join the Trust, which includes free entry to the Well, regular newsletters and discounts in the shop, and which supports the organisation in the important work of preserving this ancient site.

All the sacred places are easy to find and within walking distance of the town centre, but there are also a few tour companies that offer half-day, full-day and week-long journeys into Glastonbury's Arthurian, druidic and Christian past, which can help you delve beneath the physical level of the town and unlock the secrets within its heart. And there are many healers, both traditional and New Age, spiritual courses and workshops, as well as public gatherings, rituals and special events that take place throughout the year.

In addition there is a Goddess Temple, the first one in Britain for fifteen hundred years. Co-founded and run by pagan author Kathy Jones, it is a beautiful space which people are welcome to visit so they can meditate, soak up the divine energies of the goddess, get in tune with nature and the sacred landscape, and meet like-minded souls.

Kathy also trains modern-day Priestesses of Avalon, who undergo a three-year apprenticeship and initiation into the traditions of old, studying to reclaim the role of healers and keepers of wisdom who celebrate the cycles of life and nature. They conduct beautiful open rituals on the solstices, equinoxes and pagan cross-quarter days, and at the different phases of the moon.

They also provide healing circles and oracle sessions, and the individual priestesses (and priests) facilitate marriage blessings, naming ceremonies and divorce rituals, provide midwife services, offer correspondence courses and are pagan prison chaplains, amongst other things, as well as co-ordinating the annual Goddess Conference, a five-day celebration filled with workshops, artwork, performances, rituals and healing. They have a beautiful temple space above a shop on the High Street, as well as a goddess hall on Benedict Street, bought in 2008 to hold workshops, trainings and larger ceremonies.

The past

"Once upon a time Glastonbury was under the sea, but a stirring of geological forces pushed the Tor above the surface. For a while it looked out over empty water, then the sea-bed heaved itself up and became Somerset."

Geoffrey Ashe, British historian and author

Long ago the land where Glastonbury is located, which lies near the Bristol Channel leading into the Atlantic Ocean, was one of the few sections of solid ground in the Somerset region, an island among the flooded lowlands that have since been drained and built upon.

For thousands of years the area was inhabited by Neolithic tribes, and others before them, island-dwelling people who lived in harmony with the land, worshipped the sun, the moon and the trees as sacred and took part in rituals to honour the seasons and the landscape.

Legends persist that the earliest dwellers in Glastonbury were survivors from the lost land of Atlantis. Whether or not this is true, there is archaeological evidence of settlement in the area from at least 4000BCE, long before the time of the druids. By then the formerly flooded areas had begun to silt up, and islands had emerged amongst the marshland. A stone axe head, a goddess figurine and elaborate wooden trackways through the bogs have been found from this period, preserved in layers of peat, which provide hints of a people who worshipped the Great Mother goddess common in Europe at the time.

Later the Celts started settling in the area, building hill forts on high ground and maintaining ties with Brittany in France – a place of forests and stone circles that to this day shares stories of Merlin, Morgen la Fey and King Arthur with Glastonbury. The town was known as Avalon, and it was a centre of druidic and priestess initiation where a series of nature-based gods and goddesses were revered.

Historians can't agree on the exact origins of the word, but Avalon comes either from the name of the god Avallach or Annwn, who ruled the underworld said to reside within the Tor, or from the Celtic word for apples, the sacred fruit that grows in the orchards of the town.

Apples are symbolic of soul transformation, regeneration and immortality, thus relating to the underworld, and the apple tree was considered the Celtic tree of life. The fruit was given to the kings of Britain to symbolise their marriage to the land, which was the embodiment of the goddess. Later the Christians referred to the town as Ynis Witrin, the Isle of Glass, which developed into Glastonbury.

As Avalon it was the realm of earth mysteries, the Lady of the Lake and the deities that are still associated with Glastonbury today – the maiden Bridie, a goddess of healing and inspiration who became hidden within the legend of Saint Bridget; the nurturing mother goddesses Modron and Rhiannon, who were associated with fertility, protection and manifestation; and the crone goddess Ceridwen, keeper of the cauldron of knowledge, transformation and rebirth.

There are also legends of the Nine Morgens, the guardians of the secrets of Avalon who are said to still be present in the landscape, and who taught the priestesses the arts and sciences, including herbal lore, astronomy, prophecy, healing and music.

The most famous of them is Morgen la Fey, who became entwined in the myths of ancient Britain, claimed as King Arthur's sister-lover. She is a "dark" goddess, keeper of the deep mysteries, divination and initiation, and the shadow side of Guinevere, the "light" goddess embodied in the land and the sunshine of spring.

In 1892 some of the complex lake villages – tiny manmade islands constructed in the watery marshlands – of the goddess-worshipping Avalonians were uncovered near Glastonbury, providing a fascinating glimpse into their life and beliefs. The system of spirituality they followed revered nature and preserved the environment, and their deities were a part of the sacred landscape. They believed the planet was alive, and that they had been entrusted to keep the balance and harmony of nature. In turn the earth nurtured, fed and balanced them.

Their religion embraced tolerance, equality and the right of all people to worship in their own way. Men and women were equally respected, and they believed in both a masculine and feminine face of the divine, with a priest and priestess presiding over rituals and learning – which brought them into conflict with later belief systems.

When the Romans invaded Britain in 43CE they brought their "one true God", and killed those who would not convert to their ways. They also built an incredible network of roads across the country and drained huge tracts of land, yet Glastonbury and its surrounds remained prone to flooding from the nearby ocean, and even up to 1000CE continuous work had to be done to protect the area from the sea and keep it drained. Much of this labour was performed by the monks of Glastonbury Abbey, and the 10th century abbot Dunstan, who later became a saint, was particularly renowned for his efforts.

For a long time the Tor was one of the few pieces of land to have emerged from the waters, an island amongst the lakes. And today it remains the most significant landmark in the region, with the present-day town built in its shadow, on ground that was once underwater.

This gently curved natural hill is 158 metres high and more than twice as long, and is shaped like a teardrop, with a rounded main section that draws out to a longer, narrower part on the side closest to the town. It's comprised of layers of clay and limestone, with a harder sandstone top that has weathered erosion well. The iron-rich waters of its underground spring have also assisted its stability, as deposits of iron oxide from the water have strengthened the soil. There are strange egg-shaped boulders in the sandstone, called by some omphalos stones, as well as calcite crystals deeper within the hill.

"Saint Michael shrines are commonly set on high places, where beacon fires once blazed on the days of the festivals. The tower of Saint Michael on the Tor is one of the stations in an alignment of Michael shrines that extends along the spine of southwest England that corresponds to the path by which, according to legend, Christ once proceeded from Cornwall to Glastonbury."
John Michell, English philosopher, archaeoastronomer and author

While there's evidence of a fifth or sixth century hill fort on the Tor, attributed to Melwas, a rival of King Arthur, today it is the tall stone building that remains on top, visible from miles away, that ignites people's imaginations. This 14th century church tower is all that is left of the medieval monastery of Saint Michael, which was built on the ruins of earlier places of worship. Church records indicate a very early church and monastic settlement on top of the Tor, built by Saint Patrick, although archaeological evidence reveals that the first probably wasn't constructed until the 10th century.

This centre was dedicated to Saint Michael, who was known as the slayer of dragons to represent the Christian repression of the Old Religion that had flourished at the site previously. Pagans were symbolised as dragons and snakes by the church, thus when Saint Patrick drove the snakes out of Ireland, he was forcing the followers of the Old Ways to flee or risk being killed for their beliefs.

Building a church dedicated to the dragon slayer atop the Tor, which was sacred to those who worshipped the goddess, was a way for the Christians to publicly stamp their mark on the area and discourage alternative spiritual practices. Why else would they have built a church at the summit of this very steep hill – which parishioners would have hated to climb, especially in winter – when the beautiful Abbey in the town below was well used and easily accessible?

In 1275 an earthquake destroyed Saint Michael's church, which some attributed to the vengeful ancient spirits of the land, although science has explained that the cause of the instability was the caverns within the Tor. A new, smaller church was rebuilt on the site, which lasted until 1539, when this building, except for the tower, was destroyed during the Dissolution of the Monasteries, the four-year period when Henry VIII decided the monasteries, and the monks, owned too much land. He closed them down, seizing their wealth, selling off their land and destroying religious shrines and churches.

Today the tower adds another dimension of reverence and focus to the natural hill. Its shape is the perfect symbol of the male energy of the Tor, which contrasts with the feminine energy of Chalice Well in an alchemical marriage. And on a more mundane level it provides welcome shelter from the bitterly cold winds that howl around the top.

Winding around the Tor to the summit is the labyrinth that was carved in the side of the hill more than five thousand years ago. Labyrinths are common to all cultures, and evidence of them has been found on archaeological digs all over the world. The Tor labyrinth was a processional way related to the old goddess worship, an initiation rite symbolising the journey through life, death and rebirth, and was walked in order to communicate with the deities of the time.

Many believe it was created by the same people who built the great astronomical observatories of nearby Stonehenge and Avebury, and that it was the centre of a series of visual markers such as hills and rivers that provided sight lines so they could observe celestial events and determine seasonal midpoints and days of lunar significance, acting as an ancient calendar. There was once a stone circle on top that was part of this observatory, and an alignment of standing stones that ran down the hillside, although only a few of the latter remain.

One of the popular legends that surrounds the Tor is that King Arthur and his Knights of the Round Table rest in eternal sleep within it, and will awaken when England is in its hour of greatest need. Another states that the Tor itself is their metaphorical round table. Around it are a series of landmarks shaped by hills, waterways, roads and earthworks that correspond not only to the signs of the zodiac but also to each of Arthur's 12 loyal knights.

In this story the warriors had to go to each landmark in turn and complete a quest or an initiation – whether it was to literally slay a dragon or save a damsel in distress, or was a more esoteric mission in which they had to learn a spiritual lesson, depends on how literally it is interpreted. After successfully completing each task they would ascend the Tor through the labyrinth to attempt the final challenge.

Galahad, the son of Lancelot, is thought to have been the only one to succeed, because of his spiritual purity. He reached the top and was rewarded with the holy grail – which caused him to leave his mortal body and go into the light. For the holy grail of legend was not an object but a state of enlightenment and self-knowledge, a quest people still visit Glastonbury today to try to fulfil.

It is in fact believed that King Arthur, or a real-life man he was based on, did live in this area and unite the British people against the

Saxon invaders after the Romans departed England in the fifth century. Such a leader did have a stronghold at nearby Cadbury Castle – thought to be the site of Camelot – and there is evidence of his presence at the hill fort that existed on the Tor during this era. This was a time when goddess worship still echoed through the forests, Christianity was still establishing itself and Roman morals and codes of behaviour held influence – the chivalry that defined this period of history.

Arthur trod a difficult path in trying to reconcile the Old Ways with the new, in adopting the current religious order without betraying his people, who still saw a feminine aspect of the divine. With his death in battle, the old wisdom went underground, lost to the world and yet still energetically present in the sacred landscape of Glastonbury.

Perhaps this is why the town is emerging now as a centre of goddess worship, as the secrets of the past, of the idea of divinity being a combination of masculine and feminine, a power that is within each and every one of us, is revealed from the earth itself.

"Glastonbury Abbey is like a man struck down in his prime. The spirit of the Abbey is there, alive and energising. We have only to close our eyes to feel the atmosphere of a great church all about us. There is spiritual power there. Standing in the great nave, looking towards the high altar, we feel the movement of life."
Dion Fortune, British occultist, psychic and author

For those who prefer their religion more mainstream, the ruins of Glastonbury Abbey are renowned as the site of the first Christian church in the British Isles and the birthplace of Christianity in the country. While the pagans and New Age seekers have the Tor and Chalice Well, the Christians have the Abbey ruins, which to this day are a place of pilgrimage for believers from all over the world.

Each week services are held in the small Saint Patrick's Chapel, which was built in 1500CE and is still intact, or outside in the remains of the great medieval Lady Chapel. There are also annual summer pilgrimages to the Abbey, both an Anglican and a Catholic one, which draw people from as far away as Australia and the US.

Visitors of all faiths can wander through the sprawling, grass-covered grounds – which include the stunning ruins of chapels, altars, monks' dormitories and shrines, the still-whole Abbot's Kitchen building, an apple orchard, a sweetly scented medicinal herb garden and a duck pond – to soak up the energy and feel the power of the religious worship that's taken place here for centuries.

Church records report that Joseph of Arimathea built a wattle and daub church dedicated to Mother Mary, said by some to be his niece, on land given to him by the druids. When he arrived in Glastonbury after the Crucifixion, reputedly with the chalice of the Last Supper, the druids accepted him as a man of great learning. Legend has it that they discussed religion and theology with him, and all learned from each other and respected each other's different paths to the one divine truth. Sadly though this tolerance didn't last, and later Christians persecuted the druids, priestesses and followers of the Old Ways.

According to 12th century historian William of Malmesbury, Joseph came to Glastonbury from the Holy Land with eleven others around 63CE to start their religious foundation and spread the word of Jesus. The burned remains of their church allegedly still exist below the later constructions that made up the Abbey, and from that time onwards a community of monks lived and worshipped there.

This new religion slowly grew, continuing alongside the old in relative harmony until Roman emperor Constantine legalised Christianity in the early fourth century. He was trying to promote tolerance, because until then followers of Christ had been denied the right to practise their beliefs, but it was the death knell for the goddess religions of the country, and created a new form of bigotry.

Missionaries swept through Britain zealously preaching the scriptures, and by the end of the century paganism was illegal and the priests and priestesses of the Old Ways were killed or driven out, their sacred groves torn down and their worship outlawed.

Christianity became the official religion, and Glastonbury turned from a place of druidic wisdom to a centre of monastic glory. The popular Irish saints Patrick and Bridget both spent time in the area. Patrick arrived around 445, and declared Glastonbury "the holiest earth in England", a claim still repeated today. There are even stories that after his mission in Ireland was complete the snake-banishing cleric returned to England, gathered together the hermits of Glastonbury and became the first abbot. He's said to have been buried at the high altar – although there is some debate over whether this was the famous Patrick or another missionary of the same name.

The holy woman Bridget also visited from Ireland, in 488. She prayed at the chapel dedicated to Mary Magdalene at Beckery, on the outskirts of town atop Bride's Mound, which later became Saint Bridget's church in her honour. Before any religious buildings had existed here, the hill had been a small island sacred to Bridie, one of the primary goddesses of the Celtic world. Its well had also long been dedicated to her, but it was renamed in honour of the saint, a common occurrence in the British Isles as the world became Christianised.

Bride's Mound had been the gateway to Avalon, and a women's community existed there in both pagan and Christian times. Today goddess ceremonies take place once more on this hill, and there is a chapel in town dedicated to Bridget as both saint and goddess.

In 712 the first stone church was built in the grounds of the Abbey, which successive abbots extended, increasing the religious power of the town. In the 10th century the influential monk and court adviser Dunstan arrived in Glastonbury. He became abbot in 945, and in his lifetime he instituted Benedictine (Catholic) rule, helped the Abbey recover from the Saxon sackings, constructed sea walls to protect the town from flooding, enlarged the church and built new cloisters.

He later became Archbishop of Canterbury, the highest religious office in the land, attracting further glory to the town, and he also remained abbot of Glastonbury until his death in 988. In *The Domesday Book* of 1086, it was recorded that Glastonbury Abbey was the richest monastery in the country, and many religious men who later became saints, including David, Augustine, Collen, Paulinus, Patrick and Benignus, lived and served there for a time.

In 1184 a fire destroyed the whole complex and many of its treasures, but within a few years it had become a pilgrimage site again due to the discovery of King Arthur's bones in the cemetery, another connection that joins people of all faiths. In 1191 monks found two skeletons they claimed were Arthur and his wife Guinevere's, buried under a stone slab with a lead cross that said, in Latin: "Here lies buried the renowned King Arthur in the Isle of Avalon."

The bones were kept in the chapel for almost a century, then placed in caskets and reinterred in a black marble tomb before the high altar in a ceremony attended by King Edward I and Queen Eleanor. Pilgrimages to the site became even more popular, which has led many to question whether the monks really did find any bones and if they were in fact those of the former monarch, or whether the claims were simply a publicity stunt to draw pilgrims back after the fire.

Interestingly, the reburial of the husband and wife together, close to the point where the Mary and Michael leylines intersect, symbolises the marriage of masculine and feminine energies, another pagan concept embraced by the priests. In Glastonbury there are three energy vortexes created by the intersection of these leylines – beneath the ruins of Saint Michael's Church up on the Tor, within the Chalice Well Gardens, and at the site of Lady Chapel in the Abbey grounds.

The druids established their healing centres, initiation places and ceremonial sites at the places where leylines intersected in order to harness and make use of the amplified energy, and the monks followed their lead, perhaps unconsciously, by building Lady Chapel on the same site. Today people of all faiths feel a power there that is beyond religion, something older and deeper and more profound.

In addition, beneath the ruins of this chapel is a small dark well surrounded by ancient stones. It was once sacred to the goddess, used by the druids and priestesses for ritual and healing, and was later dedicated to Mary and Joseph, adding to the multi-dimensional power of the place. Today visitors breathe this in by spending time in quiet contemplation on this spot, finding their own sense of meaning and interpretation in this historic place.

After the fire's terrible destruction, the Abbey was slowly rebuilt. The new Great Church was consecrated on Christmas Day 1213, renewing the glory of the Abbey and making it second only to London's mighty Westminster in size, wealth and influence. The kings and queens of England often visited the area and attended services in the chapels, and the abbots wielded immense power and lived in total luxury.

This all came to an abrupt end during the Dissolution of the Monasteries. King Henry VIII stripped eight hundred religious orders of their wealth, land and churches, claiming them for his own, and forcibly converted the country from Catholicism to the new Church of England. His actions were partly due to greed and partly so he could get a divorce, which was forbidden by the Catholic church of the day.

In 1539, Glastonbury Abbey was the last to be closed. Abbot Stephen Whiting, who had long supported the king, was pronounced a traitor when he refused to join the new faith and hand over all the Abbey's treasures, and he was hanged, drawn and quartered up on the Tor as part of a terrible, senseless persecution and abuse of royal power.

Afterwards the Abbey grounds were vandalised. Arthur's tomb went missing, although the monks created another grave nearby which can be visited today. It doesn't look that impressive, just a rectangle of grass bricked off with a sign above it announcing it as the resting place of the brave king, but it is rich with symbolism, legend and history.

Glastonbury Abbey was slowly disbanded and the stones were taken away to build houses, much like the way the early church had pulled down the stone circles to construct their places of worship. It was a tragic end to one of the most powerful religious institutions in Europe, which had controlled vast lands, possessed a great library and been regarded as England's most sacred place.

King Edmund had been buried in the Abbey in 967, in 1125 it was so famous that William of Malmesbury wrote a history of it, *De Antiquitate Glastonie Ecclesie*, and 18th century English writer William Blake's famous poem *And Did Those Feet in Ancient Time*, which became the hymn *Jerusalem*, was written about Glastonbury and the legend that Joseph had taken Jesus there as a young boy.

After the dissolution, the Abbey ruins remained deserted for more than three hundred and fifty years, until in 1907 the Bath and Wells Diocesan Trust bought the site for the Church of England – a sad irony for many Catholics – and started to restore and study what was left.

Between 1908 and 1922 archaeologist Frederick William Bligh, a friend of Dion Fortune's, discovered the foundations of many old chapels and monks' cells that had been built over or buried underground, and helped reconstruct what the Abbey looked like when it was one of the most magnificent in the country. Sadly he was fired when he revealed that much of his information was channelled from a monk who had lived at the Abbey hundreds of years previously, yet his work was instrumental in restoring and rediscovering its history.

Like most of Glastonbury, the Abbey incorporates the influence of different faiths, with experts claiming the building was designed on similar mathematical principles to Stonehenge and the Pyramids, and it having been constructed along the leylines that run through town.

Today the fascinating museum just inside the entrance to the complex features a model of what it looked like in the 1500s, and presents a history of the site through all its incarnations, with stories of how the monks and abbots lived through the ages, their beliefs and challenges, the progress of this holy community and all the legends associated with it. There are also Living History characters who wander through the grounds in summer, offering unique insight into the lives of those who worked at the Abbey centuries ago.

Wandering through the ruins, which are charmingly picturesque against the vivid blue sky and lush green grass of the grounds, I could envision how it must have been in its heyday, with its soaring arches and grand construction. I walked through parts of Lady Chapel, which is open to the sky but still retains some walls and a sense of the grandeur it once had. Also known as Saint Mary's Chapel and dedicated to Mother Mary, it was built on the site of Joseph's primitive church, which was also dedicated to her.

Beneath it in the crypt is Saint Joseph's Chapel, created in the 1500s, which features an altar where services are sometimes conducted today. Other Abbey buildings are not quite as intact – some are simply foundation stones that have been dug up from the earth, some are single walls – but there is something very stirring and romantic about the old stones and the broken arches of those that still stand.

Cooing white doves nest in the ruins, and huge black ravens also swoop through the air, adding to the impression of duality, of yin and yang, of balance. There is an air of peace and tranquillity throughout the complex, and I felt that I'd stepped back in, or outside of, time. Flowers bloom, spreading a sweetness that lifts the heart, and I was blanketed by an atmosphere I could physically feel, that muffled the sound of the street outside and soothed the soul.

After a long and dramatic history, these ruins remain a beautiful, holy site. The whole of the Abbey grounds are a place of power, and while I don't follow the Christian path, I've walked through here many times and felt the echo of the beliefs that have been celebrated in this spot over the centuries and the combined energy the place still holds.

The purpose

"If I was obliged to leave Glastonbury tomorrow I would always remember the sense of a gateway that it gave me: a gateway to infinite possibilities, not abstract but right here on earth. It gives me the sense of a place set apart – a place quite other than the mundane – where I can be all I can be."
Nicholas Mann, British anthropologist and author

Glastonbury has a glorious past, myths interweaving with facts to create a rich tapestry of spirituality and history. But while people continue to debate whether it was Joseph who built the first Christian church there, if Arthur really lived and the presence of the goddess within the green hills, the most important thing is that it has the ability to transform people now. All the stories are beautiful and have deep meaning, and whether they are literal retellings of history or just symbolic parables doesn't change their effectiveness or power.

The sacred waters of Chalice Well heal, be it Ceridwen's cauldron of inspiration and immortality, the chalice of the Last Supper or a vibrational energy that will soon be measurable and understandable. The energy of the Tor opens your heart to your own deeper truths, whether it was once topped by a druidic centre, a monastic settlement or a ring of stones. Perhaps these are all simply reworkings and reinterpretations of the same archetype anyway, transformed as people change, beliefs evolve and time moves forward.

Whatever your faith, visiting Glastonbury and spending time breathing in its sacred beauty will unlock the deepest parts of your true self. Many people find physical healing here, especially in the gardens of the Chalice Well, while others experience a blossoming of their spirit and a new understanding of their own innate power. Walking in the footsteps of the people of old also activates new wisdom and knowledge, and helps you recognise the priest or priestess that lies within you, the god or goddess that is your true self – part of you, not something separate and outside of you.

For many people Glastonbury is a place of nurturing goddess energy and gentle healing power. Thousands of years ago the inhabitants worshipped the Great Mother, the spiritual embodiment of the physical planet, and today she is still revealed in the landscape of the town. The waters of the Red and White Springs are seen as her life-giving nourishment. Topographical maps of the hills and valleys of the area reveal the shape of the Mother Goddess lying on her back, her head and shoulders etched from Stonedown Hill, with Wearyall Hill as her straightened left leg, Windmill Hill her bent right leg, the Tor her left breast and Chalice Hill her pregnant tummy.

From a different angle there is another goddess shape, the crone Ceridwen flying across the town on Bridie's swan, with Wearyall Hill as the swan's outstretched neck and head, and the old woman represented by Stonedown Hill as her hunched over back, Windmill Hill her stooped head, Chalice Hill her breasts and the Tor her once-fertile womb.

The Great Goddess was considered the giver of life, the eternal mother, the source of all things, and in ancient times women were worshipped as a manifestation of her because of their ability to create and nurture life. Today the goddess-centred worship of much of the spiritual belief in Glastonbury reflects this, empowering women to follow their own hearts and decide their own path.

In the 1970s there was a thriving feminist consciousness in the town, and while its spirit remains, it has become more inclusive since then, helping both men and women find a balance between the masculine and feminine energies of their own being and learning to understand themselves through a connection with nature and the seasonal cycles of life, the earth and the divine.

In venerating the goddess in her triple aspect of maiden, mother and crone, as they did in the past and they do again now in the Goddess Temple in Glastonbury, there is also renewed respect for older women, which will hopefully radiate outwards and change perceptions. Celebrating all the cycles and ages of life changes the emphasis in our throwaway society. While in times gone by elders were held in high regard and their advice respectfully sought, in much of the western world today, from Hollywood down, older women are discarded and their wisdom ignored, while older men run companies, countries and the church.

Yet in the pagan world all people are valued and age is a badge of honour, a mark of experience and wisdom. Recognising and valuing the crone, in both a literal form and as the energy of the wise man or woman inside that everyone can access, is an important part of the energy of Glastonbury today, and the purpose of the place for many. Being here teaches you to value all people, including yourself, nurtures your individual strengths, and encourages you to explore your own path and understand what is important to you.

It also unlocks your potential and allows you to see yourself as you could be – whole, complete, with all your dreams fulfilled. It's like being in another dimension where limits don't apply. It's a place of transformation, and if you're ready to let go of the restrictions and the repressed parts of your inner self that are holding you back, the gentle energy of the place will nurture you through the healing process.

It also helps crystallise your own beliefs, and understand what's in your heart, rather than what you absorbed from your upbringing, schooling, society or friends. In Glastonbury a religious or spiritual path is a way of life rather than a system of thought and dogma, and people here come to their own conclusions through personal experiences and transformative realisations rather than rote learning.

Some say this is because of its location as the heart chakra of the world, and that the energy of the town has always been more conducive to new thought and harmony of religious expression than most.

It has been – and continues to be – the gateway of so many changes in spiritual beliefs. It was a place of goddess worship for thousands of years, the centre of druidic initiation and teachings for a millennia more, and then the birthplace of Christianity in the British Isles. And perhaps it's no accident that so many atheists are now writing books and challenging accepted worldviews in nearby Oxford, representing the birth of a new era of scientific thought.

"The spiritual power of Glastonbury changes lives. It is a natural sanctuary where the earth spirit is teacher. It comes alive in the landscape, in the peculiar shades of light, the changing seasons, the air we breathe. When people come, their intent is to live the spiritual values of caring, sharing and living lightly on the land."
Frances Howard-Gordon, local film director, author and publisher

Regardless of world events, Glastonbury is one of my favourite places as much because of what it represents to me as for the beauty and peacefulness of the town and its special sites. It has been the mirror that reflected my inner heart back to me, the place I found a name for what I believe and a connection to all I hold sacred. Over the years it has nurtured my self-reflection, activated growth and new awareness in me and held me safe as I explored my inner world.

The first time I stayed there and immersed myself in the sacred energies, I had just been to Peru. I was touched by the spirituality of the people there, and respected their history and beliefs, but their sense of deity and method of worship wasn't mine.

In the wilds of the Amazon jungles I had seen flashes of gentle green hills and ancient wells, and had visions of standing within a circle of stones, arms open to the sky, gentle sunshine caressing my face. In the meditation we did in the Temple of the Condor at Machu Picchu I kept hearing a name that sounded like Sheridan, which made no sense to the people I was with or the place I was in.

But when I walked the sacred landscape of Avalon I knew I had come home. The gentleness of nature soothed my soul, and I found peace and healing by the Chalice Well and in the sunshine, mists and clouds up on the Tor. Breathing in the energy of this land energised and inspired me, and the light and the atmosphere felt so familiar.

I went to a talk held by the Pagan Federation in a bookstore in town. As I randomly opened a book while waiting for people to arrive, Sheridan was revealed as Ceridwen, the goddess of knowledge and rebirth, and I knew this was the name that had been whispered to me in the mountains of Peru. She is a Celtic deity, symbolic of the feminine principle, of wisdom and of crone energy. Some believe Chalice Well is her cauldron of inspiration, and that those who drink from it are changed forever, even if they don't realise it at the time. I know I was.

As the talk began, I was excited to hear the articulation of the beliefs I'd always held dear. Here, on the other side of the world to where I live, the inner truths I'd always felt in my heart and mind were being expressed. I experienced a deep feeling of belonging amongst these people who also felt the magic of nature, and discovered a sense of home on the sacred hills and by the holy wells of this place.

On my way into town that night there had been a baby snake on the footpath – symbol of wisdom and healing – showing me the way forward. As I walked back to my B&B later, mind spinning, a sweet little black cat leaped out in front of me and rubbed against my legs, purring, making me smile. My pagan heart was awakening.

The following night was the full moon, and I decided to celebrate it by basking in its silvery light up on the Tor, an initiation of sorts into my own deeper magic. It would become full at 4.15am, so half an hour before that, after a few hours excitedly tossing and turning in my narrow bed, I quietly slipped on some warm clothes and crept outside, feeling like a kid sneaking out of home. I started to wind my way reverently around the ancient peak, tracing the path of the priestesses on their ceremonial processions to the top.

In awe, I felt myself absorbing the spiritual energy and wisdom of those who had lived and worshipped here before. The fact that the clouds still covered the entire sky like a dark blanket didn't bother me – I just mouthed a silent prayer to the universe and expressed gratitude for my journey. Soon I left the path and climbed straight up the steep side. At times I had to cling to the grassy hillside with my fingers and toes, stumbling in the blackness, smiling, filled with wonder at the magic of the moment and the beauty of the night.

Finally I stood on the summit, slightly breathless and shivering a little in the breeze. At the moment the moon became perfectly full I gazed up at the sky, and suddenly the clouds parted and I was bathed in silver light. I felt a power rush through me, and felt a thrill of excitement that the moon had showed itself to me in that instant. This connection to nature is the basis of the earth magic that has long been practised, and that is becoming popular again today.

The moon has been worshipped as a deity for thousands of years by people throughout all countries and cultures, with its phases echoing the maiden-mother-crone aspects of the goddess. The moon controls the tides of the oceans, the cycles of the human body as well as the emotions, and stimulates magical experiences, divination skills and the ability to go within and access the deepest intuition.

I stayed up on the Tor for hours, thinking, dreaming, meditating, staring at the sky, feeling a connection with this ancient land and the sense of the mystical feminine that is embodied in the gentle landscape and beauty of nature. I revelled in the strength and wisdom imparted by the dancing moonbeams, then gazed in wonder as the sun began to snake fingers of colour across the opposite horizon.

It was truly breathtaking – the moon peeking out from behind the clouds for me, the sky gradually lightening, and the approaching dawn painting the heavens in vivid pinks, golds, oranges and purples. I thought about the stories of the grail quest, of Galahad finding enlightenment and self-knowledge, and as I sat alone on the Tor in the misty dawn, I felt close to an illumination of my own self, my own soul, and that I was beginning to find answers to my own quest.

"It is our collective and individual responsibility to preserve and tend to the environment in which we all live. This planet is our home. Taking care of our planet is just like taking care of our own home. Our very lives depend on this earth, our environment."
The Dalai Lama, Buddhist monk, exiled Tibetan leader
and Nobel Peace Prize winner

Walking the sacred landscape of this pretty corner of England reminds me to be in tune with and aware of nature, and to slow down and breathe in the energy and wisdom of the earth, which is available to all of us on this incredible planet if we want to open up to it.

Like Machu Picchu, Glastonbury is a place where all the elements come together in a magical way. The healing waters of the Well, the mystical air around the top of the Tor, the sacred earth of Chalice and Wearyall Hills, and the fiery power of the sunshine and the inner flame of the Tor all meld together, an alchemical blending of the four elements. Absorbing them reawakens the ideals I held dear as a teenager, before work and rent and commitments got in the way – looking after the earth, seeing the trees, rocks, animals and air as sacred, fighting against nuclear bases, fundraising for peace and an end to poverty.

The earth supports and nurtures us, and we have a responsibility to treat it with respect and care, and not exploit the resources that sustain us. Some modern-day pagans believe in the literal existence of deities within the landscape while others simply revere the beauty and power of nature and the complexity and immensity of the universe, but they all feel a deep connection to the earth, and to environmental issues as a result of that. They hold the planet as sacred, and express their spiritual beliefs through protecting the land, conserving resources, campaigning for change, utilising organic agriculture and produce, and creating a new environmental awareness.

The most precious example I saw of someone connecting to the old wisdom of Avalon, and the thing that moved me the most, was not an elaborate pagan rite or glamorous ceremony. It was a man on the Tor the day after the spring equinox celebrations, picking up all the rubbish left by the spiritual revellers. I was shocked and disappointed to see all the cigarette butts, food scraps and empty bottles left so carelessly on this holy ground, so I asked him for a plastic bag and spent the morning helping him clear up the earth.

Paganism and magic isn't just about dancing naked around the fire (although that has its place for some!). It's about revering nature, assisting the earth, and connecting with it. Doing what you can for people and the world. That day I reclaimed my environmental consciousness and the activism of my idealistic youth. I went to an internet cafe and rejoined Greenpeace, adding my voice to their campaigns and determined to remember this feeling when I got home.

It made me so sad that people could desecrate such a sacred site. They went there to celebrate the vibrant new energy of spring because of the spirituality of the place, the natural beauty and strong earth energy, the ebb and flow and tides of life you can feel pulsating within the Tor, then destroyed what they love about it. But hopefully the essence of the place got through on some level to those who recognised its significance but had such little respect for it, and will help them grow, and become more aware. Glastonbury is a gentle, patient teacher, ready to aid anyone who opens their heart to listen.

I've been to the town at different times of the pagan year so I could celebrate nature with people who dance on this sacred earth with the same joy as me. I've leaped the Beltane fires alone and with new friends, burned my intentions and longings in a fiery cauldron, and whispered prayers into a candle sent to float on the vesica piscis pool with everyone else's hopes and dreams. Each time I learned something more about myself, about the world. I let go of something I no longer needed, and started to see myself more fully as the person I can truly be, filled with love and light and all the energy of the universe.

One summer solstice I found myself trapped on the Tor by the mists of Avalon, and it was beautiful. I'd climbed the hill on solstice eve to soak up the magic of the sunset, then gone down to Chalice Well for a Midsummer's Night ritual. The gardens were lit up with coloured candles, faery lights and incense, creating an enchanted, mystical land. There was a Buddhist chant at the Well, theatrical performances, songs and harp playing, and people of all faiths joined together to meditate on what they wanted to manifest in the coming year.

Then just before midnight I threaded my way back up the path to the Tor in the darkness. I found a little spot among the drummers, didgeridoo players, singers and silent watchers, and settled in for the night. By 2am I was freezing cold, having lent my scarf to a girl with fewer layers on than me, and decided to go back down and snuggle up in bed for a few hours before returning to watch the sun rise.

But by then the mists had stolen in, and the Tor was surrounded by the thickest, whitest, most magical substance. It was like the densest clouds I'd ever seen, so thick and white and full of form, but shifting and dancing and recreating itself. It seemed as though it was alive, and the whole experience was so surreal. Suddenly it was like I really was on a tiny island and was trapped there, unable to get back down and across the lake to solid ground, or reality.

It is these mists that have added to the magical legend of the town, this memory of Avalon and the dimension of knowledge and wisdom that can be accessed by slipping through this veil, which is so thin here. The usual landmarks – Gog and Magog, the church towers in town, my B&B – had all drowned beneath the mist. If it wasn't for the flickering outline of the tower on top of the Tor I wouldn't have even known in which direction anything was. There was no way I could get down without becoming lost in the mists, wandering off the path or falling off the Tor, so I sat there and shivered, smiling, dreaming, until colour stained the horizon and we all stared in anticipation.

And then everyone was awake and vibrant, calling out salutes to the sun and the solar god as solstice morning unfolded. It was 3.30am, and still incredibly cold despite it being the middle of summer, but all of a sudden there was so much hope and optimism around me. The sun took ninety minutes to rise, but it was beautiful – the slowest, most gentle sunrise I've ever seen, and it painted the mists too, spreading out in soft pinks and golds and warm lavenders and mauves.

Finally it rose fully above the horizon in all its fiery, fierce and golden splendour, warming my heart, lifting people's spirits, filling us all with joy and touching the world with its sense of radiance.

The summer solstice, known as Litha, represents rebirth and light in the sacred Wheel of the Year, in both an archetypal and literal sense. The day is about acknowledging and celebrating your achievements and setting new goals, and also recognising what isn't working in your life and letting go of negative things or purifying them to make them positive. I've done a lot of that in Glastonbury over the years, on so many levels. Somehow the powerful earth energy helps activate this change, while gently nurturing you as you grow.

"What greater thing is there for two human souls than to feel that they are joined... to strengthen each other... to be one with each other in silent unspeakable memories."
George Eliot, 19th century English novelist

My most magical, mysterious and illuminating experience happened on one of my most recent visits to Glastonbury, when I broke through the mists and wandered in the magical state of being that is Avalon. I went there for my honeymoon, to finally share my special place with my beloved, and while we were there we felt the most blissful state of sacred union, my inner heart melding with his and filling me with a sense of self so strong that I will be able to hold on to it forever.

Night had already fallen by the time we'd driven down from London and found our little cottage, but we had a sudden sense of urgency to go exploring. So we walked hand in hand up the High Street in the gathering darkness, all jetlag falling away as we passed the Abbey ruins and the Chalice Well Gardens. It was spookily dark as we turned in to the ivy-clad, tree-lined laneway that leads up to the Tor, but we stumbled our way up the stairs to the gateway, clinging together, and stepped out onto the lower slopes of the mystical hill.

Suddenly everything changed. It was like we'd stepped through a gateway and into another world, into the mists, although we didn't know it at the time. Slowly and steadily we climbed the hulking peak. I felt the steepness and paused for breath, but he didn't.

The next day when we walked up it again my beloved was surprised by how hard the climb is, but on this night he strode effortlessly ahead, with a sense of urgency that compelled him to dart upwards as fast as he could to face what was at the top. A few times he asked if I'd seen the flashes, but I hadn't. Nor did I see the same apocalyptic sky he did, or hear the voice telling him that he was going up the Tor to die.

Instead I saw a building in the sky to the left of the tower. Many people have reported seeing things there – visions of stone circles, places of learning, monks' cells, old temples, crystalline structures. It felt like a clue to what was going to come next, or perhaps to the mystery of who we had been to each other in a past life, or what had drawn us to this tiny town in this ancient land now.

When we got to the top we were blissfully alone. We stared into each other's eyes forever, and his face kept changing, as mine must have too, because sometimes he looked at me as though he didn't know who I was. For a moment two other people took us over. Or were they us too? The us we once were? The us we are becoming?

Whatever it was, something very deep and ancient was being played out between us. It was intense, and surreal, a moment outside of time and meaning. As we held hands on the summit I heard a whisper in the wind: "You've chosen well. This is a love beyond time, outside of time, throughout time." And then more mysterious words: "He was the Keeper of the Well, and now he will keep your love safe."

As I struggled to comprehend what was being said, and who or what could be saying it, my new husband was getting messages and being bombarded by feelings too. At one point he looked deeply into my soul and said, so solemnly: "Now we really are married." And it was true. At that moment we knew our vows were consecrated, in a way they hadn't been when we'd spoken them in front of the celebrant, and our union became more real, more sacred.

Standing there together, holding on to each other, in a space between the worlds, was beyond words, beyond understanding. Vows were exchanged, and something deep shifted between us, grew, bonded. The final part of our wedding took place here, as we stood together alone on a magical hilltop across the world, where it seemed we had been together before, even though in this life at least we hadn't.

The darkness was so thick and close – although for my beloved the sky was aflame, fiery red, while mine was deep velvety blue and speckled with stars – yet we could see each other perfectly. There was such overwhelming urgency and passion between us, the most sacred feeling of deepest love and connection. Heart to heart, god to goddess. Just holding each other close, or gently kissing, was a kind of magic, an initiation into the sacred mysteries of life and love.

And then, at the same instant, we understood that it was complete. We suddenly felt chilled by the freezing wind, and knew it was time to descend our faery hill, shivering as we clung together to walk back down the Tor, back into the world. Before we departed, as we passed through the tower, I felt a presence that seemed to have been there the whole time. It was a supportive, protective, feminine energy. Not a physical one, because we were alone there, but something beyond. She was crouched in the corner of the tower as we left, and I thanked her as we passed, without knowing what or who it was.

For my beloved it was a masculine presence up there, as though God himself was communicating with him, and a dreamscape that had long haunted his nights. He felt that something within him died atop the Tor, and he had been reborn. On this mystical hill all the subtle pieces of the magical puzzle that is our connection came together so profoundly, and we understood that it was the spirit of Avalon rather than the priestess in New York who had actually married us.

I don't know what happened that night, or how we passed through the mists and into Avalon. We can't explain or define it, but there was a definite magic that we tapped in to in this enchanted town, a universal force of love and connection, and the tiny web-like threads of it still swirl around us wherever we are in the world.

Scientists may not be able to measure Avalon yet, or prove it exists, but there's no doubt people have extraordinary experiences there that change them forever. Some go back in time to heal their past, others find pieces of their future selves to weave into their consciousness, and some access another dimension of themselves, or the world, to become more fully realised. Perhaps one day the reason transformation occurs so readily in this location will be understood, but until then Avalon remains alive, thriving in the physical realm where Christian and pagan still live alongside each other, balancing the masculine and feminine, the god and the goddess, in each pilgrim who journeys there.

The next day we spent hours in the Chalice Well Gardens. As we sat in the shaded courtyard by the waterfall, each look into each other's eyes seemed to be another vow, a deepening of our bond, another step through time. We heard voices again, more messages about keepers of wells and hearts, and we felt as though we belonged there, or had been there together before. And in all the photos we took by the Well we look different, ourselves yet somehow Other.

There had been serendipitous moments involving this place as we'd prepared to marry. The chalice we bought for the ceremony was from there. And when we spoke to our American celebrant she said she didn't know if we'd heard of a town called Glastonbury, but she had some water from its sacred spring that she felt guided to use in our vows.

As we ran our hands through that same water now, we refilled the chalice and drank again from the same cup, creating a new ritual. We breathed in the air scented with roses from the offerings, and felt the spirit of this place course through us, opening our hearts to the eternal truth of who we really are. As I gazed at my beloved I saw the god within him, the beauty of all that he is and the potential of everything he can be. And as I smiled into his eyes, I saw there the reflection of the goddess essence within me, and the qualities of mine that he recognised, which I had refused to see.

That is the gift of Glastonbury. It opens you up to the immensity of who you really are, and reveals the hidden, sacred parts of yourself that, burdened by daily life, are usually ignored. Its power is accessible to everyone, of all faiths. It is a connection to spirit that goes beyond religion to the very heart of belief – be that in God, goddess or the purity of nature – and the universal energy that links all things.

Being in Glastonbury will awaken the magic of Avalon within you. As you sit at the Well, drink its healing waters, gaze at its peaceful gardens, climb the Tor and watch the moon, perform sacred rituals, reflect on the history and the myths and the magic, absorb the power and beauty of the place, and the ancient wisdom in the trees, the hills, the wind and the stars, you'll integrate the magic that is so intrinsically linked to this ancient town – and realise that it's within your heart too.

The psychic connection

Quick tips to integrate the wisdom of Glastonbury

1. Read *The Mists of Avalon* by Marion Zimmer Bradley, which will touch your heart and unlock your inner priestess. Since it was first published in 1983 it's inspired thousands of people to visit Glastonbury and learn more about the area's magic, or embrace its power from home. While considered a work of fiction, the book is firmly rooted in reality. Marion studied the writings of Dion Fortune, researched magic with modern-day witch Starhawk, and spent time with local tour guide Jamie George to learn the history and myths of Avalon.

2. Open up to the faery realm. Paint, draw, write about or hang pictures of the magical winged beings that live in the mist-shrouded dimension of Avalon. Morgen la Fey was reputedly half faery, and even today it's not hard to imagine these mythical creatures flitting through the ancient trees of Glastonbury. The magic and beauty of their archetypal energy stirs something deep within you and touches the heart, bringing joy and inspiration, while their vibration can alter yours and bring lightness to your soul. Within the old faerytales there are also hidden truths (and fun!), so channel your inner faery.

3. Meditate on pictures of the Chalice Well Gardens, and let their magic change you. I don't understand how, but just seeing photos of this place has healed people of serious illnesses, without them having to be there physically. There are beautiful images on the website, www.chalicewell.org.uk, where you can buy paintings, cards and books inspired by the Well, the pools and the gardens, as well as exploring the links and finding out more about this sacred place.

4. In addition to drinking from the Well, people have used the waters of the Red and White Springs in homeopathic essences, both as a physical treatment and in spiritual rituals as a way to connect with the energies of Glastonbury and Avalon. In the Chalice Well Gardens a healing essence is made from the flowers and buds of the holy thorn tree, which helps you feel loved, discover your purpose and be supported through transformation. There's also an Essence of Avalon range you can take no matter where you live, which distils the energies of Gog, Magog, the Eggstone and the Holy Thorn into vibrational medicines to bring healing and a connection to this powerful place.

5. Explore a method of divination, be it scrying, dream journalling, tarot cards, angel oracles, psychometry or a pendulum, and spend at least a month recording the results. Becoming a professional psychic or tarot reader involves a lifetime of study, but you'll be amazed by what you can learn about yourself and how well you can develop your own abilities and connect to your intuition if you practise regularly.

The armchair traveller's way to visit

"Herbal magic is one of the easiest, safest and most joyous methods of re-establishing earth roots and of returning to a healthy and natural life. It touches the essence of life itself, and is a co-operation between plant and human, earth and heaven, a union of energies forged to produce change by methods that outsiders view as supernatural."
Scott Cunningham, American author and natural magic practitioner

The energy of Glastonbury – and Avalon – awakens the powers you have within you and allows you to see yourself as a magical being connected to the universe and to the past, present and future. While being there will nurture you as you explore your inner wisdom, you can also achieve this quest at home. If you feel drawn to Glastonbury but can't make your own sacred journey to the town to gaze into the waters of Chalice Well or sit on top of the Tor, there are still many ways you can embrace the eternal magic of this beautiful place.

One method is to channel the wisdom of the priestesses and druids who lived there peacefully for so long. They were the doctors and spiritual advisers of their communities – they healed the sick, helped women give birth, counselled the depressed, divined the future, made love potions, warded off evil, led the rituals to bless the crops, settled disputes between villagers, performed marriage and baby naming ceremonies, helped people face death and presided over funeral rites.

You can connect to this ancient wisdom by studying herbcraft, which is the basis of all magical systems. Learning about the medicinal and magical properties of herbs, and how to not only heal people of physical ailments but also to help with spiritual matters such as protection, love, working through grief and drawing love and abundance in to their lives, will fill you with the energy of Avalon.

Herbal medicine is the oldest form of health care, and has been practised in cultures throughout the world for as long as history has been recorded. Thousands of years ago physicians from as far afield as Egypt, China, Rome and India used the therapeutic properties of herbs to heal the sick, and they're also mentioned in *The Bible*.

Today eighty per cent of the earth's population still uses herbs as a major source of health care, and even in the west, where it has long been discouraged and dismissed as folk superstition, herbal medicine is becoming an increasingly respected healing tool.

Far from being an old-fashioned craft with no relevance today, herbs are the basis of many modern medicines. Aspirin was developed based on the compounds in the herb willow bark, which for centuries was used for pain relief and fever. Ephedrine, an ingredient in medications for asthma patients, is based on the herb ephedra, which has been used in Chinese Medicine for more than two thousand years. Digoxin, the life-saving heart drug, is based on compounds in the herb foxglove. And quinine, the malaria drug, is based on properties extracted from the bark of South America's cinchona tree.

There are many colleges that teach degrees in medicinal and clinical herbalism for those who want to become a practitioner and treat physical ailments with herbal remedies. There are also shorter courses and extensive reference books that introduce the basics so you can start to work with herbs for yourself. A warning though – herbs are natural, yet they are powerful healers with intense therapeutic effects, and serious medical conditions should only be diagnosed and treated by a professional. But anyone can start growing herbs and using their properties to promote health and wellbeing.

Drinking herbal teas and adding fresh plants such as parsley and basil to your food will boost vitality. Herbal compresses, ointments, massage oils and inhalations can increase healing. And aromatherapy, skin lotions and hair care products can help treat simple conditions and prevent ill health. For example, chamomile and passionflower alleviate insomnia, peppermint can be used to relieve nausea, and rosemary is a general tonic and boosts memory.

To feel the magic of the land, grow your own herbs, either in a whole garden or a single pot on a balcony or windowsill. Watching plants grow from seeds or seedlings, learning the difference between perennials and annuals and watching the seasonal shifts within your garden will attune you to nature and the cycles of the year, and connect you to the earth in a similar way to the old Priestesses of Avalon.

Learning the ancient art of magical herbalism, an important priestess craft, is another way to channel this ancient wisdom. The use of herbs to create change on a spiritual and emotional level, common to all belief systems and cultures, is one of the oldest and most powerful magical methods. From the Ancient Egyptians and Greeks to Celtic priestesses and shamans of the Americas, herbs have been used in various magical ways since the dawn of time.

Herbs each have a specific therapeutic effect, and they also have spiritual/emotional properties, such as lavender being used to calm the mind and in rituals for love, cinnamon to increase psychic abilities, ginger to attract abundance and success, and bay leaves to promote courage. There are courses and encyclopaedic books both old and new that teach these magical properties, and how to cast spells, perform rituals, create talismans and herbal sachets and enchant your life with your own magical powers and the added boost of herbs.

While old legends and literal retellings of symbolic stories have given magic a reputation as being made up or otherworldly and out of the reach of ordinary people, it's a natural part of life that can be utilised by everyone. Magic is an ancient path of wisdom and knowledge, the science of manifestation, which involves the directing of your own energies, intent and actions to achieve a desired outcome.

Magical herbalism adds the magical properties of herbs to your own innate powers, as well as the life force and energy of the universe to create real change in the physical world. It's still used in many indigenous cultures, and increasingly by modern practitioners for spiritual healing, prophecy and protection, as well as to attract love, abundance, career success and happiness.

The Priestesses of Avalon also practised scrying, a method of seeing the future by staring at a surface and taking note of the images and symbols on it. They gazed into the sacred waters of Chalice Well, but it can also be done using a bowl of water, a crystal ball (as the gypsies so famously do), a piece of black obsidian, a lake, a pool of ink or a mirror, which is the method famed seer Nostradamus employed.

To try it, fill a bowl with water, adding ink if you prefer, light a candle or sit outside under the moonlight, and stare into the water's surface. Clear your mind and focus solely on the water. Take note of any images you see, either here or in your mind's eye, and write them all down so you can analyse and start to interpret them later. Scrying requires lots of practise and patience, but can bring intriguing results.

If you're using a mirror or a crystal ball to scry, you can boost the effect by rubbing fresh mugwort leaves on the surface to strengthen its power. Magical herbalists also recommend drinking an infusion of mugwort tea before divination work to boost psychic abilities, and that you burn mugwort and wormwood incense while scrying.

Mugwort has long been revered as a powerful visionary herb, and in many ancient cultures the dried leaves were stuffed in dream pillows or sachets to stimulate and enhance prophetic dreaming. Remedially this herb has been used as a digestive stimulant and by women for general good health and female cycles, although it should be avoided during pregnancy and can be toxic in high doses.

Wormwood is also a visionary herb, with similar properties to mugwort. The priestesses of old believed it was sacred to the Greek goddess Artemis and her Roman counterpart Diana, as well as local deities, which is reflected in its botanical name, Artemisia absinthium, while mugwort's is Artemisia vulgaris. Remedially it's used for stomach and digestive disorders and migraines, amongst other conditions, but it has an unpleasant taste and can cause side effects if ingested in large doses or for more than a short period of time.

Developing your intuition is a powerful way to connect to the energy of Glastonbury and Avalon and to increase your happiness, connect to your inner truth and improve your life.

"The festivals of the Wheel of the Year are defined by the cycle of nature, by the dance of the weather gods and spirits of place. They require us to look not to the heavens but to the earth. They are set within our soul, watching the leaves on the trees, feeling the shifting temperature and the changing light, within and around."
Emma Restall Orr, joint chief of the British Druid Order,
priestess, ritualist and author

Another way to bring the magic of Glastonbury and Avalon into your life is to celebrate the eight sacred sabbats, or festivals, of the Wheel of the Year, as the ancient priestesses did – and modern pagans still do – and perform meaningful personal rituals that will inspire your own growth and the manifestation of your dreams.

In ancient times, when life revolved around agriculture and the sun and moon were considered deities to be worshipped, the Celtic people of Britain were in tune with nature. They had to know when each season began and how long it would last so they could plant and harvest crops, hunt migratory prey and prepare for the harsh winters. They divided their year by seasons, not months, and honoured each change, celebrating eight festivals that marked the turning of these seasons and the cycles of the earth.

There were four astronomical and four agricultural festivals. The astronomical celebrations were determined by the position of the earth in relation to the sun. These included the spring and autumn equinoxes (Latin for equal night), which occur when the sun is directly over the equator and the length of day and night is exactly equal, and the summer and winter solstices (Latin for sun stand still), which occur when the sun is at its northern or southernmost extreme, the furthest it ever gets from the equator. These four events are the midpoint of each season – thus the summer solstice was known as Midsummer's Day and the winter solstice as Midwinter.

The agricultural celebrations were referred to as the cross-quarter days because they fell midway between the astronomical festivals. They were tied to agricultural events such as the sowing and harvesting of crops, and marked the beginning of each season.

The ancients were very aware of when these seasonal events occurred. They watched the sky and noted where the sun rose and set each day in its arc from north to south, and observed the behaviour of birds and animals and the growth of plants. They constructed stone circles, ritual cairns and other monuments, such as Stonehenge in England and Newgrange in Ireland, which were aligned to sunrise or sunset on one of the solstices or equinoxes. These acted as giant calendars, and alerted them to these special days and the passing of time.

Even today, when we no longer live in harmony with the earth's rhythms or agricultural cycles, modern pagans celebrate the Wheel of the Year as an honouring of nature and an acknowledgement of the continuing cycle of life, death and rebirth, both literally and symbolically. Becoming aware of the seasonal shifts and the patterns of nature wherever you live, and celebrating these ancient but still relevant festivals, is a simple way to tap in to the magic of the universe and start to develop your inner priest or priestess.

Channelling this magic and creating meaningful rituals in your life doesn't conflict with any religion or require a belief system, as it's a celebration of the science of nature and the cycles of the planet. Many pagans do call on gods and/or goddesses, and have a personal concept of the divine as a universal creative force, but others don't believe in any form of deity, simply revering nature as sacred and as the source of life, and believing that divinity is an inner not an outer power, an energy within themselves and every other person alive.

Attuning yourself to nature isn't hard – simply start paying attention to the time the sun rises and sets, the phases of the moon, and the trees in your street as they flower, lose their leaves, then start to blossom again. Walk through a park or along a beach and feel the tides of the earth and the energy of the universe as it surrounds you and moves through you. The Wheel of the Year represents the eternal cycle of life, death and rebirth. Literally this refers to the changing seasons – the fertility and vibrant life force of summer, the introspection and endings (death) of winter, and the rebirth of spring.

Mythologically this was tied to the story of the god and goddess. At the spring equinox they meet and court, before consummating their love during the rites of Beltane. At the summer solstice the goddess blooms into the mother, pregnant with new life, and the sun god reaches his energetic peak. From then he weakens through the harvest time of Lughnasadh and the autumn equinox, before going to the underworld at Samhain to learn new wisdom, then being reborn at the winter solstice when the goddess gives birth to the infant sun god and the wheel turns again, playing out the cycle on and on through time.

Back then this creation story was accepted as fact. Today some pagans still believe it to be a literal retelling of a historical truth, while others feel it's a parable that humanises nature. Either way, it's now the symbolic meaning that's most relevant to our lives – planting the seeds of our dreams in the metaphorical spring, watching them grow and manifest in the world before we give thanks for our literal harvest, allow the things that no longer serve us to die off or be released, then start all over again with new dreams as we celebrate our own rebirth.

The winter solstice, known to pagans as Yule, falls around December 21 or 22 in the northern hemisphere and June 21 or 22 in the south. It's the shortest day and the longest night of the year, and marks the transition between dark and light, both emotionally and physically. It's the lowest point of the Wheel of the Year in terms of daylight and energy. The land is barren, cold and infertile, there is less light than ever, and energetically people feel tired and unmotivated.

Winter is a time to rest and reflect, to acknowledge sadness and loss – of dreams, of friendships, of parts of your self – and conserve your energy and life force. Doctors have recently discovered that the long darkness of winter can cause depression, with Seasonal Affective Disorder now a recognised medical condition, so don't be hard on yourself if you suffer a touch of the winter blues – sunlight affects brain chemistry, and its lack can impact on your wellbeing.

But the solstice is the turning point in this time of darkness, introspection and dreaming. Considered the dark night of the soul, which gives birth to the creative spark, it marks the period when the dark half of the year relinquishes its hold to the light half. From this day forward the days will slowly start to lengthen, the sun will become stronger and the energy within and without will increase and build.

In pagan times an evergreen tree was brought inside on this night as a symbol of the hope of spring's return, and Yule was a time of feasting, celebration and gift giving in honour of the birth of the sun god – traditions that live on today in the Christmas tree that's decorated at this time, the presents we put under it, the huge family meals we cook and the recognition of the birth of the son of God.

To attune yourself to the Wheel of the Year and this festival of hope and renewal, light a candle on solstice eve to symbolise the sun and its activating energy, and list your dreams for the coming year. Traditionally people stayed up all night to await the return of the light, but if you can't do that, get up for the sunrise to toast the dawn and give thanks for this energetic reawakening.

Open yourself to the promise of new growth and achievement, the rebirth of your own self and your creativity as the sun is also reborn. Symbolically and energetically it's a time to honour your inner wisdom, consider the lessons you learned during winter's introspection and integrate them into your life so you can start to initiate change.

Imbolc, celebrated in the first week of February in the northern hemisphere and the first week of August in the south, is a cross-quarter day marking the end of winter, and celebrates the return of light to the land. It's a time of hope, renewal and fresh starts after winter's sluggishness, and is the first of three fertility festivals.

Imbolc comes from the Irish word for ewe's milk, and is sometimes translated as in the belly, because sheep were pregnant at this time, swelling with new life. The first signs of winter's end appear, the first tentative flowers bloom and the sun strengthens, symbolising the return and renewal of the life force of the land and its people.

Energetically it's a time of awakening and new energy, and is the day to sow the seeds of what you want to achieve in the coming year. It's dedicated to Bridie, the goddess of inspiration, creativity and fire, who was later supplanted by Saint Bridget, whose festival is now celebrated at this time. Talk to Bridie – or Bridget or the higher self aspect of yourself – or write her a letter, and tell her what you want to create in the next 12 months. Meditate on your goals and what you hope to achieve. Don't worry about how to do it, as that will be revealed later as flashes of inspiration, guidance or outside help.

It's also a time of purification and cleansing after the long dark of winter, so clean your house and energetically clear your space, sweeping out old energy and thoughts so the new can thrive.

You can also light a candle to represent the coming back of the light, and do some candle magic. Stare into the flame as you concentrate on what you want, then blow it out, sending your desire out to the universe. Making a wish as you blow out the candles on your birthday cake is a magic that has survived from pagan times, and is a potent way to manifest your wishes into reality, whatever day it is.

The spring or vernal equinox, known to pagans as Ostara, is celebrated around March 20 or 21 in the northern hemisphere and September 22 or 23 in the south. It's one of only two times in the year when the length of day and night is exactly equal, as the sun sits directly above the equator on its journey north or south, creating equal light and dark in both hemispheres. On a personal level it's a time of balance and harmony, of union between the physical and spiritual, which can be harnessed to anchor your dreams in reality and enhance your own inner harmony as the balance of universal energies is reflected within. Relationships are harmonious too, making it a good time for weddings and for healing rifts.

It's also a time of growth and fertility, when new crops are sown, new shoots break through the earth, buds on the trees open, birds build nests and lay eggs and new life is celebrated. Thanks was traditionally given to the fertility goddess Ostara, whose symbols were an egg and a hare, and who is still honoured around the world today, albeit unknowingly, in the form of chocolate eggs and the Easter bunny.

Energetically it's also a very fertile time, as the seeds you previously sowed of your goals begin to sprout and gain momentum. Paint some hard-boiled eggs or buy or make the chocolate version, meditating on your own metaphorical fertility and your ability to manifest dreams into reality. Choose an affirmation relating to your desired outcome, write it down and pin it up where you'll be able to see it every day.

Go outside during the day and breathe in the fresh spring air, filling your heart with new inspiration as you fill your lungs with oxygen. In many ancient cultures, including the Romans whose calendar ours is based on, the spring equinox was the first day of the year, and the sense of new hope and optimism reflected in this time remains today. It's a celebration of new life, hope, passion, growth and energy.

Beltane, celebrated in early May in the northern hemisphere and early November in the south, is a cross-quarter day marking the end of spring and the start of the heat and energy of summer. The evidence of new life is everywhere, in abundant blossoms, the hatching of birds, and bees pollinating flowers, proving that time is moving forward and life is progressing along its path. Women would bathe their faces in the dew gathered from their garden on Beltane morning to harness the energy of youth, and flowers were brought inside to symbolise fresh beginnings and the power of nature.

Beltane was the major fertility festival, and lovers would leap over bonfires hand in hand to renew their vows of love, then come together in sacred union in the fields to bless the crops with fertility. Maypole dancing, representing the union of the god (the pole) and the goddess (the ribbons), was performed to join the two forces of masculine and feminine, and May Day was – and still is – one of the most popular days for marriages in the northern hemisphere. It's a time of lovers and spells to attract love, and celebrating the fertility of life, not just physically, but also of your dreams and ambitions.

Symbolically this day marks the igniting of the fires of creativity and passion, of the fertility of your dreams being made manifest, and is the time to take steps to achieve what you want. Magic can enhance and help you achieve your goals, but you still need to put the physical effort in. The energy of this day will support you as you take action. Start a new project, apply for a new job or take up a new hobby, knowing the universe is bursting with raw energy and power that you can tap in to simply by breathing it in.

It's also a powerful time to repledge your love to your partner. You don't have to build a bonfire and leap over it (although you can!). Simply lighting a red or gold candle as you stare into each other's eyes and speak your love and commitment is enough to invoke the power and passion of the element of fire. If you're single, make a commitment of some kind to yourself, such as achieving a goal or starting a project, nurture a friendship, or sing your intention and your wanting of a romantic partner to the universe.

The summer solstice, known as Litha, is celebrated around June 20 or 21 in the northern hemisphere and December 21 and 22 in the south. It's the longest day and the shortest night of the year, and marks the peak of energy and solar power for the year. On this day the sun reaches its northern or southernmost latitude before it turns and heads back towards the equator, so near the poles daylight lasts for 24 hours. Everything is ripe and abundant and life is blooming.

Universally it's a time of high, hot and active energy. Creativity and expression is at a peak, so stand in your power and express your needs, saying what you want rather than assuming people know. Whereas the winter solstice is slow and introspective, its opposite is fast and effective. Make use of the active energy – this is a time to do, to get out there and harness the energising power and make things happen. It's also a time when relationships – and you – will mature, and you'll apply new wisdom and forethought to your passion.

It's a time of celebration too, of acknowledging how far you've come and what you've achieved. Enjoy the happiness and abundance of this season and soak up the sunshine and festive atmosphere. Traditionally people stayed up all night on solstice eve, partying around the bonfires or within the sacred circles, then watched the sun rise the next morning, feeling it bathe them in warmth and light.

At dawn, stand with your arms outstretched and breathe in the sun's life-giving powers. Let it wash over you with its healing energy and burn away anything you no longer need. Take note of how your dreams and goals are progressing, and meditate on anything that could be blocking your progress. Be open to letting go of whatever isn't working so you can move forward in a new direction.

Lughnasadh, or Lammas, which is celebrated in the first week of August in the northern hemisphere and the first week of February in the south, is a cross-quarter day marking the end of summer and the beginning of autumn. It's the first harvest festival, traditionally a time of feasting and of thanksgiving for the life-giving properties of the grain, as well as a recognition of the cycle of sowing and reaping of the crops – and of the symbolic things you grow and create in your life.

It's a day of harvesting the fruits of your labours and acknowledging your successes and what you've achieved in the past year. Celebrate the goals you've reached and have your own festival of gratitude, in whatever form that takes. Toast your success, throw a party or do something special to mark the occasion. Make a list of all the things you've gained over the past year – the gifts you've been given, the new talents you've developed, the friends you've made, the experiences you've had, the healings you've received – and give thanks for it all.

Then, out of gratitude and in the spirit of the ancestors who shared the bounty of their harvest with those less well off, pass on some of your good fortune. Make a donation to a local charity, lend money to a business in the developing world or give your time to help someone, ensuring the energy of abundance continues and is strengthened. Give out of grace and for joy, not with the expectation of receiving anything in return. Work out small ways you can make a difference to the world and the people around you all year.

Now too, as the energy begins to subtly slow, it's a time to be patient and to trust that everything is as it should be, because there are still harvests to come. Not everything has to be achieved right now – some things take longer to manifest. The lesson of the Wheel of the Year is that everything continues, everything happens when it should, and everything is eternal.

The autumn equinox, known as Mabon and celebrated around September 22 or 23 in the northern hemisphere and March 20 or 21 in the south, is characterised, like the spring equinox, by the length of day and night being equal as the sun travels back across the equator to the other hemisphere. From this point on the days will become shorter and the weather will get cooler, but today is the moment of balance in nature and within – a time of harmony and gentle calm.

Mabon is the time to honour your achievements, experiences and wisdom, and to ensure balance in your life by integrating all the parts of your self. On this day, when all is balanced, witches traditionally renewed their magical commitments, and you can renew any vows you've made or pledge a new one, be it to do with magic, love, friendship, career or anything else. It's also a harvest festival, a time to further celebrate your achievements and feel fulfilment from each one, releasing what no longer serves you in order to move forward. In the wild, old growth is cleared. In your life, cut out anything that's holding you back, draining you or preventing new life and love from flourishing, whether it's work, people, a belief system, regret or the past.

As the shadows lengthen, it's also a good time to scry if you want insight into your future. If you can, light a fire and stare into the flames, allowing your mind to go blank and your vision to blur a little. Note any images you see. Or go outside and watch the clouds scuttling across the sky and analyse the shapes you see within them. Without thinking about it too much, write down what they mean to you.

Pyromancy (fire reading) and nephomancy (cloud reading) are forms of divination that have been used for millennia. You should eventually develop your own dictionary of symbols, because you know better than anyone else what each symbol means to you, but you can begin with standard readings, such as a heart indicating new romance, a cat referring to the need to trust your intuition, a tree meaning you'll make new friends and a plane foreshadowing travel.

Samhain, celebrated in early November in the northern hemisphere and early May in the south – and in popular culture on October 31 – is a cross-quarter day marking the end of autumn and the beginning of the coldness and dark of winter. Long ago, food had to be stored at this time for the cold barren months ahead, when snow covered the land and fresh food was scarce. Animals, who could no longer find grass for grazing, were slaughtered and preserved for later eating.

Symbolically this festival is about rest and renewal, of preparing for what's ahead and withdrawing a little to conserve your energy. It's also the night when the veil between the worlds is at its thinnest, and people traditionally honoured their ancestors and tried to commune with the dead. Some simply set an extra place at the dinner table for a relative who'd passed over, while others cast spells to bring their spirit back to the land of the living, or did mediumship rituals to converse. This magical time and its purpose has been conserved in the modern-day festival of Halloween, which celebrates ghosts and witches, and the Christian holidays of All Hallows Eve and All Saints Day.

It's a period of inner reflection, so spend time in quiet contemplation. If you've lost someone close to you, light a candle and remember them. Look at photos or letters and feel their presence with you. It shouldn't be morbid – you're celebrating their life and all they meant to you. Also honour those who *are* here. Call your mum and dad, visit your grandparents, write to someone who meant a lot to you when you were growing up and thank them for the moments they shared with you.

In ancient times, Samhain was the end of one year and the beginning of the next, so it's also a powerful time to let go of the energy of the old year and old memories so you can move forward with lightness and strength. Light another candle and, by its flickering illumination, write out all the worries, frustrations, regrets and seeming failures you've held on to over the past 12 months. See the candle flame burning them away and leaving you purified and refreshed, and breathe in this positive new energy. Then burn the list in the flame, releasing your attachment to those emotions and their power over you.

This is the time to prepare yourself for the rebirth you'll experience at Yule, but for that to happen there must be death – the death of your fears and doubts, and anything that's holding you back.

Postcard from Glastonbury

Colette Baron-Reid is a Canadian-born intuitive counsellor and the author of *Remembering the Future: The Path to Recovering Intuition* and *Messages From Spirit: The Extraordinary Power of Oracles, Omens and Signs*, which recount her own spiritual journey and include exercises to develop your psychic powers.

She tours alone and with US psychic Sylvia Browne, teaching seminars and giving audience readings. She is also a singer, and has released two albums of her songs in addition to the meditation CD *Journey Through the Chakras*.

Colette is now based in Sedona, USA, but has visited the magical town of Glastonbury a few times, and feels a strong past life link to it. She created *The Wisdom of Avalon Oracle Cards* to help other people connect to the energy that can be accessed in this sacred place. Visit www.colettebaronreid.net.

My connection to Glastonbury goes back a long time. When I was in kindergarten I would draw a blue crescent moon on my forehead whenever I had paints. Fast forward to my late twenties, when I first read *The Mists of Avalon* in the late 80s, and I was struck dumb by the description of the blue crescent moons tattooed on the foreheads of the priestesses, because I had such a strong memory of having done that as a kid. The story felt very familiar to me too. Not so much that I knew King Arthur, but the description of the forest, the mists and their methods of divination and scrying were so vivid to me.

Ten years after that I went to Glastonbury for the first time, but I went with a group of people, which was very distracting, and I felt really disjointed. But the land was calling me. It was a very strong magnetic pull to my psyche, and I felt this strange sense of longing and yearning, so later I went back on my own, and that was when I felt I'd come home. I could feel a presence there, something that grew around me, that beckoned to me, that was very much alive. And I heard whispers and saw buildings out of the corner of my eye that weren't there when I looked directly, but had been in the past.

My most incredible experience was at the Chalice Well Gardens. As I walked towards the Well, all of a sudden it became like a place I'd been to before, and I recognised it from a vision I'd had a few months earlier. I'd been learning reiki, but during the attunement I found myself in another dimension. My jeans became a rough scratchy dress, I smelled different, I was aware I hadn't shaved my legs, and I was suddenly in a circle around a well being initiated by a different group of women. I saw deerskins, so I thought it was a Native American past life, but then I noticed the blue moons on the women's foreheads.

So now as I was walking towards Chalice Well I was in shock, because all of a sudden I was those two women again, me in the now and me from another life, the one I'd seen before. My sense of location became altered and I felt a merging of energy inside me. I was very aware that I was in two places at once – that I was the person I am now, a Christian woman, but that I was equally a priestess worshipping the goddess around the Well. It was strange, because in the physical present world it was raining, but the other me could see through the branches above that it was sunny in the other life.

It was as though I was straddling two entire worlds, and nature was allowing me to witness myself in the two dimensions. I started to cry, and for a brief instant I had access to this well of knowledge from this other life, a clear sense of memory. It faded as I walked away, but at that moment all of it was available to me.

Chalice Well Gardens is my favourite place in Glastonbury, because I've had incredible experiences there which confirmed for me that my path as an intuitive is the right one, but I also like to walk up the Tor, and I like sitting inside the tower at the top on my own, because from up there you can see what it would have been like back then.

People have visions of the past and the future in Glastonbury because the leyline energy makes the veils between the worlds thin there. I can't explain leylines, I just know they're there, I know they pull you. You can feel their power physically, viscerally. I felt as though I was an instrument someone was playing when I was there – I really felt that I had strings. It's almost overwhelming sometimes, and you can feel a little dizzy until you adjust to the energy. But the leylines help you feel things, and if you allow your senses to open you'll have a very strong amplified sensory experience while you're there.

The wisdom of Avalon is attached to the land, so when you go to Glastonbury today you can connect to it. Anyone can go there and ask for visions and they will come. I believe you can access this wisdom from anywhere, but you will definitely have a much bigger experience if you go there, because the physical place is very important.

Spending time in Glastonbury reminds me of something, because the spirit of Avalon has never left it. I live in the city, I get caught up in my busy life and the memory fades, but being in Glastonbury opens my awareness to the deeper levels. It makes the lost sense of spirituality accessible again so I remember what is most important in life. A visit to Glastonbury also helps people to remember the sacred quality of nature and inspires a vision of eco-spirituality, which we need today for our own survival.

Postcard from Avalon

Lucy Cavendish is an Australian white witch who embraces magic as a belief system of personal fulfilment and happiness. She is the author of *White Magic* and *The Lost Lands*, and creator of *The Oracle Tarot*, *The Wild Wisdom of the Faery Oracle*, *Magical Spell Cards* and *Oracle of the Dragonfae*. She is an astrologer, ritualist and psychic, and has released the space clearing CD *As Above So Below* and the guided meditation *Return to Avalon*.

Lucy feels deeply connected to Avalon, and facilitates workshops that impart the wisdom and teachings of the druids and priestesses of the sacred isle. She took her first spiritual group to England in 2010, to explore Somerset, Wiltshire and Cornwall, and plans many more such magical pilgrimages. Visit www.lucycavendish.com.

While the geophysical location of Avalon is in the town of Glastonbury in England, there is also an Avalon of the heart, a world between the worlds that we all carry within us, and which I believe can be tapped in to from anywhere on the planet.

I first reached Avalon long before I travelled to Glastonbury. As a child I went there in dreams, and when I began practising magic I accessed this in-between world during ritual, spellcasting and chanting. Avalon is a sacred space between the worlds that is within all of us. It is another dimension where we can get in touch with our inner world, as well as the Otherworld where all knowledge resides.

Avalon is a sacred joining of the elements, our own faery self, and our connection to the highest principles of love and service, romance and magic. It's a mystical state we can go to through meditation, by communicating with the goddess or by invoking it in ritual.

In my workshops I guide people through a series of magical processes that connect them with the ancient crafts of the Avalonian priestesses and activate their psychic abilities, but you can do this yourself if you open your heart to the wisdom and purity of Avalon.

It is easier to access at the special times of the year – the enchanted sabbat nights when the veils between this world and the Other are thinner and we can communicate with spirits and elementals – but it can be reached at any time, through the power of thought and intention. Avalon can be accessed when you invoke the goddesses of the place – Bridie, Rhiannon and Ceridwen – as well as Morgen la Fey and Guinevere, the goddess who still remains to be reclaimed.

She is no tragic victim – she is a true goddess of the land, and she wants us to find her and know her again. Many of us can also access Avalon easily because we had past lives there, so we have a strong cellular memory of it. I feel the magnetic pull of several lifetimes there, where I lived and worked as part of a sacred community.

Avalon is the place where we become one with our spirit, where we can achieve great healing, see the future and manifest what we need and want. Being in Avalon healed a part of me that was wounded. Its compassion is limitless and its teachings are endless. Avalon is a dimension and an experience that can bring women and men into their power in a way that creates love and respect for the earth plane, for our beautiful planet, for our bodies and for our relationships. Avalon heals everyone, but our individual experience of her will differ according to our own unique vibrational blueprint.

It is linked to modern witchcraft because it includes the teachings of the druids and priestesses of the Celtic world, and learning to hear the voice of the earth mother. It is the belief that everything is sacred, that we are a part of nature and must respect and protect it, and that the earth is alive and connected to us. It gives us a vision of a life lived in harmony with the ancient wisdom that is in tune with the planet.

Visiting Avalon will impart to you the teachings of the druids and priestesses of the Celtic world and the sacred rites that help us to hear and feel, see and know the voice, the face, the wisdom and the knowledge of the earth mother. It also includes the teachings of Atlantis and Lemuria that survived in the apple groves, the significance of the apple – the element of Avalon that has remnants in the story of Eden and Eve – the Merlin Taliesin's sacred poetry, and connecting to the faery and elfin realms. You'll experience the difference between the "real" world that we physically live in, and Avalon – the heart place.

Dwelling so long in the dimension of Avalon, I felt a magnetic pull to visit Glastonbury, its earth plane location, and I finally went there at Beltane in 2005. How amazing it was, that I could feel so naturally at perfect ease in a place I'd never physically been. The actual landscape has true magic in it, and the water from the Well has an incredible repository of blessings within its structure that work on a physical and energetic level. Being there validated that my path, my mist-filled dreaming, is legitimate, but it also confirmed for me that the magic of Avalon is available to all, no matter where in the world you live.

Visiting this dimension today, from wherever you are, will give you access to the ancient wisdom for a more meaningful, psychically aware and healed present and future. Avalon activates your magical talents, brings a new level of awareness and purpose to all you do, and makes the everyday world enchanted and sacred. It's time to re-learn and reactivate its magic, and incorporate it within your heart and soul.

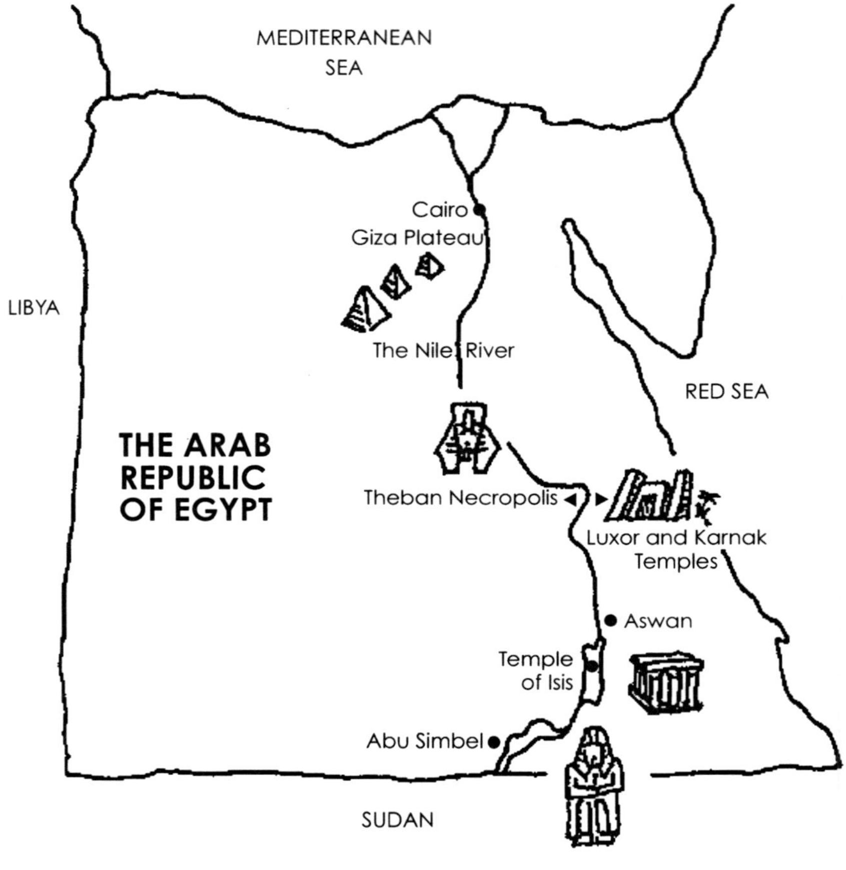

MEDITERRANEAN
SEA

Cairo
Giza Plateau

LIBYA

The Nile River

RED SEA

**THE ARAB
REPUBLIC
OF EGYPT**

Theban Necropolis ◄ ► Luxor and Karnak
Temples

Aswan

Temple
of Isis

Abu Simbel

SUDAN

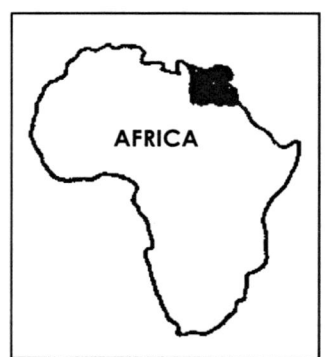

AFRICA

Rejoin the two halves of your soul in divine union

The monuments of the pharaohs
Ancient Egypt

Feel the masculine and feminine energies of the universe flowing through you as you walk in the shadow of the ancient pyramids and within the temples where Isis and Osiris were worshipped as two halves of the divine, allowing these ancient powers to unify the disparate parts of your soul, creating union and a sense of oneness.

The place

"Do you not know that Egypt is a copy of heaven or rather, the very place on earth where the forces of heaven are balanced and ordered? Even more than that, if truth be told, Egypt is the temple of the entire world."

Egyptian scribe, circa 1400BCE

Egypt, like much of Africa, is a sun-drenched, luminous land of shifting sands, vast deserts, vivid blue skies and friendly people. It's also a place of immense spiritual power, magic and history, and for centuries its ancient monuments have drawn pilgrims determined to unlock the hidden wisdom buried within the sands there.

The awe-inspiring pyramids, mysterious Sphinx statue and the sacred temples along the Nile are thought to hold the knowledge of one of the oldest civilisations on earth, although sometimes it seems they offer more riddles than answers, adding to the mystery and intrigue of this fascinating country.

It's a place renowned for its dark secrets and transformational magic, and a series of sacred sites that vibrate with a mix of divine power and earth energies. Today Egypt is predominantly Islamic, the cultural centre of the Arab world, but it has a rich history of magicians and priests, pagan cults, gods and goddesses, mighty pharaohs, invading Persians, "saviour" Romans and Coptic Christians, as well as beautiful stories of creation and magic.

For thousands of years one of the most advanced cultures in history worshipped the gods there, built structures that still confound scientists today, and lived deeply spiritual lives in tune with the earth, the seasons, the stars, and their concept of death as just part of the continuing journey, the gateway to a realm they envisaged as more enjoyable and enlightening than the mortal plane.

Not much is recorded of the lifestyle, rituals and beliefs of the people who lived in this country in prehistoric times, although there is evidence of life in Egypt even before 25,000BCE, followed later by hunters and gatherers who camped along the fertile banks of the Nile River, tribes moving nomadically through the desert oases, and the beginnings of structured societies with local chiefs holding sway.

Around 3000BCE Upper and Lower Egypt were unified under a single royal leader, and the great civilisation of the pharaohs began, leaving monuments and writings that continue to astound modern man. In particular people are drawn to Egypt by the history of the Old Kingdom era of the third millennium BCE, also known as the Age of the Pyramids, and the New Kingdom era that ran from around 1550-1070BCE, when famous pharaohs such as Hatshepsut, Amenhotep III and Tutankhamun ruled the land and built grand temples to honour themselves and the gods.

Beholding these monuments, which have weathered centuries of sandstorms, dramatic floods and the fiery desert heat, connects people with the ancient wisdom and power that is imbued in each stone. Standing on this ground, touching these buildings and praying or meditating within the temples awakens something deep within, and transforms a person's awareness and their life.

Any journey to Egypt will be filled with magical experiences. Visitors ride camels across the desert sands towards the mysterious pyramids as the sun rises, feeling the prehistoric beasts lurch beneath them as they clumsily make their way forward. They sit in restaurants on the very edge of the Nile River, watching the famous waters stream by as they sip exotic hibiscus tea and eat the spicy local cuisine. They walk in the footsteps of legendary figures such as Ramses, Cleopatra and Alexander the Great, picturing the lives of these long-ago people who helped shape the modern world.

And they stand in the shadow of the Great Pyramid, irresistibly drawn by one of the most well-known structures on the planet, and contemplate the magic of the universe. This pyramid was erected at what was believed by many to be the navel of the world, and certainly Ancient Egypt, its rulers and its grand monuments were the centre of civilisation for a very long time.

The pyramids and temples were purposely located along lines of earth energy and constructed with deep ritual according to precise religious plans, yet the sacredness of the land and its people also comes from the spiritual beliefs and actions of all those who have walked this holy ground over the past five thousand years.

The magic of long-ago priests, the sincerity of their offerings to the gods and their search for enlightenment and peace can still be tangibly felt, as can the piety of the Christians who ruled the country for centuries, and the devotion of the Muslims who have steered it into the modern world. Whatever your beliefs or quest, this energy changes your vibration, opens you up and touches your heart.

Most people who visit Egypt also spend time cruising the Nile, sailing languidly past the enigmatic monuments and temples scattered throughout this vast ancient land. This impressive waterway, the longest river in the world, has been a source of physical and spiritual sustenance to the people of Egypt for millennia, and watching life drift by as the boat sails along it is better than any movie.

There are many magical group tours available, led by spiritual teachers, healers, psychics and metaphysical authors, which incorporate ceremonies and rituals at significant sites and allow participants access to some of the sacred places not usually open to tourists. They are accompanied by local guides, who share the traditions and customs of their country as well as its history, and help people look deep within the heart of this intriguing place.

All visitors to Egypt are seeking different things – adventure, knowledge, connection to the divine, ancient secrets, self-awareness. And everyone who walks where the pharaohs once lived receives and learns more than they could ever imagine. In the incomprehensible beauty of this strange foreign land, people find themselves changed, stripped bare and laid open to the immensity of possibility held within the incredible experiences that occur there and the places of power throughout the country.

I travelled there with a fascination for the goddess Isis and the people who first worshipped her, and left with a new knowing of the masculine energy of the universe, the union of male and female, the previously unacknowledged masculine force within my own self and an increased sense of balance and confidence.

And in learning about the shifting pantheon of deities, who were recreated to suit the ruler of the day, I came to understand that there is no need for gods, because all that you require is within you, and around you, in the relationships you surround yourself with and the divine union of all parts within your self. This is the gift of Egypt, and it's a blessing bestowed on all who visit this magical land.

The present

"Egypt is the heart of Mother Earth and the beginning of most of the learned realities that we know as human beings. It is a place of spiritual emergence, with memories that are held there for all of us to discover."
Lynn Andrews, American author, mystic and spiritual teacher

Egypt – officially the Arab Republic of Egypt – is a place of burnished desert sands, ancient temples, medieval mosques, bazaars, museums, modern high-rise apartments built alongside sprawling old villas, many-laned highways where cars jostle with donkey carts, buzzing nightlife, markets, hustle and bustle, a colourful clash of cultures and the mysterious, life-giving waters of the Nile River.

At its spiritual – and tourist – heart are the ancient structures of the Giza Plateau, on the outskirts of the capital city of Cairo. The iconic shape of the Great Pyramid is the first thing you picture when you think of the country and the first sight you see as you fly in, and has become the symbol of Egypt around the world. You can feel its presence and its sense of mystery even when you can't see it, and its power holds you spellbound long after you've left this golden land.

My plane landed in the middle of the night, and I was met by a friendly local guide who accompanied me through customs, much to my relief. Many western women are nervous about travelling in Egypt alone, because it's so different culturally, which is another reason so many choose to visit as part of a group. The one I'd booked included spiritual seekers from around the globe, travelling together to take part in rituals and learn about this mystical land and its past.

I staggered outside with my backpack, stunned by the heavy cigarette smoking even inside the airport, and the night-time heat and strangeness of things. We drove through the streets of Cairo towards the suburb of Giza and the old part of the city, across the Nile and through the heart of this ruggedly beautiful and timeless place.

Even at 3am there were people around, and bright lights, noise and revelry. Discos blared music out into the still night air, palm trees appeared to float alongside the road, mosques were lit up and breathtaking, and everywhere people smiled welcomingly.

I fell into bed in a jetlagged stupor, not realising just how close I was to the Great Pyramid. But the next morning I opened the curtains and gasped, staring in wonder. It was right there! I felt as though I could reach out and touch it, or lean close and hear it whisper its secrets to me. I had a surreal moment as I marvelled that I was here, in this land of worldwide fascination, staying in a faerytale palace of a hotel at the base of the famous Giza pyramids.

While many people assume that the three structures are far out in the desert, standing alone and silent in a sandy wilderness, the city of Cairo has actually sprawled outwards to meet them, and you can see their peaks on the city skyline like any other landmark building. I wanted to rest my brow against them, and my heart, like I did with the trees below the Tor in Glastonbury, to connect physically and psychically with these incredible monuments, but I was waiting for the rest of the group I was travelling with to fly in.

I ended up having the whole day to myself, as the others didn't arrive until nightfall. I spent most of the time in the pool, gazing up in awe at the pyramids, writing postcards home (there's a pyramid in my garden!), basking in the sunshine and soaking up the sensation of being in such a sacred and timeless land. Despite the cloying heat, and my usual aversion to high temperatures, I felt very comfortable. Egypt is a paradise, with a relaxed, languid atmosphere. Birds chirped loudly in the trees and the sound of people praying drifted down lazily from the pyramids, and I felt welcome and so vibrantly alive.

Then early the next morning I finally got to touch the Great Pyramid and breathe in the desert air that has swirled around it for millennia. Out in the heat and dust of the Giza Plateau I stared up in awe, amazed that I was standing at the foot of this ancient wonder. The dry African winds burned my eyeballs and the summer sun stung my skin, but it didn't matter. Time seemed to stand still, and I was overwhelmed by the sense of history and occasion.

Cotton-draped locals gazed serenely at us as the heat washed over them and they swatted flies with graceful ease. Colourfully dressed boys led camels through the sands, trying to entice people to ride into the desert to view the pyramids from another perspective – a perspective that hasn't changed for thousands of years. One tried to scam me, but I was saved by our guide, who screeched at him in Arabic and drew me back to safety. "Trust in Allah but tie up your camel," he grinned, verbalising a long-held view from this land, that the gods watch over you, but you must also take responsibility for yourself.

The sense of antiquity at this place was amazing, especially for a girl from a country where the oldest buildings were constructed only two hundred years ago. So much history surrounds these three pyramids, which are close to five thousand years old.

I spent hours wandering between them, touching the stones, imagining their glorious pasts and trying to comprehend their immensity. Our Egyptian guide had worked at the Cairo Museum, and he filled our heads with stories of history and archaeological discoveries, hard facts and mythical tales, of scarab beetles that signify long life and beautiful plants with magical properties, as well as ancient dark sacrifices and glorious accounts of rebirth and resurrection.

Later our group performed a ritual at the base of the Great Pyramid, to anchor our energy there, to draw down solar consciousness and to open ourselves to the immense wisdom before us. There's so much to learn in this ancient country, and we wanted to suck up and savour every sight, sound and piece of information we could.

Two weeks later, on the night of the summer solstice, we returned to the Great Pyramid and climbed inside as the sun started to sink over the desert dunes, to perform a ceremony of healing and transformation in its sacred inner chamber. Occultists, theosophists and spiritual seekers have long claimed that this pyramid is a repository of secret knowledge and healing, and a place where you can commune with spirits or even people from other planets or star systems.

Shirley MacLaine spent a night here, manifesting and dealing with her fears as she lay in the sarcophagus of a long-dead pharaoh, and ceremonial magician Aleister Crowley, who was fascinated by the pyramids and their occult possibilities, stayed inside the King's Chamber on his honeymoon, bathed in supernatural light and performing black magic rituals that sent his new bride into a trance.

In a state of awe we entered the giant pyramid and slowly climbed down the tiny, narrow passageway. We had to stoop, almost crawling at some points, and the darkness and closeness of the walls gave each of us a touch of claustrophobia. But how many people get to sit within this ancient monument, on this sacred day no less, and touch these stones that have been here for centuries, watching over the desert as gods were worshipped then discarded, as armies rose and fell?

A little way in the passage divides, one path continuing downwards, a torturous hundred metres further into the earth and the unfinished lower chamber, the other climbing to the royal chambers above. We went upwards, a steep, awkward climb. I shivered as I thought of the *Indiana Jones* movies and recalled the stories we'd been told of snakes supposedly guarding the rooms from intruders, wrapped around statues of deities and ready to strangle anyone coming to disturb the pharaoh's rest, but we passed by unscathed.

There's another fork, where the tunnel either climbs higher or goes forward to the Queen's Chamber, so called even though no queen ever lay there in eternal rest. We stepped inside this limestone room, which experts believe was intended to house the pharaoh's statue. On the walls are the holes archaeologists made in the 1870s while trying to discover the ventilation shafts – which scientists recently sent robots down, resulting in the startling discovery of a secret chamber in the south of the pyramid and a tiny passageway aligned with the Dog Star,

Sirius, which in ancient times was connected to the goddess Isis, for centuries the primary deity and earth mother of this country.

We performed a chanting ritual to attune ourselves as a group and to raise energy. In this land of solar gods and sunshine, the summer solstice is a powerful time, the longest day of the year and a celebration of the sun god Re and his influence on life and death. I felt a loving feminine presence too, which filled me with strength and purpose.

Then we headed back out and climbed upwards again through the hot, airless Great Gallery, with its high corbelled ceiling, to the King's Chamber. It was eerie, lit only by the flickering of my tiny torch, and much bigger than I'd expected. Five chambers rise above the ceiling, to relieve the pressure of the immense weight of all the stones above, and although we couldn't see into them in the dark, it was within these chambers that ancient graffiti that mentioned the pharaoh Khufu's name was found, identifying the pyramid as his.

The room, made of polished red granite, was empty but for a dark lidless sarcophagus assumed to be Khufu's final resting place. Granite was used for the coffins of their beloved pharaohs because it symbolised eternity and permanence. For Khufu's a special stone was brought at great effort from Aswan, a town a thousand kilometres away, showing that only the best could be used for this exalted ruler. Once the carved coffin was situated in the middle of the room, but today it lies against a wall, no longer the focal point of the chamber.

I was seated with my back against it for our ceremony, along with another woman. She freaked out a bit, and asked nervously if we were leaning against a tomb, but since we were inside one too, I didn't think it would matter much where we sat.

Yet it's easy to be spooked within such a monument, weighed down with the ghosts of ages past, trapped within the centre of the massive stone structure. I imagine it would be frightening to anyone who suffers from claustrophobia, and when I thought too hard about how far within it we'd climbed, and the long, slow and painful crawl we'd have to repeat to get back out, I did get a small shiver up my spine.

Once we were all seated and with our collective altar set up in the centre of the room, we were plunged into a thick, breathless darkness. We meditated for a while, and I thought about the vision I'd had the day before, deep within the ancient temple of Abu Simbel, located in the hot desert sands in the south of the country.

In the vision the members of our group were sitting in the crystal-walled star chamber of the Great Pyramid, although such a place is not known to exist in "real" life. We were all holding hands around a fire, meditating much like we were now – until one of the women in the group burst into flames. Eventually the fire burned down, and she was left unscathed, cleansed and purified by the intense heat.

Two others had had very similar visions of the same person – and now, during our solstice ceremony in the pyramid, the woman we'd seen purified by flames was experiencing a disturbing image of herself drowning, before she finally emerged in a new body, transformed and free of her past issues. Being in Egypt changed her deeply, and it was fascinating that a few of us had the same visions of her process. The energy of this land really supports and nurtures spiritual growth, manifesting emotional challenges that lead to deep inner change.

Afterwards, as we made our way out of the pyramid, one of the group felt compelled to go down to the underground chamber, drawn by its lower world connotations, a realm ruled by the god Anubis. We all waited in the tunnel as he felt his way down and sat in the darkness alone. Later he told us he'd been terrified, and had had vivid flashes of being buried alive and left to die in a place just as cold and dark as the chamber. But he underwent a self-initiation process deep within the earth, calling on the ancient gods and purging himself of the fear, doubt, pain and other emotional blocks that had weighed him down for years. He felt a metaphorical rebirth as he processed the anger he'd long felt over events in his past, and as he climbed back up towards us, and the light, he felt weightless, renewed and totally transformed.

During our time in Egypt each of us had a sense of connection to a place, a period of history or a deity that resonated with us, our experiences and the aspect of ourselves we needed to heal. This holy land gives something different to each person who visits, seeming to understand exactly what is required for healing and transformation.

When we finally emerged from the monument we sat out on the desert sands, staring up at the stars, and I was filled with wonder at where I was, what it all meant, and the massive weight of history around me. What was this ancient place? Could the people who claim it was an initiation chamber or a stargate be right? Was it a pyramid of transformation? Or was it simply a tomb? If so, how incredible that one man could build himself a burial chamber that would last more than four thousand years and be known throughout the world. I hoped he'd found his way to the afterlife he'd been so desperate to reach.

I also thought of the indigenous people of other cultures, who don't need physical constructions to make a memory or achieve immortality. It intrigued me that so much of the power and spirituality of Ancient Egypt is linked to buildings and monuments, not trees, rivers, rocks or desert sands. So like the Christians and their cathedrals or the Muslims and their mosques, which seem to hold the power of their prayer and devotion and the spirit of their times. People must leave something of their beliefs and spirit within each stone, pressed into the walls, or the triangular sides as in these pyramids, which seem to pulse with the energy of ages past.

"Though its proportions are colossal, the outline is pure and graceful. The expression of the head is mild, gracious and tranquil – the character is African, but the mouth and lips, which are thick, have a softness and delicacy of execution truly admirable. It seems real life and flesh. Art must have been at a high pitch when this monument was executed."

Baron Denon, 18th century French painter and archaeologist

Further mystery surrounds the other major monument of the Giza Plateau, the enigmatic Sphinx. It's one of the largest single-stone statues on earth, more than 70 metres long, and 20 metres tall at its highest point. It has the face of a man and the body of a lion, representing a divine being with the intellect of the former and the strength of the latter. It was carved as a depiction of royal power, although it's believed by many to have a deeper meaning.

I was a little surprised when I got up close to it, because pictures and its international fame and significance led me to expect this statue would be enormous. Yet next to the might of the pyramids it seemed smaller than I'd imagined. It's also not as well preserved as I'd thought – the Sphinx's eyes were pecked out over the centuries, and Napoleon's army is blamed for much of the more recent damage after allegedly using the grand statue for target practise when the French army invaded Egypt in 1798.

But it remains incredibly regal – even its missing nose and partly destroyed face can't dim its incredible presence. It still wears its kingly headdress folded out to the side of its face, although the royal uraeus, the sacred cobra, on its brow and the ritual beard on its chin fell off long ago. Some parts of these are housed in the British Museum, while others have yet to be found or are lost forever.

Not much is known for certain about this iconic leonine statue – who the face was modelled on, who built it, why or even when – yet it's one of the world's most-visited wonders, and a thing of great power, mystery and beauty. The head was carved out of a hard natural rock outcrop on the lower slope of the Giza Plateau, while the body and its paws, claws and tail were sculpted out of the limestone bedrock after stone blocks were quarried from around it, possibly for the building of the first pyramid. The harder rock of the head has made it more resistant to erosion (if not bullets!), while the softer body has weathered away a little over the centuries.

Most experts have concluded that the Sphinx is related to the solar worship of the early Egyptians, and may have been built, or at least acted, as a guardian of the pyramid tombs behind it. It faces east, which they believed was the direction of the Land of the Living, and gazes at the rising sun, which they considered a god.

But the enchanting Giza Plateau is not the only place of ancient monuments in this fascinating land. While the three pyramids of Giza are the grandest and best known in Egypt, there are a hundred more pyramids throughout the country. Twenty-five of these are considered historically significant, and most of them are quite close to Cairo, so their evolution can be traced in the surrounding desert landscape.

One of the most impressive sites is at Saqqara, 20 kilometres south of Giza through the sea of sand. This was the burial place of most of the pharaohs of the Old Kingdom, when the nearby settlement of Memphis was the country's capital. The pyramid complex is west of the town, in the direction of the Land of the Dead, and boasts many fascinating architectural discoveries, including the first-ever pyramid, the Step Pyramid of the pharaoh Djoser, who ruled around 2650BCE.

He began the building of his royal tomb in the traditional way, as a mastaba, a flat-roofed structure with sloping sides. He had grand plans of making a three-tiered step tomb, but by the end of his reign it had grown to a 62-metre-tall, six-tiered construction – the largest building in the world at that time.

It was designed by the architect, priest and physician Imhotep, who was deified centuries later, and has been described by some as the starting point of architecture. It was literally a stairway to heaven for Djoser to ascend to the afterlife, built atop a complex series of inner corridors that led to a burial chamber dug deep within the earth, which represented the underworld that souls must travel through.

Nearby are several fascinating tombs and five other pyramids, as well as the intriguing Serapeum, which held the mummified bodies of the sacred Apis bulls, the earthly manifestations of the god Ptah.

Another significant pyramid complex is at Dahshur, a little further south, where Djoser's successor Snefru built the famous Red Pyramid around 2600BCE. He was the first pharaoh of the Fourth Dynasty, and is credited with several pyramids, an unusual feat. His first was the Maidum tomb, 50 kilometres south of Dahshur, which was abandoned fifteen years into construction when he moved the royal court.

He then commissioned the structure known as the Bent Pyramid, so called because it began with very steep sides, which represented the rays of the sun the pharaoh's soul would use to reach heaven, then halfway up changed to a more gentle slope due to instability in the base, creating an odd looking bent triangle and a pyramid that was much shorter than planned. And even before this one was finished he began work on the nearby Red Pyramid, so named because the exposed limestone sides glow red in the morning and afternoon sun.

We climbed inside this one too, down a steep, narrow passageway where we had to stoop then practically crawl, clutching desperately to the handrails. It's made up of a burial chamber – although today there is debate over where Snefru was actually buried – accessed through two smaller chambers. Lower down is another tiny, rock-strewn chamber where the priests and nobles went to fast and pray in total blackness. It's dark, dank and cold in here, and a little spooky, but what would you expect from a tomb?

In Dahshur there are also pyramids from the Middle Kingdom, circa 2000-1800BCE, when this burial style had a short revival of popularity in royal circles, before it died out. Commoners continued building smaller man-sized pyramids after this though, such as in the workers' village of Deir el-Medina, where they laboured on their own tombs in time off from digging the new style of underground burial chambers for the pharaohs. For while there's a royal pyramid at Abydos that was built by Ahmose II around 1550BCE, by the time of the New Kingdom era he ushered in, the pharaohs had decided to hide their tombs in the hills surrounding the royal centre of Thebes, where Luxor now stands, in what's known as the Valley of the Kings.

"I inserted the candle and peered in. At first I could see nothing, the hot air escaping from the chamber causing the candle flame to flicker, but presently, as my eyes grew accustomed to the light, details of the room within emerged slowly from the mist. Strange animals, statues and gold – everywhere the glint of gold."

Howard Carter, English archaeologist, on discovering Tutankhamun's tomb on November 22, 1922

The Valley of the Kings, also known as the Theban Necropolis, is near Luxor, a short flight from Cairo. It has revealed many ancient secrets to the world, including the treasure-filled tomb of the boy pharaoh Tutankhamun, who reigned in the 14th century BCE. While so vastly different to the pyramids, hidden away rather than displayed for all the world to see, this burial place of the pharaohs of the New Kingdom reveals that their obsession with death and the afterlife had not waned.

The bodies of the kings were still mummified in elaborate rituals then buried, protected by the gods and accompanied by riches, but their tombs were sunk deep within the ground in the bleak and desolate hills of the Valley of the Kings. It wasn't modesty though, for the pharaohs also built huge, elaborate mortuary temples on the plain below their tomb, across the river from the royal capital of Thebes, to display their importance and enable people to worship them after their death.

In ancient times all Egyptian burials occurred on the western bank of the river, because the east was considered the direction of growth and birth, as the sun god rose there every morning, while the west was the direction of death and resurrection, as that was where the sun god sank every evening, dying before his rebirth the next day. They believed that in order to make their way to the afterlife and be resurrected, they had to be buried on the side that symbolised rebirth.

Known as the Place of Truth, the dusty, sun-baked Valley of the Kings was an attempt to preserve the bodies of the pharaohs more effectively than the pyramids had managed to, and they were successful. Last century many incredible tombs were uncovered for the first time, which have shed new light on our understanding of this enigmatic country, its people and their customs.

We went inside three tombs, an experience that had its moments of creepiness. I don't know how the grave robbers braved these dark, mysterious caverns, not knowing what would be in there or how far down into the earth they'd have to go – but it was amazing to be inside, imagining how ingrained the belief in the afterlife must have been for these people to have built such incredible monuments for the dead.

The mysterious funerary texts were painted or carved on the walls. Awesome pictures and hieroglyphs, some of them now covered by glass to protect them from the humidity and the breathing of eager visitors, tell the stories of the lives of the kings and queens who ruled more than three thousand years ago, as well as their religious ceremonies, deities, concepts of the afterlife, burial practices, battles, agricultural methods, pastimes, clothes and lifestyle.

First we descended into the tomb of Ramses IV, who died around 1150BCE, marvelling at how bright the colours on the walls still are. Painted across the ceiling of the burial chamber is a depiction of the sky goddess Nut, while images of Isis and Nephthys were carved into the sarcophagus to protect the body of the pharaoh.

Then we climbed the ninety steps down into the earth and along the corridor that leads to the vestibule of the complex tomb of Amenhotep II, who died around 1400BCE. There are beautiful paintings on the walls and brilliant stars etched on the ceiling – these tombs really are works of art. From here more steps descend to the burial chamber itself, which still houses the sarcophagus even though the body of the pharaoh, which was here when the tomb was first opened, has been removed, along with six other royal mummies that had been stashed in this tomb for safe keeping when their own were invaded.

The most famous tomb is that of Tutankhamun, who died around 1325BCE. It's renowned not for its size or grandeur – other tombs are more impressive – but for its relatively recent discovery and the incredible treasures that were revealed when it was opened in 1922. The amazed archaeologist found a solid gold coffin and funeral mask, several gilded shrines and lots of jewellery. He also unleashed the legend of the Curse of Tutankhamun, which began when Lord Carnarvon, who financed the excavations, died in Cairo a few months after the tomb was opened, followed by five others involved in the dig.

More than sixty tombs have been discovered in the Valley of the Kings so far, although not all of them are open at any one time, with research and restoration an ongoing adventure. But all of these burial places are fascinating, impressing with the sense of history and the richness of the spirituality and beliefs represented within them.

The remains of the workers' village of Deir el-Medina are nearby, where the craftsmen who laboured on the tombs lived and died. This gives amazing insight into the everyday life of Ancient Egypt, which is sometimes overlooked in favour of the rich lifestyles of the pharaohs.

A short distance away, past the ever-present hawkers, is the Valley of the Queens, also called the Place of Beauty, which includes the tombs of queens, royal children and officials of the era. We descended slowly into the darkness of the tomb of Queen Nefertari, who died around 1250BCE. She was the wife of Ramses II and considered his equal – and as a result her tomb is the most beautiful in the valley.

The ceiling is painted like the night sky, and there's a vestibule and antechamber with steps leading further down to the burial chamber, where the rebirth of the dead was believed to take place. This is one of the most-valued tombs, partly because of the quality of the paintings, which offer the most detailed source of information on the Egyptians and their journey towards the afterlife. There are beautifully rendered extracts from *The Book of the Dead*, a copy of which was placed in every tomb, and depictions of the ceremonies that followed Nefertari's death and the tests she had to undergo before reaching the next life.

Later, down on the river plain below the necropolis, we visited Deir el-Bahri, the mortuary temple of Queen Hatshepsut, who died around 1458BCE. She was the first female pharaoh, who encountered massive opposition and was murdered for being a woman – or for being ruthless, depending on your source, although the latter wasn't a crime for male pharaohs. She was a successful and prosperous ruler, and some say she invented women's lib. Our guide told us her name was pronounced "Hot Chicken Soup", although others prefer "Hat Cheap Suit".

It's a stunning temple, set in a natural amphitheatre and designed with terraces and colonnades that contrast with the stark and dusty hillside. Carvings on the walls tell the story of her life – she was the daughter of Thutmosis I, and married his successor, her half-brother Thutmosis II. When he died she made herself regent for Thutmosis III, her husband's son by another woman, and ruled for years in her own right. After she died her stepson destroyed her images and deleted all mention of her, so her story was lost to history for centuries, until she was rediscovered by archaeologists and her life was reconstructed.

As we approached her temple I felt really sick – weak, feverish, dizzy and nauseous – yet as soon as we left I felt fine again. This was the place where fifty-eight tourists and four guides were massacred by

Islamic extremists in 1997, and I wondered if the sense of grief and fear from that event could have soaked in to the ground or hovered in the ether and be affecting future visitors. It makes sense that in the same way magic and worship can seep into a place and make it sacred, terrible pain suffered there could also remain trapped within the earth, the stones and the very air, able to be felt by people who visit the area.

One of our group performed a beautiful ceremony here, raising power and sending it into the ground to try to heal the pain inflicted on the area. Some locals still won't go near the place, and it's so sad that so much fear still lies so palpably over this beautiful site.

Once the temple boasted an avenue of sphinxes running up from the Nile, and scores of amazing carvings and hieroglyphs on the walls. While nearly every image of Hatshepsut was defaced, in order to strike her from memory and history and affect her journey to the afterlife, many of the other murals depicting life in those times remain, as well as intricate depictions of gods and goddesses, of the queen's birth at the hands of these deities, and the elaborate offerings she made to gain their favour. There's also a chapel dedicated to Anubis, the god of the dead, and one to Hathor, the goddess of healing.

Close by is Medinet Habu, the mortuary temple of Ramses III. The whole complex is surrounded by high enclosure walls, and two statues of the goddess Sekhmet stand at the entrance. Within is a small, older temple built by Hatshepsut, as well as the Chapels of the Divine Votaresses, which were added later. The votaresses were priestesses and princesses of the royal house, "married" to the god Amun.

I felt really drawn to these, and was intrigued to discover that long after the main temple was abandoned, locals still went to these tiny chapels to pray. There's also a sacred lake, where women made offerings to Isis and bathed in the waters in the hope of conceiving, and people still believe the whole site is imbued with deep magic.

The temple itself includes a palace where Ramses often stayed, several chapels dedicated to gods including Osiris, Ptah and Sokar, and chambers that once held treasure but now simply tease with wall murals that boast of gold, lapis lazuli and other valuables. In the centre is the sanctuary, which enclosed the pharaoh's funerary chamber, and several altars where offerings were made. It's an incredible complex, and I was awed by the sense of divinity within these walls, which remains even after all these centuries.

"It flows through old hushed Egypt and its sands,
Like some grave mighty thought threading a dream,
And times and things, as in that vision, seem
Keeping along it their eternal stands."
James Henry Leigh Hunt, 19th century British poet

Another amazing Egyptian experience is to cruise the Nile. After visiting the Theban Necropolis and the temples of Luxor and Karnak, we set sail for the Upper Egypt city of Aswan. Cruising this ancient waterway, with the ship's magnificent views and luxurious airconditioned cabins, is a great way to evoke the colonial tradition made famous in so many books and films, and watch the daily life of the Egyptians as you float by. Men farm their land, women pass by with huge bundles, and children play in the shallows or kick a soccer ball around, all with a languid grace that belies the heat.

Feluccas, the sailboats of the Nile, can also be used to travel along this famous route, and there are three-night cruises that involve river travel by day and campfires and camping on the shore by night, the way people have travelled the Nile for thousands of years.

Departing from the town of Luxor, the first major stop is at Edfu, where we journeyed by caleches – little horse-drawn carriages – to Edfu Temple, the best-preserved cult temple of the ancient world. It was consecrated to the falcon-headed god Horus, the son of Isis and Osiris and the embodiment of kingship and divine order. Further along the Nile is the town of Kom Ombo and its sacred site. Like Edfu, the temple of Kom Ombo was built in the Ptolemaic era, circa 305-30BCE, and finished by the Romans. It's located on a bend of the Nile, and the ruins look stunning as you drift slowly towards them.

At the top of the Nile is Aswan, the southernmost city of Egypt and a popular tourist place and meeting point. Historically it was a frontier town, the border between Egypt and the region of Nubia, a country of immense wealth due to its gold, ivory, gem and slave trade. Since pharaonic times Nubia has been conquered and divided, with some of the land being absorbed by Egypt and some by Sudan, but the people of the region still consider themselves Nubian, speak their own language and maintain their traditions.

Their presence brings a rich cultural flavour to the town of Aswan, and reinforces the African essence. It's easy to forget, watching movies and walking around Cairo, that Egypt is an African country, and the pharaohs, until the last few kingdoms, weren't the pale-skinned Europeans depicted in Hollywood retellings.

Aswan's tiny Elephantine Island, just over a kilometre long and 400 metres wide, was the site of the Egyptian-Nubian fortress, and was believed to be the home of Khnum, the ram-headed river deity who controlled the Nile. The first temple constructed here in his honour dates back to 3000BCE, although the current ruins are from a later rebuilding. Elephantine Island is also famous as the site where third century BCE geographer and astronomer Eratosthenes concluded that the earth was round, and was able to calculate its circumference, simply by watching the sun's rays in a well there.

Visitors can catch a ferry to the island to stay at the resort there, go over to explore the Aswan Museum, see the traditional Nubian House and walk through the temple ruins, or take a felucca ride and see it all from the water. We each climbed aboard one of these tiny boats and set out on the famous river at sunset, a noisy, vibrant, exciting trip where we got caught up in the energy of life on the Nile and swamped by the colour, sights and sounds of this thriving town.

Sailing also provides great views from the river of the mausoleum of the third Aga Khan, situated on the west bank with the Tombs of the Nobles, and the Christian monastery of Saint Simeon, which can be reached by camel. We also drifted around beautiful Isis and Amun Islands, which both have hotels on them, and the Island of Plants, which boasts an incredible tropical botanic garden.

Aswan is also the base from which to explore the legendary Temple of Isis, one of the most significant in the country, and the striking grandeur of Abu Simbel, a startling temple monument that sits in the blazing desert sun near Egypt's border with Sudan.

In the town itself is the acclaimed Nubia Museum, the Unfinished Obelisk, the Sculpture Park, the Fatimid Cemetery and the luxurious Old Cataract Hotel, where Agatha Christie wrote *Death on the Nile* in the 1930s and which has accommodated everyone from Tsar Nicolas II, Sir Winston Churchill and Margaret Thatcher to Jimmy Carter, King Farouk and Princess Diana over its many years of existence.

Aswan is also famous for its bazaar, which we visited in the blessed coolness after dinner. It was so colourful, alive, loud, vibrant and exotic, and certainly reinforced that we were in Egypt. Traditional clothes, like galabiyya robes, scarves and vivid shawls, fight for space with art, handicrafts, carved stone scarab beetles, jewellery, piles of pungent spices, flowers, dyes, basketwork and rugs.

At the end of the night we sat down to rest at a tiny outdoor cafe and drank karkaday, a delicious tea made from hibiscus flowers which is especially popular in Aswan, and smoked a sheesha water pipe (when in Rome!). Tobacco flavoured with apple, mint, strawberry or apricot is now common, but the traditional way is ma'azil, tobacco mixed with molasses. Later we discovered that it's unusual for women to smoke the unladylike sheeshas, or to visit tea rooms and coffee houses, because in Egypt these are male pursuits. However more and more cafes are now springing up that welcome both men and women.

The customs and traditions of this land are so different from the west, and it's fascinating to learn about them and try to understand the people and their monuments and sacred landscape. One of the most valuable parts of travelling is opening yourself up to new experiences and realising that your ways and beliefs are not the only ones, and that there is so much out there you have yet to discover.

The past

"The Ancient Egyptians are still fascinating to people today because theirs was a civilisation that has left such magnificent monuments, which have intrigued us and tickled our imagination. The size and splendour of their achievements are rarely matched by other civilisations."
Professor Fekri Hassan, modern Egyptologist and author

It's now known that humanity's ancestors first emerged from Africa millions of years ago. And Egypt, in the northeast of the continent on the Mediterranean Sea, has been inhabited for longer than we can comprehend by people who left little evidence of their existence.

Around 6000BCE their Nubian neighbours built the stone circle at Nabta Playa, a hundred kilometres south of Abu Simbel, which is the oldest known solar calendar in the world. However it wasn't until the reign of the Egyptian pharaohs commenced three thousand years later that written records of their civilisation began.

The glory of the Pharaonic Age ran from 3100BCE until 525BCE, when Persia conquered the land, adding it to their expanding empire and integrating many of their customs and beliefs into Egyptian life. Two hundred years later military leader and Ancient Greek king Alexander the Great overthrew the Persian Empire, and Greek culture spread throughout the ancient world. In 323BCE one of his generals, Ptolemy Soter, was installed to rule Egypt – and two decades later he declared himself a pharaoh, founding the Ptolemaic Dynasty that ruled for three hundred years. Ptolemy retained the religion of Egypt yet gave land grants to fellow Greeks, creating an upper class of foreigners and moving the royal capital to the new Greek city of Alexandria.

Centuries of infighting, sibling marriage and family murder culminated in the reign of Cleopatra, the last pharaoh of Egypt, from 51BCE. Warring with her brother-husband Ptolemy over the throne, she sought out Roman emperor Julius Caesar, who became her lover, fathered her child Caesarion and restored her right to rule. After Caesar was assassinated, Cleopatra reigned with the support of Roman leader Mark Antony, with whom she had three children.

However Caesar's adopted son Octavian, later Emperor Augustus, saw them as rivals. Seeking sole rule of the mighty Roman Empire, he declared war on them. He defeated Antony in 30BCE, which led Cleopatra to commit suicide with an asp, and Egypt became part of the fold, providing grain for Rome and soldiers for their campaigns.

Christianity was introduced around 33CE and the country slowly converted to the new religion, although worship of the goddess Isis persisted until the fifth century, at which time all the temples of Ancient Egypt were abandoned and the priesthoods died out, leaving no one to make offerings to the gods or able to decipher the hieroglyphs.

Around 619 the Persians took over again and ruled for a decade, before the lands were won back by the Eastern Roman Empire. Then in 639 an Arab army from Palestine entered Egypt and waged a battle that resulted in them taking power. The country was transformed from Christianity to Islam, and several dynasties rose and fell until the country was conquered by the Turkish Ottoman Empire in 1517.

In 1798 Napoleon Bonaparte brought the French army to Egypt and defeated the Turks at the Battle of the Pyramids – in which the Sphinx suffered some bullet wounds – but French rule was short lived. Four years later the British assisted the Ottomans in their reconquest of Egypt and then departed, leaving a power vacuum. Soon Muhammad Ali, an Albanian officer in the Ottoman army, took control. While he initiated industrialisation – including the still-famous Egyptian cotton industry – and is known as the founder of modern Egypt, his reign was bloody and brutal. He expanded into Sudan, Ethiopia and Syria, and proclaimed the right of hereditary rule of Egypt for his successors.

The British Empire invaded in 1882 and oversaw the country for a time. They finally granted the nation independence in 1922, when King Fouad then his son Farouk ruled, with the British maintaining control of the Suez Canal and strategically using Egypt in both World Wars.

In 1952 new leaders were elected. General Gamal Abdel Nasser took power, the monarchy was abolished and British troops were ordered to leave. A year later the Egyptian Arab Republic was declared, and since then Egypt has become one of the most powerful countries in the Middle East, while retaining friendly relations with the US.

Yet to most people who visit Egypt today, the last two thousand years of history have little bearing on their fascination with the place. They go to embrace the memory and wisdom of the pharaohs and the gods of Ancient Egypt. For almost three thousand years this culture flourished, with unique religious customs, deities, artwork and language, and today it remains one of the most-studied civilisations of all.

It began around 3100BCE with the unification of Upper Egypt, which covered the southern desert region, and Lower Egypt, which included the Nile Delta region in the north. Scholars can't pinpoint exact dates for all the historical ages because some of the papyrus scrolls that recorded the pharaohs contradict each other or are partially destroyed. But the Early Dynastic Period is considered to span the First and Second Dynasties of pharaohs, from 3100-2700BCE. Not much is known of these kings, who ruled from Thinis in Upper Egypt.

The Old Kingdom Period spanned the Third to Sixth Dynasties, from around 2700-2150BCE, and was run from the royal capital of Memphis. It marked a golden age of achievement and complexity, including the building of the pyramids, governmental reform and a peak of civilisation. During this era the pharaoh, whose main responsibility was to preserve justice and make offerings to ensure the growth of crops and the annual flooding of the Nile, was considered an actual god and was worshipped in the same way, ruling by divine right.

Djoser was the best-known pharaoh of the Third Dynasty, while the Fourth boasted Snefru, Khufu, Khafre and Menkaure, the builders of the famous pyramids. The pharaohs of the Fifth Dynasty increased the importance of the sun god Re and later Osiris, while in the Sixth Dynasty the power of the kings was diluted by a new noble class and a period of national drought, which was blamed on the royals.

This led to the decline of the Old Kingdom and the start of the First Intermediate Period, a time of political upheaval and a split between Upper and Lower Egypt. Little is known of the pharaohs during this era, although earlier ones continued to operate out of Memphis, while later rulers moved to Herakleopolis, the capital of Lower Egypt.

The illustrious Middle Kingdom Period was ushered in by the 11th Dynasty, which ruled from Thebes, and continued until the end of the 14th. It ran from 2050-1650BCE and was characterised by the reunification of Upper and Lower Egypt, national prosperity and the winning back of much of the land lost in the previous era. Trade connections were extended, and a system of co-regencies ensured the handover from one pharaoh to his successor went more smoothly.

Another age of disunity, the Second Intermediate Period, followed, and the country was ruled for a century by the Hyksos invaders, who established their centre in Memphis. But around 1550BCE Pharaoh Ahmose I drove them out and took control, founding the 18th Dynasty that began the golden age of the New Kingdom. This ran until 1070BCE, and included some of the best-known pharaohs in history, including Tutankhamun, Hatshepsut, Ramses the Great, Thutmosis III, Amenhotep III and Akhenaten and his wife Nefertiti. The royal capital moved again, from Memphis to Thebes, which is today called Luxor.

The death of Ramses XI, the last king of the 20th Dynasty, sparked another decline, the Third Intermediate Period. The capital moved from Thebes to Tanis, and the pharaohs ruled only the northern lands of Lower Egypt, with the priests controlling the rest of the country and distilling the power of the kings. The country splintered and rival leaders fought for power, leading to instability and civil conflict. Rulers from Nubia, Libya and Assyria took the throne at various times.

The Late Period of 670-332BCE was characterised by Egyptian rule interspersed with periods of Persian occupation. The first occupation was relatively peaceful, the second, shorter one was vicious. For this reason, when Alexander the Great invaded he was welcomed to Egypt as the great liberator and saviour, despite the fact that his conquest made the country a Hellenistic state, with Greek customs, traditions and language, and ensured the final pharaohs, the Ptolemaic Dynasty, were foreigners who intermarried to maintain their Greek heritage.

"One of the first acts of Osiris was to deliver the Egyptians from their destitute and brutish manner of living. This he did by showing them the fruits of cultivation, giving them laws and teaching them to honour the gods. Later he travelled over the whole earth civilising it without the slightest need of arms."
Plutarch, first century CE Greek historian

The history of Egypt is intimately woven with the gods and goddesses believed to have created life and controlled existence. The Egyptians worshipped them, made offerings to them and called on them for help. Part of their devotion to these deities came from their identification with them as human – they were beings who loved, lost and suffered like they did. They also believed there had been an earlier golden age when these gods had walked the earth, teaching people language, agriculture, art, science and the laws of civilisation, before they removed themselves to the heavens or the underworld to rule from afar.

There was a whole pantheon of deities, some still recognised today, others lost forever in the mists of time. One of the most important and enduring was the sun god Re, also known as Ra, who was considered the father of all the gods, a solar deity and the sole creator. At various times he was also merged with other gods, becoming Atum-Re and later Amun-Re as different beliefs and regions took precedence, and in some periods of history his name was changed completely.

Early in the Pharaonic Age the legend of creation told of the sun god Atum, who appeared out of the chaos of the primordial waters at Heliopolis, where Cairo now stands, and manifested as the first mound of earth, pyramidal in shape, from which all life came. He then created the air god Shu and the water goddess Tefnut, who gave birth to Geb, the earth god, and Nut, the sky goddess. Nut in turn gave birth to the four central deities of Egyptian belief – Isis, Osiris, Nephthys and Set – who populated the land with humans.

A different creation myth came from Hermopolis in Upper Egypt, which claimed that before existence there was chaos, not water, and that out of this chaos had come four pairs of deities – Amun and Amunet, god and goddess of invisibility; Nun and Naunet, god and goddess of the primordial waters; Heh and Hehet, god and goddess of infinite space; and Ket and Keket, god and goddess of darkness.

A third story, originating in Memphis, merged the other two legends, claiming that Ptah was the creator god and had called the world into being with the power and magic of his word – a concept echoed in other world religions – and contained within himself eight other deities, including Atum, Thoth and Horus. With his wife Sekhmet and son Nefertem, the patron of healers, he formed the holy trinity of the city.

During the Old Kingdom, Atum was the primary deity, worshipped throughout the land. The pharaohs claimed they descended from him – many included "son of Atum" in their title – and they made daily offerings to him on behalf of their people. It was also believed that Atum took the soul of the pharaoh from his pyramid to the heavens after death.

But as power shifted between dynasties, the gods also shifted. When the royal capital moved to Thebes at the start of the Middle Kingdom, the local deity Amun was elevated to national prominence. People began worshipping him as the creator god, with his wife Mut becoming the divine mother and their son Khonsu, the moon god, completing the holy triad. Massive temples were built in their honour at Luxor and Karnak, and centuries later, when the Ptolemaic pharaohs ruled the country, they identified Amun with Zeus, the king of their Greek gods.

During the New Kingdom, Isis and Osiris took their place as the primary deities of Egypt, along with their son Horus, although recent discoveries of ancient artefacts show they had always been important. Their story of life, death and rebirth became the blueprint of Egyptian beliefs, and an archetype that has roots in every civilisation.

In a long-ago age when the gods walked the earth, Osiris and Isis were happily married and wisely ruling the country, the first king and queen of Egypt. But their jealous brother Set murdered Osiris and took the throne for himself, unleashing a time of cruelty and pain.

Isis desperately searched for her husband's body, recovered it, and used deep magic to bring him back to life and conceive a child. Enraged, Set butchered Osiris into fourteen pieces, but Isis found them and took them to Anubis, who put Osiris back together and wrapped him in linen – creating the first mummy. He couldn't come back to literal life, but he was transformed into the god of the underworld.

Isis gave birth in secret, and her son Horus grew up to avenge his father's death. He defeated Set in a great battle, but his eye was injured – when it was restored it became a symbol of protection and perfection, and depictions of the Eye of Horus are still used as amulets today. Many see Horus and Set's fight as a symbolic and constant war between good and evil, order and chaos, balance and change, which plays out eternally, maintaining the yin-yang balance of the universe.

There were also local deities who were popular with the common people, but the major gods, associated with the pharaohs and divine rule, were known throughout Egypt and are still worshipped today.

Anubis: Originally the god of the underworld, he became the conductor of souls when Osiris usurped his position. He weighed the hearts of the dead, judging a person's worth for the afterlife, and was associated with mummification. He was depicted with the head of a jackal.

Bast: An ancient protector goddess who was defender of the pharaohs, she later merged with other deities. She was a fierce warrior depicted with the head of a lion, representing courage, but was later portrayed in a more gentle form with a cat head, as the goddess of fertility.

Hathor: A protector goddess and mother of the pharaohs, she ruled love, joy and music. She was associated with the Nile River and thus fertility, and had a mother aspect. She was shown as a woman with a cow's head or wearing cow horns with a sun disc between them.

Horus: The only son of Isis and Osiris, he represented divine kingship and was the guide and protector of the pharaohs. He had many forms, and represented new beginnings, the rising of the sun and power and responsibility. He was depicted as a falcon or a falcon-headed man.

Isis: The queen of the heavens, she was considered the great mother of all creation. She was associated with healing, divination, dream interpretation and magic, and parallels have been made between her and the Virgin Mary, especially when depicted nursing her son Horus.

Ma'at: The personification of law and morality, she kept chaos at bay, regulated the cycles of time and was the feather that balanced the scales of the dead. She was the principle of justice as well as a goddess, and was shown as a woman with an ostrich feather for her head.

Nephthys: A deity of the dead, she brought comfort to those in mourning, and was considered the mother of Anubis. She was wife to Set, but when he killed their brother Osiris she helped Isis bring him back to life. She and Isis were beloved sisters who possessed great magic.

Osiris: He ruled the earth with his wife Isis and taught the people agriculture, then later became god of the underworld, overseeing the phases of life, death and rebirth. While Horus embodied the pharaohs in life, Osiris embodied them in death on their journey to the afterlife. He was depicted wearing the crowns of Upper and Lower Egypt.

Re: The ultimate sun deity and creator, he was represented by the sun itself or his solar boat, which he sailed across the sky each day. He was also sometimes depicted in human form with a falcon head, which was crowned with a sun disc encircled by the sacred cobra.

Sekhmet: A fiery goddess of war and vengeance, she was also a deity of healing. Doctors invoked her and people petitioned her for cures. She was a solar goddess, depicted with a sun disc atop her head and a cobra at her brow, or as a lion-headed woman carrying an ankh.

Set: The god of chaos and disorder, in his battles with his brother Osiris and then his nephew Horus he became the principle of evil, but he was also seen as a balancing force against their good. Also known as Seth, he was represented with the head of a mythical beast.

Thoth: The god of wisdom and truth, he was credited with the invention of language, writing, magic and religion. He spoke the words of Re that created life and was a moon god, portrayed with the head of an ibis or a baboon, and considered the masculine counterpart of Ma'at.

"The Pyramids of Giza are sacred and divine. This is a site we visit to learn about history, about a great people and their achievements. The pyramids have magic and mystery. Many people even dream about them! And I believe we've only found thirty per cent of the monuments. Much of Egypt is still hidden beneath the sands."
Dr Zahi Hawass, archaeologist, author and
head of Egypt's Supreme Council of Antiquities

Egypt's most enduring mystery is whether the Great Pyramid is simply the tomb of an ancient king, as history has recorded it, or, as many people suspect (or hope!), something more spiritual. According to historians, the famous structure is the burial place of Khufu, who was later called Cheops by the Greeks. He was the second pharaoh of the Fourth Dynasty, who ruled during the Old Kingdom Period, some time between 2600 and 2550BCE. He was not the first pharaoh to erect a pyramid – his father Snefru built three, and Snefru's predecessor Djoser built one before that – but Khufu's was the largest and grandest, and was located at the most impressive site, on the banks of the mighty Nile on the outskirts of what is now the country's capital.

The Great Pyramid was constructed from more than two million stone blocks that weighed an average of 2.5 tonnes each. When it was built it was 146.5 metres high – the tallest manmade structure in the world until the spire of England's Lincoln Cathedral topped it by four metres in the 14th century – and was covered in bright limestone casing, which made it even more impressive than it is now, shining and sparkling in the desert sun, vivid white against the deep blue sky and golden sands. The casing was later removed to build the mosques and palaces of medieval Cairo, making the pyramid a few metres shorter and exposing the bare granite understones.

The pyramid was part of a larger royal burial complex that was typical of the age. These were made up of the main pyramid tomb, a valley temple where the body was prepared for burial and a mortuary temple where he was later worshipped, as well as a courtyard, smaller subsidiary pyramids and family tombs, and a miniature version of the main structure, known as the cult pyramid. This tiny replica housed the pharaoh's ka, his soul, while the larger monument held his body.

Khufu's cult pyramid was recently uncovered near the southeast corner of the Great Pyramid. To the east are the remains of three smaller pyramids, a fifth of the size of the main one, believed to have housed Khufu's mother Hetepheres and two of his wives. Other family tombs lie nearby, and there's a cemetery to the west that was for the burial of priests and court officials. The entire royal necropolis was a bit like the pharaoh's palace when he was alive – in death he still had his family and officials surrounding him.

Today there's also a small museum to the south of the pyramid, which houses one of the solar barques that was found nearby in more than a thousand pieces and reassembled. Barques were a type of boat that were buried with the king for his use in the afterlife, to ferry him through the underworld or float his soul to heaven.

When the Great Pyramid was built, a causeway approached it from the east, the Land of the Living, leading from Khufu's valley temple down near the Nile to the mortuary temple right next to the main structure. Today the foundations of this mortuary shrine and a small part of the causeway remain, but the valley temple is buried beneath the desert sands, with the village of Nazlet el-Samman erected on top.

When the pharaoh died his body was ferried across the Nile from the palace to the valley temple, where it was purified, embalmed and mummified by priests. It was then carried in an elaborate funeral procession up the 800 metre causeway – which back then had walls, a floor and a vaulted roof – followed by mourners. Next the mummified body was taken to the mortuary temple where further religious rites took place, before it was interred within the pyramid.

From that day forward the pharaoh was worshipped as a god, and a cult grew up in his memory. People said prayers and left offerings at his two temples and his cult pyramid, and the priests performed rites there on special days. Just as the deities had their grand temples at places like Karnak and Dendara, so too must the pharaoh. Khufu's mortuary temple no longer stands, but in its day it was a lavish, magnificent building to reflect his stature and the power of his rule.

The Egyptians believed that some of the soul stayed with the body after death, so both had to be looked after properly to ensure the smooth progression of the pharaoh to the afterlife. Any failure to do this could bring down the wrath of the gods and disaster on the country, so they built elaborate tombs to protect both body and soul.

The pharaohs were also buried with the four protective goddesses – Isis, Nephthys, Selket and Neith – carved into their sarcophagus and with statues of them surrounding their canopic jars, the vessels that held their embalmed organs, which were removed from the body before it was mummified. The four sons of Horus – Imsety, Hapi, Duamutef and Qebehsenuf – appeared on the lids of the canopic jars.

Ironically, given that his pyramid is famous throughout the world, not much is known about Khufu. Only one statue of him has been found, whereas many statues and likenesses of other pharaohs exist. No one knows whether others of Khufu were destroyed at some point, simply haven't been found yet or were never created in the first place.

Two other pharaohs also left their mark, and their quest for immortality, on the Giza Plateau. Less than 200 metres southwest of the Great Pyramid is Khafre's Pyramid, which is also known as the Middle or Second Pyramid. This king, who was later referred to as Chephren by the Greeks, was one of Khufu's younger sons, and ruled Egypt after the death of his older brother.

His tomb appears taller than the Great Pyramid, but it's actually a few metres shorter – the illusion comes from its intact summit, steeper sides and location on slightly higher ground. Some of the original casing stones remain near the top, which gives an idea of how the pyramids looked when they were first built and a few more clues to their construction. For a long time it was believed that this monument had no entrance, and one was actually dug into it at ground level. But in the early 1800s a sealed portal was blasted open on the north face, revealing the original entrance – and the fact that tomb raiders had already found a way in and stolen whatever was once inside.

In contrast to the lavish interior of Khufu's Pyramid, with its Great Gallery and Queen's Chamber, the inside of this one is quite basic, with simply constructed corridors, a plain burial chamber and a small second chamber that housed the burial tools.

Yet while the interior is unassuming, Khafre's pyramid complex, the best preserved of the three on Giza Plateau, is extensive. His valley temple, situated next to the Sphinx, was built of limestone and covered by polished pink Aswan granite, with floors of white alabaster, which represented purification. It featured two river entrances, one dedicated to the goddess Hathor and one to Bast, a vestibule, inner chamber and small storage areas. It was covered by the desert until being reclaimed in 1852, so it hasn't worn away over time as the others have.

Several beautiful statues of the pharaoh have also been found, with niches for many more. This is not the sign of a megalomaniac though, but of a culture that held the pharaoh as sacred, the reincarnation of a deity. For them, worshipping their king was a way to worship god.

Khafre's mortuary temple, to the east of the main pyramid, is also relatively intact. It has an entrance hall, decorated granite pillars, an open courtyard, niches for more statues, storage areas and an offering hall, as well as boat pits nearby, which once held his solar barques.

The Third Pyramid is Menkaure's Pyramid. This pharaoh, known as Mycerinus to the Greeks, constructed a much smaller monument than his predecessors, at just 66 metres high. But while Menkaure's tomb is smaller, its interior is more interesting and more complex.

There's a succession of rooms, including a mysterious first chamber whose purpose is still not understood, an antechamber reached by another corridor, two passageways, the burial chamber itself, and a smaller one off that with niches for the canopic jars. A dark basalt sarcophagus was discovered in the burial chamber, although it was lost to the world – and to further investigation – on its way to the British Museum, when the ship that was carrying it sank.

Menkaure's mortuary temple is well preserved, and three smaller pyramids along the south side of the main one still stand, although his valley temple was buried beneath the sands a long time ago. New research has discovered that the decreased size of this pyramid may not have been a reflection of the waning power of the pharaohs, as earlier assumed, but instead represented a changing emphasis that gave higher priority to the royal temples than their burial tomb.

Every year new understanding is gained about the people and beliefs of Ancient Egypt. It was long thought (if you dismissed the alien builder theories!) that slave labour was used by cruel pharaohs to create the pyramids, yet it's now known that there was a high-level class of architects, engineers, builders and astronomers who lived nearby and worked year-round on their construction. In addition, during the yearly late summer flooding of the Nile when work in the fields halted, farmers were paid in food to labour on the monuments. It was a kind of national service and a sacred duty, a way to ensure your own happy afterlife, much like other civilisations felt that it was an honour to take part in the construction of cathedrals.

Pyramids are thought to have taken between twenty and thirty years to complete, with work on the Giza Plateau continuing for almost a century. Twenty thousand workers were involved in this national government project, with four thousand core staff and the rest working seasonally. They're believed to have used ramps around each pyramid to construct it, and to have taken advantage of the annual flooding to shift stones downstream from Aswan, and move blocks from the quarries right to the base of the pyramid when the river was high.

While it seems a little creepy to us, with our modern fear of death, to spend your whole life constructing your tomb – and for it to be the life's work of the common people to help you build it – to the Ancient

Egyptians it was sacred. Politically it was a pharaoh's main duty during their reign to have their tomb constructed, as a way to ensure their elevation in the afterlife and their resulting ability to intercede with the gods on their people's behalf. It was a community project that created employment and celebrated architectural and building skills.

Pepi II, the second pharaoh of the Sixth Dynasty, inherited the crown at the age of six and ruled for ninety years – and the community broke down because there was no employment and no purpose for the people. His pyramid was completed by the 30th year of his reign, leaving up to sixty years with no national project for the country to work on. Combined with a famine and several years without the optimum Nile inundation – which was blamed on the pharaoh – his extended reign marked the end of the Age of the Pyramids.

But in Khufu's time the Giza Plateau was a thriving community. His palace was nearby, and people lived and worked around the complex of the Great Pyramid while it was being constructed and stayed as it was maintained. When he died this area became a place of worship, and his successor Khafre and the local community began work on the Middle Pyramid nearby. And when he died, work began on the Third Pyramid while worship of the previous two rulers continued.

This was borne out by the discovery of the remains of a town around the pyramids, with huts, workshops, a bakery, butcher, hospital and grain storage areas, as well as a cemetery for priests and workers.

"Externally the pyramid symbolised the creative principle of nature and illustrated the ideas of geometry, mathematics, astrology and astronomy. Internally it was a majestic temple in whose sombre recesses were performed the Mysteries, and which witnessed the initiation scenes of the royal family. The sarcophagus was the baptismal font, upon emerging from which the neophyte was 'born again' and became an adept."

Helena Blavatsky, 19th century Russian author
and founder of the Theosophical Society

While most visitors to Egypt accept the official history of the pyramids, their sheer size and grandeur has left others convinced that they couldn't have been built by human hands, and mystery and legend continue to surround them. The fact that they're bare inside, with no treasure, no carvings and no hieroglyphs – unlike the elaborate later tombs in the Valley of the Kings – adds weight to the theory that these were not burial tombs but something far older and more complex.

To some, the only explanation for their construction is a superhuman or alien race with knowledge and methods far superior to ours. One popular theory is that the people of Atlantis came to Egypt when their land sank beneath the waves, around 10,500BCE, and designed the pyramids as well as building a Hall of Records within the Giza Plateau that contained all their secrets. American trance channeller Edgar Cayce excited people in the early 1900s with his prophecy that this room would be discovered by the end of the century. Officials deny it exists, but a few archaeologists insist it was found and covered up.

Others believe the pyramids were a connection between humans and the star beings of Orion and Sirius, which could explain the intriguing shafts within the Great Pyramid that align with certain stars. In both the King's and Queen's Chambers there are two narrow shafts which, at just 20 by 20 centimetres, are too small to be passageways.

The shaft in the south wall of the King's Chamber points at Orion, the constellation connected with Osiris, while the one in the northern wall points to Alpha Draconis, which in the time of the pharaohs was the North or Pole Star, one of the brightest in the sky and associated with the hippopotamus goddess Tawaret. In the Queen's Chamber the southern shaft aligns to Sirius, the star associated with Isis, and the northern one to Beta in Ursa Minor, related to the goddess Hesmut.

These alignments have inspired the hypothesis that the pyramids of Giza are not burial chambers but stargates through which the souls of the pharaohs could shoot into the sky to meet with Isis and Osiris and enter the magical realm of the heavens. *The Pyramid Texts*, a collection of Old Kingdom religious texts carved on the walls of the pharaohs' tombs, also revealed the Egyptian belief that the destination of the king's soul in the afterlife was Orion. Others believe these shafts weren't so the pharaoh's soul could journey to the stars, but to allow communication with beings from Sirius and Orion, who sent knowledge and healing light to the earth through these portals.

Another theory is that the Great Pyramid, like many other ancient sacred sites, was designed for astronomical purposes. Its sides are perfectly aligned to the four directions, and it's used as a reference for true north by compasses. Along with the original temples, tombs and courtyards of the complex, the pyramid was used as an enormous sundial, with the shadow to the north and its reflected sunlight to the south marking the annual solstices and equinoxes. Due to its angles, size and location, it casts no shadows at midday of the equinoxes, similar to the Intiwatana Stone at Machu Picchu.

Those who study sacred geometry and understand the principles of Pythagoras claim that the pyramid's precise measurements make it a calendar, able to mark out the seasons and measure the length of the year to an accuracy of 365.2422 days, which is as exact as any modern instrument. And calculations of the length of the base and the angle of the sides also apparently reveal that the builders knew the length of the earth's orbit, its distance from the sun and even the speed of light.

Pyramids have also been used throughout time by many cultures to meditate within and to gather and amplify energy, and today people have started using such structures again as a tool for healing and to channel life force. Some even believe that pyramids can be used to collect and distribute solar power. The Great Pyramid has been described as a device to focus and amplify energy, and could have been used in ancient rituals for healing and peace.

An increasing number of spiritual teachers feel that the Great Pyramid was used as an initiation chamber where priests and nobles were taught the Mysteries, with the King's and Queen's Chambers utilised for different functions in an apprentice's years of study towards enlightenment. Today many take groups within these chambers and re-enact these rites for healing and spiritual growth.

Many also believe there is secret knowledge encoded in the walls that can be accessed by going inside, and that you can expand your awareness and learn about life, healing and the energy of the gods by opening yourself to the wisdom that's been there for thousands of years, waiting until humanity is ready to access it again. Meditating within the inner chambers is certainly an incredible experience, and many people have had huge shifts in consciousness while inside.

Although they are protected now, and people despair at the sacrilege done in destroying any part of them, the true meaning of the pyramids began to be lost just a few hundred years after their construction, and by the first millennium CE, when new religions had swept through the country, little significance was attached to these monuments.

It breaks my heart to hear of people lighting fires to heat the stones covering the pyramids then pouring vinegar on them to split and dislodge them, but no one realised at the time how highly regarded they would become. They have impressed sightseers throughout the years, but it's only with new archaeological insight and the weight of history and perspective that their true value has been recognised.

The Pyramid Fields from Giza to Dahshur were declared World Heritage Sites in 1979, for representing a masterpiece of human creative genius, bearing testimony to a civilisation that has disappeared, and being associated with ideas, beliefs and artistic work of universal significance. This listing saved the Giza Pyramids when they were threatened by a highway project near Cairo in 1995, because UNESCO negotiated with the Egyptian Government and helped find an alternative that would not impact on these ancient monuments.

In Victorian times travellers to Egypt climbed the Great Pyramid, helped by porters because the blocks are almost as tall as a person. In the 1800s French writer Gustave Flaubert was hauled up the steps by Arab guides, while famous nurse Florence Nightingale boasted it was an easy climb, and English novelist Amelia Edwards, helped by three men, ascended to describe the view from the top. Before that, Greek historian Herodotus visited in the fifth century BCE, and Mark Antony scaled the heights when he was with Cleopatra. Today climbing is banned to protect the pyramid – and the tourists! – but a limited number of people each day can go inside, which is far more exciting.

"A little way to the southward, from the midst of a sandy hollow, rises the head of the Sphinx. Older than the Pyramids, older than history, the monster lies couchant like a watch-dog, looking ever to the east, as if for some dawn that has not yet risen."
Amelia Edwards, 19th century British novelist and Egyptologist

Not far from the pyramids is the mysterious Sphinx statue, which conventional scholars assume was carved in the same era as the great pyramids behind it, and others believe was constructed as early as 10,500BCE. One school of thought claims it was built by the pharaoh Khafre, owner of the second pyramid, as part of his attempt at immortality. The location of his valley temple right next to the Sphinx led to the conclusion that he'd built the massive statue too, but others insist the bend in the causeway that links his two temples is proof the Sphinx was already there and had to be worked around.

Others consider that the statue was fashioned by Khafre's father Khufu as part of the Great Pyramid project, while new research reveals that it could have been constructed by Khufu's older son Djedfre, who died after only a few years of rule, who modelled the face on Khufu to reinforce the belief that his father was the sun god Re.

Still others insist that Khufu merely unearthed the statue, which had already existed for centuries, when he was building his pyramid, and repaired it in honour of the sun god. The Inventory Stele, an inscribed stone slab, describes Khufu's discovery of the damaged monument and the restoration work he did, and oral traditions handed down by villagers in the area date the Sphinx to at least 5000BCE.

Whatever its origin, when the royal capital moved away from Cairo after the glory days of the Giza Pyramids, the Sphinx was buried up to its neck in sand by time and the hot winds, which protected it from further erosion. It stayed that way for a millennium, just a lonely head gazing out over the desert, but in the 15th century BCE a young prince fell asleep under the shadow of the statue's head.

He dreamed that the Sphinx spoke to him, instructing him to clear away the sand from its body and promising in return that it would make him king. The boy obeyed, revealing the body of the statue, and the Sphinx kept its side of the bargain too – according to the Dream Stele, an inscribed stone found between the Sphinx's paws from that period, the boy grew up to be Pharaoh Thutmosis IV.

The original purpose of the statue was unknown, and the Sphinx was simply worshipped as a depiction of the sun god. At this time different gods had developed that were identified with the solar phases – Khepri was the rising sun, Re was the sun's zenith and Atum was the sunset. Combined they represented the creation and sustenance of life, and offerings were made and rituals enacted in temples across Egypt to ensure the sun returned each morning.

Like many of Egypt's monuments, the Sphinx was part of a complex that consisted not only of the great statue itself but also of two temples and some smaller structures. The original temple lies between the lion's great paws, and had a central court, an altar for offerings, cult statues, pillars and two entrances. There were twenty-four columns, believed to be for each hour of the day, and because of this some consider it the first solar temple in Egypt. Another temple was added by Thutmosis's father Amenhotep II northeast of the Sphinx's left paw, and its ruins can still be seen today, although little remains of the actual building.

Because of Thutmosis's discovery, throughout the time of the New Kingdom the entire statue again gazed out across the Nile at the rising sun. Later however it was buried again, and historical accounts of the statue describe it simply as a lion's head coming out of the sand.

The body was dug out once more in 1925 as part of a major operation, and between 1990 and 1997 it underwent serious restoration, with a hundred thousand blocks of stone added to its body. Today there is great concern over the protection of this landmark, and its gradual deterioration, caused by increased humidity, water infiltration and air pollution, is a problem many are working to solve.

Sphinxes had great religious significance in Ancient Egypt. Although this one was the largest and is assumed to have been the first, there were many similar statues throughout the country. They were usually designed in pairs, and often guarded the entrances to temples. Whole rows of them would line the processional walkways – the path between the temples of Karnak and Luxor boasted more than ninety ram-headed sphinxes, rams being common in statues representing the god Amun.

Yet like the pyramids there are other theories about the origins of the Sphinx. Many have been rejected by academics, but who knows? Until compelling evidence is found to prove any single theory and explain the inconsistencies, people will continue to debate and wonder.

The lack of any markings, tiny statues of it or recorded history on the origins of the Sphinx make it particularly mysterious. Some cite its deep water erosion as proof it was on the Giza Plateau long before the pyramids were thought of. Geologists say the wear could only be from severe flooding, which most recently swept Egypt after the last Ice Age, some time before 10,000BCE. There was serious climate change then, which led to increased rainfall, the creation of desert oases and a newly fertile Nile Valley, and ushered in a new era of agriculture and the beginnings of farming and permanent settlements.

This supports the claim that the Sphinx's lion shape is a reference to the constellation of Leo, and that it was carved in 10,500BCE, in the Age of Leo, as an astronomical marker of the period. The great Ages of Man, known as the Precession of the Equinoxes, have been recorded in the religious and spiritual texts of all cultures, and mark the 26,000-year cycle of the earth moving through the heavenly constellations.

Each age, which spans around 2160 years, has been typified by huge shifts in thought around the world. The Age of Taurus, represented by the bull, ran from around 4380-2220BCE and was characterised by the start of the agricultural age. It was marked by bull cults in Crete, Assyria and Egypt, Hindu cattle worship in the East, the secret religion of Mithraism, symbolised by a bull, and in Egypt the veneration of the sacred bull Apis and the cow goddess Hathor. Statues of bulls abounded throughout different cultures during this era.

When the Age of Aries began, it marked a period of empire expansion, violence and conquest. Moses threw out the golden calf and called for ram horns to be put in the temples. Judaism became the primary religion, and ram-headed sphinxes were constructed in Egypt, where the god Amun went from being known as Amun-Min, the bull that serves the cows, to Auf-Re, symbolised by the wearing of ram horns.

The most recent era, the Age of Pisces, began just before the time of Christ and was represented by the fish. It saw a shift to Christianity – which uses the fish as its symbol – Islam and Buddhism, and religion through fear. Now we're on the brink of the Age of Aquarius, which supposedly marks the end of superstition and dogmatic religions and will usher in a time of peace, spirituality and new consciousness.

The Age of Leo ran from 10,860-8700BCE, which coincides with the idea that the Sphinx was created in 10,500BCE as a complete lion statue, and later had its head carved into the likeness of a pharaoh.

Some people also believe the layout and orientation of the Sphinx, the three pyramids of Giza and the Nile River reflect the constellations of Leo, Orion and the Milky Way as they appeared in the sky back then. It's also claimed that the placement of the three pyramids mirrors the position of Orion's Belt, the three main stars in the Orion constellation, which could explain why the smaller third pyramid seems out of alignment with the other two.

There are also a few passages within the Sphinx. Tales abound of underground chambers that hold the secrets of the universe, treasure or knowledge, but most experts dismiss this as fanciful. Yet nothing is certain. All we can do is read all the stories and studies about this statue, consider the evidence, feel what seems true to us as we stand in its shadow and listen to its ancient whisper, and keep an open mind.

The purpose

"One wonders that people come back from Egypt, and live lives as they did before."
Florence Nightingale, 19th century English nurse, traveller and author of Letters from Egypt

For centuries people have been lured to Egypt by the mysteries of the pyramids, the exotic foreignness of the country and the deep magic that seems to be such an integral part of the wind that blows across the hot desert sands. Gods and goddesses, ancient healing methods and talk of extraterrestrial contact have captured the imagination of spiritual seekers from around the globe.

The intricate hieroglyphs and artwork of the Ancient Egyptians reveal a civilisation that had a deep belief in magic, and practised it as a normal part of life. They didn't separate their spiritual and everyday existence – instead every moment was sacred and enchanted, something many people today crave in their own lives.

They revered a host of gods and goddesses who inhabited the earth, the sky and the underworld, and interacted with them on a daily basis. These deities looked like people, yet they had superhuman strength, power and abilities, and could shapeshift to take on the appearance and qualities of the animal kingdom. They were also very human – they fell in love, had children, got angry, developed friendships, were betrayed, and mourned their dead. The Egyptians believed the gods were like them, and as a result they saw themselves within the divine, a quality that was later lost as people were taught that God was outside and above them, separate rather than a part of them.

Ancient Egyptian spiritual beliefs also embraced both the good and supposedly bad aspects of life, the totality of experience. Chaos was celebrated alongside order, life alongside death, healing alongside war, light alongside dark. And their understanding of the divine incorporated both the masculine and the feminine. They had both male and female gods, not just a male, and all the deities were important, with their own role to play in the well-ordered running of people's lives.

The Egyptians also revered their ancestors, who they imagined had gone to live with the gods but could interact with their family members, invisible to humans but still a part of their world. They believed in the resurrection of the body in a glorified form, and that they would live for eternity in another realm with the gods and goddesses they felt they knew. They thought that the physical body had to continue to exist on earth after their death, hence even the commoners built elaborate tombs and mummified their dead to assure their proper progress through the afterlife. They also buried food, jewellery, furniture, tools and other objects they might need there so they would be prepared.

They believed that magic – heka – was a gift from the gods to them, an empowering force that protected them from harm as well as the energy that animated the world and linked intent and action to outcomes. The ceremonial magic of modern paganism and witchcraft owes much to the rites of this ancient land and their belief in rebirth and initiation into secret knowledge. The Egyptians had faith in spells, rituals, amulets to protect against evil, prayer and words of power.

This magic was made manifest in the pharaohs, who were seen as the embodiment of the gods. These earthly representatives communicated with the deities, asking them for guidance and wisdom. They made offerings to them and performed daily ceremonies to ensure the rising and setting of the sun, the turning of the seasons and the flooding of the Nile, thus ensuring the survival and prosperity of their people.

Over time however the influence of the pharaohs waned. They were seen as chosen by the gods rather than descended from them, and the priests increased their power and started acting as the intermediaries between heaven and earth. They were thought to be able to heal illness and cast out evil with a word, and many priests devoted their lives to worshipping the gods and being of service to the people of Egypt.

But there were also periods when black magic was performed by too-powerful priests who made sacrifices for unholy purposes and hid in temple chambers to enact the voices of terrible gods. In one temple we visited we were shown the secret room where they would sit, pretending to be gods and pronouncing punishments and judgement through a tiny hole in the wall to the people who had come to pray.

Remnants of rituals we may never understand give intriguing glimpses of a deeper, darker plane of existence. I really felt this dimension, a heaviness and sense of darkness that hovered on the edge of my consciousness as I walked through the ancient temples. I have no doubt there are powerful, ancient secrets, hidden in subterranean chambers and encoded in writings we can't translate, and it's this tantalising thought of magic and hidden wisdom that draws so many to the country. A lot of people experience a fear of Egypt, perhaps sensing this darkness, yet also a deep fascination. I had moments of terror, of feeling an oppressive presence, which was mixed with awe and wonder at the incredible energy imbued in this land.

There have also been many claims of UFOs spotted in Egypt, particularly over the pyramids. As we approached Djoser's Step Pyramid everyone in the group – except me – saw a silver craft in the sky, which hovered near the pyramid then went behind it, split in two then disappeared. Our very conservative guide was shocked. Having never believed the stories, he'd now seen one with his own eyes, and seemed transformed by the experience.

There are depictions of what look, to some observers, like extraterrestrials engraved in the ceiling at Abydos and incorporated in some of the temple artwork – such as carvings of people with strangely elongated heads and long fingers in flying machines – and a picture in a tomb in Saqqara that many believe is of a grey alien.

In the 1980s NASA announced it had discovered three pyramids on Mars constructed in the same configuration as the Giza monuments, adding more intrigue to the link between Ancient Egypt and ETs. And there are claims that the topography of the Red Planet includes a region that looks like Queen Nefertiti in profile.

Combined with the thousands of UFO sightings reported over Egypt, many people are convinced that star beings from the Pleiades, Sirius, Orion and other constellations are visiting earth now, and have been for thousands of years, imparting wisdom and technology and helping us evolve spiritually.

"The temples trained priests and priestesses in all the great mysteries and were a place of initiation. Within the temples worship of the deities was continuous from early morning until late at night, which energised and protected the surrounding land and people and brought a state of balance (maat), health, truth and harmony to the whole country."

Elisabeth Jensen, Australian healer, writer and creator of the **Isis Lotus Oracle Cards**

The experiences that most opened my heart and mind and offered opportunities for growth and healing took place in the temples of this ancient land. For me Egypt was a place of balance, of merging the masculine and feminine energies of my self and the universe, and it was within the temples and in the stories of the gods and goddesses the early Egyptians worshipped that this was most apparent.

The temples were dedicated to different deities and built as homes for them. And as I walked amongst these stone ruins, gazing on massive pillars carved with incredible hieroglyphs and beautiful symbols, the energy and sense of awe they inspired was tangible.

While they were each different, most of the temples had some aspects in common. Surrounding the complex was a wall to keep everyone out, because unless it was a special occasion usually only priests and pharaohs were allowed within the holy grounds. At the front were two gated pylons, massive structures with bold carvings of the pharaoh who commissioned the temple, the god it was dedicated to or both. Many temples had a series of pylons that got smaller as they progressed inwards, built by different pharaohs over many years.

Open courts flanked with carved columns continued towards the series of chambers preceding the inner sanctuary, each one smaller and darker than the last to indicate the movement towards the divine mysteries at the centre of the complex. It also symbolised the progression from the sunshine and light of Egypt to the darkness and secrecy of the holy rites within. This inner sanctuary housed a statue of the god or goddess, which was elaborately cared for by the priests.

There were also different chapels and chambers for worshipping secondary deities, preparing offerings and storing sacred robes and ointments. Sometimes the temple was not only a place of worship but also acted as a fortress, palace, royal retreat or administrative centre.

Two of the most breathtaking temples in Egypt, Karnak and Luxor, are situated in the town of Luxor, which was previously called Thebes. This was the capital of Egypt during the Middle Kingdom period, which ensured that local god Amun became the premier deity, and his temple the most significant. His glorious home was Karnak Temple, which was dedicated to the powers of creation, and is considered by scholars and spiritual seekers to be as important as the Giza pyramids.

Karnak was the most magnificent of all the places of worship, spread over more than two hundred acres – the largest temple complex ever built by man – and filled with soaring columns and beautiful shrines and chapels. Begun around 2100BCE, it was constructed and expanded over a period of thirteen hundred years, and for a time it controlled immense wealth and was the religious centre of the country.

There are three main temple enclosures, the most impressive being the Precinct of Amun, complete with a sacred lake, several chapels and temples and a sanctuary dedicated to the god that only the pharaoh or his high priest could enter. There is also a Temple of Mut, in honour of Amun's wife, and a Precinct of Montu, the god of war who was worshipped there centuries earlier. Much of the Karnak complex is in ruins, but wandering down the ancient corridors past courts, columns and obelisks is an awe-inspiring experience, and I could picture where the temples and altars had been located, and why it was once called Ipet-Isut, the Most Sacred of Places.

My favourite moment at Karnak Temple was our ceremony in the Chapel of Sekhmet. This goddess represented the duality of war and healing, of balancing peace and its opposite to find your inner power – again, the blending of two seeming opposites to be whole. She was the lion-headed sun goddess who embodied the strength of that regal creature, and her name means the Powerful or the Mighty One.

While she was sometimes considered vengeful by the Egyptians, who didn't require or expect perfection in their gods, Sekhmet was also the patron of doctors, and her priests were renowned as powerful healers. Although her ancient cult centre was in Memphis, near the modern-day city of Cairo, she was known throughout Egypt, and is still recognised today by pagans as a goddess who can be called on when protection, courage and strength is required.

On this day I felt so connected to her. I'd been struggling with anger at someone over the previous days, and tapping in to the energies of the Sekhmet archetype helped me realise it's okay to feel mad about a situation, that I have the right to experience and express my anger, and that it doesn't cancel out my gentleness or make me a bad person.

Life is all about balance – being a healer and nurturer when needed, but allowing yourself to go into battle and fight injustice when that is the more effective and heartfelt course. Expressing anger constructively is far better, and healthier, than suppressing it, and finding your own power is about embracing every part of yourself – the light and the dark, the healer and the warrior.

Three kilometres south of Karnak Temple, and once linked to it by an avenue of lion-sized ram-headed sphinxes, symbolic of Amun, is the spectacular Luxor Temple, which we visited one night as darkness was falling. The beautiful columns and ancient hieroglyphs were illuminated by golden beams of light, and we approached along the sphinx avenue, the way pilgrims arrived millennia ago.

This temple was dedicated to Amun, his wife Mut and their son Khonsu, and was the home of Mut and her child while Amun resided at Karnak. In spring they were reunited in the fertility festival of Opet, when priests took the statue of the god to stay with his spouse at Luxor. This symbolic ritual was played out every year, as they believed it would maintain the connection between heaven and earth, ensure the fertility of the land and keep the gods happy.

Construction at Luxor began under Amenhotep III, circa 1400BCE, and was expanded by successive rulers, including Ramses II, who added massive statues of himself to the entrance, the Ptolemies and the Romans, who built a chapel dedicated to their emperor Hadrian. Stunning carvings and scenes of the pharaohs making offerings to Amun and Mut, and the story of Amenhotep's divine birth, adorn the walls. Some of these are really well preserved because, like much of Ancient Egypt, the temple was buried by desert sands for centuries.

There's also a mosque near the entrance, which makes the complex even more intriguing, a melding of Egyptian, Greek, Roman, Christian and Islamic methods of worship, sitting side by side, hewn from the same rock and built on the same soil, which touched me deeply.

Luxor Temple has a strong feminine vibration, while Karnak feels deeply masculine. The avenue of sphinxes that links them is the connection between the two energies, and walking this pathway became a solemn ritual that provided union of these two halves, a sense of completion and wholeness. One of our group led us in a spiral procession through the illuminated temple and along the avenue, which took each of us deep within our own soul and triggered healing and acceptance of the personality traits within our selves that we'd struggled to accept.

Both Karnak and Luxor Temples are located across the Nile from the Valley of the Kings and the Theban Necropolis, so while the dead pharaohs were worshipped on the west bank of the river, on the east bank the gods dwelled in their beautiful temples.

"The old physician priests and priestesses who practised in the Egyptian temples under the protection of the deities understood what modern doctors are only just rediscovering – that the mind and spirit are crucial to healing even the most physically based problems. Healing was part of the whole spiritual concept, with prayers, rituals and spells an integral part of a remarkably advanced medical knowledge."

Cassandra Eason, Celtic witch, teacher and author

Sixty kilometres north of Luxor is the beautiful and well-preserved Dendara Temple Complex. There have been places of worship on this site since the Old Kingdom, circa 2500BCE, and it was once considered the Lourdes of Egypt. There are several beautiful chapels and shrines, a sacred lake, a well, a sanatorium which pilgrims would visit to seek healing for all manner of physical ills from the goddess Hathor, two birth houses with incredible reliefs of gods and goddesses within, and a Coptic Basilica dating from the fifth century CE.

But the central feature of the complex is the beautiful Hathor Temple, consecrated to the goddess of healing and love, who was also celebrant and mistress of the cycles of time. A shrine to this goddess has existed on this spot since prehistoric times, but construction on the current temple only began around 125BCE, at the behest of the Ptolemaic pharaohs, who identified Hathor with their goddess Aphrodite. When the Romans conquered the country a century later, these new rulers continued to add to the temple and worship here.

The carvings on the walls are a mix of hieroglyphs, depictions of Hathor and other gods, winged sun discs, scenes of Egyptian life, an image of Cleopatra and her son Caesarion, and the Romans and their emperors. The ceiling of the great hall boasts splendid carvings of the sky goddess Nut, the heavens and the constellations of the zodiac, and there are richly decorated offering halls and sanctuaries.

Further north is the Abydos Temple Complex, consecrated to Osiris, the god of resurrection and the underworld. This is the place where his head is said to have been buried after he was dismembered by his brother Set. Their playing out of the cycles of life, death and rebirth represented the beliefs of the early Egyptians, and the battle between order and chaos as well as the redemptive power of love. This also ensured Osiris's eternal life and importance, for he rose from being a simple human-like agricultural god of Lower Egypt to become the god of the dead, their most valued realm, for the whole country.

The Temple of Abydos was built by Seti I in the 13th century BCE. Rather than being dedicated to a single deity, as was common, this complex pays homage to several gods of death, resurrection and the underworld, which isn't as creepy or morbid as it sounds – the Ancient Egyptians saw death as a part of life and the beginning of a new existence, which was something to be celebrated and worshipped.

The complex is also famous for the Abydos King List that is carved in the wall, which lists the cartouche names of seventy-six pharaohs and has been invaluable to historians in identifying the country's long-ago rulers and the order of their succession. And behind the temple is the Osireion, thought by some to be a fake tomb for Seti and by others to be the aforementioned burial place of Osiris's head.

Abydos was a place of pilgrimage for the Egyptians, who endeavoured to visit once in their lifetime as a matter of religious duty. Those who were ill also made their way here to pray for a miracle, because of the healing energies. Today many experience it as a place of deep mysteries and initiation, where they can descend to the metaphorical underworld, battle their demons and be reborn. One of our group had an intense experience here, connecting to the energy of Osiris, and while it was scary at the time, he was lighter and happier for the rest of the journey.

Another of the major stops along the Nile is Edfu Temple, dedicated to the falcon-headed god Horus. Construction began in 237BCE under Ptolemy III, and was continued by his successors. Today the golden building is surrounded by mudbrick houses, children playing games in the dust and the teeming village that relies on tourists for survival.

In the courtyard there are immense black granite falcon statues of Horus, while the temple features amazing wall carvings of him with his wife Hathor, the pharaohs in battle, instructions on rituals and the preparation of offerings and anointing oils, and depictions of Horus's triumph over Set. The temple is thought to be located on the site of their ancient battle, where Horus defeated his uncle to avenge his father's death. Set represents the "negative" aspects we all have within us, and our own battle with our dark side in order to integrate it into our self so we can manifest our life purpose and allow our light to shine.

Once inside the temple we wandered through several different chambers before going deep within to the holy sanctuary of the god, where there is still a pedestal for offerings, and behind that a large black granite shrine with a niche where the statue of Horus once sat.

We all took part in a ritual around the altar and touched our brows and hands to the shrine. I immediately started shaking, and felt dizzy and nauseous, as though I'd been hit in the stomach. I was relieved when we went to another room to meditate, but I struggled to breathe there too, gasping for air and starting to feel quite scared.

I walked outside to get some fresh air, but one of the men who haunt the temple led me behind the shrine and told me to put my brow against it again – which made all the strange sensations even stronger. Some say this temple is about letting go of the past, that its energy nurtures you and allows you to go within to work out what you no longer need, and I wondered if some part of me was being stripped away.

Further along the Nile is Kom Ombo Temple, which was also built in the time of the Ptolemies. Much of it is now in ruins, with parts of it having slipped into the dark river waters at some point during the last two thousand years, and further damage being done by an earthquake in 1992. Kom Ombo was a double temple dedicated to both Horus the Elder and Sobek the crocodile god, with twin entrances and twin sanctuaries, and halls that divide down the middle.

It was also a healing temple and hospital, and it's covered with fascinating hieroglyphs of medical instruments such as scalpels, bone saws, suction cups and dentistry tools as well as procedures that are performed today – surprising in a temple built more than two thousand years ago. There's even a room where they used to do brain surgery, as well as the place they locked people to convince them of the god's presence, and a sacred well, a chapel dedicated to the healing goddess Hathor and a pool where they raised crocodiles in honour of Sobek.

Others claim the temple was dedicated to Horus and Set, and represented the continual battle of good versus evil, order versus chaos and life versus destruction. Today its purpose is still related to balance, to reconciling the positive and negative aspects and bringing your two halves to wholeness, and we did a moving ceremony there to help each one of us find our own sense of completion and unity.

"I am nature, the Universal Mother, mistress of all the elements, primordial child of time, sovereign of all things spiritual, queen of the dead, queen also of the immortals, the single manifestation of all gods and goddesses that are. Though I am known by countless names, the Egyptians who excel in ancient learning and worship call me by my true name, Queen Isis."

Lucius Apuleius, second century CE Roman writer

The most powerful place for me was the Temple of Isis, on an island in the Nile River south of Aswan. Isis was the divine mother and giver of life, the goddess of nature, women and purity, and the patron of magic, healing and spiritual science. She's even credited with inventing marriage, through her union with Osiris, and remains a symbol of enduring, eternal love because of her devotion to him even in death. Her ability to resurrect him and conceive their child also connects her with deep, ancient magic and the power of love.

Her religious complex was built on the Island of Philae over a period of eight hundred years, beginning in the fourth century BCE. But it was damaged when the first Aswan Dam was created in 1899, which submerged the island for half the year and washed away the paintings on the walls. When construction began on the second one, the Aswan High Dam, in the 1960s, the temple and its shrines were threatened with complete ruin, and UNESCO stepped in to save them. A mammoth international rescue operation began – the island was surrounded by dam walls, the water was pumped out and every stone block of the buildings was numbered and removed to the higher ground of nearby Agilika Island, where they were reconstructed exactly as they'd been.

The new island was renamed Philae and landscaped to resemble the original, and approaching it across the ancient waters of the Nile is like stepping back in time. It's the most beautiful sight, with palm trees waving against a perfect blue sky and the golden temple walls contrasting with the shining river. It has remained a magical, enchanted place, full of power, and a site of sacred pilgrimage.

The main temple begins with an open court and progresses through a series of vestibules that get smaller and darker before opening into the sanctuary, which I entered with a feeling of awe. There's a stone altar that once held Isis's barque, and wall carvings of the goddess feeding her baby Horus and enfolding her husband Osiris protectively with her wings, an image seen often throughout Egypt. I could feel the presence of something divine here, a tangible sensation of the sacred.

The impressive complex also includes the remains of an earlier temple to the goddess Hathor, a shrine to Horus, a chapel dedicated to Imhotep and a birth house. Upstairs from the main temple there are rooms dedicated to the story of Osiris's death and rebirth, and his beloved wife Isis's part in his resurrection and remembrance.

For centuries local people and later travellers from across the Mediterranean visited Isis's temple as a pilgrimage to pray for miracle cures, and today great healings still reportedly occur in her inner sanctuary. Her cult spread throughout the empire to Greece, Italy and even Britain, but in the sixth century CE Emperor Justinian forbade worship of Isis and any rituals in her honour. After this, Coptic Christians made use of her temple, carving crosses in the walls alongside the old murals, before it was abandoned and forgotten altogether.

The temple site was rediscovered in the 18th century by British adventurers, and today Isis has been embraced again as an iconic goddess embodying the energies of Quan Yin, the Buddhist deity of compassion, and the Christian Mother Mary. More than any other in the pantheon of Egyptian gods, Isis has transcended their ancient culture to be worshipped by modern spiritual seekers around the world.

In the ruins of this beautiful temple was my chance to make a connection with her. Instead of a group ceremony, this time we all did our own ritual, finding a unique way to connect. I slowly entered the shrine and stood within the holy sanctuary, filled with reverence and great humility. It's a place of magic and healing, of the divine feminine, of strength and beauty, and each of us, regardless of religious persuasion, was deeply moved by the power that resides there.

I breathed in the great feminine energy of the temple, and of the earth, and was overwhelmed by a sensation of immense love. I felt enfolded within Isis's wings as Osiris had been, protected from anything that could harm me, and so nurtured and loved. I was supposed to summon Isis, yet I realised she is in me and I am in her – we're all connected in a web of oneness and wholeness, and the divine spark of the gods and goddesses are simply aspects of our own inner selves.

After a while one of the other women entered, and I took her hands and willed my image of the goddess to her. Later she told me I was surrounded by blue light and my face looked really different, and I did feel an immense sense of calm as I stood on the sacred ground of Egypt, slowly beginning to accept a masculine side to the divine energy that flows through the universe, while in turn helping this woman find a feminine side to her God. We smiled with recognition, understanding and a deep sense of our own inner wisdom, which had been locked within us through this lifetime but was slowly beginning to re-emerge.

After two millennia of patriarchal religion, perhaps this new age needs a return to the feminine – the feminine in the form of a power totally in tune and in touch with itself and its masculine aspects. Isis did not exist alone, as a female god, instead she was part of a pair with her husband Osiris, and their story is one of love, redemption and eternal union and faithfulness, representing the universal balance of yin and yang. If there is a god, surely it must be both masculine and feminine, as the energy of the universe is. As we all are.

The last temple complex we visited was at Abu Simbel, a striking monument to past glories in the one-time region of Nubia, near the border with modern-day Sudan. Massive statues of Pharaoh Ramses II rise up out of the desert sands, protecting the entrance to this huge and elaborate sun temple. Getting there involved a ferry, a bus and a plane from Aswan, but it was worth the trouble to wander through this old site and soak up the atmosphere and mystery of ages past.

Like Philae, Abu Simbel was cut from the rock of its original location and moved to escape the rising waters of the Aswan Dam, another massive operation. Funds were raised from around the world to move it to higher ground, such is its significance and sense of history.

There are two temples at Abu Simbel, which were built in the 13th century BCE by Ramses II to prove his power and divinity to anyone approaching from the south, and to remind the world of Egypt's might.

On the outside of the Great Temple are four 20 metre high statues of Ramses, but inside are the true mysteries. Like other ancient temples and monuments, this one also marked the passage of time. Twice a year the sun's rays reached the inner sanctuary and illuminated the four statues – one of the pharaoh Ramses, the other three of the creator gods Ptah, Amun-Re and Re-Horakhty.

The Small Temple was dedicated to Ramses's favourite wife Nefertari. On the outside are six statues that dwarf the entrance, four of the pharaoh and two of his wife, and inside is a temple dedicated to Hathor, built by Ramses to honour the goddess of healing and also to recognise his wife as a goddess in her own right – for this reason there is also a statue of Nefertari dressed as Hathor.

For me, it was this eternal knowledge and acceptance of the yin and the yang of life, of people, of ruling and of divinity, that touched me the most in Egypt. Thousands of years ago they embraced both the masculine and the feminine within their gods, and most importantly within themselves. Their local deities ruled as husband and wife, equal, with a child to complete the holy trinity.

There was even a deity who had aspects of both male and female – Hapy, the god of the Nile in flood, was an androgynous figure represented as a man with breasts and a swollen belly, symbolising the fertility of the land and the balance of all things.

To find balance in our own lives involves an acceptance of all aspects of the inner self – the aggressive and the gentle, the protector and the nurturer, the positive and the negative, the masculine and the feminine. Today so many people deny a part of themselves, afraid to be considered too girlie or too tough, too emotional or too driven. But getting in touch with our inner selves and all aspects of our personality is crucial to being the best and most effective person we can be, to achieving our dreams and finding true love and contentment.

Relationships work best when we are balanced, and have accepted both the masculine and feminine within our hearts. Seeking our opposite aspect in a partner instead of within means we've lost a part of our self, and will never be truly balanced or at peace.

It was hard for me to say goodbye to this ancient land. My time there was amazing – both challenging and fun, difficult and deeply magical – and as I flew away, watching the pyramids grow smaller out of the window of the plane, I felt a new lightness and a new sense of my heart and my self as whole and complete.

The psychic connection

Quick tips to absorb the power of Egypt

1. The energy of Ancient Egypt is one of the easiest to connect with. You can study the history as a conventional subject at universities and colleges around the world, or via the internet and the vast array of books on the topic. In addition there are many esoteric mystery schools and online institutions that offer metaphysical degrees and initiations, with teachings on the deities of the country and the high ceremonial magic the priests engaged in, and you can also learn Egyptian healing methods and be attuned to this ancient energy.

2. There are plenty of movies that can transport you to the ancient days of Egypt, from adventure flicks like *Death on the Nile*, *Sphinx*, *Raiders of the Lost Ark*, *Cairo* and *The Mummy*, to historical films such as *Cleopatra*, *The Curse of King Tut's Tomb*, *Antony and Cleopatra* and *Queen of the Nile*, biblical epics including *The Ten Commandments* and *Prince of Egypt*, and the more esoteric, such as *Stargate* and *The Fifth Element*. They're not necessarily factual, but they are based on the mystery and intrigue of the country, and portray some of the potent themes and historical moments that enchant people to this day.

3. Meditate in a pyramid. Studies have shown that it's quicker and easier to enter an alpha state of consciousness while sitting within a pyramid. A four-sided panel-less pyramidal structure made from brass or copper rods or crystal-filled quartz tubes will amplify and focus the energy within it, enhancing meditation and relaxation, cleansing the energetic body, alleviating stress and pain, deflecting negative energy and increasing concentration and intuition. It's even claimed you can charge crystals, purify water, boost plant growth and keep food fresher by putting them within such an object.

4. Long before the Inkas proclaimed themselves the Children of the Sun, the Egyptian pharaohs claimed that they were the sons of Re, the creator of the world and the solar deity of their country. They considered the sun a powerful, life-giving force, and while we now know that it's not actually a god, it *is* a source of life and energy. Climbing a hill or going to the beach to watch the sun rise over the horizon is a powerful, beautiful way to breathe in the energy of the sun and feel its power, and energise yourself for the coming day.

5. Work with an Isis crystal, holding it while you attune to its energies and meditate on its meaning. An Isis crystal is any kind of quartz with a five-sided face. It can bring polarities together, balance duality and unite opposing aspects of your self in order to create completion and harmony. It also helps women regain their power and embrace the masculine within them, and men to tune in to their feminine side – much like the energy of this ancient country.

The armchair traveller's way to visit

"Water symbolises the whole of potentiality; it is fons et origo, the source of all possible existence."
Mircea Eliade, Romanian philosopher, historian and professor

While the people of Peru worshipped the mountains and the deities who resided on them, to the Egyptians the mighty Nile River was the source of their spiritual sustenance. It was considered the pathway to the afterlife and the boundary between the Land of the Living and the Land of the Dead. It was also their physical life source. The flooding along the banks created the only fertile land in this desert country, while the river provided water, fish and a trade route. They believed the Nile was ruled by Hapy, the god of fertility, and they made elaborate offerings to him to ensure its free flow and the vital annual floods.

One way to attune to the energy of Ancient Egypt is to connect with the element of water at a place near you. Sit on the bank of a river or stream, or any body of water, and focus on the sounds of the rhythmic flow, lapping or gurgling as it moves. Still your mind, then let it follow the water. If you're worried about anything, find a leaf or a pebble, hold it in your hand and send your thoughts into it. Then throw it in the river and watch it float away, taking your troubles with it.

Ancient Egyptian life revolved around the cycles of the Nile, and you can also connect with them. While Celtic cultures had four seasons divided by eight festivals, Egypt had three – Akhet, the time of the flood; Peret, the time of growth; and Shemu, the time of harvest.

Akhet marked the new year and the beginning of the heavy rains that caused the Nile to flood. It started around the time of the summer solstice, which falls in late June in modern timekeeping, and lasted around four months. During this season the river would overflow its banks, leaving a thick, fertile black silt. This rich muddy soil was perfect for growing crops, but farmers had to wait until the flooding had ended and the waters receded before they could plant their seeds.

Akhet was dedicated to Hapy, and offerings were made in the hope that the inundation wouldn't be too low, which would prevent an abundant harvest and in extreme years lead to drought and famine, or too high, which would wash away the fertile soil and wipe out entire crops, wreak havoc on the mudbrick homes along the banks of the Nile, and destroy the paths and canals built to irrigate the fields.

While they waited until they could sow their seeds, the Egyptians mended tools, fished, looked after their livestock, laboured on the pyramids and temples and performed other works for the pharaoh.

When the floodwaters subsided, the growing season of Peret began, and continued for around four months, depending on the weather. The sun shone, the fields dried out and the ploughing of the soil and sowing of the crops got underway. They planted grains such as wheat, barley and corn, as well as flax to make linen. They also grew vegetables, fruits and vines, irrigating the fields with canals leading from the Nile.

Next was the harvest season of Shemu. Crops were cut and gathered, and the canals were repaired in anticipation of the next flood. It was a time of dryness and sometimes drought. The priests who studied astronomy and the cycles of the seasons discovered that the appearance of the star Sirius coincided with the beginning of the Nile flood each year, so this star became the marker of the end of Shemu, and the start of Akhet and the new year, a time that became associated with the goddess Isis, who was linked to Sirius.

Although Egypt is no longer connected to the cycles of inundation and growth, since the creation of the Aswan Dams ended the yearly floods, you can symbolically align yourself with their ancient Wheel of the Year. At the beginning of the rainy season, which may be winter in your part of the world, celebrate Akhet by working with the element of water, which is associated with emotions, cleansing and letting go.

Stand outside in the rain, arms outstretched to the sky and face gazing upwards, and let the water wash away any fears, regrets, sadness or painful memories of the past. There's something incredibly liberating about standing outside in the wildness of a storm and letting the elements wash away all that you want to let go of, but you could also dive into the ocean or a river, or soak in a warm scented bath, to feel yourself symbolically cleansed and reborn.

Akhet is the time for washing away what is no longer necessary and creating a fertile base from which to move forward. Get in touch with the things you want to change in your life, whether it's finding a new job, meeting someone, moving house or transforming your spiritual life. You can't achieve your goals until you're certain of what they are. Call on Tawaret, the hippopotamus goddess of fertility and the birth of children, ideas and new projects, to help you, or simply listen to your inner voice and pay attention to the feelings you've long buried.

At the start of the growing season, which may coincide with spring where you are, celebrate Peret by connecting with the energies of new growth. Plant the seeds of the things you want to achieve in the coming year, which means being clear and taking action to make what you want happen. Crops don't grow unless you sow the seeds, and dreams don't come true until you start working to make them happen.

If you want a new job, rewrite your resume and send it to companies you want to work for, or do a course that will qualify you for the career you aspire to. If you want to meet a partner, deal with any issues you have from past relationships and let go of bitterness, anger and regret. Forgive your exes, and yourself. Make your own happiness your priority, because when you're the best person you can be – content, at peace, doing what you love to do – you'll attract someone with the same qualities. You can also plant a seed or a tree and nurture it, seeing your own progress symbolically reflected in its growth.

At the beginning of the harvest time, which may be your autumn, celebrate the energy of Shemu by giving thanks for all you have achieved over the past year. Write a list of the things you've gained and the things you've let go of. Have a party to honour your achievements, or reward yourself for your hard work with a gift you've long wanted, some time off to rest and chill out or even a trip away.

Acknowledge what you've done and share your success with others, because you'll inspire people with your breakthroughs and the stories of how you overcame obstacles, helping them realise they can also make it, and encouraging them to follow their dreams. Every success you have will inspire your friends to know they can do it too, and could give them the motivation they need to get moving.

"Isis is the Egyptian moon goddess who fosters our development of inner wisdom. She opens us up so we can trust our insights and understand the truth of all matters. With Isis energy, intuition rules – decisions become clear, clarity replaces clutter and calm overcomes chaos. Her ancient temples were places of wisdom and teaching, which we can still access today."
Anita Revel, Australian author and creator of www.goddess.com.au

Another way to connect to the country's energy is to commune with Isis, the archetypal mother goddess and Queen of Egypt. She was goddess of the heavens and the moon, and aligned with deep magic and initiation into the mysteries. Her role as grieving wife made her an icon to all women who suffered pain, and her desperate search for her husband's body and determined efforts to bring him back to life made her a goddess of love, romance and devotion, as well as a powerful healer. Her actions in conceiving her son Horus and protecting him from his uncle also made her an inspiration to all mothers and to women in childbirth, and she was petitioned for help by both.

Whether you believe in her as a person who once walked the earth, a goddess who ruled the fortunes of Egypt or simply an archetypal energy that can be tapped in to, invoke Isis and see what she has to impart to you. Start by researching her and discovering the aspect of her powers that most resonates with you. For me it was healing, but for others it's love, fertility, motherhood or divination.

Draw a picture of her or buy a painting or statue, and meditate on her image. Or call on her and ask for guidance. Sit quietly and visualise yourself surrounded by blue light. Picture Isis or simply repeat her name as a mantra. Ask a specific question, then write down, draw or speak into a tape recorder everything you feel, see or hear. Some people are more visual – clairvoyant – and will see images in their mind's eye in response to the query. They may see flashes of the future, a person who can help or a solution to a current problem acted out.

Some people are more clairaudient and will hear the answer as an internal or external voice – they may channel Isis, or other deities, or hear their higher self or spirit guide offering answers. Others are more clairsentient, which means clear feeling, and will receive guidance through feelings and sensations. They may experience a sudden understanding of something they weren't previously aware of, be overcome by emotion or have a gut feeling or prophetic dream.

The goddess Isis can also be invoked to increase your powers of divination or to help with healing work – many people experience this as a blue light that envelops them and increases their own methods of healing. Call on her energies, or those of any of the Egyptian deities you have an affinity with, for healing, transformation and initiation into the mysteries of the spirit and the unseen world.

The Ancient Egyptians had a deep belief in magic, and as well as petitioning the gods for assistance they also used specially charged talismans and amulets for protection, health and luck. They would imbue a small object, such as a crystal, statue of a deity or wax figure, with power and healing energies – by chanting a spell over it, engraving it with symbols, invoking a god or plunging it through incense – then carry it with them so they could access the power of the spell.

Women in childbirth would cling to a tiny statue of Hathor, Tawaret or Isis, as they were thought to contain the energy and power of the particular goddess. Workers would display an idol of their patron deity, and many people wore pendants with protective symbols carved in them or carried a tiny lion-headed sphinx statue to endow them with the wisdom of man and the strength of a lion. Statues of animals were also believed to bring protection and the power of that creature, such as a snake for wisdom or a scarab beetle for immortality.

The easiest way to create an amulet is to get a small piece of crystal suitable for your purposes, such as citrine for abundance or onyx for protection. Purify it by leaving it out under the light of the full moon or charging it with the sun's rays, then smudge it with sandalwood incense. Next, hold the crystal in your non-dominant hand – your left if you're right handed – and concentrate on your aim. It can be as simple as repeating a word, such as protection, over and over again, or as complex and specific as you like: "Amun, Re, Ptah, gods of the sun, please charge this crystal with your powers of strength and protection. Charge it so I am kept safe from harm as I face [state your issue]..."

You can also engrave animals, shapes, words or hieroglyphs on a silver pendant and wear it close to your skin, or embroider them into a garment, bag or piece of cloth. Alternatively, carve the symbols in a candle, so that as it burns the power of the charm will be released.

Egyptian magic was highly ceremonial, with elaborate rituals, invocations and altars. They placed the element of fire in the south, because that was the direction of the equator and the fiery sun, represented by a candle. In the west they had water, in the north was earth, represented by a pyramid or a dish of sand, and in the east was the element of air and new beginnings, symbolised with incense.

Incense has been used throughout history for religious purposes and magical rituals, and the priests of Ancient Egypt perfected its use in the temples, where it was burned in their daily offerings to the gods as well as in the elaborate funeral rites that helped the pharaohs reach the afterlife. In the famous *Pyramid Texts*, reference is made to incense alongside other rituals, religious beliefs, scientific lore and history.

Inside the pyramid of the pharaoh Unas is a prayer that begins: "The fire is laid, the fire shines, the incense is placed on the fire, the incense shines." In another, a line reads: "They take you to heaven, to heaven on the smoke of incense." Not only was it believed that burning incense would help a soul reach the afterlife, it was also offered to the gods in the hope that the perfume would please them.

The temple incense was handmade by the priests, with great ritual intent, out of special herbs and resins, and used in purification ceremonies, at festivals and during processions. They thought the scented smoke took their prayers to the heavens. Perhaps more importantly, it also purified the air, physically and etherically, and masked the pungent smell of the animal sacrifices.

The priests would burn frankincense during morning prayers, myrrh at noon and Kyphi at dusk. The first two are the resins (dried sap) of the frankincense and myrrh trees, which were later gifted to Jesus by the Three Wise Men, and are still used in many cultures as a holy offering and to transmute negative vibrations in the atmosphere.

Frankincense, burned for purification, is associated with the sun and masculine energy. Myrrh has similar properties but a more feminine energy, so it is used in healing rites and to attract things.

Burning Kyphi, which is made from a blend of herbs, resins, honey, wine and raisins, can help you attune to the energy of Ancient Egypt. Greek historian Plutarch wrote: "Kyphi gives forth a sweet emanation by which the air is changed, the body acquires a temperament conducive to sleep, and the strain of our daily cares relax and loosen without the aid of wine. Its aromatic substances lull to sleep and allay anxieties."

He also noted that it was used medicinally as a potion and as a salve to cleanse the internal organs and heal snakebites, asthma and anxiety. And when first century Greek physician Dioscorides wrote *The Materia Medica*, an encyclopaedia of herbal knowledge still quoted today, he too described the preparation and medicinal uses of Kyphi.

This incense was said to "brighten dreams like a mirror", and as another job of the Egyptian priests was to interpret dreams and provide oracles, it was burned in the temples to heighten mystical experiences. Before consulting a priest, people would sleep within the temple complex, where the scent made their dreamscapes more vivid.

There are a few different versions of the Kyphi recipe recorded. Plutarch said it had 16 ingredients – honey, wine, raisins, cyperus, resin, myrrh, aspalathus, seselis, mastic, bitumen, rush, sorrel, larger and smaller juniper, cardamom and calamus – added in a specific order and blended while sacred writings were read to the priest creating it.

While all Kyphi recipes mentioned wine, honey and raisins, others also included herbs such as cinnamon, cassia bark, lemongrass and cedar, and resins such as frankincense, gum mastic and benzoin. Below is a simple version that uses herbs and resins readily available today.

Put 12 raisins, 1 tablespoon of honey and 2 tablespoons of wine in a small jar and leave in a dark place for a week. With a mortar and pestle, grind together 1 teaspoon each of cardamom, calamus, cinnamon, galangal, juniper berries, orris root and lemongrass. Add 3 teaspoons each of ground frankincense, myrrh and benzoin. Separate the raisins and the wine, grind the raisins and mix with the dry ingredients. Blend with your hands, adding the honeyed wine as necessary. Shape into tiny balls or pellets and allow to dry for a few days, then burn on charcoal blocks and let the scent transport you back to the temples of Ancient Egypt.

You can buy commercial Kyphi incense and oils from specialty shops, but it isn't as powerful or sweetly scented as handmade incense, because it includes chemicals that interfere with the vibration of the herbs.

Incense can be burned to invoke gods and goddesses, aid concentration and attain ritual consciousness, consecrate ceremonial tools and purify temple rooms, shrines and altars. Making your own incense can be as simple as burning a sprig of sage to purify a room or sprinkling dried lavender on a smouldering charcoal block for healing, or as elaborate as creating your own unique Kyphi blend.

"Past life therapy results in healing at all levels, including the physical, emotional and spiritual. When traumatic events are brought to the surface, interpreted and integrated, clinical improvement results. People also often lose their fear of death, so the process helps them to focus on the important issues in their current life."

Dr Brian Weiss, American psychotherapist and author

Many people journey to Egypt today because they think they've lived past lives there, and feel a strong connection to the religious and spiritual beliefs of this ancient civilisation. I've always been a little sceptical that so many people claim to have had prior incarnations in Egypt, yet past life therapists say this makes sense because the Age of the Pharaohs spanned such a long period of history.

Tapping in to past lives can be very therapeutic, and you don't have to leave home to achieve the benefits. There are many CDs and books that can help you carry out your own session, or you can see a practitioner to not only discover the lives you've lived, but to learn how this information can be used for deep healing in your current life.

Past life therapy involves a kind of self-hypnosis, a mild trance state similar to deep meditation in which you are able to tap in to the memories locked in your subconscious. So, whether it's an actual past life you're seeing or simply issues expressing themselves in that form so you can better understand them, it can be very powerful.

A few years after my trip to Egypt I had a PLT session. After a preliminary discussion, I followed the therapist's voice as she guided me through a meditation that enabled me to access my subconscious in a way I usually can't. Then she asked me what I saw, and I panicked. All I could see was blackness. I was worried I wasn't going to see a past life, that I was wasting her time and I wouldn't experience anything.

"What do you feel?" she prompted.

I shrugged. I was about to say "nothing", when I opened my mouth and a voice said: "Fear."

And then it unfolded. I'd seen blackness because I'd been left in the dark, bound and terrified, to be sacrificed on an altar. Although I'd been hoping for a Celtic life, I saw myself inside the Great Pyramid, in a larger chamber than the one I'd been in when I was there. Light flickered down a corridor, and then I was surrounded by white-robed priests.

Their leader – someone I was with in Egypt – held me down and forced me to drink poison, which made my head hurt, then watched me struggle until I died. I described the scene, surprised. I was aware of what I was seeing and what I was saying, but I didn't know the answer to anything the therapist asked until it came out of my mouth. I was also aware that the voice sounded different to my own, which freaked me out a bit. Words were coming out of my mouth that I wasn't conscious of, I was vocalising thoughts I'd never had before, and the attitudes I expressed about death are not what I feel in my "waking" life.

She asked why I felt fear, and the voice I seemed to have no control over answered again: "Because they've left me here."

Why are they sacrificing you? "The men are supposed to learn something from my death. But they didn't, they're all confused."

I watched myself as the scene unfolded below me, looking down at my limp body and their puzzled faces. This other me was floating free, laughing, because it felt it had discovered the secret – that death is not really the end, that all things, even people, continue to exist in some form, like matter that transforms from liquid to gas and back to solid, never disappearing but instead eternally changing composition.

How do you feel about your death? "It doesn't matter. What they did doesn't matter. I learned something from it and am moving on," replied the mysterious part of me that I'd now unlocked.

After I described "my" death and floated upwards, the therapist spoke to my subconscious, utilising a tool known as parts therapy to discover the reasons it had shown me that life, how those events have a bearing on my life today, and how I can work through the issues and improve my health and happiness in the now.

In some ways past life therapy is like conventional psychotherapy or psychoanalysis – it brought to my conscious mind things that I knew on some level but had ignored or not really paid attention to. I understood that the notion of being sacrificed, and of thinking back then that it was a good thing, was connected to my current life and behaviour. Even the fact that my head hurt in the vision I saw was interesting, because today I suffer from terrible migraines.

Many therapists extol the virtues of PLT to assist with issues ranging from claustrophobia and anxiety disorders to physical problems such as asthma, chronic pain and infertility. They claim it can help unlock the reasons behind physical and emotional conditions and provide deep and lasting healing. It can also connect you to a different place and time and give you access to information from there.

No matter how you do it, the most important aspect of connecting with the energy of Ancient Egypt is in connecting with your own inner self, and acknowledging and embracing the different aspects of your personality and the duality within your soul – and you don't have to fly across the world and walk the desert sands to do that.

My experiences in Egypt were about darkness and light, yin and yang, and the union of the male and female within the divine as well as within the everyday. The deeper lesson was to be conscious of the balance of masculine and feminine in my own life, and ensure that I'm not denying one of them and thus rejecting a vital part of my true self.

Postcard from Egypt

Elisabeth Jensen is an Australian healer and psychic medium. She is the founder of the Angel Miracles and Isis Mystery School courses, and teaches around the world. She was a nurse and midwife, but now trains people in a system of spiritual healing she developed during her time in Egypt. She has also created the *Isis Lotus Oracle*, a set of divination cards based on the deities of Ancient Egypt, and produced three meditation CDs which help listeners manifest healing and access past lives.

Elisabeth has long had a passion for Egypt, and the energies of this ancient land and its deities influence her healing methods and her life. She takes spiritual groups there each year and guides participants through rituals and ceremonies at some of the country's most sacred sites. Visit www.isismysteryschool.com.

Egypt is such a spiritual place because the ancient temples and Great Pyramid are still energetically alive. The veils between realms are very thin there, and you can access past and parallel realities easily due to the intense spiritual and energetic work performed in the temples many tens of thousands of years ago. Spiritual healing and psychic abilities are magnified when you're near the Giza Plateau – although it's hard to sleep due to the constant energy buzz and spiritual visitors!

This power comes from the energy from the past that was encoded within every temple and tomb. I believe that Egypt has existed for almost fifty thousand years, and that it was once a truly magical place, like heaven on earth. Much energy was rebuilt again, but it has been lost over the past two thousand years. It is the people who lived there ten thousand years ago and longer that give it its power today – most present-day people in Egypt are not aware of their own power.

What makes Egypt so special to me is that you have the ability to connect very closely with the divinities there, especially Isis, the ancient Egyptian goddess of healing, science and magic. She still has immense significance today. She is a huge and very powerful healing and balancing force whose memory and energy were almost lost for thousands of years. Her mythological story of overcoming great personal loss is inspiring, but really she is our divine mother coming back to reteach us how to live in an energy- and karma-based world.

I first visited Egypt in April 2003, because I'd received guidance from Isis that I needed to be there to receive a new system of healing she would give me. As I sat meditating in the Queen's Chamber of the

Great Pyramid I experienced the most powerful blue healing light enter me, and this energy is within me still. Since then I've been another five times, taking spiritual groups there, and I plan to go again soon. I'm Australian, but Egypt is my soul home. My physical body lives in Australia while most of my spirit, soul and consciousness is in Egypt.

My favourite place is the Queen's Chamber of the Great Pyramid, also known as the Isis Chamber. It's one of the earth homes of Isis. I feel that part of my soul lives there too – I live in Adelaide and the Great Pyramid at the same time, and am fully conscious of both existences, but only feel complete and "home" within or near the Great Pyramid.

The King's Chamber is also powerful – true alchemy is possible there because of the connecting leylines that run through it, plus the effect of the pyramid's power, which is maximised in the sarcophagus. It's possible to physically dissolve people there, then see them reform. The Great Pyramid connects heaven and earth energetically and allows access for the white light beings to enter and leave the earth plane.

The temples along the Nile also remain significant. They were training and living centres for the priests and priestesses, and the ceremonies performed in them led to the Nile providing both water and energy to all of Egypt, keeping it in a state of maat or balance. Ancient priests and priestesses still do rituals in the temples, especially at those reasonably untouched ones, such as the Temple of Bast, the cat goddess, in the ruins of the ancient city of Bubastis, near today's town of Zagazig. There are thousands of cat-like beings there as well as spiritual priests and priestesses living in beautiful etheric temples.

Visiting Egypt can really enhance lives and spiritual beliefs. I see huge shifts in people's spiritual awareness and an increase in psychic and healing abilities. Even people unaware of the country's power are affected by the energies and have some kind of awakening, or at least are inspired by their visit. Everybody is touched in a positive way, although the average tourist can be overwhelmed by the security measures and those trying to make money off them. When I take spiritual groups we visit the temples at 5am or late at night to avoid this.

Spending time in Egypt deepens and enriches my work and my understanding, and strengthens my connection with the divinities as well as my ability to communicate with them. The ancient pharaohs used to undergo ceremonies to test their ability to lead their country – taking groups to Egypt is my way of testing my ability to be a high priestess of Isis and lead my own mystery school. Plus I just love to assist others to have their own special experiences there.

Even if people can't travel there, they can incorporate the wisdom of Egypt into their life by reading spiritual books about the country or studying courses based on Ancient Egyptian wisdom and healing energy, in order to incorporate the immense wisdom and knowledge.

THE HAWAIIAN ISLANDS

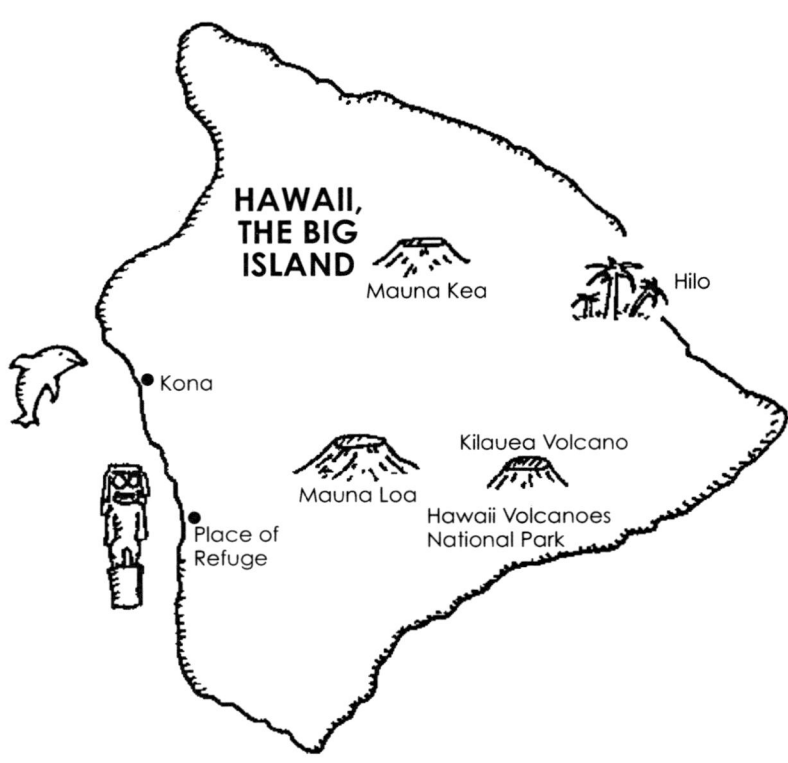

HAWAII, THE BIG ISLAND

Mauna Kea

Hilo

Kona

Kilauea Volcano

Mauna Loa

Hawaii Volcanoes National Park

Place of Refuge

*Find healing and happiness
in the Aloha State*

The Big Island
Hawaii, USA

Feel your soul being cleansed by the fiery and passionate
volcanic energy of this tropical island, and your heart
opening up to joy as you climb sacred mountains,
bathe in crystal waterfalls, swim with dolphins and
feel the presence of ancient gods and goddesses
in a paradise of sunsets and deep healing.

The place

"Hawaii offers the sensual delights of any tropical paradise, then adds a quality of rejuvenation. The islands' healing energies are abundant, and can be felt by any sensitive soul, simply by smelling the air or touching the sand. In Hawaii we call it mana – the spiritual force of the islands."

Nancy Kahalewai, Hawaiian lomi lomi teacher and author

Hawaii is an island paradise, a place of perfect golden beaches, lush rainforests, beautiful flowers, vibrant colours and sweetly fragrant air. It's relaxed and informal, with shorts and t-shirts the standard dress code, and the concept of time and deadlines a million miles away.

It's famous for its spirit of aloha, which translates as "to be happy with", and sums up an attitude of unconditional love and acceptance typified by tolerance and courtesy, broad smiles, fragrant plumeria leis, friendly locals and open-hearted welcome. To Hawaiians, aloha is a guiding principle for living in harmony with each other and the earth.

While it's the most isolated landmass on the planet, Hawaii is the world's most popular tourist destination, constantly topping polls of the place most dream of visiting. More than seven million people arrive each year in search of sun, sand, surf and, increasingly, the unique sense of spirituality that pervades the islands and draws those yearning for healing and transformation.

For those wanting rest and relaxation, there are hundreds of stunning beaches, peaceful bays and palm-fringed lagoons in which to swim, suntan, snorkel and dive. Luxury resorts cater to every whim, with a range of spas offering Hawaiian massage, native plant lotions and potions and other healing therapies. The slow, gentle lifestyle of the islands is conducive to recharging your batteries, and the beautiful scenery soothes the soul.

For adventure seekers there are coastlines with the biggest waves on earth, wild rivers to raft down, rugged canyons to hike through, big game fish to catch and dramatic volcanoes, some of them still active, to explore. The incredible climatic contrasts mean you can go snow skiing on a mountain in the morning then drive down to the bay to swim in the warm seas in the afternoon. It's also the perfect place for a family holiday, with resorts offering beautiful pools, child minding and kid-friendly activities, while those seeking solitude can find windswept, desolate peninsulas and coves or hike through forests without seeing another soul for days at a time.

The tropical beaches, bright sunshine and perfect weather have made Hawaii the location of many famous TV shows, from *Hawaii Five-O* and *Magnum PI* to *North Shore* and *Lost*, and movies ranging from the classics *From Here to Eternity* and *The Old Man and the Sea* to modern flicks such as *Jurassic Park* and *Waterworld*.

But while it's been a US state for fifty years, Hawaii remains its own unique cultural entity. It has a history of Polynesian settlers, native kings and queens, hard-working Asian immigrants and shamanic wisdom keepers known as kahunas, while today Buddhist temples sit side by side with Catholic churches, and Chinese New Year is celebrated alongside Jewish and pagan holidays.

Although Christian missionaries banned the dances, healing methods and storytelling of the Native Hawaiians, there is now a cultural renaissance underway, and they are reclaiming their lost traditions and sharing their rich spiritual history. Hula dances, melodic religious chants, kahuna massage and luau festivities are drawing visitors in to their exotic world, and the old knowledge is beginning to fill a new generation with light.

It's this resurgence in spirituality and the connection of the people to their land that attracts modern-day pilgrims to Hawaii. There's also an incredible, tangible power exuded from the volcanoes that make up most of the islands. Some are still active, spewing forth torrents of boiling lava, and this energy of creation inspires transformation and reflection. The leylines that crisscross the land have a powerful effect as well, activating energy and wisdom deep within.

Hawaii is located in the middle of the Pacific Ocean, 4000 kilometres southwest of the United States and just below the Tropic of Cancer. The Hawaiian Island Chain includes more than one hundred and thirty islands within its archipelago (which stretches for more than 2000 kilometres and includes Papahanaumokuakea Marine National Monument, the largest marine protected area in the world), however most of them are tiny and uninhabitable.

Only six of the eight most southerly islands receive visitors, and it's these that most people identify as Hawaii – Oahu, the site of the state's capital of Honolulu, Hawaii, known as the Big Island, and

Maui, Kauai, Molokai and Lanai. The other two southern isles are Kahoolawe, off the coast of Maui, which remains uninhabited after its seventy-year use by the US Army to train troops and test weapons, and the tiny island of Niihau, off the coast of Kauai, which has been a private residence since the mid-1800s.

Sun worshippers head to the perfect white sand beaches of Waikiki on Oahu, which is known as a mecca for shopping and nightlife. Surfers go to Maui, the adventure island that boasts myriad water sports and other activities. Nature lovers head for the unspoiled wilderness and magnificent scenery of Kauai, the wettest, lushest and prettiest place on earth. Those in search of the old Hawaii go to Molokai, with its large ranches and traditional way of life.

But for spiritual pilgrims the Big Island is the place to be. It's there that Pele the volcano goddess works her fiery magic, adding to the size of the island with her constant eruptions. It's the ancestral home of Hawaiian royalty, and hidden temples and ancient places of refuge are markers of an old, seemingly more primitive, way of life. Beaches of white, black, green and gold sands stretch for miles in splendid isolation, and dolphins and whales splash around in the shallow, sun-kissed waters, interacting with swimmers in a deeply healing way.

Wherever you go in the Aloha State, you will be reminded of how beautiful and sweet and full of mystery and magic life can be. Sitting under a swaying palm tree in a peaceful garden, breathing in the balmy tropical air, smiling up at the half moon or the radiant sunshine, assailed by the fresh, salty scent of the sea and the pretty fragrant flowers, you realise that this earth is a paradise, and each part of the planet has its own enchantment.

In Hawaii you'll feel overwhelmed by the love and welcome of the islanders, the sacred earth energy running through the land, the cleansing, healing pull of the pure ocean waters, and the immense joy that its incredible beauty instils within your heart and soul.

The present

"Hawaii has a unique gift to offer the visitor – the ability to quiet the mind, heal the heart, relax the body and feed the soul. It's on a vortex of spiritual energy along the leylines of the earth, and the result is an environment nurturing, supportive and healing."
Laura Crites, director of Hawaii Wellness Tourism Association

All the Hawaiian Islands are blessed with incredible beauty, spiritual power and a sense of the sacred, but the Big Island possesses an extra layer of mystery and healing energy. There's a wild and untamed quality to it, a sense of space and diversity. Although you can drive right around the island in a day, it has within it twenty-one of the world's twenty-two climate zones, with golden beaches not far from snow-topped mountains, and eerie lava fields, stark desert areas and tropical rainforests. Energetically it combines the four elements of water, air, earth and fire with its beautiful coastline, pure winds, sacred mountains and the fiery aspect of its still-active volcanoes.

Hilo, the biggest town on the island, is on the windward east coast, a rugged stretch of beaches with pounding surf, verdant forests, soaring cliffs, stunning valleys and waterfalls sparkling with sunlight. All the Hawaiian islands have a windward and a leeward side – the windward is along the east and northeast coast, and is wetter, greener and more moderate in temperature, cooled by the trade winds and lush from the night-time rain, while the leeward side is along the west coast and is the hotter, drier and sunnier part of the island.

The settlement of Hilo, built on a half-moon bay and guarded by two mountains, is full of gorgeous gardens, testament to the combination of tropical sunshine and high annual rainfall. While it rains often here, the showers never last long, and each one is followed by a breathtaking rainbow, making every drop worthwhile.

It's the oldest city in Hawaii, with immense charm and personality. When a tsunami in 1960 destroyed the newer section of town, the locals decided not to rebuild, turning the low-lying bayfront area into memorial parks and leaving the character-filled old quarter to define the place. In Hilo Bay is tiny Coconut Island, known to Hawaiians as Mokuola, which means island of life. A narrow footbridge extends from Liliuokalani Garden to the island, where people used to flock to drink the water in the sacred spring and touch the ancient healing stone.

Kona, also known as Kailua-Kona, is on the hot and dry west coast, and is the other main town. It has an incredibly different atmosphere, energy and appearance to Hilo. Although smaller, Kona is the tourist town, a sun-drenched paradise of turquoise waters, pale sand beaches, ancient fishponds, whale watching cruises, coffee houses and health food stores. People stay in this lively seaside location to enjoy the heat and the stunning sunsets, swim with dolphins, snorkel or go deep sea diving, and generally relax and restore their energy.

It's also the entrance point to the Kohala Coast, which stretches northward in a golden splash of natural beauty. From the road the area looks like a blackened lava wasteland, but once you turn off to the beaches the bright sands and tropical palm trees expected of Hawaii suddenly appear. Protected from storms by volcanic peaks, this strip is the driest and sunniest part of the island, a tourist mecca that offers crystal clear lagoons in peaceful bays, luxury hotels with indulgent spas and emerald green golf courses.

While the resorts of the Kohala Coast are out of the price range of most people, they boast hidden charms that are freely accessible to all travellers, such as the amazing Kaupulehu Cultural Center at the Four Seasons Resort Hualalai, which includes hula lessons, Hawaiian language classes and cultural demonstrations. At the Eva Parker Woods Cottage at the Mauna Lani Resort, cultural advisors share the area's rich history and show people the rock carvings known as petroglyphs and the ancient caves that are accessed from the hotel. The same resort also has a magical full moon event, Twilight at Kalahuipuaa, which celebrates Hawaiian traditions on the Saturday closest to the full moon and is open to everyone, not just hotel guests.

The Big Island was formed by five volcanoes, which creates an intense earth energy that has immense healing power. Mauna Kea and Kohala are dormant, but Kilauea, Hualalai and Mauna Loa are still considered active, and all five have a revitalising atmosphere and pure air that invigorates and cleanses emotionally and physically.

Mauna Loa, the Long Mountain, is 4170 metres tall, and is the world's largest volcanic mountain by volume. To the north is Mauna Kea, the White Mountain, which is 4205 metres above sea level but rises almost 10,000 metres from the ocean floor, making it the tallest mountain in the world when measured from its base.

Both were profoundly sacred to the early Hawaiians, and were considered the home of the gods. They're so high that they get snow in winter – a strange prospect on this sunny, tropical isle – but while Mauna Loa is still active, with its last eruption recorded in 1984 and scientists predicting it may soon re-awaken, Mauna Kea is considered dormant, having last erupted more than four thousand years ago.

This makes it the perfect location for astronomical observatories, and the summit looks like a strange space station, with massive white domed telescopes operated by nations from all over the world exploring deep space. The light-gathering power of these instruments is sixty times greater than the Hubble Space Telescope that orbits the earth, making it scientifically significant, but even with the naked eye, stargazing from this mountain is extraordinary, partly due to the clear, unpolluted skies and inky blackness undisturbed by city lights.

There's also a cairn of stones, a cinder cone and a sacred glacial lake at the summit of Mauna Kea, and some of the most breathtaking views on the planet. Getting to the top is almost impossible without a four wheel drive, but most cars can make it to the Onizuka Visitor Information Station three quarters of the way up. Each night the centre runs stargazing programs with powerful telescopes, knowledgeable guides and free lectures, and there are tours to the top.

Because of all the volcanic activity and the spreading lava flows that reach right down to the sea, the tropical golden beaches Hawaii is famous for are not as common on the Big Island. Instead there are amazing black sand beaches, formed from ground-down lava, which sparkle in the sunlight and soothe your feet when you walk on them, and stunning green sand beaches created from the presence of peridot, a shiny green crystal also known as olivine.

Pu'u Mahana, Green Sand Beach, is located near the southernmost tip of the island, and has long been considered a sacred place. Peridot, known to the Ancient Romans as Evening Emerald and to Hawaiians as Pele's Tears, is formed during volcanic eruptions and contains a fiery energy. It's a powerful cleanser and purifier, both physically and emotionally, and helps to release guilt, resentment and negativity.

South of Hilo, on the Puna Coast, is the secret hideaway of Ahalanui Pool, also known as Pele's Bath. Swaying palm trees ring this large volcanically heated pool, which is separated from the sea by a manmade lava wall. It's a beautiful experience to watch the waves crashing on the nearby shore as you float around on the gentle surface, marvelling at the nurturing sensation and the tiny coloured fish that swim around with you. The water, half from a fresh spring and half from the ocean, is almost as warm as a spa, and soothes and relaxes body and mind. When the surf is big enough to crash over the wall, fountains of water add mist and rainbows, making the spectacle even more magical.

To the north is Waipio Valley, the sacred Valley of the Kings where many of the earliest chiefs ruled from, which is reputed to be the cradle of Hawaiian civilisation. It was the site of many important temples, although a tsunami in 1946 destroyed much of the valley and forced many of the families who had lived there for generations to move out.

The lookout gives spectacular views, and visitors can hike down the soaring cliffs – or take a mule tour – to get closer to the lush jungles and waterfalls that have made this picturesque place the location of many legends and so popular with film crews.

"The past is very important. Don't go back, but remember the past. Preserve the past, but improve yourself. We have to keep respecting those things that our kupuna – elders – had. We still carry today our aloha for our temples, even though they're destroyed. Our aloha for all these things is still with us. It never will be gone."
Charley Keau, Hawaiian archaeologist and historian

One of the most emotionally charged places on the island is the mysterious Pu'uhonua O Honaunau, the Place of Refuge. Built in the 1500s, it was a heiau – a temple – as well as a royal complex and a city of refuge. In those days there was a strict system of rules, known as kapu, with some crimes punishable by death, but if the lawbreaker could make it to a place of refuge they'd be forgiven, their sin forgotten and their soul wiped clean. It was no mean feat – the refuges were built close to the water's edge and the approach was through often treacherous seas and a shoreline of sharp black lava rocks, but the chance of redemption meant many people, from those sentenced for a crime to those defeated in battle, fled there for the chance of a new life.

A place of refuge was sacred – the Hawaiians understood this was not an excuse to get away with a crime and then reoffend, but that the nature of their absolution meant they should grasp this second chance with their whole heart and start their life over. It was a place of grace, and I could feel the sense of sacredness as I wandered through the grounds. Some visitors feel the echo of tall, solemn guards, the ghosts of the guardians of old, while others feel a sense of protection that emanates from the religious buildings and platforms or the land itself.

There is also a healing energy within the earth, and many people do their own ceremonies of releasement here, protected by the sanctuary that for centuries was a place of safe haven and new beginnings. Watching the sun set over the horizon as you exhale your pain and breathe in the pure air, feeling cleansed by the power of the ocean and the energy of this powerful site, is an intense, moving experience.

Today, in a Hawaii trying to reconnect and remember its roots, it remains one of the island's most important places, and an example of the forgotten side of the kapu system – the kapu akua, or law of the gods, which provided mercy and pardon. Local artists have restored the complex to the way it was at the height of its use, rebuilding some of the temples, houses, storage shelters and even canoes of a bygone era.

The sanctuary begins with the Palace Grounds, a beautiful, tranquil spot where waves lap the shore of the coconut palm grove and endangered green sea turtles swim languidly in the tiny cove that was once the royal canoe landing spot. Further out on the peninsula the Great Wall that separated the royal compound from the refuge still stands, more than three metres high and six metres thick.

On the other side, jutting into the ocean, is the Place of Refuge itself, a haunting site where I could feel the spirits of ages past. Fierce looking ki'i, wooden images of the gods, still stand watch throughout the grounds, whispering their stories of the past. Several are on guard outside the reconstruction of the Hale O Keawe Heiau and mausoleum, which housed the bones of twenty-three alii, the chiefs who ruled the island. The mana – spiritual power – within their royal bones made this place even more sacred, and added to its protective powers. Long ago, daily offerings were placed on the wooden towers, and now they're being made again, with a riot of flowers swamping the heiau when I visited.

It was in reaching this temple that refuge was won, but there are the remains of other heiaus on the peninsula too, which served various religious purposes and still have a powerful energy. There's also the Keoau Stone, which Mark Twain reported was the favourite resting spot of the then-chief, and the Kaahumanu Stone, a seven tonne rock which a long-ago queen hid under when she swam to the site following fights with her husband. In 1819 the Place of Refuge was abandoned, but in recent times its significance has been re-embraced. Today there's a temple priest who oversees the complex in the manner of old, and the spirituality of the past continues in the present.

In addition to this amazing shrine, the ruins of some of the most impressive heiaus in Hawaii are situated on the Big Island. These sacred temples, where the kahunas, or priests, would communicate with the gods on behalf of the chiefs, have been found to align with heiaus on the other islands, and were built on lines of earth energy that the kahunas were attuned to. This is partly why such a surge of power can still be felt amongst the remains of these old places of worship.

Temples were located at sites of special power, such as cliff tops, where the mana could be harnessed. They varied in size and structure, from simple stones that served as altars for offerings to the fishing or harvest gods, to the massive, intricate stone platforms that were the foundations of buildings where elaborate rituals were performed.

Mo'okini Heiau, on the northwest tip of the island, has a strange, eerie atmosphere. Located on a windy hillside, the three-storey temple was constructed around 480CE, and is the oldest on the island. Centuries later it was rededicated by the priest Pa'ao, who introduced human sacrifice to the island, and transformed into a luakini, a temple where people were offered to the gods. Many visitors claim to have seen ghosts there, or etherically witnessed the sacrifices of the past, and there's an intense energy that emanates from the stones.

Today it's protected by Leimomi Mo'okini Lum, who's taken on the role of guardian priest from her father, continuing an unbroken hereditary line that spans centuries. She prays there, leaves offerings to the gods and organises a monthly clean-up which volunteers can join in with. Leimomi, who has written a book about the site, says the heiau is now a place of healing, and she has sworn to protect it.

The 18th century warrior Kamehameha, who united the Hawaiian Islands, was born next to Mo'okini Heiau, and his birthplace, commemorated by a statue, is also a place of significance. Before his birth a kahuna had prophesied that the son of a Kohala chief and a Kona chiefess would grow up to kill the ruler and reign in his place. To prevent the prophecy being fulfilled, the then-chief murdered any boys born of noble blood. But Kamehameha's mother ran away and gave birth in secret, leaving her son with a trusted servant to raise.

As an adult Kamehameha used Mo'okini Heiau as his place of worship, until his kahuna advised him that if he built a new one dedicated to Ku, the god of war, he would rule all the islands. So in 1790 Kamehameha ordered construction of the massive Pu'ukohola Heiau to the south. It was the last sacred site built before the coming of the westerners who dramatically altered Hawaiian society, and has been carefully preserved, making it a fascinating place to explore.

Another important temple is Kona's Ahuena Heiau, a 15th century shrine that was rebuilt by Kamehameha after he'd united the islands and retired to the seaside town of Kona to rule from there. The heiau, on tiny Kamakahonu Bay, was dedicated to the god of healing. The king built his royal compound next door, and Ahuena became his personal place of prayer. Today the reconstructed heiau is in the grounds of the King Kamehameha Hotel, and people are welcome to visit.

Across the bay is Hulihee Palace, built in 1838 of coral, lava rock and native woods, which hosted many of Hawaii's kings and queens. It was restored in 1927 and is now a museum, filled with traditional as well as monarchy-era artefacts and crafts. Opposite it is Mokuaikaua Church, the oldest Christian house of worship in Hawaii, which offers a different historical slant on the islands.

"It's considered blessed to see a rainbow because it represents the power of the spirit to unite separate spheres, including life and death. A rainbow is a symbol of someone's passing. The opening of the colours of light represents the expansion in consciousness that happens when the spirit is freed. It's a visible bridge between the physical and spiritual."
Dr Rima Morrell, European writer, huna teacher and anthropologist

My spiritual connection came amidst the rugged grandeur and primal energy of Hawaii Volcanoes National Park, where the magic of creation takes place every day as the lava from two active volcanoes spills down to the sea and creates new land. The Big Island is actually increasing in size, the only place on the planet where this happens.

While Mauna Loa is part of the 333,000 acre park, the central focus is Kilauea Volcano and its massive central summit caldera, which has within it two craters, Kilauea Iki and Halemaumau. Here the lava lurks, bubbling below the surface, its presence never far from conscious awareness. Clouds of steam billow upwards from the vents in the caldera, and hardened lava swirls in intriguing patterns from previous flows. This volcano displays all the brutal force of nature, occasionally wiping out homes, roads, forests and even towns as the molten fire explodes upwards from inside the earth then spills down, covering all in its path. It's the most active volcano on earth, and is a fascinating vortex of energy.

It's also the legendary home of Pele, the goddess of fire and volcanoes, and the incredible natural force that Hawaiians worship for her powers of both destruction and renewal. And it's where I decided to do my ceremony for a friend who'd taken his life just before I flew to Hawaii. As his close-knit circle prepared for the funeral in Australia, I calculated the time difference and made my way down into the volcano for my own farewell, and to link up energetically with those left behind.

One trail was closed – which often happens when the underground lava activity gets a bit heavy – but a massive rainbow was stretching up from the other side of the crater, so I headed over there and began to climb down into the volcano. It was a beautiful walk through dripping rainforests, ferns and flowering ginger on a path along the edge of the crater, and I said my prayers on the way down, asking Pele to guide my friend safely on his way and help him find peace, and to give strength to all those who were suffering without him.

As I got to the bottom the rainbow got brighter, huge and vivid in the sparkling, rain-fresh air, and its beauty touched my heart and made me feel more connected to my friends on the other side of the world. I walked out onto the volcano floor, marvelling at the strange, eerie moonscape. The cracked grey lava stretched ahead as far as I could see, and the billowing steam from vents further out and the tiny pools left from earlier rain made it look like a sci-fi wasteland.

I found a tiny fern that had fought its way up through the tough basalt, and placed the red velvet-wrapped bundle I'd brought with me, a spell of release, transformation and hope, at its base. There was no one else down there, which made it even more spooky and desolate and perfect. The sense of loss and waste at my friend's death was overwhelming, highlighted by the wasteland where I stood, and I was overcome with sorrow and regret – and the certainty that we must tell people how we feel about them because they don't always know.

Our friend had no idea how much he meant to so many people, how devastating his death was to them, and the emptiness they felt at his passing. Many of them wondered if they could have prevented it, which isn't the case, but they all wished they'd been more open in expressing their love for him. If anything came from his tragic death, it was that they all made sure their friends knew how much they were loved. And while it's sad that it took such a loss to realise the importance of this, it's a lesson that will stick with us forever.

As I climbed back out of the crater it rained again, a cleansing rain that washed away my tears, and by the time I got back to the car the sun was shining again and the rainbow had returned. Throughout my weeks in Hawaii I was constantly surrounded by these beautiful vivid arches. They showed me the way to go when I was lost, pointed me in interesting directions, and made me smile as I remembered my friend.

Pele's volcano was the perfect place to say goodbye to him, and the perfect place to start my journey. The primal energy here activates and awakens everyone who walks this land, and the goddess – or the forces of nature she represents – brings emotions to the surface to be examined and released. It isn't an easy or gentle process, because the magnetic force of the leylines and the fiery nature of the lava bubbling underground create a surge of power that is like a jolt of electricity, initiating you into a new state of being. Spending time here is a powerful catalyst for change, inspiring you to open up to your own inner awareness and shed any pain you've held on to.

The park has been designated an International Biosphere Reserve, and is Hawaii's only World Heritage Site. There are fantastic hikes across the still-steaming floors of the volcanic craters, mountain treks, places to camp and more than three hundred archaeological sites. The visitor centre provides background on everything from the geology of the park to the enchanting legends of Madame Pele, with documentaries that capture flowing lava rivers and spectacular molten fountains, and frequently updated information on current danger spots.

Across the road from Kilauea Caldera are the Sulphur Banks, strange piles of steaming rocks where the volcano lets off steam, depositing sulphur as it reaches the surface. It has a unique smell, and the thick fumes can be dangerous. A new word, vog, has been coined to describe the volcanic smog that sometimes envelops the park, which is caused when volcanic gases react with moisture, oxygen and sunlight.

Further around the caldera is the tropical rainforest that leads to Thurston Lava Tube, which highlights the savage extremes of this dramatic region. The lush green ferns, tall trees and thick mosses provide some respite from the harshness and heat of the lava beds and volcanic wastelands, and a home for chattering birds.

A trail winds through this cool, wet environment and down to the entrance of the lava tube – a huge black tunnel that curves into the earth, like a cave or the inside of a monster worm's stomach. Lava tubes are the shells that remain from the underground passageways that molten magma – the name for lava before it reaches the surface – once flowed through. This one is at least four hundred years old, and the tree roots that stretch down through the roof and the cobwebs that cling to the sides add to the sense of history and age.

It's slightly unsettling to walk through it, but meditating in a lava tube opens your senses and plunges you deep into your own inner universe, allowing you to tap in to the cleansing power of the darkness and the hidden recesses and potential of your own mind. There are many lava tubes throughout the islands, forming labyrinths under the ground, and being inside any one of them is a strange, silent experience that has been likened to being in a flotation tank, a deep meditation that soothes the soul and quiets the mind.

In sharp contrast to Thurston's lush greenery is nearby Devastation Trail, which crosses an area that was turned from forest to desert fifty years ago when a lava eruption buried its trees. The path follows the old road, which was replaced with a diverted new one when this stretch was totally covered by lava – winding across an eerie landscape known as the dead zone. It's a burned-out wasteland, stripped of all life and colour, with the odd bare bleached tree trunk starkly white against the ash-covered floor, and a blanketing silence adding to the desolation.

There's also the Pu'u Loa Petroglyph Trail, a short walk that leads down to a field where more than fifteen thousand petroglyph images were carved into the surface of the lava by the early Hawaiians, who left this unique artwork all over the islands. There are etchings of people, animals, boats, hunting, fishing and sports, as well as various patterns and designs. It was a very sacred place, and according to legend, if a father buried the umbilical cord of his newborn child in a tiny lava hole here, the baby would have a long and healthy life.

"The vast floor under us was as black as ink, and apparently smooth and level, but over a mile square of it was ringed and streaked and striped with a thousand branching streams of liquid and gorgeously brilliant fire! It looked like a colossal railroad map done in chain lightning on a midnight sky. Imagine it – a coal-black sky shivered into a tangled network of angry fire!"
Mark Twain, 19th century author and father of American literature

Kilauea Volcano has significantly altered the landscape of the Big Island. In modern times there have been two violent eruptions, in 1790 and 1924, and for the past twenty-seven years it's been constantly active. This latest eruption began in January 1983, and has continued for a record-breaking period, with lava spewing forth at various rates – sometimes a trickle, sometimes an angry molten flow. It's covered about 20,000 acres of land, blocking the coastal road to Puna in 1988, and two years later burying the entire town of Kalapana, which has been hidden forever under the lava. Other villages have also disappeared beneath the volcano's fury, along with hundreds of houses, several shops, churches, a visitor centre, beaches and even an ancient heiau.

Driving there from Hilo, I came to a spot where a lava flow had wiped out a whole section of the road. The highway abruptly ended, and I had to pull up quickly and retrace my steps. There were mailboxes and street signs and a bit of car wreckage poking up from the swirling rock – it was totally surreal, but nothing out of the ordinary in Hawaii.

Beautiful Lava Tree State Monument is another haunting reminder of the harshness of nature. It's a ghostly field of lava shells shaped like trees, created in 1790 when an ohia forest was engulfed by lava and the trunks burned away inside, leaving the lava moulds in their place.

But while Kilauea has destroyed so much, it has also created new land, reinforcing the primal energy of this island. More than six hundred acres have been added to the southeast coast, and the map at the visitor centre is constantly being updated. The current lava flow is not from Kilauea Caldera itself – which has crusted over, the stinky breaths of steam exhaled through vents the only hint of its volcanic action – but from Pu'u O'o vent, a crack in the southern slope of the mountain where lava erupts and flows down the cliffs to the ocean.

This can be viewed along Chain of Craters Road, which winds downwards to the sea and ends dramatically in a shiny new lava flow that has made this street even shorter, gobbled up greedily by Madame Pele. If Kilauea is in an active phase, it's the most spectacular sight on earth. Molten lava pours down from above and into the ocean, exploding with passion, energy and a steamy hiss into the dark swirling waters of the Pacific. Often the clouds above turn red, reflecting the lava lakes in the park, and the lava tubes glisten with devilish hues.

It's best seen at night, when the fiery, fountaining lava gleams red against the darkening hillside, contrasting deeply with the inky blackness of the sky. Here you stand on the edge of creation, peering into the earth to see the molten magma swirling in its path to the surface – which some have likened to the pits of hell. This is the astonishing process that creates new land, a mind-blowing notion.

It can be dangerous though, and the advice of park rangers and tour operators should be heeded. In 1993 a tourist died when the new ground he was standing on, not yet hardened and fully formed, broke off and fell into the sea. More recently two hikers died from steam inhalation near where the lava hits the ocean, and another received third degree burns when he fell into hot magma after venturing into a closed off area. And the extreme sports surfers who recently began riding the massive waves where lava meets sea risk being badly burned or dragged under and drowned in Pele's churning cauldron.

There are full-day tours from Hilo and Kona that travel around the park by day then down to the lava flows at night, picking the best places to view the eruption sites or the bubbling lava cascading into the sea. You can also take a helicopter tour – one of the best ways to see it all and get a greater perspective – or hike in on your own, checking in with the rangers for updated details on flows. To explore further you can camp within the park boundaries, stay at historic Volcano House, on the rim of Kilauea Caldera, or in a range of hotels and B&Bs in the tiny village of Volcano, just outside the park.

Viewing the lava as it flows down the hill or crashes into the ocean is a truly spectacular event, but there are no guarantees it will be active on a given day. Sometimes the hot molten magma shoots metres in the air before streaming downhill in red rivers, and at other times it's slow and quiet, with little to see. Some days the flow is easily accessible, near the road or a place you can hike to in order to view it, and at other times it flows underground or far from sight in the wilderness.

But no matter when you visit and what the volcano is up to, this place will overwhelm you with its power and passion. Be wary if you're not ready for emotional and spiritual change, because the ancient energy fires you up, and unless you're focused – be it on healing the past or starting a new project – the forces of nature could be too much, creating chaos rather than action in your life.

The energy of this region is tangible, fiery and deeply cleansing. There's something primal about this place, and the whole of the Big Island, a feeling of restless intensity that can be sensed beneath the beauty of the rainforests and the tropical splendour of the beaches. It is definitely a place of spirits. Not faeries and gentle nature sprites, like in the British Isles – Hawaii is savage and beautiful and strong and wild, and you'll be re-energised and inspired by its incredible power.

"To greet the sun as it rises, this was the tradition of the ancestors. Everyone would turn to the sun with prayers of love and gratitude, because native practitioners believe with the coming of the sun the mana, spiritual life force, returns to earth each day. With mana comes healing, growth, life itself, for all creatures and the earth."
Lanakila Brandt, Hawaiian kahuna and temple priest

The other islands also have their share of magic. Maui, known as the Valley Isle, is full of glorious beaches, stunning waterfalls, artfully restored heiaus in wild botanic gardens and rocks considered stepping stones to the Otherworld. It also boasts the beautiful, cliff-hugging Road to Hana, 80 kilometres of ocean views, waterfalls, lush jungles and one-lane bridges, which winds its way along the northeast coast from Kahului to the village of Hana and the Seven Sacred Pools.

Maui is also the location of Haleakala, the world's largest dormant volcano. This was the home of the gods, like Mount Olympus to the Ancient Greeks, and was considered one of the most sacred sites in the region. Legend tells of the god Maui, creator of the Hawaiian Islands, standing atop Haleakala and lassoing the sun to strike a deal with it on behalf of his mother, the goddess Hina, who was frustrated that there wasn't enough heat in the day to dry the cloth she was making. The sun agreed to shine longer for half the year, creating the seasons, and Haleakala got its name, which means House of the Sun.

In the past, this sacred mountain was used by the kahunas for meditation, prayer and communing with the gods. It was a place of initiation rites and manifestation rituals, and the remains of three hundred heiaus on the east side of the mountain add to its spiritual significance. The volcano's high iron content and density also make it a vortex of electromagnetism, and the leylines that run through it create a powerful activation in people who spend time there.

Watching the sun rise from the summit above the clouds is a breathtaking, transcendental experience. One morning I dragged myself out of bed at 3am and made my way to the top, driving up the steep, winding road in the darkness, with mist and occasional rain splattering down. I got out in the chilly pre-dawn and saw a few shooting stars light up the heavens, which made me smile even as I pulled my beanie lower and my scarf tighter.

It's really cold at the top, a surprise in tropical Hawaii, and the crisp, clean air is slightly thinner, making breathing laboured. But it's worth the freezing temperatures and the long drive – two hours from the west coast resorts – to witness the splendour of the sky colouring and the whole world waking up for the day.

When I was there nature's dramatic show went for more than forty minutes, with the volcano rim casting long shadows and the crater filled with fluffy, billowing clouds that seemed to dance through the air below, at times a deep blue, later streaked with gold, then settling into a vibrant snowy white. In the distance the two highest peaks of the Big Island could be seen. Closer in, the details of this unique volcano, which rises more than 3000 metres above the lowlands, were hidden then slowly revealed in the shadows of this enchanted hour.

Finally the sun rose in a huge ball of golden fire, and it seemed as though it was coming up out of the crater itself. As the sky coloured, with bright slashes of deep orange, red, yellow and hints of pinky purple, the warmth of the sun flooded the summit and people began peeling off layers of clothing. Below, the lower mountain slopes slowly became visible, stripped of the mist that had shrouded them, along with the little bays and islets that stretch along the coast and the toy towns that huddle close to the ground.

As the sun's rays crept over the land and kissed the top of the volcano, they also crept within my body, warming and energising every cell and awakening my heart. I was overwhelmed with a sense of being deeply connected to the earth and the cycles and moods of nature, at one with this beautiful, peaceful world.

As the sky became bluer, many of the onlookers jumped on pushbikes and flew back down the steep hill. This thrilling 45 kilometre ride is one of Maui's most popular tourist attractions, descending quickly through the clouds and down to the ocean's edge.

I chose instead to walk down into the crater and hike 20 kilometres across its floor, a surreal, spectacular adventure that pushed me to the limits physically, liberating my mind to soar above the world and contemplate its deepest secrets. This was one of the main things I'd come to Hawaii to experience, and although I could barely walk for days afterwards, and lost a toenail or two after the blisters finally settled down, it was definitely worth it.

Sliding Sands Trail begins steeply, descending down through desert sands and past towering cinder cones and volcanic vents that add to the eeriness and wonder. The looming shapes and swirling red-black sands, highlighted with shades of pink, purple, orange, silver and gold, are totally Otherworldly, and crossing the crater is like marching across the surface of a distant planet. The view is breathtaking, with dramatic rocky headlands and bluffs up ahead, ever-changing colours and the crater rim outlined starkly against the vivid sky.

On the valley floor the scenery changes. The ground becomes a bed of black lava rock, the flatter surface a relief after the steep slopes. It stretches ahead, hazy in the shimmering heat. In the distance the mountainous sides loom above, and the bizarre rock formations and their strange silhouettes rear up. The only vegetation in this section is an occasional silversword, a rare and delicate plant made up of a clump of cactus-like leaves with a flower stem rising from the centre.

Gradually the huge red cinder cones and black lava fields give way to dirt, and a scrubby kind of vegetation emerges, peeking out of gaps in the earth before – much later – an almost lush greenness takes over, with patches of grass covering the ground and bracken ferns and even flowers surviving in the barren heat.

While the scenery is desolate, it is stunning too, filled with subtle changes of colour, texture and elevation. I'd pictured the crater floor being flat, yet it's not – there are hills and even steep exhausting climbs in parts, so the perspective is always changing.

Most significantly, when I walked there wasn't a single sound. Down in the crater it was absolutely silent – no birds, no people, no cars, just my footfalls and the soft exhalation of my breath in the warm air. The whole landscape was so sparse, bereft of life and noise, which was a hauntingly beautiful experience. The aloneness of the trek was wonderful. It was totally solitary, giving me time to think and dream, and contemplate the world and my place in it. Even the physical pain was part of it, allowing my mind to detach and float free while I pushed through the aches and strains riddling my body.

After five hours I finally got to the other side, completely exhausted, and contemplated the exit – a sheer cliff. My feet were sore and blistered, and the midday sun was extremely hot, but I stubbornly began climbing the countless switchback trails. Little did I know it would take another two painful hours to actually make it out of the crater, but it didn't matter. This journey was absolutely stunning, beginning with the soul-soothing sunrise and continuing through the desolate, mind-expanding hike, and I'll always remember it with joy. The energy of the Haleakala volcano is subtle yet intense, and I felt so connected to the land and its harsh beauty as I walked through it.

There are more than 40 kilometres of hiking trails within the crater, as well as two camping sites and three cabins. For those who can't face the whole walk there are pony rides down Sliding Sands Trail which let the horse do the work, leaving you free to take in the breathtaking scenery and immense peace and tranquillity. There are even full moon hikes into the crater, a truly magical experience.

It was on the slopes of Haleakala too that I had my own brush with Pele, as I spent the day with a friend who was living in Hawaii. Legend says that the volcano goddess appears in human form as an old woman just before one of her mountain peaks erupts. People who show her kindness are spared from the flowing lava, but anyone that refuses to come to her aid will lose their home or even their life when the mountain explodes. This is the basis of Hawaiian hospitality, which treats everyone as a god or goddess and welcomes them warmly.

After spending the morning meandering along the beautiful Road to Hana and swimming in the Seven Sacred Pools of Oheo Gulch, we drove back the other way, along the tiny gravel road rental cars aren't allowed on. Marvelling at the stunning archways that extend into the ocean, the awe-inspiring *Lord of the Rings* valleys, the waterfalls, coastal cliffs and lava fields, we stopped to offer a lift to an older, grey-haired hippie-ish woman. She was picking noni fruits, which are used in herbal medicine in Hawaii, but she accepted a ride to her home several kilometres away, and blessed us as she left.

My friend and I laughed as I recounted the Pele legend – but that night, while we were still struggling to get back along the single-lane gravel path that passes for a road, there was an earthquake. We didn't know about it at the time, but when we found out later we breathed a sigh of relief and smiled happily at having helped Pele, and ensured our safety from the power of nature.

"The political and journalistic world can boast of very few heroes who compare with Father Damien of Molokai. It's worthwhile to look for the sources of such heroism. He's an inspiration."
Mahatma Gandhi, Indian political and spiritual leader

Molokai, known as the Friendly Island as well as the Most Hawaiian, is an unspoiled wilderness with very few inhabitants and hardly any tourists. It's the least developed and most traditional, and its rural feel encapsulates the last vestiges of the Old Hawaii that once spread across all the islands. Half the population has Native Hawaiian ancestry, a result of the 1921 Hawaiian Homes Act which tried to redress the dispossession of the indigenous people by providing land grants.

In legend Molokai was the child of Hina, goddess of the moon, making the island a good place to get in touch with your intuition and inner self, and there are traditions of sorcery and spirits. It's sparse and windswept, although it has its share of pretty beaches. The main town, Kaunakakai, was once the summer residence of the king, but now looks like it's straight from the set of a dusty western. It features Church Row, where seven churches, each a different denomination, stand next to each other, a fascinating glimpse at Hawaii's missionary past.

The east coast is ruggedly beautiful, with massive cliffs, hidden valleys, groves of sacred trees, tiny one-lane roads and an impressive heiau. On the western side there are gently sloping hills, old-style ranches, golden beaches and the island's only resort. And in the north, home to Ka Ule O Nanahoa, the fertility stone where women used to spend the night in the hope of falling pregnant, there are lush, impenetrable rainforests and towering sea cliffs.

This stunning backdrop hides a dark secret that stirs the soul and inspires with its tales of human endurance and hope. At the base of one of the cliffs, accessible only by walking or riding a mule down the twenty-six steep switchbacks, is the Kalaupapa Leper Colony. Leprosy, now called Hansens disease, was unknown in Hawaii until 1835, when immigrant workers brought it to the islands. With no known treatment, and concerned that it would become an epidemic, in 1865 the king signed a bill to quarantine anyone with the condition.

Ten thousand people throughout the islands were ripped away from their families and sent to the tiny colony on Molokai's Kalaupapa Peninsula. It was an effective prison, hemmed in by rough oceans on three sides and the highest sea cliffs in the world on the other. No one left the settlement, and visitors weren't permitted. Such was the overwhelming fear of the disease that boat captains would throw the patients overboard and make them swim rather than land anywhere near the colony. Those who made it to shore had to fend for themselves, with no medical assistance or food and few provisions supplied.

It was a desolate, hopeless existence, until the arrival of Father Damien de Veuster, a Belgian priest who, after eight years on the Big Island, requested that he be sent to the leper colony to minister to those who'd been cut off from society and left to die alone. People thought he was mad, but in 1873 he moved to Kalaupapa.

He built a church and three hundred houses for the residents, who'd sheltered in caves until then, constructed a water system, conducted services, nursed the sick, buried them when they died, and petitioned the government for resources. He lived in the community for more than fifteen years, increasing the quality of life for the patients and changing the perceptions of the illness in the outside world. Although Hansens disease is almost never contagious, Damien did develop it – the only one to do so of the more than a thousand volunteers who worked in the community over the course of a century – and died there in 1889.

A cure was discovered in the 1940s, and the laws of enforced isolation were repealed in 1969. No one has been sent to Kalaupapa since then and the residents are free to leave, although most still live in the community. Some have nowhere else to go, and others bear the scars of their illness and find it too difficult to assimilate into society. When the last person passes away or moves out, however, the place will be closed down, and the area will become a national park.

Those who live in the community allow people to visit as part of a tour to learn about the segregation and suffering that was endured there and break down the misinformation that still surrounds the condition. It's a heartbreaking tour, which inspires reverence for the bravery of the people who dealt with their illness, as well as anger at the way they were shunned and left at the mercy of the elements. Tours are led by a resident who shares the history of the colony, the discrimination they faced, how they live today and the heartwarming stories of friendship, love and hope that survived in this isolated spot.

It's very moving to stand in the church built by Father Damien and think of the sacrifices he made to help these cruelly discarded people. The cemetery beside it is also a touching site, and Damien's grave has become a place of pilgrimage. He was buried there after his death, but in 1936 the Belgian government requested the return of his body, so it was exhumed and re-buried near the village where he was born. Yet at the ceremony of his beatification in 1995, the first step on the road to sainthood, the bones of Father Damien's right hand – the one he blessed his parishioners with – were presented to the people of Hawaii as a sacred relic and returned to his original grave at Kalaupapa. In July 2008, Pope Benedict XVI announced that another "miracle" had been determined, and the Belgian priest will be declared a saint.

The Damien Tour is confronting, encouraging contemplation and challenging your ideas about disabilities, illness and human strength.

I was frustrated by the tragedy of Hawaii and its people being decimated by introduced diseases, and the pain inflicted by rulers unable to deal with the tragic situation. And I was moved by the kindness of the many people who followed in Father Damien's footsteps to do what they could to alleviate suffering and live their own version of aloha.

"We consider the environment sacred. Not to be polluted and desecrated, but to be treasured. Aina, our term for land, means 'that which feeds'. Aina feeds us. If we don't take care of it, we'll perish. The earth is our mother. To Native Hawaiians, everything is alive and everything is communicating with us. All we need to do is open up our receptors."
Dr Kekuni Blaisdell, Hawaiian doctor and sovereignty activist

The island of Oahu, known as the Gathering Place, is most famous for beachside Waikiki, a suburb of the Hawaiian capital of Honolulu. It's renowned for its tiny bikinis, fruity cocktails and nightlife, yet it's so much prettier and more spiritual than I expected. High-rise hotels crowd along the beach and vast shopping malls pump out cheap goods, loud music and junk food, but there are also coconut palms, golden sands and mystical stones. The sun sets over the ocean in the most magical explosion of colour and light, and there's a sense of serenity as the waves lap against the shore and honeymooners walk hand in hand in the vibrant twilight, city on one side, beach on the other.

On the sand at Waikiki are the four Kapaemahu Healer Stones, known as the Wizard Stones, which after years of being buried under a bowling alley have finally been accorded a place of respect on a lava rock platform, with an altar that's usually draped with floral leis and other offerings. According to legend, hundreds of years ago four powerful kahunas lived nearby, healing the sick, advising the chiefs and teaching medicine. Before they returned to Tahiti, they spent a month transferring all their healing powers into these stones so locals could maintain their health and wellbeing simply by touching them.

Nearby is historic Iolani Palace, the only royal residence in the United States. Visitors can take a tour through the house to see the fascinating displays of photos, paintings, ancient regalia and crown jewels, while the Royal Hawaiian Band performs free concerts in the grounds and quilting and genealogy classes are offered.

A few streets away is the Royal Mausoleum, Mauna Ala, the final resting place of Hawaii's monarchs. This haunting, history-drenched site is one of the most sacred burial places in the islands. A pretty chapel sits alongside the crypts in the shade of the gently waving palm trees, with gold lettering spelling out the names of Hawaii's much-loved royals. A kahu – caretaker – lives on the grounds, descended from the first great chiefs and determined to protect the bones of the ancestors and the mana that radiates from them into this hallowed earth.

Overlooking Waikiki's beach is Diamond Head Crater, a volcanic cinder cone so named because the British mistook the calcite crystals in the lava rock for diamonds. There's a fairly easy path to the summit, which has spectacular views of the entire island. Standing here I was filled with the amazing sensation of looking out over the whole world, with waves crashing below, the blue sky stretching out forever and the sweet tropical breeze cooling my cheeks.

In the centre of the island, which symbolises the navel and thus birth, are the Kukaniloko Birthstones, where royal women had their babies and generations of leaders were born. At this complex of almost two hundred stones, in use since the 12th century, expectant mothers would sit in specially carved rocks to give birth, watched over by thirty-six chiefs to assure the status of the baby (no private maternity suite for them!). As soon as the child was born it was taken to nearby Ho'olonopahu Heiau, which no longer stands, for purification rites and ceremonies.

There is still a sense of spiritual power at Kukaniloko, hovering in the atmosphere, and some women even experience birthing pains when they visit. The site is on a fertile green plateau surrounded by mountain peaks, eucalyptus trees, pineapple fields and coconut palms, which provide a beautiful tranquillity and strong earth energy. It's known as Hawaii's Stonehenge, as it's believed the stones were used to mark the changes of the seasons, map stars and foretell the royal child's future.

Ulupo Heiau, in the southeast of Oahu, is one of the best-preserved archaeological sites. While this agricultural temple fell into disrepair long ago, it remains a part of the sacred landscape and has become a focus of spiritual activities, cultural celebrations and educational tours. I drove there along Pali Highway, taking in the breathtaking views from Nuuanu Pali Lookout, then looped up to Keaiwa Heiau, the remains of a 15th century healing temple, school and medical centre. This is where initiates were sent to train in the healing arts, and a few of the many medicinal plants they cultivated still grow here.

On the west coast is the 11th century Kaneaki Heiau, dedicated to the harvest god and once a place of refuge. Well restored, it consists of three platforms surrounded on three sides by the swirling ocean. And on the northwest coast is Pu'u O Mahuka Heiau, Oahu's largest ceremonial site and a national historic landmark. The sacred buildings have long since perished, but a stone platform the size of two football fields remains, and there's a wooden altar that was covered in flowers and fruit, offerings left by the local people, when I visited. Situated on a cliff overlooking Waimea Bay, it has stunning views that sweep from the north of the island to the most westerly tip, Kaena Point, where souls reputedly made their leap to the Otherworld to meet their ancestors.

Waimea Valley, known as the Valley of the Priests because it was the home of the highest kahuna, is the site of Hale O Lono Heiau, an excavated temple dedicated to Lono the agricultural god. It's been restored to the way it once looked, with grass huts and wooden altars, and is set in a valley of waterfalls, forests and botanic gardens.

It was on the North Shore that I connected with Oahu. I drove up the east coast from Waikiki in a rented convertible – the poshest car I've ever been in, and a little nerve-wracking at first as I was driving on the "wrong" side of the road – marvelling at the beautiful beaches on my right and the lush, forest-clad mountains to my left. I wandered for hours through the plumeria grove in Koko Crater, enchanted by the heady scent and the vividly coloured varieties, with each tree flowering in a slightly different sunset shade of pink, creamy yellow or gold.

Later I pulled off the highway to swim in the tranquil waters of a shallow green bay, basking in the sparkling sunshine and surrounded by tiny tropical fish. And in the afternoon I arrived on the famous North Shore, where massive surf breaks – Pipeline, Sunset and Waimea Bay – capture the world's imagination, and where my dad surfed in the 1960s when he competed professionally. For months he slept under the stars and lived off fruit from the plantations, spending his days catching waves, at one with the spirit of this glorious ocean.

To surfers, wave riding is not sport but a spiritual pursuit, the most peaceful feeling on earth and a connection to the soul of the universe. Dad described it in an interview as: "The ultimate liberating factor. You're working with nature in the raw when you catch a wave," and fellow surfer Ted Spencer declared: "When I surf, I dance for Krishna."

Surfing is believed to have originated in Hawaii. Captain Cook's crew reported the phenomenon in the late 1700s, but local chiefs had been doing it for a millennium, and there are legends of the gods and goddesses surfing at the dawn of time. And while it was banned by the missionaries for almost a century, in the early 1900s Native Hawaiians started a revival at Waikiki, and it caught on all over the islands.

American author Jack London wrote about surfing after trying it on a visit to Hawaii, and local board rider and Olympic swimmer Duke Kahanamoku, known as the Father of Surfing and immortalised with a bronze statue at Waikiki, introduced it to Australia and California, which, along with Hawaii, have been at the centre of its development.

The Hawaiian Islands boast more than sixteen hundred quality surf spots, the first ever surfing contest was held at Oahu's Makaha Beach, and the North Shore breaks where they take place today are synonymous with wave riding. Spending time up there, watching the waves thunder in to shore and absorbing the raw power of nature, made me feel so close to Dad, as I retraced his steps and sensed the magic that had drawn him across the world to live off the land on this enchanted isle.

The past

"Before the last Hawaiian island had assumed its dominant shape, men had erected in Egypt mighty monuments. While volcanoes still played along the island chain, China developed a sophisticated system of thought. These lands were the youngest part of the earth's vast visible surface. They were new. They were raw. They were empty. They were waiting."

James A Michener, American academic and author

The geological history of Hawaii is fairly recent, as such things go. The main islands are the tops of a series of massive volcanic mountains that rise from the ocean floor, and are part of a long chain of isles and atolls that stretch northwest through the Pacific Ocean. The first of the islands didn't even begin to form on the sea floor until seventy million years ago – two hundred million years after the formation of the continental landmasses – and it was millions of years more before it reached the ocean's surface and took shape as an island.

Usually volcanoes occur on the edge of tectonic plates – the Pacific Plate has more than three hundred volcanoes around its rim, hence its name the Ring of Fire – but the Hawaiian Islands are near the centre of it. Instead of being the result of friction at the edge of the plate, they were formed by the actions of a hotspot below the ocean, a weak point in the crust of the earth where magma wells up, over thousands of years, then bursts through the plate to create underwater volcanoes. Sometimes, with enough eruptions and other geological forces in play, they will slowly (and I mean slowly!) grow to form islands.

Yet the Pacific Plate drifts a few centimetres northwest each year, which means that over time the volcano, and the island that has formed from it, are no longer above the hotspot. The volcano becomes extinct, and a new one starts to form in its place. This has resulted, over millions of years, in an island chain more than two thousand kilometres in length, which varies wildly in age and volcanic activity levels.

To the north are the remains of the earliest islands, which have now worn down to sea level, with some just a small chunk of lava rock or an atoll in the ocean. In the south are the newest islands, those known as Hawaii. Of these, the northernmost one, Kauai, is the oldest, around six million years old. Its volcanoes are long extinct and deeply eroded, leading to the immense lushness and fertility of the island.

In contrast, the Big Island is the youngest. Its oldest rocks are only seven hundred thousand years old – with some of the land just a day old!

Its current position over the hotspot is the reason most of its volcanoes are still active – but the cycle is continuing, and soon they too will be dormant. Now a new volcano off its southern shore, Loihi, is erupting and growing under the ocean, and it's thought this will – thousands of years from now – grow large enough to form a new island.

Scientists believe the entire island chain will eventually erode away and fall back into the sea, and it's this constant energy of physical destruction followed by creation that makes the power and impact of Hawaii so unique, as the islands constantly recreate themselves.

The recorded history of Hawaii is also very recent, with historians and archaeologists claiming the first inhabitants only arrived in the fifth – or even eighth – century CE. Yet the Polynesian ancestors of the Hawaiians have a long and rich cultural tradition, beginning thousands of years ago in the islands between Australia and Asia and spreading eastward through the Pacific Ocean to New Guinea, Fiji, Samoa and Tonga, and later to Tahiti, the Cook Islands, Bora Bora and the Marquesas Islands. Later they migrated even further, settling Hawaii, Easter Island and New Zealand, which mark the corners of the triangle of more than a thousand islands that make up modern Polynesia.

The Polynesians were incredible sailors, navigators and astronomers, with an amazing knowledge of ocean currents, seasonal patterns, the stars, migratory birds and marine life, which enabled them to travel vast distances throughout the Pacific and settle far and wide. It's even said that they could navigate between islands simply by tasting the sea water, which allowed them to pinpoint their exact location.

They rowed huge distances to Hawaii in small double-hulled outrigger canoes, centuries before Europeans made their first tentative forays around the world. They landed at South Point on the Big Island, then slowly spread northwards to inhabit the other isles. There's still debate about the exact origins of the first Hawaiian settlers, but most evidence points to people from the Marquesas, part of an island group in the southern Pacific that includes Tahiti.

Hawaiian culture and spiritual belief systems are thus Polynesian in origin, with similar gods and a close link to the land, the ocean and the natural world. The early inhabitants lived simply – fishing, gathering seaweed, growing fruit and vegetables and tending the chickens and pigs they'd brought from their homeland.

For while Hawaii enjoys a perfect tropical climate, there was little natural vegetation when the first settlers arrived, and few sources of water. There was no metal or pottery, making survival difficult, and no horses or cattle to develop agriculture. Yet they improvised, perfecting a form of tidal pool fish farming still practised today, creating taro farms with complex irrigation systems and becoming skilled in woodwork and the carving of stone and shells.

They worshipped a range of nature-based deities, saying prayers and leaving flowers and food at local shrines as offerings to ensure abundant fishing, a good harvest, and health for their family members. They lived a peaceful existence in harmony with nature and each other, and their aloha aina – love of the land – permeated everything they did. These early people defined themselves by their interconnectedness with all things, and their relationships with each other and their families, their ancestors and the land.

Chiefs known as alii, who were the wisest and strongest warriors, administered their local area, but everyone shared the land, working together to grow food and raise children. Each community had a kahuna, a healer-priest who fulfilled a similar role to the shamans of other indigenous cultures, advising the chiefs, communicating with the spirit world, studying the stars to see the future and healing people and animals. They maintained and nurtured their collective history through storytelling, chants and the dance known as hula. They also developed a therapeutic form of healing, herbal medicine and massage that's now being adopted around the world.

Some historians believe there was a second wave of settlement from Tahiti around the 12th century, with the new inhabitants overpowering the peaceful locals. Oral history records that a Tahitian high priest named Pa'ao came to Hawaii at this time. Disappointed by the relaxed society, and believing the chiefs had grown lax in their rituals and watered down the bloodlines by marrying "lesser" people, he instigated a stricter form of governance.

He sent for a "pure" Tahitian chief named Pili, who began a new line of Hawaiian royalty. Together they took over the Big Island, instituting a new system known as kapu, which involved a series of strict laws and taboos, many of them punishable by death if broken. They forced a new, more literal observance of a more aggressive array of gods, and built the first luakini heiau, a temple of human sacrifice, which was previously unheard of by the gentle Hawaiians.

Many of the surviving chants speak of the time before Pa'ao as a golden age when all people were equal, and all were connected to nature and the god source. They worked in the fields for the chiefs, but all shared in the abundance of the islands. They performed beautiful ceremonies, danced joyously, feasted well and enjoyed the spirit of aloha they had created in a land considered a paradise.

But Pa'ao ushered in a new age of war, power-hungry chiefs and intolerance. No one was allowed to touch, approach or interact with royalty or high kahunas, look at them or enter their space. A strict class system was enforced, and human sacrifice became commonplace. Women were suddenly forbidden from eating with men, were no longer allowed to consume certain foods, and became second-class citizens. Some places became out of bounds, and new gods were introduced. Significantly, Pa'ao transformed the benevolent god Ku into a bloodthirsty war deity.

The royal dynasty begun by Pili and Pa'ao ruled the Big Island of Hawaii for almost seven centuries, and their system of kapu took hold throughout the islands. Later kings traced their ancestry to Pili, and the kahunas who worked with them claimed descent from Pa'ao. Today however many consider the pair oppressors who fundamentally changed Hawaiian culture and spirituality – a spirituality that has only recently begun to return to the light, being revived and relearned as the elders come forward to share their knowledge and pass on the old healing methods, chants and dances to a new generation.

Some people link Hawaii to the mythical sunken continent of Mu or the lost land of Lemuria, claiming ancestors that go back thirty thousand years. There are also legends of the menehune, or little people, who would help humans by building fishponds and walls and working the fields by night, then hide during the day. Some believe they were a magical race related to the leprechauns and faeries of Ireland, and that they intermarried with the Hawaiians and live on to this day.

Others think the term menehune was the word for a people already living in the islands when the first Polynesians arrived, who were chased into the shadows by them. Still others say the name derives from the Tahitian word for commoner, and simply referred to people small in status and social standing, not size – the Marquesan inhabitants who were overthrown by the second wave of migration.

"When we sent our gods into the mists of the wildwoods so many years ago, they went and waited while we ran off into a strange world, seeking truths we already had. Our heritage was there all along. It's still there. My family's beliefs were based on the beauty and power of nature, the complexity. All the love and the truth and the beauty. That was our religion."

Winona Kapuailohiamanonokalani Beamer,
Hawaiian advocate, educator and hula teacher

The Hawaiians worshipped the forces of nature, such as volcanoes, storms and the sun, and deified the elements of earth, air, water and fire. Their primary deities were Kane, Ku, Lono and Kanaloa, but there was a whole pantheon of other gods and goddesses too, likened to those of the Ancient Greeks. They had human characteristics, falling in love, having children, suffering jealousy and rage, and working hard to create food, clothing, shelter and community. They looked after the people and taught them how to survive and thrive, and within the legends of their existence were guidelines for living well.

Ku: The king of the gods and ancestor to human kings, his wife Hina was the queen of the goddesses. They symbolised balance, embodying the masculine and feminine principles of existence, with Ku the sunrise and Hina the sunset. Ku incorporated many aspects, including Ku-ula, god of fishing and the seas, and Ku-kailimoku, god of war.

Kane: The god of procreation, he was the source of life and the creator god who breathed life into man, associated with the sky and the sun. Married to the fertility goddess Haumea, their children included Pele, Hiiaka, Laka and Kamohoalii the shark god, although in other legends Papa the earth mother and Wakea the sky father were their parents.

Kanaloa: The god of the ocean, symbolised by the octopus, he taught the kahunas their spiritual practices. He also oversaw departed spirits, which led to his alignment with hell by the Christian missionaries, who declared him Satan. But this was never his role – Milu was the god of the underworld, and even he had nothing to do with the devil.

Lono: The god of the harvest, the weather, the elements and nature, he was a fertility god with similar qualities to the agricultural deities of other cultures, and people prayed to him for abundant crops, plentiful animals and long, healthy lives. He was also the god of peace, prosperity and abundance, and in his weather aspect he was associated with storms, rain, wind, thunder, clouds and rainbows.

Pele: The goddess of volcanoes, she was associated with the element of fire and was the deity of transformation and fiery passion. Early Hawaiians lived in awe of her physical and emotional powers of destruction and creation, and left offerings to her in the hope of staying safe from her eruptions. Pele was the keeper of the sacred fire, and filled with compassion for her people. She is still worshipped today.

Namakaokahai: The goddess of the sea, she was associated with the element of water. She fought her younger sister Pele for seducing her husband, chasing her across the oceans and down through the Hawaiian islands. Their battle is still played out today in the fiery explosion that occurs when the lava of the volcano rushes down into the sea, a collision between the two primal forces of fire and water.

Haumea: The goddess of marriage, birth and rebirth, she was the earth mother, linked to the element of earth. An ancient goddess, she was known to some as the mother of Pele and Hiiaka, to others as the earthly manifestation of Uli, the creator of all life. She was the divine midwife who helped women in childbirth, and a goddess of fertility.

Hiiaka: The goddess of healing and dance, she was associated with the element of air. The beloved sister of Pele, she brought the volcano deity's true love back to life with her power to heal and restore. She was guardian of the sacred groves, invoked in herbal medicine, and associated with many plants. With Laka she was patron of the hula.

Laka: The goddess of love, legend also stated that she gave birth to the famous hula, the heartbeat of Hawaiian culture, in Molokai. Held within these languid dances is the history of the islands and the cultural and spiritual beliefs of the people. Dancers learning the ritual steps were under Laka's protection, and made offerings to her.

Poliahu: The goddess of the snow, she lived atop sacred Mauna Kea, the mountain of clarity. She had a fiery relationship with Pele, who would cover the land in lava while Poliahu smothered the flames in ice in a continual battle to master the elements and the Big Island. Her clothes were the snows of the mountain peaks, which fed the streams, and thus the people, and ensured the valleys remained fertile.

Hina: The goddess of the moon, she embodied the principles of life and fertility. She was the sacred guardian of the heavens, and was invoked for healing and balance, and for help in moving forward emotionally and putting new ideas into action. She was also worshipped by fishermen and associated with fish and seaweeds, and it is from her name that the Hawaiian word for woman, wahine, comes.

Maui: The god of magic, he was considered the father of the Hawaiian islands – according to legend, he caught them with his fish hook and dragged them up from the ocean floor. The son of the goddess Hina, he captured the sun and forced it to shine for longer, lifted up the sky so there was more room on earth, and taught men to make fire.

Koleamoku: The god of healing and patron deity of kahunas, he was called on to cure the most serious illnesses. Depicted as the tallest ki'i at many of the heiaus and places of refuge, he was a messenger of the chiefs, and was thought to be reincarnated or embodied in the golden plover birds known as kolea who adorned his statues in the temples.

Gods and goddesses were known as akua, and controlled the major aspects of life – they made the sun rise, ensured the land was fertile and assisted in childbirth. On a more personal level, the aumakua were the spirits of the departed ancestors who were worshipped by their families and called on in times of need. They were believed to help with problems, watch over the family and warn of danger, give advice and assist with healing. They could appear in animal form or in dreams. Some families on the Big Island considered Pele their ancestor and thus their aumakua, but to most people she was, and remains, an akua – Hawaii's most popular deity.

"The consolidation of the islands by Kamehameha into one kingdom was one of the greatest achievements in Hawaiian history. He possessed all the qualities of a strong leader. Powerful in physique, agile, fearless and possessing a strong mind, he easily inspired loyalty in his followers. Though ruthless in war, he was kind and forgiving when the need arose."

Richard Wisniewski, author of
The Rise and Fall of the Hawaiian Kingdom

After centuries of living in harmony with the land and each other, change came suddenly and dramatically to Hawaii on two different fronts. In January 1778 English explorer Captain James Cook, on a voyage to find the fabled Northwest Passage, landed on the island of Kauai to restock. He was the first westerner to visit Hawaii, and he reported that the locals were happy to see him and trade with him. He named the archipelago the Sandwich Islands after John Montagu, the fourth Earl of Sandwich and a lord of the British admiralty.

A year later, on his journey home, Cook returned to Hawaii, this time landing at Kealakekua Bay on the Big Island. His arrival coincided with the Makahiki festival dedicated to the god Lono, and the locals greeted him ecstatically. It had been foretold that their god would return on a floating island with white sails during the festival, and with Cook's ship looking uncannily like the prophecy and he being tall and pale like the god, some believed him to be the reincarnation of Lono.

Cook and his crew were treated to endless feasting, celebrations and women, and they spent a month there, enjoying the tropical idyll and replenishing their provisions. But on their departure they angered the Hawaiians by taking the carved wooden prayer poles from Lono's temple instead of cutting down trees for firewood.

When a storm broke their mast and Cook limped, ungodlike, back into the harbour a few weeks later, the welcome was not so rapturous. Relations broke down further when the Hawaiians took a boat and Cook tried to capture the high chief as a hostage. Fighting broke out, the crew shot one of the chiefs and all hell broke loose, with Cook being stabbed to death in the melee. It was an ignominious death for the explorer, yet his discovery of Hawaii marked the beginning of foreign visitors and a western influence that transformed the islands.

It also coincided with the evolution from a system of many smaller chiefs governing local communities to one great king who ruled the whole island chain. On the Big Island there had long been a legend that a great leader, whose birth would be foretold by a comet streaking across the sky, would unite the islands. In 1758, as Halley's Comet lit up the heavens, a boy known as Kamehameha was born to a minor chief. The then-ruler had ordered that all children of noble blood be killed, but his parents spirited him away to be raised in secret.

Kamehameha grew up to be a powerful warrior, and became part of the regional chief's court, even meeting Cook as one of the official party. But when the chief died in 1782, Kamehameha's weaker cousin inherited the reign, and he was relegated to spiritual guardianship of Ku, the god of war. Believing he should be the ruler, Kamehameha challenged his rival, and within a few years he had become alii nui, chief of the whole island, through cleverness, intrigue and battle.

He dreamed of controlling all of the islands though, and soon assembled a massive army to carry out his plan. In 1790 he conquered nearby Maui, and within five years he'd also united Oahu and Molokai under his rule. He was helped by his favourite wife Ka'ahumanu, the guns he'd acquired after Captain Cook's visit and the prowess of two westerners who trained his troops to use firearms.

His attempts to take over the islands of Kauai and Niihau were hampered first by geographical difficulties and a perilous storm, and later by an outbreak of a fatal illness amongst his warriors, but he continued his campaign. In 1810, facing another onslaught, the chief of Kauai pledged his allegiance through treaty to avoid the bloodshed of his people, and Kamehameha founded the Kingdom of Hawaii.

In Cook's wake the new king developed strong ties with the British, adopting some of their political institutions and unifying the legal system. He maintained Hawaii as an independent rather than a colonial power, refusing to allow foreigners to own land. Today he's remembered as the great warrior king who united the islands, and is celebrated on Kamehameha Day on June 11 every year.

This first monarch was a follower of the traditional Hawaiian religion, but after his death in 1819 there was huge social upheaval. His son Liholiho, known as Kamehameha II, inherited the crown, but it was his widow Ka'ahumanu who ruled the islands, declaring that the king had wanted his wife and son to share the office. The role of kuhina nui, the equivalent of a prime minister, was created for her, and she enacted laws and governed the people as queen regent.

She fought for Native Hawaiian and women's rights, and the continuation of the unification of Hawaii. When she feared Kauai would break its treaty, she kidnapped the chief and forced him to marry her, keeping him a subject of the monarchy. And just six months after she and Kamehameha II took power, she convinced him to have a public meal with her – violating the ban on women eating with men.

This event marked the end of the kapu system instituted by Pa'ao, and caused a crisis of faith amongst Hawaiians. They began to question their gods, challenge the laws and dismantle many of the heiaus. When the first Christian missionaries arrived a year later from Boston (led by Hiram Bingham, whose grandson would later rediscover Machu Picchu in Peru), they found the islanders in a spiritual void.

Queen Ka'ahumanu befriended the missionaries and allowed them to build churches and preach their gospels throughout the islands. Within four years she had publicly announced that she had joined the Protestant faith, and was encouraging her subjects to do the same.

There were positives – the missionaries built schools, created a written language based on spoken Hawaiian and provided medical care to the locals, many of whom were suffering from smallpox, cholera, measles, tuberculosis, syphilis and influenza that had been brought to the islands by whalers, sailors and merchants.

On the flipside, horrified by what they considered lewd behaviour, the missionaries banned the hula dances and chants that were such an important part of Hawaiian tradition, outlawed the healing methods of the kahunas and forced their own conservative morals – and dress – on the islanders. They told them that the spread of the new diseases, such as leprosy and smallpox, was God's punishment for their sins, and they convinced Ka'ahumanu to expel their rival Catholic missionaries and forbid Catholic worship.

By 1824 Hawaii had become a Protestant Christian nation. Kamehameha II, who refused to give up the old gods, died of measles, which he had no immunity to, when he and his wife sailed to England to meet King George IV. He was succeeded by his younger brother Kauikeaouli, who became King Kamehameha III and ruled for almost thirty years. He too maintained his own traditional beliefs, but he legalised Catholicism and decreed that all religions be tolerated.

During this time Hawaii had become a popular stop for traders. Livestock was brought to the islands, and from 1825 to 1870 it was the whaling capital of the Pacific. The sugar industry also began, and soon sugarcane plantations covered the islands. It became the economic mainstay for a century, and also transformed society. With up to two thirds of the Native Hawaiian population wiped out by introduced diseases, the plantations began importing cheap foreign labour from Japan, China and Portugal, and later the Philippines and Korea.

This led to the unique melting pot of cultures that Hawaii is celebrated for today, and introduced new traditions borrowed from Buddhism, Judaism, Islam and other world religions. Today the Hawaiian people embrace a varied spirituality that ranges from Christianity and Buddhism to Islam, Wicca, Scientology, Hinduism, the Bahai faith and atheism, and incorporates sixty ethnic groups.

"The King is the sovereign of all the people and all the chiefs. He shall be the chief judge of the Supreme Court, and it shall be his duty to execute the laws of the land, form treaties with the rulers of all other kingdoms, have the power to make war in time of emergency, and be the commander-in-chief."

Constitution of the Kingdom of Hawaii, 1840

Kamehameha III created a progressive kingdom. By 1840 he'd written a constitution and created a House of Nobles and a House of Representatives made up of elected officials, which gave political power to the common people while confirming the rule of the king and his heirs. He moved the royal capital from Lahaina in Maui to Oahu's Honolulu in 1845. Three years later he presided over a series of land reforms known as the Great Mahele, which was intended to make things fairer for all, but in fact left Native Hawaiians homeless and allowed foreign businessmen to buy up land and take control of the islands.

In 1852 he was pressured to amend the constitution to increase the powers of the elected legislature, and American plantation owners, the children of the missionaries and other outsiders all increased their political influence. Tourism began – author Mark Twain spent five months in Hawaii in 1866, traipsing around the volcanoes, attempting to surf and writing glowing, adventure-laden articles for US journals that attracted more and more visitors to the islands. And the Americans continued to increase their own profits while eroding away the rights and way of life of the Native Hawaiians.

In 1874 King David Kalakaua took the throne. Known as the Merrie Monarch, he was celebrated for reintroducing cultural practices such as the hula, kahuna healing, surfing and the martial art of lua. He fought for the independence of the islands and the welfare and wellbeing of his people. But the plantation owners wanted one of their own in power, so lawyer Lorrin Thurston, the grandson of Christian missionaries, formed the revolutionary Hawaiian League, which planned to overthrow the monarchy so they could control the wealth.

In 1887 they forced King Kalakaua to sign a new constitution, known as the Bayonet Constitution for the threats of violence that obtained his signature. It reduced him to a figurehead, created a new cabinet comprised of league members and gave foreigners the vote while stripping it from most locals, diminishing the voice of Native Hawaiians within politics and thus putting an end to self-government.

In January 1891 King Kalakaua died, and his sister Queen Liliuokalani took the throne. She was determined to wrest control back for the people of Hawaii, but Thurston and his cronies were too powerful. They plotted to overthrow the monarchy and annex the islands to the United States – a move backed by US president Benjamin Harrison.

When Liliuokalani wrote a new constitution to restore the power of the throne and the rights of Hawaiians, the insurgents sprang into action.

On January 17, 1893, the Hawaiian Kingdom was overthrown in an armed coup backed by the US Marines. Liliuokalani gave up the crown to prevent bloodshed, assuming the US government would soon restore order. The American flag was raised over the palace, and Thurston set sail for Washington to have the annexation approved.

President Harrison sent it to the Senate, but he lost office before it was passed and his successor, Grover Cleveland, withdrew the treaty and mounted an investigation. He proclaimed the Hawaiian takeover unjust, the intervention of the US Marines unauthorised and the military demonstration an act of war. He promised to reinstate the queen – but Thurston and his comrades refused to give up power.

They proclaimed a new constitution, cutting Native Hawaiian rights even further, and on July 4, 1894, Thurston's colleague Sanford Dole declared himself president of the new Republic of Hawaii.

"We want to conserve our people and our lands, our traditions and our language. We cannot let them be wiped out. To us it's very clear, it's part of the process of strong, distinct self-identity. I consider myself to be speaking like my ancestors, from our ancestors, because of our ancestors."

Dr Kekuni Blaisdell, Hawaiian doctor and sovereignty leader

In January 1895 the Hawaiians rebelled, but their leaders were arrested and Liliuokalani was imprisoned. When she was finally released two years later and went to Washington to appeal for the restoration of her kingdom, it was too late – President Cleveland was out of office, and his successor William McKinley had approved the annexation. While Cleveland maintained: "I am ashamed of the whole affair," and Native Hawaiians complained that their rights had been trampled, on July 7, 1898 the island kingdom became the Territory of Hawaii, a US possession similar to a colony – although the legality of this takeover remains in question today.

This move allowed plantation owners to again exploit cheap foreign labour. They started planting pineapples, which soon rivalled sugarcane as Hawaii's best cash crop. In 1922 farmer James Dole – Sanford Dole's cousin – bought the whole of Lanai and transformed the entire island into a pineapple plantation that employed a thousand workers and their families. Further plantations were established, and for a long time Hawaii grew more than eighty per cent of the world's pineapples, with labour provided by low-paid immigrants.

The economy and the government were ruled by the "Big Five", sugar companies that oversaw all business and controlled elections, forcing their workers to vote the way they wanted and creating an oligarchy, a form of government controlled by the rich elite. They ensured only white Republicans had power, and turned the rest of the population – Native Hawaiians and those of Chinese, Japanese, Filipino, Portuguese and other ancestry – into a poor underclass with few rights.

In 1920, with the first non-stop flight to Honolulu from the American mainland, the islands became a major tourist destination. But it was the events of World War II that convinced the US that Hawaii should become a state. On December 7, 1941, the Japanese bombed Honolulu's Pearl Harbor, killing more than two thousand American soldiers and forcing the US to join the war. Today the USS Arizona Memorial at Pearl Harbor is a haunting reminder of the war and a top tourist attraction.

On August 21, 1959, Hawaii was proclaimed the 50th US state by President Dwight Eisenhower, and it has remained so ever since – although there's now a strong movement dedicated to restoring Hawaiian sovereignty. In 1993, a hundred years after the overthrow of the monarchy, the US government made the Apology Resolution, passed by Congress and signed by President Bill Clinton, which apologised to Native Hawaiians for the overthrow of their kingdom and the deprivation of their rights, and admitted that the US minister involved had conspired to overthrow the indigenous and lawful government of Hawaii.

It also acknowledged that the health and prosperity of Native Hawaiians is intrinsically tied to their deep attachment to the land, and that the economic and social changes of the 19th and 20th centuries were devastating to their physical and spiritual wellbeing.

Along with the campaign for sovereignty, there's also been a strong push to preserve the traditional culture of the islands. Like indigenous communities around the world, the loss of their land, spirituality and language led to disadvantage in terms of education and health care, with higher rates of homelessness, substance abuse and incarceration.

The Office of Hawaiian Affairs was created in 1978 to promote the language and culture and better the conditions of the islanders through political, legal and educational channels – what the old monarchs had been fighting for. America recognised Hawaiian as the second official language, after English, and young people began learning it again.

At the same time a resurgence in traditional wisdom began, with elders sharing their knowledge and teaching such culturally specific traditions as hula, native healing and chanting. While the increase in tourism in the 1960s saw sacred sites levelled to build fancy resorts, by the 1980s there was a groundswell of people concerned with conserving their history and their sacred places, which continues today. Native Hawaiians have a new pride in themselves and their history and traditions, and the world is finally realising the importance and immense beauty of a culture and spirituality with so much to offer.

The purpose

"The Hawaiians have that joy and appreciation for living in their blood. There's something pure about them and the simple way that they still live life that draws me to them. It's the mystique of joy they exude in living a fuller life, which I can talk about but not stay in touch with, let alone exude from my innermost being, as I witness in the Hawaiian people."

Pila Chiles, Hawaiian resident, huna teacher, author

People are drawn to Hawaii by its incredible beauty and the sense of joy it encapsulates. It's the dream destination for honeymoons and fantasy vacations because the islands represent love and happiness, which comes from the spirit of the people as well as the land itself. Everything from the strength of the sunshine to the cleansing purity of the waterfalls and the gentle colours of the sunsets seems designed to reconnect visitors to a state of joy.

Some people attain this simply by soaking up the blissful relaxation of this tropical paradise and its beaches, massages and slowed-down pace. Others find it through absorbing the transformative earth energy and ancient wisdom of the place and visiting the sacred sites. And many are uplifted by the stunning beauty of nature and the healing power of the islands. Hawaii is blessed with crystal clear oceans that cleanse and soothe, bounteous sunshine that warms heart and soul, warm trade winds that keep the islands free of pollution, and pure air that revitalises and awakens all who breathe it in.

Air contains positive and negative ions. Positive ions make you feel tired, sluggish and depressed, while negative ions energise and refresh you emotionally and physically. Negative ions are most abundant in nature – in tropical thunderstorms, high in the mountains, down at the beach and beside thundering waterfalls – which is one more reason that spending time in Hawaii makes you feel so alive and exhilarated.

Another of nature's joy-inspiring gifts is the rainbow, and one of my overwhelming memories of Hawaii is of how many I saw, and the incredible happiness they instilled in me. Few things can lift the spirits as easily as these gorgeous arcs, which touch the soul with the harmony of their hues and the deep vibration of each colour. They've been described as the most spectacular light show on earth, and have inspired centuries of poets with their mysterious, fragile beauty.

To the Ancient Greeks, rainbows were known as the path between heaven and earth, and the symbol of Iris, the messenger of the gods.

In Norse legend the rainbow joined the realm of the deities with that of humans, in China it was used by the creator goddess Nuwa to seal the sky after calamity, and in Australia the rainbow serpent was the initiator of life. Christians believed a rainbow was a covenant between them and their god after the flood, and to many cultures it was the route to the afterlife – the pathway of souls to Native Americans, the floating bridge of heaven in Japan and the way to the upper world for Polynesians – while in Ireland it was the road to the pot of gold the leprechauns had hidden, symbolic of the fulfilment of dreams.

In Hawaii, where rainbows are known as anuenue, there's a legend about Kahala the Rainbow Maiden, the beautiful daughter of the wind and the rain. After being killed by a jealous suitor, she was brought back to life by her true love and his kahuna brother, and resided with him forever in their home in Manoa Valley, the royal palace of rainbows, with the colourful arch stretched permanently above to show their love and happiness to all.

Throughout these tropical islands, where the heavenly prisms dance constantly across the skies, rainbows were considered a representation of the goddess Hina, and a truly magical occurrence. Hawaii is known around the world as the land of rainbows, and its people long referred to themselves as the Children of the Rainbow. The goddess Anuenue is said to have saved the life of the rain god Ua by catching him in her coloured arch and breaking his fall, and chiefs were believed to be accompanied by rainbows throughout their lives.

At Rainbow Falls near Hilo on the Big Island, countless beautiful rainbows appear in the mist and across the curtain of cascading water. It's not the biggest waterfall – nearby Akaka Falls is five times the size – but it has a beauty and delicacy that touches the heart. The sparkling waters of Wailuku River rush over the edge and drop more than 25 metres into the large, dark lagoon below. This turquoise pool, fringed with wild ginger, mango trees and vines and lit up by rainbows, is surrounded by a deep, verdant gorge, and it's easy to forget how close you are to the city as the tranquillity washes over you. Behind the curtain of the falls is a deep cave where the goddess Hina once dwelled, which adds to the sense of mystery and magic.

It's especially beautiful there in the morning, when the sun rises from the ocean and shines its golden light onto the misty water, creating the most vivid, enchanting rainbows. It's also stunning after rain, when the river swells and the water plunges down into the pool in a thundering torrent that fills you with respect and love for all of nature and its impressive, soul-soothing power.

Rainbows have always fascinated me. The only lesson I remember from my first year of school is learning the colours and their order, Roy G Biv – red, orange, yellow, green, blue, indigo, violet – and being intrigued by the beauty of the shades melding together. I love that they're part of nature's alchemy, created by light being reflected and refracted within water droplets, and present wherever there's water in the air and sunlight behind the person observing.

Rainbows are common in waterfalls, mist, the spray of ocean waves and when the sun appears after rain, which is why there are so many in the watery, sun-drenched paradise of Hawaii. And while they don't really exist in the physical – they're an optical illusion unique to the observer – their ephemeral essence doesn't diminish their romance or impact, it just adds to their power and beauty.

Meditating on the colours of the rainbow and breathing in their vibration is energising and uplifting. Nature is mind-blowing and incredibly healing, the highest form of magic there is, and definitely worthy of the reverence in which cultures such as Hawaii's held it.

"Chakras are bright wheels of energy spinning within your physical body. Your chakra system holds within it your ancestral records, relationship history, beliefs about yourself and your power and connection to the divine. The health of your chakras is therefore directly linked to your physical, mental and spiritual wellbeing."
Natalie Southgate, Australian psychotherapist
and founder of Chakradance

In addition to the rainbow connection, the seven main islands of Hawaii are being linked to the seven chakras of the human body. Chakras are energy centres that absorb light, vitality and energy from the universe, nourishing you emotionally and physically and helping balance body, mind and spirit. Long identified in eastern philosophy, they are slowly becoming more widely accepted in western belief systems. They each have a physical location in the body and are associated with organs and bodily functions, but are more etheric in composition. They can be visualised as a lotus flower, a sparkling jewel or a fan spinning around within you – the word is Sanskrit for wheel, and some traditions describe them as spinning wheels of light.

The chakras are aligned vertically, with the first one at the base of the spine, the next ones spaced out along it and the top one at the crown of the head. In a similar layout, the islands of Hawaii correspond to each chakra, beginning with the Big Island at the base and stretching northward to Niihau, the crown chakra. Interestingly, the colours that have long been attributed to each island through its official flower and its hula school also coincide with the colour of the related chakra.

Spending time on the Big Island then moving northwards through the other islands, focusing on the issues of each chakra as you absorb the corresponding earth energy, is an amazing healing journey.

The Big Island corresponds to the first or root chakra, known as Muladhara in Sanskrit, which is positioned at the base of the spine. Its colour is red, and it's associated with the element of earth. It's the chakra centre most attached to survival, security, self-protection and having physical needs met, and is the foundation of existence. Its main purpose is to ground you physically, and it channels energy from the earth up into the body, and also returns the toxicity of unwanted emotions and past pain to the earth for transmutation.

The Big Island, with its fiery power and energy of creation and new beginnings, is aligned with this purpose. Spending time there grounds you physically and helps you realise the things you no longer need and then release them. There's a destructive element to this energy that can be harnessed for personal growth, because the volcanic eruptions wipe out whatever is in their path and leave a fresh slate. The flames, fire and flowing lava activate the life force of the land, and your soul.

The base chakra is also where the kundalini life force resides, the cosmic energy that helps you fulfil your dreams. When awakened, it sends the energy of potential up through the body and washes the other chakras with happiness, love and light. In much the same way the Big Island, as the root chakra of Hawaii, purifies and cleanses the other islands with its fiery energy, and blesses visitors to its dramatic shores with healing, grounding and balance.

Maui aligns with the second or sacral chakra, known as Svadisthana, which is located in the navel region about five centimetres below the bellybutton. Its colour is orange, and it's associated with the element of water. It's the centre most attached to giving and receiving love and the ability to see yourself as loveable, and is related to relationships, sensuality and sex. Healing an imbalance in this chakra can require coming to terms with feelings of guilt and pain regarding sexuality, and learning to see it as a form of spiritual union and a connection with the universal energies, rather than something fearful or wrong.

In this way Maui is the perfect fit. Considered the pleasure isle of Hawaii, it's filled with lush jungles, invigorating waterfalls, languid heat on white sand beaches and a nightclub strip that inspires steamy sensuality. Visitors to Maui spend much of their time in the water too, swimming, surfing, kiteboarding and windsurfing, while its sacred mountain Haleakala warms the soul with its incandescent sunrises.

When this chakra is balanced you experience unconditional love, the state of aloha so prevalent on Maui. It's also the energy centre of self-expression and joy, so being creative – whether it be through art, dance, singing, writing or cooking – helps activate it. While many healers have moved to the Big Island, it is artists who are drawn to Maui, and the energy of the island is inspiring to all who travel there.

Lanai, off the northwest coast of Maui, connects to the third or solar plexus chakra, known as Manipura, located about five centimetres above the navel. Its colour is yellow, and it's associated with the element of fire. This energy centre defines your self-esteem and personal power, and the small island of Lanai, which translates as day of conquest, relates to this. It's long been owned and controlled by one company, and only slowly is power being diluted and redistributed.

Power is the key issue of this chakra, and if you can balance yours, by transforming controlling tendencies to confidence, it will activate your own inner fire and burn away all obstacles to achieving what you seek. Many people visualise this chakra as an inner sun within the abdomen, drawing in solar energy to revitalise the body. Lanai, which is known as the Pineapple Isle and is famous for its sunny golden beaches, corresponds to the colour and element of the solar plexus.

This is the location of the "gut instincts" that are constantly received yet often ignored, and developing its intuitive powers can increase your wellbeing and help you manifest. Spending time at Lanai, famous for its laid-back resort lifestyle and gentle water activities, helps reawaken this chakra and inspires a sensation of calm centredness so you can feel strong and powerful within yourself.

Molokai corresponds to the fourth or heart chakra, known as Anahata, which is located in the centre of the chest. Its colours are green and pink, and it's associated with the element of air. This energy centre is all about love, including unconditional love and compassion for all things, and an interconnectedness of spirit and aloha that transcends the physical. It's the central chakra, bridging the physical elements of the lower three with the spirituality of the upper three, and is aligned with spiritual inspiration and universal love.

Appreciating and connecting to nature is a simple way to open up your heart chakra, and the island of Molokai, a sparsely populated, old-world place, is the perfect location for this. It's covered with beautiful green forests, stunning cliffs that can be climbed down or kayaked around, and gentle rolling hills. Many consider Molokai the heart of Hawaii, the least affected by invasion and foreign influence, and the most true to the feeling of the islands.

If your heart chakra is blocked you can feel fearful, drained of energy and withdrawn from the world. Breathing also becomes shallow as you forget to connect with this most essential of energies, but simply inhaling fresh air and flooding your body with oxygen can activate this energy centre. The air on Molokai is clear and pure, and you can breathe it in while walking through the rainforests or along the beaches to connect with the heart chakra, the flowing energy of your body and the compassionate love that's the centre of your being.

Oahu relates to the fifth or throat chakra, known as Vishuddha, which is located in the area of the neck and shoulders. Its colour is blue, and its element is spirit as well as sound. It's concerned with self-expression and communication, and helps you define and affirm your life and the feelings of your heart. It's also linked to authenticity and speaking your truth, and a sore throat or lost voice can result if you aren't expressing your inner thoughts and beliefs or being true to yourself.

Oahu, known as the Gathering Place, is recognised as the voice of the islands. It's where more than seventy per cent of Hawaiians make their home, and is the location of the government, universities and primary industries. It's the place where Queen Liliuokalani cried out to the world for justice for her people as the monarchy was being overthrown, and today an increasing number of elders are coming forward here to communicate the old wisdom of this beautiful island.

It is within the throat chakra that the possibility for transformation, change and healing resides, but it's also the place where many people hold anger and repressed thoughts, so it's important to balance its energies by expressing your truth and higher wisdom. This allows your inner light to shine, which inspires others too. You can awaken the throat centre by absorbing the earth energy of Oahu, or by chanting, in the way the Native Hawaiians once did, singing or even screaming.

Kauai aligns with the sixth or brow chakra, known as Ajna and the third eye chakra, which is located in the centre of the brow, between and slightly above the eyes. Its colour is indigo and it's associated with the elements of ether and light. It's linked with intuition and clarity, and can be activated through meditation. When balanced it helps purify and transmute negativity, and activates higher levels of intuition and psychic skills such as clairvoyance, prophecy and channelling.

Traditionally Kauai was a retreat centre where initiates went to study the healing arts and develop their psychic powers on their path to becoming a kahuna. In the stillness of this lush garden island meditation was – and still is – more easily achieved, and the deep connection to nature that is so tangible here helps open the third eye chakra and connect you to the spirits and the Otherworld. If you are too caught up in the modern world and too cut off from the peace and tranquillity of nature you could have blockages in this area, and need to slow down, breathe deeply and go outside for a while to rebalance.

Today there's a Hindu monastery on the island as well as many spiritual retreats, continuing the tradition of contemplation and opening to the divine source. Many people also find inspiration and insight while walking through majestic Waimea Canyon, visiting the enchanting gardens and breathing in the pure air, the power of the crashing waves and the many rainbows painted across the heavens.

Niihau, a tiny island off the west coast of Kauai, connects to the seventh or crown chakra, known as Sahasrara, which is located at the crown of the head. Its colour is violet, and its element is thought. It's the centre of pure consciousness, a balance of masculine and feminine, sun and moon, and a higher consciousness not often accessed. It's the centre of spirituality and enlightenment, and some believe it's where the soul enters the body at birth and leaves at death. Its issues relate to inner wisdom and transcendence of the self.

Niihau is known as the Forbidden Isle, and represents the hidden wisdom of the Native Hawaiians. In 1864 it was bought by a Scottish widow, Eliza Sinclair, and since then it's been cut off from the influence of the outside world, which has protected and conserved the Old Ways. Access is limited to the family and the few hundred Native Hawaiian residents who work their ranch. Everyone who lives there speaks Hawaiian – it's the only island where it's the primary language – and all the children learn the customs and rural lifestyle that's been typical of these islands for more than a thousand years, fishing and farming to survive, with no electricity or running water.

Eliza's descendants have continued the tradition of protecting the culture and spiritual wisdom of Niihau's residents, making it a unique, valuable and mysterious place. Very limited day tours of this pristine, undeveloped island can be arranged, although they're restricted to a helicopter tour of the island and landing on one of the beaches, which maintains the mystique and spiritual purity of the place.

While the base chakra grounds you in the physical, the crown chakra is the place of spirit, of higher consciousness and connection to universal wisdom. When all the chakras are balanced and activated, people describe a kind of bliss, an understanding of the self as part of the universe, and a wave of love and compassion that embraces all of life. Perhaps Hawaii's ability to align the chakras in those who visit is one more reason that spending time in the islands is so healing.

"As humans we want happiness – the dolphins have found this. We want peace of mind – when we swim with wild dolphins, we find it with them. They have a twinkle in their eyes that says: 'Let's play!' They're intelligent friends who exemplify qualities we value – co-operation, harmony, peace, joyfulness, good health, beauty, wisdom, grace and unconditional love."
Joan Ocean, Hawaiian dolphin researcher, psychologist and author

Swimming with dolphins, which has been shown to transform, heal and fill you with joy, is another motivation for many people to visit Hawaii. There is something so beautifully uplifting about swimming with these gentle sea creatures, and the crystal clear, sunlight-dappled waters of the island chain, especially off the Kona Coast of the Big Island, are the perfect place to experience it.

Just watching them dance in the ocean, catching waves, leaping in amazing acrobatic feats and playing with each other with such grace and warmth touches the heart, and immersing yourself in their world and swimming alongside them is even more powerful and magical. Staring into their eyes fills you with the most overwhelming sense of love, peace and acceptance you can imagine. Many people cry, and others laugh almost hysterically, when a dolphin gazes at them. It feels as though they're looking deep within your soul, filling any emptiness with joy and replacing any pain with love.

One of the most beautiful experiences I've ever had was swimming with dolphins in their natural environment, which has become a very popular activity in Hawaii. As the boat sailed out from the shore and our small group sat listening to the captain talk about marine conservation, and the local dolphins and their particular traits and personalities, right on cue two began keeping pace with us. They raced alongside the boat, spinning over and over and showing us their bellies, and we laughed joyously at their beauty and friendliness.

I slipped into the water with a facemask and snorkel and stared down in wonder at the majestic creatures beneath me. The playful mammals allowed us to come very close, and it was amazing – they looked bigger underwater, and even more graceful and effortless in their movements. There were three at first, twisting and turning below us, peeking curiously up at us then swimming alongside us. They jumped around a fair bit and frolicked so joyously amongst us, arcing through the air, diving down beneath the surface, swimming off to catch a fish then returning to where we were treading water.

Later, as we spread out a bit, one came over to me and stopped right below me, suspended in the golden green water, so big and gentle and full of grace. I peered down and watched in awe as he hovered there under me, smiling upwards and slowly spinning around and showing me his white tummy. He was so close I could have touched him, but I didn't, I just stared in wonder, and he stared right back. I felt a jolt, a shiver of total peace and acceptance, and a wash of emotion that made me warm and happy inside. I could feel love radiating out from him, right to my heart, and I had a strong feeling that he was trying to tell me that everything would be okay. I had a vivid flash of my friend who had died, and the dolphin seemed to smile at me and nod. It was so touching. I felt really teary, but in a happy way.

I could sense this creature's child-like joy in just being alive – he was so playful, and it was contagious. I laughed out loud, and later the others said they too had been overcome with giggles as they swam alongside these happy, loving, peaceful mammals. We often forget how to have fun and enjoy life, too bogged down in details and situations that seem so worrying, but which stressing over doesn't actually improve. This is one of the gifts of the dolphins, to reawaken happiness within us and remind people of the importance of play.

Afterwards I felt joy simply by looking out at the ocean and picturing the dolphins dancing beneath the waves. And even now, a few years later, I can still recapture the feeling of happiness and peace I experienced with them. The unconditional love and acceptance they exude opens the heart and improves physical and emotional wellbeing – hence the smile I couldn't wipe off my face for days after my swim!

On the Big Island, local swimmers have forged loving relationships with the dolphins off Kona, interacting with them daily, calling them by name and developing a way of communicating with them and learning from them. Some of the dolphins have even approached these human friends for help when they've had fishing line wound around them, been tangled in plastic bags or had fish hooks embedded in their skin.

A few people in Kona facilitate dolphin swims, and through their daily interactions with these beautiful sea creatures they know where they're most likely to be at a certain time. However their protection and wellbeing is the main priority. They are wild animals, and all human-dolphin encounters take place on their terms. Our boat never chased them – we let the dolphins come to us, and were filled with gratitude and love that they did grace us with their presence.

Swimming with the dolphins is a beautiful, spiritual experience, which touches your heart and opens you up to a new way of seeing the world. Dolphins are renowned for their abilities as healers and communicators, and generate an awesome feeling of wellbeing in everyone who encounters them. Their healing transmissions affect people on all levels – physical, emotional, mental and spiritual. Increasingly those with illnesses and chronic disease go swimming with wild dolphins as a type of therapy, with Hawaii and Florida prominent destinations, and new research is also uncovering ways to duplicate the therapeutic effects of the dolphins in a lab or pool, so this healing can be accessed anywhere.

Dolphin Assisted Therapy is becoming popular around the world, with some medical professionals acknowledging the powerful benefits of interacting with these beautiful mammals. Amazing healings have been reported by people suffering from autism, cerebral palsy, ADHD, depression, multiple sclerosis, Down syndrome, stress, phobias, addiction, arthritis and many other conditions. And incredible emotional healings have occurred when *Law & Order: SVU* star Mariska Hargitay, whose work on the TV show inspired her to create the Joyful Heart Foundation to help victims of sexual assault recover, organised Hawaiian retreats so these women could swim with dolphins.

Recent studies have shown that interacting with dolphins increases the production and uptake of neurotransmitters such as dopamine and can trigger the production of neurochemicals. Interacting with dolphins also influences and changes human brain patterns, creating a more restful, relaxed state conducive to healing. The dolphins' sonar is believed to stimulate the immune system, resonate against and heal the spine, skull and brain, and zap infected cells or diseased parts of the body. The animals are often drawn to the person in a group who is sick, seeming to scan their body then send a burst of healing energy to them. Perhaps it works in the same way as other vibrational therapies, raising a person's vibration to a more healing level.

Dolphin expert and psychotherapist Olivia De Bergerac has been studying these creatures and their interactions with humans for more than fifteen years. She takes people on overnight trips to swim with them in Australia, and has recorded hundreds of cases of physical as well as spiritual and emotional breakthroughs. In addition to keeping detailed journals and conducting follow-up sessions with participants, she uses an electroencephalograph (EEG) machine to monitor changes in people's brain activity before and after a dolphin encounter.

The human brain operates at different frequencies of electrical activity. Usually it's in the beta range, a higher frequency that helps you focus, concentrate and take action – but which can lead to anxiety and stress if not balanced by also spending time in a more relaxed, alpha frequency state, which is conducive to good health, and can be achieved through meditation and relaxation techniques. An even slower frequency, theta, occurs in the time between waking and sleeping or in deep meditation, and helps you access the subconscious, grasp elusive ideas and experience deep healing.

Olivia noticed a change in people's brains, from stress-related beta brainwaves to alpha or theta waves, after they swam with dolphins – which helps explain the sense of peace and wellbeing felt when interacting with them. And she found these states could be accessed again, long after leaving the water and returning to daily life, by simply recalling the dolphin encounter – which was certainly true for me.

Swimming with dolphins is transformative and healing, and can help you overcome fears and self-limiting thought patterns. People often experience an intense emotional release after being in the water with these beautiful creatures, and manage to let go of pain, grief, loneliness and anger. This helps you reconnect to your true self, attune to and increase your intuition, remember who you really are and realise your full potential. Dolphins are a catalyst for emotional change, physical healing and regeneration, and a reminder of the importance of play. They will open your heart, fill you with an overwhelming feeling of love, and leave you in a state of joy.

The psychic connection

Quick tips to soak up the essence of Hawaii

1. Learn to surf. Surfing was a central part of traditional Hawaiian culture, a spiritual as well as physical endeavour, and is believed to have originated here. Long ago the chiefs would ride a wooden board across the face of a breaking wave, mimicking the gods, and although the missionaries banned it for a time, the locals later began a revival. Spending time out in the ocean, at one with the forces of nature and connected to the wind and waves, is a thrilling, liberating and spiritual pursuit, and those who do it consider it a near-religious experience.

2. Get a hula hoop and rediscover the joyful abandon of this child-like pursuit. While it isn't strictly Hawaiian, it got its name from the 18th century sailors who visited the islands and were amazed by the similarities between the hula dancing of Hawaii and the practice of hooping. Now it's been embraced as a fitness activity to tone the tummy and increase circulation, but it's also great fun, reconnecting you to the happiness that is the foundation of health and the mind-body-spirit philosophy of Hawaii, and opening and balancing the chakras.

3. Meditate on rainbows. These graceful arcs represent harmony because they incorporate all the colours of the light spectrum, flowing into each other and blending to create new hues. They uplift the spirit with their beauty – the rainbows that dance around my office, created by sunlight shining on a spinning crystal pendant in the window, are a constant source of delight, and you can also absorb rainbow energy by painting them, displaying photos or stickers, working with a moonstone crystal or a prism, or simply dressing in bright clothes.

4. Breathe! If you're stressed, anxious or just not paying attention, your breathing can become shallow, the automatic bare minimum to stay alive, rather than the deep inhalations that re-energise, invigorate and connect you to your inner self. The Hawaiians have always known the importance of breath. Aloha, their word for love, literally translates as "with breath", while haole, foreigner, translates as "without breath", because when the missionaries arrived locals were surprised by their lack of spiritual power and assumed they lacked mana, the breath of life. Doctors have found deep breathing can lower blood pressure, decrease stress, ease panic attacks and induce a state of calm and clarity.

5. Swim with dolphins. There are now many places around the world where you can interact with these incredible sea creatures, from Australia and the Bahamas to Israel and Russia. You can also align yourself with their healing energies and joyful emotions by watching them leap around in the ocean and play in the waves, listening to dolphin sounds, viewing documentaries about them, creating or buying dolphin artwork, connecting with them through guided meditations or doing something to help conserve their habitat.

The armchair traveller's way to visit

"A kahuna is a priest or priestess, a spiritual teacher. They act as human bridges between the spiritual world and its laws and the material world with its trials, sadness and problems. Kahunas were common to all Polynesian societies, similar to your medical profession. An essential part of native life and social structure, a kahuna might be a judge, doctor or head of a church."
David Kaonohiokala Bray, Hawaiian kahuna and author

The Native Hawaiians were deeply connected to the earth and nature, so studying their spiritual philosophy is a good way to connect with the energy of their land. The kahunas were the keepers of spirituality and wisdom, knowledgeable in many areas, and variously defined as priest, sorcerer, wizard, minister and expert. Master canoe makers, temple builders and navigators were also called kahunas, but today the word is more commonly associated with healing and spirituality.

Like the shamans of other indigenous cultures, kahunas were primarily healers and counsellors, who treated the sick, promoted wellbeing, advised the chiefs and the community, and foretold how best to farm the land and harness the forces of nature. The highest ranked kahuna was second only to the royal chief in status and authority – he was an influential and powerful high priest who worked with the alii, while other kahunas were more like family doctors, offering physical and emotional healing to their village.

While they all had a wide general knowledge of healing, like modern GPs they often specialised in one area, be it the field of their ancestors, who handed down their wisdom within the family, or something they had a special affinity with. There were more than twenty different types of healers, including experts in herbal medicine, childbirth, bone setting, massage, diagnosis and emotional healing. And, in a time when illness was often attributed to the anger of the gods or a sorcerer's incantation, there were also those who specialised in communicating with the spirit plane and returning the illness to its source.

Today Hawaiian herbalism – called la'au lapa'au – is undergoing a resurgence as people experience the effectiveness of the remedies and western medicine studies it for clues to fight modern diseases. Herbal remedies can be blended to treat a wide array of physical ailments, and are often prescribed in a holistic manner that includes prayer, exercise and massage. Many healers from around the world are now finding common ground between ancient and modern medical methods, and are combining and sharing the wisdom of each.

Hawaiian massage, known as lomi lomi, is also becoming popular for its power to soothe and heal on many levels. A simple way to connect with the energy of the islands is to indulge in a treatment, or learn how to perform this unique form of massage yourself.

The aim of lomi lomi is to release physical and energetic blockages, which is achieved with a combination of long, gentle, flowing strokes and deep therapeutic pressure, using the hands, forearms and elbows on the full length of the patient's body. It has immense physical benefits, soothing aching muscles, draining toxins from the lymphatic system and correcting skeletal imbalances, and people report feeling energised rather than lethargic after one of these massages.

But lomi lomi is much more than just a physical treatment – it has been described as a journey to emotional and spiritual healing. It's a connection of the heart, hands and soul, and practitioners seem to dance around the table, entering a deep meditative state that connects them to the client and unleashes subtle healing energies.

The latter was intrinsic to Hawaiian healing, which is very much a melding of body, mind and spirit. The lomi lomi kahuna created a spiritual connection with their patient through breath, dance and aromatherapy, and worked on their emotional being as well as their body. Mana, the spiritual life force, can be generated through breathing, so linking their own breath with that of the person they were treating allowed the patient to heal on several levels.

Today, Hawaiian belief systems and healing practices are referred to as huna, although this term was only coined in the 1930s when Californian Max Freedom Long moved to Hawaii and began studying the kahunas and the secret science behind their miracles. Because native wisdom was banned then, with healers facing huge fines or jail terms if they practised their art, he named his teachings after the word for hidden. In the islands, if they used a word at all for a system that was as much a part of them as breathing, it would have been ho'omanamana, which means "creating life force", and which involved healing and empowering physically, spiritually and emotionally.

These spiritual beliefs and practices went underground following the death of King Kamehameha in 1819 and the arrival of the missionaries soon after, when spiritual healing, prayers to the old gods, hula dances, religious chants, sorcery and even herbal medicine were criminalised. Sixty years later King Kalakaua, intent on preserving Hawaiian culture and wisdom, documented the healing remedies, prayers, chants and dances in his book *The Legends and Myths of Hawaii*.

The increasingly Christian legislature was horrified by this show of native pride and knowledge, and reinforced the ban on native healers – even as recently as 1953 kahuna David Kaonohiokala Bray was arrested for performing a Hawaiian chant at Hulihee Palace in Kona.

Some of the kahunas continued to work in secret though, healing friends and family and passing the knowledge down when they could find someone who wanted to learn. In the 1970s the laws were finally overturned and herbal medicine, lomi lomi and other healing techniques became legal again. Today many elders have reclaimed the word kahuna, and the wisdom that had been hidden for so long is re-emerging. They're reviving their healing methods and passing on their skills, and many westerners have also embraced the knowledge and are writing books and teaching courses on this beautiful philosophy.

Learning the secrets of the kahuna can improve your health, heal old hurts and help you find the beauty, deep love and aloha of life. It is then, some say, that Hawaii becomes not a place across the ocean but a place within you, a state of being where you are happy, healthy and in tune with the divine power of the universe.

"The hula is Hawaii. The hula is the history of our country. The hula is a story itself. And the hula, to me, is the foundation of life. It teaches us how to live, how to respect, how to share. The hula is the ability to create one's inner feelings."
George Na'ope, Hawaiian hula master and historian,
and founder of the Merrie Monarch Festival

You can also capture the spirit of the islands by learning to dance the hula. The word itself means dance, but it was much more than that. The rhythmic movements of the hula, which holds within it the soul of the people who performed it, not only praised the chiefs, described the forces of nature and told the stories of their history, but were a prayer to the gods and a way to communicate with them.

In hula, the dancers became one with nature, the land and the gods. The best dancers were regarded as mystics, enchanters and priestesses, able to educate, entertain and create magic with their routines, and were highly acclaimed and respected. They were graceful and expressive, the result of years of study, meditation and prayer.

The hula was banned by the missionaries for being lewd, which struck at the heart of Native Hawaiians, destroying their sense of self and spiritual practice. But the experts held it in their hearts and kept it alive. In the 1950s Hawaiian hotels started using hula as a type of entertainment, which brought it into the world's consciousness, while behind the scenes the deeper meanings of the dance were revived and passed on. It's now being studied seriously by scholars, and events such as Hilo's famous Merrie Monarch Festival are reintroducing the beauty and wonder of this ancient art form to a new generation.

Today the hula is primarily, to visitors, a form of entertainment, but it holds a very deep, important place in the culture of Hawaii. Those learning the sacred dance were sequestered in special schools, halaus, and gave their life over to perfecting the intricacies of movement and story, dedicating themselves to their teacher and the goddess Laka for many years. The hula was a strong part of Hawaiian religious life, and was danced to ensure abundant crops and the successful outcome of a battle, and at weddings, funerals and other significant events.

Learning to hula dance not only connects you to the Hawaiian culture, but provides a gentle workout. It increases spinal flexibility and strengthens your core, boosts rhythm and co-ordination, helps re-align the body and improves posture. It's also used as a form of physical therapy for the elderly and people recovering from surgery or cancer, as it's been found to stimulate the lymphatic system. There are courses and classes held all over the world, in gyms and community colleges, and even a fitness video, filmed in Hawaii, based on the traditional dances.

The skill involved in mastering the basic foot, hand and hip motions that tell the stories makes it a great mind-body exercise, and it also helps open up, activate and balance the lower chakras. On a more emotional level, hula dancing releases endorphins that make you feel joyful, provides you with an inner radiance and grace and is deeply meditative, boosting wellbeing and lowering stress. And it's a spiritual pursuit that aligns you with the wisdom and history of the islands.

Associated with the hula are the chants that traditionally accompanied the dance. Without a written language, all knowledge in early Hawaiian times was passed down orally, in elaborate chants that charted epic events and the genealogy of the chiefs as well as the commoners. Some were recited alone, the voice taking on the aspect it was describing, from crashing waves to bird song, and others were performed accompanied by music and elaborate dances.

There were chants that were prayers and poems of praise, and others that were lullabies, love songs or emotional eulogies. They were all filled with spirituality and meaning, and those who were drawn to the art apprenticed for years with the kahuna mele, the chant expert. In a performance not a single word could be changed, and the learning was – and is again today – taken very seriously.

Chanting is used in many cultures as part of their religious beliefs, as a connection to the divine source and a way to attune everyone present to the same wavelength. In addition to that, it increases wellbeing because the vibrational essence of the sounds has a healing effect on the body as well as the mind. It's a powerful method of self-expression, allowing you to get your feelings and emotions out and activate the throat chakra, releasing blocks in that area. You can chant yourself, or play tapes of traditional chants, which will not only impart the wisdom of the Hawaiians but also align you vibrationally with the intent and energy of their spirituality.

An increasing number of people also visit Hawaii today to enjoy the incredible wilderness and absorb the unique environmental wisdom of the elders, and channelling their conservation beliefs and methods of protecting the islands is a good way to connect with the power of the land. Biologists are now seeking answers from the elders, employing a new strategy in their attempts to save the environment, which is based on Native Hawaiian knowledge and is called ahupua'a.

In western terms it means ecosystem restoration, and it incorporates the old tenets of caring for the earth, regulating land use, controlling access to resources and respecting and creating balance in nature. Many groups have formed to protect the unique environment of the islands, and there's even a new form of tourism emerging where visitors can spend time in nature, helping replant native flora, remove alien species, work with the community and learn about indigenous culture and traditions – something you can do in any part of the world.

In the old days, when people shared rather than owned the land, agriculture was sustainable and strictly regulated. They rotated crops, grew only what was needed for food, and everything was interconnected. The fishponds fertilised the taro patches, animals were slaughtered only when needed and every part was used, and the chiefs oversaw and protected the section of land – and especially the precious water resources – they ruled over. The kapu system, while strongly criticised for its apparent harshness, was environmentally sound. It was forbidden to take too much water from an area, cut down protected trees, pollute the wilderness or over-fish the oceans.

But when westerners flocked to Hawaii they cut down the trees and sold the wood to China, and stripped the earth to create cattle ranches and plant sugarcane. The delicate ecological balance was destroyed, and native plants and animals died out as their habitat was decimated. The new crops exhausted water supplies, cattle ate the vegetation meant for other species, and the natural balance was so damaged that today Hawaii has to import most of its food. In the 20th century alone, more than a hundred species of plants became extinct.

You can make a contribution to the wellbeing of the planet by becoming environmentally aware, because the easiest way to connect to the soul of Hawaii is to reawaken your own relationship with the earth.

The people of the islands are energised by the sunlight that warms the land, cleanse themselves energetically in the waterfalls and pure ocean waters, and breathe in the colours of the sunsets and rainbows from the top of sacred mountains. They sense that their own energy is drawn from the earth, and that they have a responsibility to protect it, love it and enjoy every moment on this beautiful planet – a form of wisdom you can adopt right now and start integrating into your life.

"Pele is the personification of majesty and power. Possessing the power to create new land, she has a volcanic personality – an impetuous and lusty nature, jealous, unpredictable, capable of sudden fury and great violence. Yet she can also be gentle, loving and as serene as her forests of ferns and flowering trees."
Herb Kawainui Kane, Hawaiian artist, historian and author

Another way to connect with the healing power of Hawaii is by working with Pele, the goddess of fire and volcanoes. She's said to live in the crater of Kilauea Volcano on the Big Island, but her energy permeates the whole island chain, and you can access her power and communicate with her from anywhere in the world. She has immense strength, and brings balance to all things, drying out too much water and warming when it's cold. Legend records her lover as Kamapua'a, the god of rain and fertility who appeared as both a handsome warrior and a pig.

Within their relationship they balanced the island with water and fire, moisture and heat, fertility and barren dryness, and it was his love for Pele that transformed her lava lands to fertile ground and allowed forests to grow. But theirs was an ill-fated romance, and he finally retreated to the cool wet valleys of the north of the island while Pele remained in the south in the fiery heat of her volcano.

Whether you feel Pele is an archetypal energy or an actual being, she represents power and life force, and a revitalising of your path and purpose. Being near her volcano and feeling her energy is an initiation of sorts, but you can invoke her no matter where you are. She's a goddess of transformation and change, and many women in particular find her strength inspiring. She represents a primordial energy of creativity and purification, which cleanses you, your emotions and your life so you can rebuild it the way you want it.

She's often portrayed as angry and destructive, being both creator and destroyer, yet she's simply full of passion and creativity. She has a fiery, active energy, and challenges you to wake up, look within, burn off the dross that has dragged you down and awaken the powers and emotions that lie dormant within you. This goddess is a true manifester, and will help you create and draw to you what you desire.

Pele can be called on to clear and purify anything that's no longer needed in your life – guilt, pain, sorrow, procrastination, the past. Ask her to help you release these things by writing to her, invoking her presence and conducting a formal ritual, or simply lighting a red candle and burning a symbol of what you want to leave behind in its flame.

She also helps you deal with, express and direct your anger, so you can use it as a powerful motivating force. When she's upset she shoots out a stream of lava that covers the earth, burning away everything in her path – but the fiery destructiveness also leaves behind a shiny new land that sparkles with beauty and potential.

Anger itself is not a bad thing, it's what you do with it that can be damaging. Some people lash out instantly without considering the consequences, while others have been taught to swallow their anger, to repress it or hide it or deny it completely. But not expressing it leaves it to eat away at your insides, which can manifest in cancers and other illnesses, or bubbling away until it final erupts like a volcano and consumes you – and often others too.

Pele teaches you how to use anger as a positive force. Understood, harnessed and expressed well it can help you change your life, release people, situations or things that don't serve you, and create new beginnings. You can use it to transform, allowing it to destroy what doesn't work for you, clearing and cleansing so you can rebuild on a stronger, more positive foundation. Pele, after helping you clear the bad from your life, will also fill you with the power and focus to rebuild, and this energy of creation is just as important as her destructive force.

Being at Pele's home and feeling her fiery energy can help you connect to her, but you don't have to go to Hawaii to do so – just looking at paintings of the goddess, invoking her in a ritual or meditating on her meaning and purpose will unlock her archetypal power. You can also work with the crystal peridot, also known as olivine, which is called the Luck of Pele. Carry a piece with you to soak up the energy and power that emanates from it, wear it in jewellery, keep a piece under your pillow or create a ritual bath with it to soak up its energies.

Another powerful Pele crystal is black obsidian, a dense volcanic glass made from molten lava that cooled too quickly to crystallise. It's produced on the Big Island, forged from the heat and vibrations of this unique land, and known as the kahuna stone. It's protective and grounding, and acts as a mirror to the soul, helping reveal your flaws and emotional blocks then providing support while you deal with them, release them and move on. It absorbs negativity from the environment as well as from people, and detoxifies the physical and emotional body, making it a powerful support in times of transformation.

Like the volcano, the energy of obsidian can sometimes be a little too cathartic, but ultimately that's a good thing, if you're ready to let go of the things holding you back and embrace the joy of life.

Postcard from Hawaii

American author Doreen Virtue teaches people around the world to communicate with the angels, increase their intuition and heal physical and emotional issues by opening up to spirit.

A psychic, former psychotherapist and fourth-generation metaphysician, she's written many inspiring books, including *Healing With the Angels*, *Divine Magic* and *The Lightworker's Way*, as well as the novel *Solomon's Angels*. She's also created several beautiful oracle card decks, such as *Messages From Your Angels*, *Saints & Angels* and *Archangel Raphael Healing Oracle Cards*, that help people tap in to their own inner wisdom with the help of angels, faeries and ascended masters.

Doreen fell in love with Hawaii as a child, and now divides her time between California and her home on the Big Island, where she communicates with the menehune, swims with the dolphins and teaches her Angel Therapy Practitioner courses amidst the powerful energy of the islands. Visit www.angeltherapy.com.

My first trip to Hawaii was when I was six. My mother took me to Honolulu, and we spent a magical time on the white sandy beaches and exploring the windy mountains and magical waterfalls. I fell in love with Hawaii right then. Although I was raised as a Southern California beach girl, I'd never seen water or sand like Hawaii's – the ocean had the most magnificent clear colours I'd ever seen, and the sand was like sugar, white and so fine and soft.

Each Hawaiian island has its own energy and personality, and I've since spent a lot of time visiting each one. I love Maui for its beautiful beaches – it's the best place on earth to go swimming! – and Kauai is magical and mysterious, but a bit too rainy for me.

In contrast to the green lushness of Maui and Kauai, the Big Island is relatively barren. When you land at the airport in Kona you feel like you're landing on the moon, because all you see are these big lava rocks. So the beauty of the Big Island is more subtle than the other islands – but for me it's the most powerful because of its rawness. The lava meeting the vivid blue ocean creates a powerful yin-yang effect, which is the basis of divine magic.

The Big Island is the only place on earth that I've experienced Mother Earth inhaling and exhaling beneath my feet. Part of its healing power comes from it being so close to nature, and I believe its raw natural surroundings – the wildness of the growth, the magnetic lava rock, the star, sun and moon light shining without the filter of air pollution, and the salty ocean water – create a metaphysical energy chemical reaction that everyone can feel and enjoy.

The goddess Pele is a big part of the island, and it's impossible not to connect with her when you're there. Her energy is Hawaii's lava, which is the physical foundation of the islands. Pele's reputation as a dark mother goddess comes from lava having magnetic qualities. This lava magnifies your thoughts and feelings, so if you're in a good mood you'll be euphoric – but if you're in a bad mood you'll be in a really foul mood! On the Big Island you instantly manifest what you're thinking about, and karma is also instant. It seems there's a mother energy there making sure you walk the straight and narrow.

I also feel Michael the Archangel very strongly when I'm there, as the island is similar to his strong and loving power. Both Michael and the Big Island are simultaneously gentle and strong. And I feel the spirit of nature – the Hawaiian faeries called menehunes – very strongly when I'm in the wilderness too.

The wild spinner and bottlenose dolphins who are always near the Kona coastline are also healing. I've been in the water with them many times, and these amazing beings are definitely teachers and healers. They're exquisitely psychic, and stay away from people who are chasing them. Dolphins help those who are sad or in need of healing, and love to be around people who have their hearts wide open with love.

One of my most profound experiences with the dolphins was after I'd spent the morning cleaning up fishing line while scuba diving, which I call underwater housekeeping. After I got back on the boat a pod of dolphins surfaced nearby. I jumped back in the water without my scuba gear, and had three dolphins with me, one on each side and one beneath me. They were thanking me for cleaning up the fishing line! We swam around and around for ages, then they escorted me to the stairs of the boat to climb back onboard.

Being in Hawaii deepens and enriches my work because everything about it helps with intuition and psychic abilities, including the island's fresh air, warm sunshine, clean ocean salt water, open-hearted people, sun-ripened fruits and vegetables, fragrant flowers and the slow pace of life. And when I teach in Hawaii my students' readings go really well, because the island opens your natural spiritual gifts.

But you don't even have to go there to experience all of this – you can "visit" Hawaii energetically by simply looking at a photo of a Hawaiian beach or sunset and imagining you're there. Allow all of your senses to experience the sensations, sights, sounds and smells of Hawaii in this visualisation. And breathe deeply, because the aloha spirit is all about breath and having an open heart full of love for yourself and everyone around you.

GREAT
BRITAIN

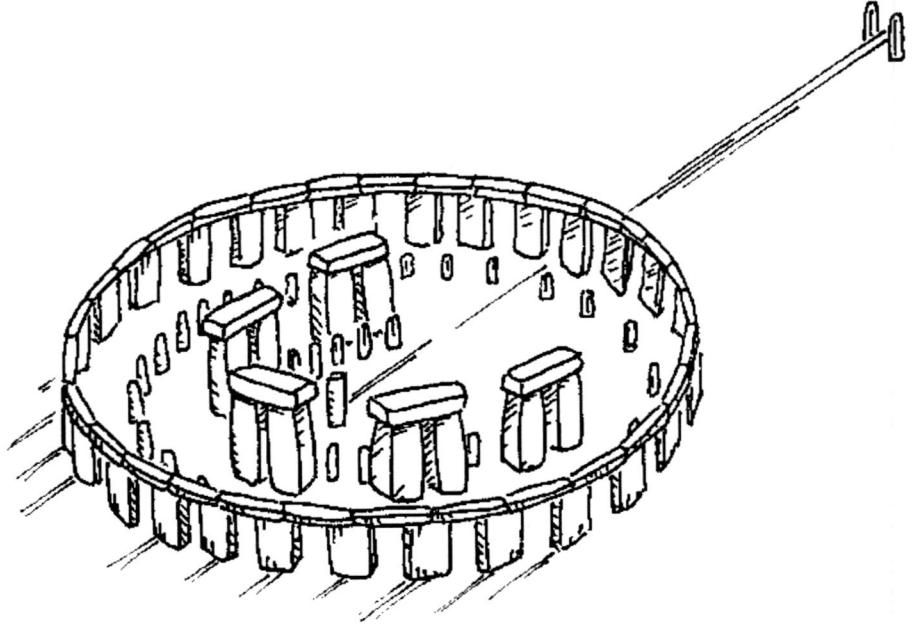

*Dance within a stone circle
and absorb its ancient wisdom*

Stonehenge

Salisbury Plain, Wiltshire, England

Unlock the secrets held within these ancient stones
and connect to the energy of the cosmos, drawing
on the wisdom of the past and the power of the earth,
moon and stars to release and fulfil your deepest
potential and create your own meaning and purpose,
and your own monument across time.

The place

"From a distance, its appearance is stately. As you advance nearer, the greatness of its contour fills the eye in an astonishing manner. When you enter the building and cast your eyes around the yawning ruins, you are struck into an ecstatic reverie, which none can describe, and they only can be sensible of it that feel it."
William Stukeley, 18th century English antiquarian

Stonehenge, the legendary circle of stones set in a green field in the pretty English countryside, is the national temple of ancient Britain, as famous as London's Westminster Abbey and instantly recognisable even by people with no interest in spirituality or historical monuments. There are hundreds of stone circles across the country, but the sheer size of this one's towering monoliths, the ingenuity of its construction and the way the stones are joined together by huge rock slabs to form enchanted doorways make it truly unique.

Today only half the monument survives, but it still has a rugged, stately grandeur, and somehow its ruined state makes it even more hauntingly beautiful. There are several fallen monoliths lying in the middle of the circle, including the Altar Stone, which is cracked in half and pinned beneath another. They all lie scattered unceremoniously in the grass, broken and chipped, part of this majestic graveyard of long-ago dreams. You can picture how it looked in its glory days from the upright stones that remain and the shells at their feet, while the weight of history adds to its physical and emotional presence.

Stonehenge is the centrepiece of England's rich history, and has become a symbol of the ancient wisdom of the early inhabitants of the British Isles. For a long time people believed the circle must have been constructed by "less barbaric" foreigners, because of its beauty and sophistication, but archaeologists have now discovered that it was built by the indigenous Neolithic people over a long period, beginning around 3100BCE and continuing for fifteen hundred years.

Located on windswept Salisbury Plain in Wiltshire, near the pretty cathedral town of Salisbury and just an hour and a half drive southwest of London, Stonehenge is surrounded by a sacred landscape of burial mounds and ancient earthworks. Yet it's the monument itself that inspires the most awe and wonder, capturing the imagination and touching the heart on a deep, soulful level.

The circle stands on a vortex of leylines, which flood the earth with energy and have given rise to many stories of intrigue and strange phenomena in the area. Some people have seen lights hovering above it, and others feel strange sensations and dimensional shifts when they stand within it. It's certainly fascinating to watch a dowser demonstrate the power of the magnetic flow as they walk across the ground with divining rods, which swing wildly as they interact with the ley energy, or to hold them yourself, knowing there are no tricks being played, and mesmerised by their mysterious movement.

A hundred years ago Stonehenge stood alone on the grassy plain, with animals grazing within the circle, visitors wandering between the stones as they pleased and druids welcoming the summer solstice sunrise with great ceremony. But today it has been roped off to protect the monument, and a busy highway roars past, polluting the air with fumes as well as noise. Busloads of tourists descend at the same time – up to two thousand an hour during the busiest periods – and many people claim the atmosphere and energy has been destroyed.

Yet the magical light that has so enchanted people throughout the centuries still illuminates the circle, and the power of the stones remains tangible. Standing with your back to the road, the noisy modern world falls away and you journey back in time. The grassy plain stretches out into the distance, and the immense presence of these ancient monoliths moves everyone who contemplates them. The stones still speak, if you're willing to listen, reaching out across the rope that protects them from the public. And anyone who wants to can go within the circle and touch them, as part of a spiritual tour or by booking a time through the guardians of the place, which I have done a few times now, at different times of day and year.

Stonehenge became a World Heritage Site in 1986, and is the most popular tourist attraction in the UK, with more than a million people flocking there each year. Over the centuries it has been visited by royalty, political leaders, painters, archaeologists, writers, rock stars, druids and witches. It has become a symbol of British culture and history, used as a logo for historical societies, on coats of arms and even as the name of a navy submarine. There are countless paintings of the iconic structure, and it features in several books, including 19th century local author Thomas Hardy's classic *Tess of the d'Urbervilles*, whose climax is set within the ring of stones, and contemporary American writer Erica Jong's novel *Fanny*.

Many advertising campaigns have included the instantly recognisable image, including ones for Pentax cameras, Benson & Hedges cigarettes and the Shell oil company, and an environmental group uses it as their symbol. The Beatles performed in front of the monument in their movie *Help!*, Dr Who and his alien enemies met there for a galactic showdown, and it's been sent up in the comedies *This Is Spinal Tap* and National Lampoon's *European Vacation*, adding a sense of fun and modern pop culture to its spiritual significance.

Stonehenge remains one of the most intriguing of the sacred sites of the world, with the people who built it and the purpose of its construction still shrouded in mystery. Some believe it's an old ruined temple, others that it was a massive stone calendar or a court of justice. For centuries it was thought to be a druidic ceremonial site – and it has become one today – while before that it was associated with the legendary King Arthur and his magician Merlin. Others claim it was a memorial to the dead, a power place built by the survivors of the lost land of Atlantis, a landing pad constructed by aliens or a stargate for humans to communicate with them.

It has archaeoastronomical significance, with its geometry aligned to key rising and setting positions of the planets, and the sunlight through the stone doorways marking out the seasons. There are also whispers of magic in its creation, as the stones seem too heavy for mortal men to have lifted – and some of them come from a place 250 kilometres away in Wales, a feat hard to explain or even imagine.

Whatever its origins, today Stonehenge is a place of worship for thousands of druidic and pagan spiritual seekers, who make a pilgrimage there at the solstices and equinoxes to pay their respects and perform their rituals within its hallowed ground, dancing inside the enchanted stone circle to connect to the earth and humanity's ancestral past. Standing within it and breathing in this energy will align you to this ancient wisdom, open you up to your deepest potential and unlock your purpose and inner meaning.

The present

"It is indeed immensely picturesque. I fancy that I can sit all a summer's day watching its shadows shorten and lengthen again, and drawing a delicious contrast between the world's duration and the feeble span of individual experience. There is something in Stonehenge almost reassuring. The immemorial grey pillars serve to remind you of the enormous background of time."
Henry James, 19th century American novelist and travel writer

The first time I saw Stonehenge, from the window of a bus, I was a bit disappointed. This small pile of rocks on the side of a busy highway was the mythical stone circle at the heart of ancient Britain, a magical temple that still inspires reverence and a sense of worship in people today? I had expected it to be bigger, or to be presented with more of a sense of occasion perhaps, a little further off the beaten track, away from civilisation and the steady stream of traffic hurtling past on the highway from London.

As I paid my money at the ticket booth and walked through the concrete tunnel under the road and into the fenced-off enclosure opposite the car park, I wasn't expecting much. But as I emerged into the sunlight and headed towards the majestic ruin, my mood lifted. And once I stood in the field surrounding the stones, the din of the traffic faded and the monument seemed to grow in stature. It dominated the landscape, rearing up from the ground like an ancient dragon and drawing me towards it with a magnetic power.

I put the audio tour device to my ear and walked slowly around the circle, listening to the history of the place, the stories of its construction, and the wild tales of magic and myth that have always clung to these ancient stones. Later, marvelling at the play of light and shadow as the sun moved overhead, and watching birds swoop down onto the taller stones and flit between the archways, I began to fall under its spell.

I felt sad that it's now roped off from the public, because I longed to touch the stones, to feel their ancient energy and the secrets they hold inside. I'd just spent time at the grand stone circle of Avebury, a little further north, where you can wander freely amongst the monoliths, rest your forehead against them and place your hands on their roughened sides, and it seemed such a shame that Stonehenge has been cut off from the people who seek to merge with its energy, worshipping it and learning from it, and absorbing and exchanging wisdom and power with the stones.

Yet I understand. This monument has been chipped away at, trodden all over, graffitied and worn down over the last century, and it needs to be protected. Countless feet tramping between the uprights has loosened the foundations, increasing the risk of stones falling over or cracking, and necessitating the securing of some of the slabs in concrete footings. Besides, as I followed the pathway around this tumbled down plaything of giants, past the guard posted to watch over his charge, I could feel its energy reaching out regardless. It is still there, still alive, even if it is cut off from human touch and regarded more as a museum piece than a living, breathing entity.

Over the years I've returned to Stonehenge several times, alone and with other people, and each time I sense a different mood, a different energy. I've sat for hours on the grass nearby, staring up at the stones, daydreaming of a life and time so different to ours, imagining the circle's ancient splendour and mysterious purpose. I've seen it lashed with rain, illuminated with summer sunshine and brooding in the mists of autumn. I've watched it in the warm glow of early morning, the harsher glare of noon and at nightfall, huddling in the dark on the grassy, windswept plain. It remains an enigma, unfathomable, a puzzle that touches you deeply yet is impossible to solve or explain. On one level it is just a pile of rocks, yet they overwhelm you with awe and inspire a questioning of your place in the universe.

When I went there on my honeymoon, I was a bit nervous that my husband wouldn't be as impressed as I'd always been, but I needn't have worried. The power of it reached out for him before we even got there, as we approached along the highway, and it took his breath away. It's such a surreal sight, the ancient monoliths sitting so casually on the side of the road, locals barely giving them a second glance and most people rushing past on their way somewhere else.

He'd been told it is underwhelming in real life, yet for him it was the opposite. He was gripped by its size, by an energy he could feel but not explain, and by the mystery of its making and the people responsible. And I was gripped anew by its sweet magic, excited to see it again and stand so close to the majestic stones. For while Stonehenge has been roped off for the past 30 years, it's just a thin cord, knee high, designed to mark out the sacred space rather than obstruct the view or interfere with your experience. And on the western side the path runs quite close to the monument, so you can see detail and texture, and gaze through the outer doorways and into the inner sanctum.

We walked around the circle holding hands, staring in wonder, feeling the energy of the earth and the revitalising power of the fresh winds that sweep over the plain. It's such a mysterious, ethereal, beautiful structure, and showing it to my beloved added another layer of meaning to it for me. I wondered whether we had once danced together within its ancient walls, or prayed in the shadow of its stones. Was there a time when we had understood its purpose and been at one with the cycles of nature it reflects? We were disappointed that we couldn't go inside the circle this time (although a few years later we did), but we could feel its power from the pathway, and the magic it was wrapping around our hearts.

As we followed the path around the monument, I also pondered the mystery that people are guided around it in an anticlockwise direction, veering off to the right as they approach it. In the northern hemisphere anticlockwise is against the sun, known to pagans and magical practitioners as widdershins. In magical rituals a circle is cast, a sacred space is consecrated and power and energy are raised by moving deosil – with the sun, which is clockwise in the north – while moving widdershins will close a circle, banish power and lower energy.

In ancient times, people walked ceremonially around a stone circle in a deosil direction to tap in to the earth energies within the sacred space, awaken and activate them, and direct them throughout the area to increase crop growth and heal the land and its people. Even in Christian times it was considered unlucky to circle a temple or monument in a widdershins direction, and there are many folktales – and indeed modern stories – of people who accidentally summoned the devil, found themselves in another dimension or even died after circling a stone or a church anticlockwise. Could this be the reason that some people claim Stonehenge is today low in energy, because thousands of people a day are decreasing its power?

On one of my visits to the mystical circle I went with a mother and daughter from Germany who were staying in the same B&B as me in Glastonbury. At breakfast they were talking about how excited they were that they'd finally get to see the monument – and were devastated when the owner told them there was no public transport from the town to the circle. I hadn't planned to go to Stonehenge on that trip, but since I had a rental car I decided to revisit it with them, and we set off on our magical mystery tour. I surprised myself by offering to go. I would never have volunteered to spend a day with strangers before, but it seemed right somehow, part of the process of my slowly opening heart. And maybe it was destined in some way. They had been wanting to visit Stonehenge for years, but had always imagined that there would be three of them when they did. And so there were.

We drove through the grey countryside, under clouds threatening rain, breathing in the clean, crisp air and chatting about the world. The car park was empty when we pulled up, which was a blessing, because when the monument is alone on the plain it has a haunting and desolate air that touches me deeply, a very different feel to its more vibrant demeanour when surrounded by people and sunshine.

As soon as I walked up from the tunnel I felt the energy hit my solar plexus chakra like a blow, and the whole time we were there I could feel the presence of the stones in a really physical way. It was just starting to rain, with a sharp, cold wind blustering around us and thick grey skies overhead, so we had the place to ourselves. And it was beautiful, the stones looming at us out of the mist, huge black birds circling above us, and the peacefulness brought about by the wintry conditions making our spirits soar.

One of my new friends said we had to walk around the pathway in the opposite direction, deosil, because that's the way it used to be done, and I smiled because it had always seemed to me to be the right way too. She was flooded with visions and messages, and described the circle as it had once been, with all its lintels in place, the setting sun streaming through one archway, the rising full moon through another, people reverent as they stood in the shadow of these humbling giants. She paused at the fallen monolith known as the Slaughter Stone and said that it had been the waiting stone, where others could venture to watch the rituals taking place within, but which only the priests and priestesses could go past, further into the stones.

As we continued around the monument, the air thick with mist and the pale stones looking like bleached bones through the rain, I could feel the energy coursing up through my feet from the ground below and heating my whole body, and it seemed I could see the whole web of leylines that intersect in the circle as they crisscross the earth.

Soon the clouds grew blacker and more threatening, and the day became ominous. Thunder roared, lightning split the sky and the air crackled with tension. Soaking wet but filled with joy and energy, we ran back through the tunnel to the little protective bubble of our car, leaving the melancholy ruin to its isolated splendour as the rain lashed down, and marvelling at the eons it has weathered and the extremes of the English seasons it has survived.

"Stanenges, where stones of wonderful size have been erected in the manner of doorways, so that doorway appears to have been raised upon doorway, and no one can conceive how such great stones have been so raised aloft, or why they were built there."
Henry of Huntingdon, 12th century English historian and clergyman

Today, more than five thousand years after construction began, Stonehenge still holds a deep fascination to so many people, partly because it's so different to every other stone circle ever erected. There are around a thousand scattered across the British Isles, but while some are bigger or more dramatically located, not a single one is as impressive as Stonehenge. It is more complex in everything from its design and execution to where its stones were sourced from, and it's this uniqueness that adds so much to its mystery.

The intriguing concentric layout is arranged within a henge, a circular area a hundred metres in diameter that is surrounded by a bank and ditch that looks like a moat. The ditch, which was once two metres deep, has filled in over time and the bank has eroded away, but you can still discern the outline and picture how it once looked.

Within this earthwork, Stonehenge itself is comprised of four alignments – two circles and two horseshoe shapes – placed within each other. There are also a few outliers, large standing stones erected outside the monument, positioned along the axis that runs through the centre of the circles in a line from southwest to northeast. Half the stones are sarsen, a form of sandstone that's stronger than concrete and harder than granite, and the other half are bluestone, a type of igneous rock imported from the Preseli Hills in Wales.

Most arresting as you approach is the outer stone circle, 30 metres in diameter, which once boasted thirty massive sarsens more than four metres tall, over two metres wide and weighing up to 50 tonnes. They were topped with thirty lintels, horizontal slabs of curved stone that joined the uprights together, forming a series of magical doorways in to the heart of the mystery and a continuous flat platform around the top that was suspended almost five metres above the ground.

The stones were fitted together with expert precision using mortice and tenon joints, with no mortar required. Each of the uprights had two small domed projections called tenons on their top, while the lintels had two rounded holes known as mortices carved in their bottom, which fitted snugly on a tenon. Each lintel capped half each of two adjacent uprights, like Lego blocks. In addition, each lintel was joined to the one next to it by a toggle joint, similar to a jigsaw puzzle. Many of the lintels have now fallen off, and lie in the grass where their carved out mortices, as well as the domed tenons exposed on the uprights they fell from, can be clearly seen.

The skill involved in fitting these massive stones together and creating circular patterns from rectangular blocks is almost beyond comprehension, especially given the rudimentary nature of the builders' tools – deer antlers for digging and concrete-hard balls of sarsen called mauls with which they shaped the uprights – and the hardness of the stones. They are so strong that to break one required lighting a fire along the place the split was required, then pouring cold water on this line and frantically hammering away at it.

Today seventeen of the thirty uprights of the sarsen circle still stand, including a section in the northeast where eleven adjacent stones remain in a consecutive pattern with three of their lintels still in place, which gives the best idea of how this elaborate circle once looked. At first glance the sarsens seem grey, but they have immense depth, with shades of white, brown and pink running through each one, and they all sparkle and glisten when the sand within them catches the sun.

Just inside this outer arrangement is a circle that once contained sixty bluestones, each as tall as a person and evenly spaced. Today only six of them remain upright, with others leaning over, some broken on the ground and a few missing altogether, taken away long ago to build houses and roads. They are each around two metres tall and a metre wide, and seem less remarkable than their bigger brothers. Yet it was these stones that were dragged hundreds of kilometres from a special spot in neighbouring Wales, across country and up river in a mammoth undertaking, so they were obviously highly valued, and are even today reputed to have healing powers and magical properties.

They turn blue when wet, hence their name, and are flecked with pink, white and gold from the crystals of quartz within them, which sparkle like stars in the night sky. This was no doubt part of the attraction to the ancient builders, who worshipped nature and the heavens. These stones are warmer to the touch than the sarsens, which you can test out on the two large chunks of rock, one bluestone and one sarsen, near the ticket booth, erected here so people can feel them both and experience the difference in texture and temperature.

In the centre of Stonehenge's two circles are the massive trilithons, individual structures made up of two huge sarsen uprights crowned with a stone lintel, a shape that has become synonymous with the monument. The term trilithon, from the Greek for three stones, was coined by English historian and field archaeologist William Stukeley to describe these hulking freestanding constructions. Unlike the outer sarsen doorways, which you can walk through into the heart of the circle, the trilithons have only the tiniest gap between their uprights, just wide enough for a beam of sun or moon light to shine through.

There were five trilithons, arranged in a horseshoe shape with the open side in the northeast, facing the monument's entrance. They were placed symmetrically, with the smallest two on each side of the open end, the next biggest beside them and the single Great Trilithon erected in the middle of the horseshoe's curve. This lone towering structure was eight metres tall, and it was between its uprights that the rays of the rising sun on summer solstice morning – and the setting sun on winter solstice night – shone.

Today three of the trilithons are still standing in their original form, while the other two – the Great Trilithon and one of the smaller ones – have just a single upright remaining, with the other one and the lintel lying in the grass. Like the outer sarsen circle, the trilithons were also echoed with bluestones, with a horseshoe arrangement of nineteen pillars, although only six of these remain standing in place.

In the middle of this, at the centre of the whole monument, is what's referred to as the Altar Stone, a huge monolith that now lies on the ground, embedded in the earth under a fallen lintel. Early archaeologists named it this because they believed Stonehenge was a druidic temple, and that this five-metre-long stone had been placed flat on the ground for use as an altar. However recent evidence shows that it once stood upright, and played a central role in the measurements and alignments of the circle.

Two outlying stones are also an important part of the configuration. On the edge of the henge, in the opening in the bank and ditch, is the fallen monolith known as the Slaughter Stone. Early investigators thought it had once been an altar where human sacrifices were performed, but it too originally stood upright. And further out, past the ditch, is the Heel Stone, which was once half of a pair of monoliths erected on the ceremonial Avenue that approached the circle.

Today the path that visitors follow around the monument passes midway between the Heel and Slaughter Stones, and if you pause in that spot you can picture the way the ancients approached their temple, passing these sentinels on their way. The Heel Stone was one of the most significant parts of the early structure, but today it looks lonely, pressed up against the wire mesh fence that separates Stonehenge from the highway. This busy road cuts through the Avenue and races past perilously close to the stones, and it's a strange juxtaposition to see a car or truck in the same frame of your camera as this ancient monument and its rolling green fields.

"When I saw them behind the rope I wept for the death of the temple, because the place seemed at best hibernating, at worst dead. But when I did a dawn ritual within the circle I realised Stonehenge is not dead at all, but very very aware. The stones seemed to welcome and accept us. I prepared myself for a zap of power from the land – what did happen was a subtle, slow process of feeling very good about myself and the group and the land."
Clare Prout, British pagan and co-ordinator of Save Our Sacred Sites

The last few times that I visited Stonehenge I finally went inside the circle and touched the stones, and it was as magical and spiritually uplifting as I had always imagined it would be. I'd discovered that English Heritage, which protects the monument from wear and tear, allows special access to the inner circle before and after the normal opening hours throughout most of the year. It's a little known fact that you can apply through the organisation's website to be allocated a date that you can go within – which, depending on the time of year, you might share with several others or have all to yourself.

You can also go on an inner access tour through one of the small companies that books some of these slots and provides a local guide and transport from London or Salisbury, or join a week-long spiritual tour that includes a ritual within the stones as part of the itinerary.

The first time I went inside the circle and touched the stones was on a late summer afternoon, as the shadows were lengthening and the crowds had just left for the day. It was that special time when day is approaching night, the light becomes golden and the whole world is transformed. At this enchanted hour anything seems possible, and as I approached the monument my head was awhirl with excitement and half-remembered tales of Merlin, giants, witches and faeries.

I stepped over the rope and into the sacred sanctuary it protects, overwhelmed that I was approaching this greatest of mysteries. There is something holy about this ancient temple, and while I'm not religious, it speaks to my heart with its simple yet powerful connection to the earth and the past. I wandered across the soft green grass towards the bank and ditch, feeling the power and energy that runs through the land, then stood at the Slaughter Stone, gazing up at the full sweep of the monument ahead of me.

From this point the entranceway to the outer sarsen circle is directly ahead, and I walked slowly towards it, retracing the footsteps of the ancients along the ceremonial Avenue to their sacred place. The path is worn down and faint now, but you can still feel an echo of the old energy as you stand on it, and the whisper of people past, those who walked this ground with reverence and spiritual conviction.

This processional route has been walked since before the pyramids of Egypt were built, before the Colosseum became an icon of the Roman Empire, before Machu Picchu was ever dreamed of by the Inkas. It was the path the sun traced out on the morning of the summer solstice, creeping across the land and warming the hearts of those who lived according to its rhythm. And from the other direction, along this same path, shone the light of the setting sun on the night of the winter solstice, an event just as vital to these solar worshipping people because it symbolised the promise of the return of spring and the renewal of crops, and rebirth for both the land and themselves.

The people of long ago had approached this huge temple with prayers in their hearts and awe in every fibre of their being, and I stared at it in wonder too, feeling tiny and insignificant in comparison to these enormous ancient stones. But I was also filled with an immense sense of connection to the past, and to the people and rituals that had played out on this sacred ground thousands of years ago.

As I stepped through the entrance, which is marked by a slightly wider doorway in the outer circle, and looked up at the massive stone lintel above my head, I was stunned and a little surprised. Although

I'd adapted my first impression over the years, I was still amazed at the sheer size of each stone. I was dwarfed by each one of these hulking upright pillars, and the ingenuity of the people who constructed it became even more apparent.

I reached out and placed my hand on the roughened rock face, and was overwhelmed by a flood of emotions and flickering visions as I touched its weathered sides. I felt dizzy for a moment, hot and cold at the same time and momentarily uneasy, but the feeling passed and I stepped eagerly inside the circle. I peered excitedly around me, sizing up the remaining stones, picturing how they had once stood, and intrigued by the doorways that seemed to open on to each other.

For a while I skipped around like a little kid, so excited to be up close, racing around to explore each stone, wind through each archway, investigate each fallen pillar. Then I slipped into a kind of daze, mesmerised by these ancient stones and feeling their energy and strength within my very bones. I slowed down and started again, taking my time as I went back to each stone, reaching out to them with my hand, my mind, my heart.

I stood with my right hand on a sarsen upright, and my left palm started throbbing. I could feel the energy rushing through me, and when I put my heart against the rock it started to beat faster, while my breathing became deeper. Then, standing with my back against another, feeling the warmth within its cool exterior, it suddenly seemed that these stones contained the wisdom of the ages, with the power to reawaken our own wisdom from deep within us.

Quartz, which is used today to store information in computers and watches, runs through many of the stones in this monument. Perhaps the ancients also used it to hold knowledge, and we're able to download it when we touch the quartz-rich pillars or stand in their shadow. Some regard these stones as the keepers of the planet's wisdom, and think that, like crystals, they can channel the healing power of the land.

Stones also have a unique ability to ground us energetically, to bring us back to earth and anchor us in the physical. As I stood in the centre of the circle I could feel a subtle hum within the ground where the lines of energy crisscross the axis. It made my head spin, but when I reached out and touched one of the fallen monoliths lying in the middle, I instantly felt centred and calmed.

"The sun dropped and lay like a great golden globe in the low west. In that singular light every little tree and shock of wheat drew itself up high and pointed; the very clods and furrows in the fields seemed to stand up sharply. I felt the old pull of the earth, the solemn magic that comes out of those fields at nightfall."
Willa Cather, US novelist and Pulitzer Prize winner

Suddenly a beam of light hit my face, flashing across my eyes and warming my cheeks. The sun, shining between two of the pillars, was starting to sink, and I turned to the western part of the circle. When I'd arrived the late afternoon sun had been strong, casting a warm glow over the site, but now it was becoming darker and deeper in colour as it slid towards the earth, framed between the famous stone arches.

This was the spectacle that the ancients had watched – the golden disc of the sun god slowly slipping downwards through the velvety sky, framed between two uprights of their incredible monument, and descending through a different doorway at different times of the year.

I was awestruck by this natural magic. To the common folk it must have seemed the work of the gods, the sun controlled by their priests, and I was just as impressed at the amazing beauty of this moment. Watching the sun rise or set from within this magical circle has inspired people for thousands of years, and today, when our beliefs are so different from those of our long-ago ancestors and we worship technology rather than nature, it still has the power to instil wonder.

As the sun disappeared and the sky started to deepen from pink and purple to twilight blue, the guard who had watched from afar came closer and gently told us it was time to go. I didn't want to leave, and I lingered as long as I could, breathing in the ancient presence of this enchanted place, staring intently at each stone and each angle as I committed them to memory. I finally headed to the tunnel, casting longing looks back over my shoulder as I went, and very grateful that I'd been allowed within the sacred stones of this hallowed ground.

The next time I stepped within the circle it was in the misty pre-dawn, all moody and swirling with the crisp chill of autumn. I went with a friend on an inner access tour from London, setting out in the inky blackness of night, the small minivan racing through the darkness, past deserted city streets then green fields shrouded in rolling clouds of fog. Even the name of Stonehenge still evoked feelings of mystery and magic to me, of ancient secrets and untold power, and I stared eagerly ahead for the first peek of the shadowy, majestic monument.

The sky started to lighten as we approached, and the brooding huddle of stones was silhouetted against the faint colours of dawn. As we drew closer they loomed out of the mist, and I felt a shiver of anticipation and joy, like greeting an old friend. The morning was cool and grey, with clouds overhead, mist snaking between the monoliths and an icy wetness permeating the air, so different to the summer sunset of before. The grass was covered in dew, soaking my feet and my skirt, and the stones were cold to the touch, with an invigorating, revitalising energy.

I was amazed that our small group was alone there, allowed access to this millennia-old mystery and able to wander inside the roped-off area without the noise or crowds that come later in the day. It was so beautiful – atmospheric and eerie, with mist enveloping each huge upright and rolling across the ground and into the ditch.

I walked along the processional way, imagining those who did it five thousand years ago, who walked along the same cold ground, through the same ethereal, swirling mists we were experiencing now. This thick white mist added a magical, surreal quality to the stones, and the early morning light had a strange, pale edge to it, weak and watery, yet illuminating in a different way to the glorious sunset I'd seen before.

Most of the time I ignored the guide, entertaining and knowledgeable though he was, and simply wandered around between the rocks, soaking up the energy and peace. It felt so remote and tranquil, cut off from the world, as though we were in another dimension. I placed my hands on the stones, first on the huge sarsen uprights and then on the smaller bluestones, and they did feel different. The taller, greyer ones had an immense presence about them, and a strength that long-ago people must have tried to invoke for themselves by touching them, drawing in their solidity and permanence. And the bluestones had a surprising warmth, even on this cold morning, and I felt a soothing, calming essence wash over me as I placed my palms on them.

Later I rejoined the group, and listened spellbound as a local man who's worked on the archaeological digs talked about the history of the area and the new information that's coming to light from excavations at nearby Durrington Walls, the site where the builders of Stonehenge are believed to have lived, which was only discovered in 2007. Afterwards, as we had breakfast in a quaint pub down the road, he continued this discussion, handing around some of the finds and explaining the changing perceptions of the monument and its context within the landscape of ancient burial mounds and earthworks that surround it.

More recently I explored this landscape on one of his tours, visiting Durrington Walls – which admittedly doesn't look like much, but the *idea* of it, and the images conjured by his stories of the dig, are amazing. I was so moved by his passion as he breathlessly described the dwelling floors and hearths they found, and the indentations in the earth made from the knees of some long-ago man kneeling to tend his hearth fire or pray to his gods. Then we visited nearby Woodhenge, before investigating some of the burial mounds in the field below Stonehenge. We wandered along the mysterious Cursus earthwork, then walked right up the length of the Avenue, marvelling as the huge pillars of the stone circle came slowly into sight over the crest of the hill, a little at a time.

Then, as we finally stood within the stone circle, he pulled out two small metal dowsing rods, and people took turns walking around the centre, crossing over the lines of earth energy within the inner sanctum. I did it too, as did my hubby, and we were baffled that they did always move as we crossed the same spot inside the circle. Our scientifically

minded guide is sceptical of leylines and other geomantic principles –
and yet he's continually amazed and a little awestruck that every time
someone crosses a particular spot the rods move dramatically,
indicating lines of energy. He can't explain it, he's not sure he wants
to believe it, yet it has happened every single time he's been within the
circle. Just one more mystery of this beautiful sacred place...

One of the best ways to experience Stonehenge is to stay in
Salisbury, the beautiful old English town 13 kilometres south of the
monument, so you can visit the site at different times of day and
spend time examining the surrounding area. Another good base is the
tiny village of Amesbury. It's harder to reach by public transport, but
there is an incredible walk across the fields to Stonehenge, which
passes many burial mounds and other features of the sacred landscape.
Or you can drive down from London for the day, or visit as part of a
tour that takes in other sights such as Bath and Windsor Castle,
which was built from the same sarsen stone as Stonehenge.

There are many buses and trains from London to Salisbury, and a
bus service to the monument from there. There's lots of accommodation
in the town, as well as the famous Salisbury Cathedral, which is located
on a leyline connected to Stonehenge. It has the tallest spire in England,
and houses one of only four surviving copies of the Magna Carta, the
eight-hundred-year-old document that western law is still based on.

There is a wonderful museum too, with displays dedicated to the
history and construction of Stonehenge, from now-disproved theories
of how it was made to ancient tools and pieces of pottery that were
discovered at the site. There are sections that trace the development
of the people who have lived in the area over the past several thousand
years, from Neolithic hunters to Roman soldiers, and a fascinating
model that simulates the path of the sun and the way it lights up the
monument at sunrise on the summer solstice.

Salisbury is also the location of Old Sarum, a three-thousand-year-
old earthwork that has played an important role in England's rich
history, from the time that Bronze Age people constructed a fortress
there through to the Norman kings who built the castle whose ruins
can still be seen, and later the priests who established Salisbury as a
cathedral town. Additionally there is a thriving arts community,
character-filled old pubs that serve pots of tea as well as beer, colourful
local markets, a pretty river and lush gardens and parklands.

And the town is a good base for visiting the grand stone circle of
Avebury, the mysterious burial mound of West Kennet Long Barrow,
the intriguing magnetic mound of Silbury Hill and the other incredible
ancient sites scattered throughout Wiltshire. The countryside in this
part of England is so beautiful, with charming medieval villages,
restored castles and prehistoric monuments dotting the landscape.

The past

> **"The mysterious monument of Stonehenge, standing remote on a bare and boundless heath, as much unconnected with the events of past ages as it is with the uses of the present, carries you back beyond all historical records into the obscurity of a totally unknown period."**
>
> *John Constable, 19th century English painter*

The history of Stonehenge is shrouded in mystery, and has been revised and updated many times, with ongoing research sure to add even further to our understanding of it – as well as raise more questions. Only a few hundred years ago it was thought to have been built by the Romans when they invaded the country in the first centuries CE, because no one could conceive of there having been people in existence any earlier than that – or believe that the supposedly savage and barbarian British could have created something so brilliant.

Later experts claimed that it was built by the Phoenicians, the Myceneans, the Saxons, the Danes, the druids or even the Hindus, but slowly the timeline was pushed backwards, a few centuries at a time, until the recent discovery that the monument is much older than anyone has ever imagined – older even than the Pyramids of Egypt and the sophisticated civilisation they represent.

It's now accepted that Stonehenge was constructed by many different tribes, over a very long period of time, beginning around 3100BCE and being added to and reworked until around 1600BCE.

The beginning and end of historical ages varies from country to country, depending on the inhabitants's methods of survival and development of technology as well as the scientist doing the research, and many seem to overlap and continue alongside each other before one finally replaces the other. In Europe, the Mesolithic (Middle Stone) Age began after the last Ice Age, around 10,000BCE, and followed the earlier Palaeolithic (Old Stone) Age that had stretched back for up to a million years, before humans had fully evolved from apes.

The Mesolithic Age marked a new era of human evolution characterised by more sophisticated stone tools for hunting, the domestication of wild dogs and a more advanced social structure. The people of this era were hunters and gatherers, with small groups moving across the countryside according to the season, following the migratory paths of the animals they hunted and the growth cycle of the plants they ate and used for healing.

The earliest evidence of ritual use at Stonehenge comes from this period. Around 8000BCE four holes were dug in an east-west alignment to hold massive pine posts. These later rotted away in situ, leaving proof of their existence if not their purpose. It's speculated that they may have been part of a ceremonial procession, or a marker for the equinox alignments. The modern car park now covers them, but large round discs in the bitumen mark where they once stood, introducing the sacred landscape of the site as soon as you pull up.

Around 4500BCE the beginning of farming ushered in the Neolithic (New Stone) Age in Britain. This new agricultural knowledge was introduced by settlers from Europe, and soon the hunter-gatherer lifestyle gave way to a far more settled existence, with native people adopting the new practices and intermingling with the newcomers.

Permanent settlements were built and the landscape was transformed by farming, with huge areas of woodland cut down, fields of crops being planted and cattle grazing over huge tracts of land.

It was these Neolithic people who interred their dead in the communal long barrows that still dot the landscape. These fascinating stone burial chambers, such as nearby West Kennet, which you can still walk inside, included an entrance area with several "rooms" coming off it where the bones of the dead were placed. The structure was then covered with a mound of white chalk, which grass later grew over, with the entrance left open for future burials.

They also built the first of the monuments, stone circles and henges that so fascinate us today. The earliest ones, circa 3800BCE, are known as causewayed enclosures or camps, and were a precursor to Stonehenge. They were settlements built within a protective circular bank and ditch, where communities would gather for festivals and to exchange livestock. Trading between regions became common, and many far-flung tribes worked together to build these sites, which were aligned to the solstices and equinoxes, indicating a knowledge by these early people of the patterns of the seasons and the celestial bodies, and a strong connection to the land and nature.

It was the Neolithic people who began work on Stonehenge. First, around 3100BCE, an earthwork now known as the Cursus was built just to the north of the future monument site, along with a causewayed enclosure, Robin Hood's Ball. Many long barrow tombs were also erected on the surrounding plain during this time.

A hundred years later the earthwork that forms the basis of Stonehenge was constructed – a circular area 110 metres in diameter which was surrounded by a massive bank and ditch. The chalky earth was dug out with deer antlers and the shoulder blades of oxen to form the ditch, then piled up to form the bank. Access to this inner area was through a main entrance cut in the bank in the northeast section, which was aligned with the path of the sun on the morning of the summer solstice. There was also a smaller entrance in the south. This ritual space was clearly delineated from the surrounding area, and would have looked impressive, with the sparkling white chalk of the ditch and bank contrasting with the vivid green of the grassland.

Such enclosed structures, now called henges in honour of this most famous one, were typical of the time – although Stonehenge broke with tradition by having the ditch on the outside and the bank on the inside, rather than the reverse.

Also around this time, circa 2900BCE, a ring of fifty-six pits, now known as the Aubrey Holes, were dug just inside the bank. The holes were a metre in diameter and a metre deep, and evenly spaced around the circle. Archaeologists believe they initially held wooden posts that were either the foundation of a roofed timber building or formed a lintelled wooden circle like nearby Woodhenge, with its massive oak tree posts. Such ritual circles, made of timber rather than stone, were common in ancient Britain, particularly in the early Neolithic period.

Others claim that the holes were dug to hold stones or poles which acted as astronomical markers. In the 1960s, physics professor Gerald Hawkins declared that the monument was a Stone Age computer, and the fifty-six holes were used to calculate the dates of lunar eclipses, which repeat in a pattern every 18.6 years, with three cycles taking fifty-six years. While much of his work, which was published in the book *Stonehenge Decoded*, has now been debunked by scientists, he inspired a new investigation into the possible archaeoastronomical use of Stonehenge that continues to this day.

Recent carbon dating of cremated human remains found in the Aubrey Holes has revealed that several hundred years after they were first dug, the pits were reused for burials, probably by a new group of people with different beliefs. Thus at one time at least part of Stonehenge's purpose was as a memorial to the dead, making it the earliest cremation cemetery in the country.

Not long after the Aubrey Holes were made, a number of timber posts were erected in the middle of the henge, indicated by another series of post holes in the ground. They may have been the foundations of a small wooden building and a covered walkway to it, or have been erected over a period of many years to mark the extremes of the moon's rising and setting points, in order to record time and calculate the correct positioning and angles of the stones that later stood there.

Some experts believe this was also the period when many of the outlying features were added, including the Avenue, the 20-metre-wide processional path defined by a parallel bank and ditch on each side, which ran for more than 500 metres along the circle's axis before turning and continuing for two kilometres down to the Avon River.

Although barely discernible today, and covered in part by the road, some of it can just be made out in the field past the ticket booth.

Across the entranceway where the Avenue met the henge, three huge upright marker stones were placed, but the fallen Slaughter Stone is the only one of these that remains. Another two massive pillars were erected about 25 metres down the Avenue, one on each side of the axis, yet today only one, the Heel Stone, still stands, its partner long gone. Between these two sets, another few monoliths are thought to have once stood, possibly as astronomical markers.

Some time later, four sarsens known as the Station Stones were erected along the circumference of the circle of Aubrey Holes, forming a rectangle whose angles marked out many solar and lunar alignments. Only two of these stones are still at the site – one a stone stump in the west, just outside the modern walkway, and another that now lies on the ground between this path and the monument. The other two, which stood on small mounds surrounded by ditches, have been missing for centuries, although their holes have recently been excavated, revealing a little more information about their age and purpose.

"To me Stonehenge is the physical manifestation of the ingenuity, the determination, the spirituality and the genius of our prehistoric ancestors. I love it, and I love the feeling that I will never fully understand it."
Julian Richards, British archaeologist, broadcaster and writer

The next and most significant stage of construction, the one that remains today, began around 2550BCE. Eighty bluestone boulders were brought from the Preseli Hills, 250 kilometres west of Stonehenge, and erected within the henge. This was at least four hundred years after the first stage of the monument was begun, and was performed by different people with a different purpose. This is one of the hardest concepts to grasp when trying to understand the mystery of Stonehenge – that it wasn't built by a single society or civilisation but by many, over a period of fifteen hundred years. During this time religious and spiritual beliefs changed and communities came and went, so the site was reworked several times to suit the needs of the day.

The bluestones were arranged in two concentric circles, the inner one with a diameter of 20 metres, the other slightly larger. Not much is known about this structure because it was later dismantled, but the pits the stones stood in have been excavated, and dubbed the Q and R Holes. The monolith now referred to as the Altar Stone, a green sandstone slab that also came from Wales, was erected at this time too.

Around 2400BCE these bluestone circles were removed and the great sarsen structures were raised – the huge outer circle composed of uprights joined together by lintels, and the five massive trilithons in the centre. The stones they used for this originated closer to home, dragged from a quarry near Avebury, 30 kilometres to the north, where a series of grand Neolithic circles had already been constructed.

The trilithons were erected first, transforming the former lunar observatory into a solar calendar and temple. Now at sunset on the winter solstice the sun's rays pierced through the centre of the Great Trilithon, a phenomenon witnessed as people walked up the Avenue into the circle, and at sunrise on the summer solstice the Heel Stone and its pair served a similar purpose, marking the time of year.

Two generations after that, around fifty years later, a new group erected the outer sarsen circle, which maintained these alignments and added new ones. It was a massive project of mathematical and engineering genius, and incredible hard work and manpower. The mortices and tenons that linked the stones were ground out and carved into shape, the huge stone uprights were smoothed and trimmed so they were slightly narrower at the top, to create the illusion of balance and uniformity, and the outer edges of the lintels were curved so they would create a smooth, rounded line around the outside of the circle.

Each sarsen was also carefully selected and sized to compensate for the uneven surface of the plain, which slopes gently downwards to the river. The taller stones were erected on the lower ground, decreasing in size at the highest ground level so the top of the circle was even and the lintelled platform that joined the stones was perfectly flat.

Not long after this, around 2300BCE, new people arrived in the British Isles, and the Neolithic Period began to give way to the Bronze Age, which was characterised by metalworking and textile production, with woollen tunics and pants replacing more basic fur garments. The new tribes assimilated peacefully with the locals, and much remained as it was, with henges still being built and established farming practices continuing. But smaller round cairns began to replace the communal long barrows of their predecessors, with single burials becoming more common and graves now filled with precious gems and gold jewellery.

Ritual use at Stonehenge also started to change. Around 2150BCE the bluestones of the Q and R circles that had been removed were re-erected in the arrangements we know today, with the circle of sixty stones inside the outer sarsen circle and an oval of bluestones within the trilithon horseshoe. A century later some of the stones were removed from one end of this oval and it was reshaped into a horseshoe pattern of nineteen stones, which reflected the layout of the trilithons.

Around 1900BCE, the foundations of a new structure were begun. A circle of twenty-nine pits, dubbed the Z Holes, were dug two metres beyond the outer sarsen circle, with a second circle of thirty pits, dubbed the Y Holes, outside that. There's no evidence they were ever filled –

it's assumed that two stone circles were started but never completed, and that they were perhaps planned as part of a lunar calendar.

A lunar calendar is made up of months that echo a cycle of the moon, and as a moon cycle is 29.5306 days long, the months alternate between twenty-nine and thirty days to even this out, which could explain the planned Y and Z circles. However a lunar calendar of twelve months runs eleven days short of a solar year, so to keep them aligned, intercalary months are added in a pattern of seven every nineteen years, which could be why the bluestone oval was reduced to nineteen stones, and indicate a link between the Y and Z circles and the inner bluestone horseshoe. In Ancient Babylon they used such a calendar from 3000BCE, so it's not inconceivable that the British could have marked the passing of time in the same way.

Whatever their purpose, the Y and Z Holes were the last of the work at the site, and some time afterwards it fell into disuse. All the great megalithic monuments of Britain, including Stonehenge and Avebury, appear to have been abandoned around 1500BCE, and the beliefs of the builders, and the purpose of their ritual places, were lost.

Around 750BCE the Iron Age began and new communities were established, enclosed in hill forts and earthworks. The Celts and their druid priests arrived in the country and merged with the local people, and it's speculated that they may have used Stonehenge in their study of the heavens and the omens written across the night sky – although they primarily worshipped in groves of sacred trees, which represented life to them, while stones symbolised death.

This period, typified by the use of iron, which was easier to work with than bronze and more effective in battle, continued until 43CE, when the Romans invaded, taking power and ruling for almost four centuries. Their occupation was marked by the rise of more military forts, the establishment of major towns such as London, and vast systems of roads that remain to this day. Initially the Romans followed their own pagan gods, and used some of the local sacred sites for their own purposes. But when Emperor Constantine converted to Christianity in 312CE he made it the official religion of the empire, and outlawed the druidic goddess worship of the British.

People did live in the area around Stonehenge during this period, but it's generally assumed that by this time no one knew what the great circle of stones was for, and that it was no longer used for ceremony or celestial observation. There is no documented history from this time, and little archaeological evidence of what went on from the monument itself. No one knows what happened to the brooding stone giant when it was left alone on Salisbury Plain at the mercy of the elements, as the Dark Ages spread across the country, and people started worshipping in churches rather than outside under the sky.

Recent history

"The stones and circles of Britain are absolutely central to who we are today. They have defined and shaped our society, and our understanding of them makes us who we are."
Julian Cope, British musician, author and modern antiquarian

The first mention of Stonehenge in the modern era was by Henry of Huntingdon, an archdeacon who published a book in 1130CE called *Historia Anglorum* (History of the English), in which he described the mysterious pile of stones. He referred to it as Stanenges, from the Old English stan, meaning stones, and either hencg, meaning hinge because of the lintels, or hengen, meaning gallows, as some thought the lintelled stones looked like a hanging place.

A few years later clergyman and historian Geoffrey of Monmouth wrote his book *Historia Regum Britanniae* (History of the Kings of Britain), which claimed that the stone monument, which he called Stonehenge, had been magically transported to Salisbury Plain from Ireland by the wizard Merlin, King Arthur's adviser. This story was believed for a long time, partly because Monmouth was a noted historian (although he's since been discredited), and partly because no one could imagine how else the circle would have been erected.

In 1620 King James visited Stonehenge, and was so fascinated by it that he commissioned royal architect and surveyor Inigo Jones to carry out the first official investigation of the site. He concluded that the Romans had constructed it as a temple, because he considered the local people too barbaric and unskilled to have created such a sophisticated monument. His architectural blueprint drew parallels with famous Roman buildings, creating angles and geometric symmetry that didn't actually exist, and assuming that the inner horseshoe of five trilithons had once been a circle of six, to better fit his theory.

In the 1660s, British antiquarian John Aubrey, who had mapped and recorded Avebury in his manuscript *Monumenta Britannica*, investigated Stonehenge. He wrote of the existence of a series of depressions just inside the bank and ditch earthwork, although this was overlooked until the 1920s, when they were rediscovered and named the Aubrey Holes in his honour. The first to use fieldwork, surveys and observation rather than studying old texts to try to unlock the secrets of the megalithic monuments, he came to the conclusion that Stonehenge and Avebury were ancient druidic temples.

In 1719, enchanted by Aubrey's tales of ancient ruins and druidic worship, local historian and scholar Dr William Stukeley began visiting Stonehenge, and carried out detailed examinations over many years. He discovered the Avenue, the Cursus and many of the burial mounds around the site, and was the first to work out, by excavating some of the holes left from monoliths that had fallen over or been removed, how each of the stones had been erected.

First, a deep rectangular hole was dug in the ground, up to a third of the stone's height, with a diagonal slope forming a ramp on the side of the hole that ran along the outside of the circle. The stone was laid flat on the ground then pushed down this ramp into the hole, then pulled upright with ropes and pulleys – and a lot of manpower – before the ramp and the gap around the base were filled back in with the chalky earth, the sarsen tools they'd used to shape the stones and some of the rock chips that had flaked off during this process.

Stukeley also realised that the monument was aligned with sunrise at the summer solstice, which he took as proof that it was a place of druidic worship. And while his written notes and detailed sketches provided valuable practical information about the site that is still referred to today, his research was overshadowed by his desire to prove his theory. He declared – incorrectly – that the druids had built Stonehenge as a temple to hold their annual rituals within, and that it was the centrepiece of the indigenous religion of the country. Thanks to his book *Stonehenge: A Temple Restored to the British Druids*, which was published in 1740, the druids became recognised as the builders of the circle, an association that still remains in the minds of many.

He became so enamoured of the priestly druid scholars he was studying that he became one himself, adopting the name Chyndonax after a fabled French druid. He wrote at length about this nature-based spirituality, which combined science and the natural world, and was instrumental in reinventing druidry as a religion. Inspired by his work, the Ancient Order of Druids formed in 1791 as a secret society, and even today a picture of Stonehenge adorns their website.

The next significant study of the monument was carried out in the first decade of the 1800s by local man William Cunnington and his benefactor Sir Richard Colt Hoare, who also investigated the burial barrows of the surrounding area. They began to realise that people had lived in the region for thousands of years, not hundreds, and started to unravel the characteristics of the different ages, such as Stone, Bronze and Iron, coming closer to deciphering Stonehenge's real age.

They discounted the druids as the builders when they discovered that the monument predated the arrival of the Celts in Britain. They also discovered that the Slaughter Stone had once stood, and that it turns red in parts after rain because of the iron content in the rock itself, not from old pools of blood left from druidic sacrifices.

Meanwhile, Stonehenge was growing in fame. A train service from London to Salisbury began in 1857, making it easier to visit. Families would picnic at the stones, sketching the looming silhouette while their children played hide and seek. Tours were arranged, a caretaker was employed to watch over the site, and it became a major attraction.

While the public latched on to the romanticised druidic associations, others were determined to discover the truth of its origins. Young English archaeologist Flinders Petrie, who later achieved fame as an Egyptologist, investigated Stonehenge in the 1870s, attempting to decipher the measurements of the alignments and thus who had constructed it.

He was followed a few years later by naturalist Charles Darwin, who was dabbling in archaeology to investigate the part worms played in the burial of ancient buildings, and more specifically the way they had preserved the stones of this monument in their upright position.

In 1901 Professor William Gowland was brought in to straighten the remaining monolith of the Great Trilithon, which was leaning wildly, tilted at an angle of sixty degrees. He spent a month excavating a small space around its base, and confirmed the way the holes for the stones had been dug, where the stones were shaped and how they were erected, and came even closer to the date of construction.

By this time the white-robed druids had attached themselves to Stonehenge, travelling there from the 1870s onwards from all over England to celebrate the summer solstice and other seasonal events. In 1905 the Ancient Order of Druids performed an initiation ritual within the stones, and rival spiritual group the Church of the Universal Bond also enacted public and private ceremonies there.

However the preparations for World War I interrupted all excavations and ceremonies. Military camps sprang up dangerously close to the monument, and the stones trembled when mines were exploded, equipment was fired and tanks rumbled past. The army, which still owns much of the surrounding land, was responsible for destroying some of the nearby earthworks, but at least it didn't succeed in levelling the famous circle, which army bosses proposed during the war because it was deemed to pose a danger to low flying aircraft!

"The more we dig, the more the mystery seems to deepen."
Colonel William Hawley, English archaeologist

Until this time Stonehenge had been on private land, although most owners allowed public access. In the early 1500s it was part of Amesbury Abbey, but in 1540 King Henry VIII took the Abbey and its land from the church and gave it to the Earl of Hertford. Over the next few centuries it changed hands a few times, including fifty years in the possession of an American, until in 1824 Sir Edmund Antrobus bought the estate, and it remained in his family for almost a hundred years.

Fortunately all the early owners, while happy to possess the ancient relic, were reluctant to make improvements to it or farm the surrounding plain, which would have resulted in all the barrows and burial mounds being levelled and possibly even the stones themselves being taken down to provide grazing land. Many of the other ancient monuments around Stonehenge were destroyed by farmers who saw no value in keeping them and simply ploughed through them to plant crops.

Antrobus, and his sons after him, also refused permission for antiquarians to excavate around the stones, which researchers today are grateful for, because their clumsiness would have destroyed all the valuable evidence that modern archaeologists, with far more advanced equipment and methods, have found so important.

They did allow tourists to continue visiting, although when a gale blew over one of the outer stones and a lintel on New Year's Eve 1900, Edmund's grandson – also Edmund – fenced Stonehenge off and began charging a small admission fee to raise funds so he could restore a dangerously leaning upright and employ a guardian whose job was to stop people hammering off small pieces of the stones as souvenirs.

The family always allowed the druids access at the summer solstice and other ritual days, but in 1913, when they refused Edmund's request for a small donation towards restoration work, he denied them entry. The druids, who had become very possessive of the monument, cursed him – and publicly claimed the credit when he died in 1915.

The landowner's death without an heir saw Stonehenge put up for auction, and there were rumours that an American wanted to buy it and transport it across the sea in its entirety. Fearful that this very British piece of heritage would be exported forever, local man Cecil Chubb bought it in order to prevent this happening.

Three years later he presented the monument and the surrounding land to the Ministry of Works "for the benefit of the nation". It became safe from development, the public was guaranteed permanent access, and Cecil was rewarded with a knighthood for his generosity.

In 1920 the government authorised the restoration of a few of the leaning uprights, which were straightened and given concrete foundations for safety reasons. Colonel William Hawley oversaw the work, and spent time from 1919 to 1926 excavating and studying the site. He identified the Aubrey and Y and Z Holes and discovered the cremated remains, which proved the monument's funerary aspect. He also unearthed many rock samples, arrow heads, coins and other items, many of which are displayed in museums today, and took copious notes which are still referred to by modern archaeologists.

Ironically though, the more that was learned about Stonehenge, the more the mystery deepened. In 1923 Dr HH Thomas worked out that the bluestones were from the Preseli Hills in Wales, and had somehow been transported across the country more than four thousand years earlier, adding a new puzzle to the site that remains to this day.

And two years later a pilot noticed a pattern in a nearby field that led to the discovery of Woodhenge, the similarly styled wooden construction from the same era as Stonehenge, which gave new context to the stone structures as well as creating even more intrigue.

In the 1940s local archaeologist John Stone excavated the Cursus earthwork, establishing its age and how it was made. After that, with friends and fellow archaeologists Richard Atkinson and Stuart Piggott, he excavated Stonehenge, identifying the different phases of its construction and getting closer to correctly dating it.

Twenty years later, in the 1960s, the biggest breakthrough came with new innovations in radiocarbon dating. It was discovered that rather than metal and stonework having spread from Mediterranean societies to the "barbaric" tribes of Britain, many of the latter's monuments and tools actually predated their supposedly more sophisticated cousins. This refined the methods of calculating historic age, and young researcher Colin Renfrew, who later became a pioneer in radiocarbon work and a professor of archaeology at Cambridge, was able to identify Stonehenge as a Neolithic rather than Bronze Age construction, and finally unlock the secret of just how old it was.

Another major discovery was made in 1979, when a massive hole was uncovered next to the Heel Stone, proving that it had once stood as half of a pair. While the belief that the monument was erected so the sun would rise directly over this stone on midsummer morning still persists, this demonstrated that it actually rose along the circle's central axis and between the two marker stones, in the same way it set between the uprights of the Great Trilithon on midwinter night.

As these new insights revealed more about the site – as well as adding further to the mystery! – Stonehenge became one of the most popular tourist attractions in the country, and was also a favourite with the "alternative" of society. While evidence that the druids hadn't actually built the monument increased, modern druids adopted it for their own, performing ceremonies there from the 1950s onwards.

Pagans, hippies and New Age performers were drawn too, and between 1972 and 1984 the Stonehenge Free Festival was held every June, culminating with the summer solstice celebration. Bands played, fires were lit, campsites were set up in the surrounding fields, and people danced within the stones on Midsummer Night's Eve then sat solemnly on the monoliths to watch the sun rise the next morning.

This all ended in 1985, when police clashed with a large group of travellers, modern-day gypsies who camped in forests and parks in caravans and buses. The festival had been banned, and the police set up roadblocks to stop a group of several hundred travellers who were heading to Stonehenge. In the ensuing melee, men, women and children were assaulted by police, caravans were destroyed, many travellers ended up in hospital and more than two hundred were jailed in an incident that came to be known as the Battle of the Beanfield.

There has long been tension between those charged with protecting Stonehenge and those who believe they have the right to do whatever they want there, but in recent times this seems to have settled down.

English Heritage, which now looks after the monument, is coming to understand the reverence in which so many people hold Stonehenge, and their desire for access on important days of the seasonal year, while spiritual seekers are beginning to accept that the site does need conserving. Since the year 2000 the circle has been open all night for the solstices and equinoxes, with pilgrims allowed to gather within the stones to celebrate as long as they respect the rules made to protect it.

The new battle is between the government and UNESCO, which has threatened to revoke Stonehenge's World Heritage Site listing if the British government doesn't do something to relieve traffic congestion and other environmental concerns believed to be damaging the structure and its outlying monuments. Plans to close the road, create a tunnel bypass for the highway and move all visitor facilities much further away have long been discussed – so the stones have a chance to breathe clean air and be reunited with the sacred landscape that surrounds them – but as at 2010, no action has been taken.

Meanwhile, research into the site continues. In 2007 the settlement of Durrington Walls was unearthed just three kilometres from Stonehenge, and is being closely studied. It's the largest Neolithic village ever found in Britain, built within a massive henge and featuring many houses as well as the remains of two timber circles, which indicates it was a settlement as well as a ceremonial complex.

It's been dated to 2600BCE, and archaeologists believe it's where the builders of Stonehenge lived. Professor Mike Parker Pearson, who leads the ongoing excavation, thinks the sites were linked both physically, by the processional routes that wind up to each of them from the Avon River, and ritually, with the timber temples of Durrington and Woodhenge a monument to the living, and Stonehenge a monument to the dead.

In May 2008 a new excavation took place within the inner sanctum of Stonehenge, the first in almost fifty years, which revealed it was used as a burial place, possibly for royalty, from as early as 3000BCE. A year later the foundation of another stone circle, dubbed Bluehenge, was found down by the river at the start of the Avenue. And in July 2010, just weeks into a new three-year study, geophysical imaging techniques revealed the base of a late Neolithic monument less than a kilometre from Stonehenge, on the same orientation as, and similar in size to, the iconic circle. Such discoveries add new possibilities and speculation as to the purpose of the monument, and mean the history of Stonehenge will continue to unfold and reveal itself to a new generation.

The purpose

"Stonehenge is a synthesis of geometric types and proportions, an acknowledgement of all the gods in nature, designed to attract and harmonise the forces of the cosmos for the benefit of life on earth. It is a cosmic temple, an image of the created universe and its microcosm, the human mind."
John Michell, English philosopher, archaeoastronomer and author

Stonehenge is one of the most enigmatic, inspiring and sacred places on earth, not just because of its artfully shaped stones, unique lintels and sophisticated design and geometry, or because it's been a place of ritual and ceremony for thousands of years, but because even today it provides different things to different people.

Some identify with Stonehenge as part of an ancestral connection to a time when humans were at one with the earth, others feel the power of the leylines at the site and the healing energy of the stones themselves, and there are also those who regard the monument as a holy place, a temple where they can worship the powers of nature.

Stone circles were constructed throughout the British Isles from around 3200-1500BCE, which marked the beginning of agricultural settlements. These circular spaces had an astronomical alignment to indicate the cycle of the seasons, and were also used as ceremonial sites and gathering places to celebrate religious rituals, births, deaths and marriages, and in some places they acted as burial grounds too.

Stonehenge, the most impressive of them all, has been all of these things at different times, and may have been other things as well. No one knows the exact purpose – although we're a lot closer to the truth than previous generations, who have had some wild ideas about how it was built and why, describing it as a faery ring, a fortress, a fertility temple, the coronation place of kings, a druid college, a space ship and even a galactic telephone.

In one legend, a group of giants were turned to stone while dancing in a circle with their arms linked, resulting in the position of the uprights and their lintels, and reflecting the Latin name Chorea Gigantum – the Giants' Dance or Giants' Round. A related theory was that the monument had been built by a race of giants and transported by them from Africa to Ireland, where Merlin the magician plucked them away into thin air, to re-emerge at their present location.

Another story was that the devil tricked an Irish woman, who had the stone circle in her backyard, into giving it to him. He offered her a huge bag of gold coins and told her to take as many as she could count in the time it took him to remove the stones. She grabbed the bag, and the devil instantly magicked the entire structure away from her, reassembling it on Salisbury Plain without having to pay a cent.

This also explains how the Friar's Heel Stone got its name. Apparently a friar saw the devil land the stones, and taunted him. Enraged, he threw one of the rocks at the friar, where it struck him on the heel and bounced off, landing outside the circle, where it remains to this day. Some claim there's still an imprint of the friar's heel on the stone, hence the name, although others say it's more likely to come from the Celtic Welsh term ffriw yr haul, which translates as "appearance of the sun".

Another retelling is that the devil challenged the locals that they couldn't accurately count the number of stones. The friar correctly answered: "Too many to count," which infuriated the dark lord and made him throw one at him. A related myth, that no one could arrive at the same number twice, persisted throughout the 1700s, with warnings that a person would go to hell, or just go mad, if they tried and failed.

The Romans, who ruled Britain from 43CE until 410, believed Stonehenge was the burial place of the rebel queen Boadicea, who led a famous uprising against them in the early years of their occupation and remains a potent symbol of Britain today. Roman historian Cassius Dio wrote that the locals had buried their warrior queen in a lavish ceremony befitting a Celtic monarch, with the druids constructing Stonehenge as her tomb and memorial. Today it's thought she was actually buried at the top of London's Parliament Hill or under what's now platform eight at King's Cross station, but even as late as the 1600s historian Edmund Bolton claimed Stonehenge as her grave.

Others believed the monument was built as the tomb of Aurelius Ambrosius, the famous fifth century king of Britain and supposed uncle of King Arthur. In the 12th century Geoffrey of Monmouth stated that this was the purpose, which was accepted for hundreds of years, with Italian-born historian Polydore Vergil describing the circle as "a royal sepulchre in the fashion of a crown of great square stones" in his 16th century opus *Historia Anglica*.

A related version of this story maintains that after a legendary battle against the Saxons around 450CE, Ambrosius wanted to build a grand monument on the site to commemorate all his brave soldiers who had died in combat. He asked his adviser Merlin for suggestions, and the wizard told him to send his troops to Ireland to bring back the stone circle known as the Giants' Dance. When the king's men couldn't move the stones, Merlin transported them by magic.

Another theory holds that the stones were erected with a different kind of magic – levitated into position with the vibrational power of music and voice by priests from Atlantis. A similar idea is connected to the Egyptian pyramids, which were constructed, according to some, by people using sound and light to move the stones, a form of vibrational energy we no longer know how to access.

Some spiritualists suggest that specially trained Atlantean choirs were able to sing the stone circle into place, breaking down the force of gravity and the dense matter of the slabs with the pitch of their voices to lift them into position. Others feel Stonehenge is an Atlantean monument, created by the survivors of this ancient lost land to resemble their city of origin, and some even link Merlin to Atlantis, claiming that he became a druid priest in Britain after his old home sank beneath the waves, neatly linking the two theories.

There are also those who believe that Stonehenge is a stargate, a transdimensional portal where you can communicate with extraterrestrials and other dimensions. Tradition speaks too of the places where the veil between the worlds is thin, sites of heightened energy where people with psychic ability can communicate with the dead or beings from other realms. Some feel that the monument is a doorway where the energy and magnetism of the earth opens up gaps and can transport someone bodily to, or at least allow them to access information from, the spirit world or other dimensions.

"Sacred spaces are associated with specific times – Stonehenge with summer solstice, Newgrange with winter, Solomon's Temple with the equinoxes. This creates a massive increase in the energy available at that power centre at that time. This alignment enhances the energies for healing, for foretelling the future, for fertility or for general growth in spiritual consciousness."
Sig Lonegren, US-born English-based geomancer, dowser and author

One of the most popular theories today is that Stonehenge was built as an astronomical observatory, an intricate map finder that mirrored the constellations and predicted the movement of the heavens, including the daily, monthly and yearly phases of the sun and the moon, lunar eclipses, solstices and even the appearance of meteoroids.

This concept was developed by English astronomer and scientist Norman Lockyer in the early 1900s. He believed that the circle was an ancient Celtic temple aligned to the seasonal ritual days in order to serve the people of the time's religious purposes, and many spiritual seekers today identify with this purpose, feeling a connection to those who lived in harmony with the earth and its seasons and revered nature as worthy of worship.

Since then others have elaborated on this idea. In the 1950s Scottish engineer Alexander Thom studied many of the monuments of the British Isles and found that they were all orientated to the sun or the moon.

He discovered a form of measurement he called the megalithic yard, which he believed all stone circles – including Stonehenge – were based on, and was astounded that, two thousand years before Pythagoras, the ancient builders had grasped and utilised the geometric and mathematical principles the Greek philosopher later made famous.

In the 1960s astronomer Gerald Hawkins reinvented Stonehenge as an incredibly advanced Stone Age computer, able to calculate lunar eclipses and other astronomical events by measuring alignments between the Aubrey Holes and the Station Stones. British cosmologist Fred Hoyle also championed this lunar theory. He believed that Stonehenge phase one – the bank and ditch earthwork and Aubrey Holes – was an instrument that proved the builders possessed an amazing astronomical knowledge, far removed from the simple-minded, barbaric characteristics previously attributed to Neolithic man.

But while the archaeoastronomical aspects of Stonehenge remain the most inspiring and intriguing purpose to spiritual pilgrims today, many of the assumptions they're based on are inaccurate. The main issue is that several of the calculations of sight lines rely on multiple parts of the structure working together, such as the Station Stones and the Aubrey Holes, yet not all of the features were present at the same time, so they couldn't have been used together to form the alignments.

In addition, the weather in England has long been rainy and grey, with sunrises and moon orbits often totally obscured by clouds, so such precise measurements would have been almost impossible to calculate. Today there are instruments that identify the exact moment of solstices, equinoxes, moon phases and eclipses with pinpoint accuracy, without need of observation, but back then it was the recording of events over many years that created a pattern. So as intricate and amazing as Stonehenge is, it's not specific enough as a marker of time or celestial events to be considered a computer device.

It's more likely to have been a cruder astronomical calendar that enabled the ancients to follow the progress of the seasons and know when to plant and harvest crops and hunt the animals they relied on for food. The building of Stonehenge coincided with the beginning of agriculture and permanent settlements, when people stopped moving around the countryside to survive and began transforming the landscape to support them. Being aware of how many days until winter began or spring returned was crucial to their ability to sustain themselves.

Yet there are much simpler ways to mark the seasonal days than lugging massive rocks hundreds of miles across the country and erecting them, and the ritual importance of the monument should not be underestimated. Many experts now believe the site was used primarily for religious ceremonies, and that its astronomical qualities were a tool to assist in their timing, rather than the main purpose.

As the burial mounds and barrows of the same era demonstrate, Neolithic people were deeply attuned to the physical and etheric energies of the seasons, and placed deep ritual significance on them. Their long barrow burial chambers were orientated to sunrise on the winter solstice, the day of rebirth and new beginnings, when the sun returned and the soul was believed to be birthed into a new life.

Other stone circles and structures were aligned to other seasonal days, which reflected not only the turning of the Wheel of the Year, but also the emotional and energetic changes that take place as the seasons change, the phases of the god and the goddess they worshipped through their interaction with nature, and the cycle of a human life.

They were also attuned to the energies of the earth, and used standing stones and megalithic circles as acupuncture needles to unblock, regulate and activate the flow of power across the land. Stonehenge was built on a hub of leylines, the magnetic lines of energy that run through the earth linking sacred sites, which makes it a very potent place, literally buzzing with energy.

Constructing such a massive and sophisticated stone monument on this grid of leylines would have focused and contained the life force and strength of the earth, which means Stonehenge may have been a power station of sorts, a battery to store the energy which could then be tapped in to on special days, empowering rituals and boosting the strength of the people and the land. Funnily enough, the layout of the monument actually looks like a power point when viewed from above – a modern construct, but an interesting coincidence.

Such an energy centre is the perfect place for communing with the gods, raising consciousness and manifesting things into the physical, because leylines activate and increase your awareness, which could be the reason the ancient builders chose to construct their circle on this otherwise unremarkable plain.

While leylines aren't yet fully understood, you can see their effect when you walk around Stonehenge with a pair of metal dowsing rods, which swing wildly in certain places as the earth energy influences their movement. A scientific project testing the magnetic fields at the site uncovered some anomalies that appear related to this hub of energy lines, and you can also feel the shifts of energy yourself, physically within your body, as you wander around inside the circle.

There are several major leys that run through Stonehenge. One runs from a mound to the north and passes through two of Stonehenge's Station Stones then down to Old Sarum, Salisbury Cathedral and other historic earthworks. Another proceeds along the axis of Stonehenge, continuing for 35 kilometres and connecting several ancient monuments. This one, which passes through a major long barrow, up the Avenue and into the circle, may have also been a spirit way, an etheric path that the mourners, and the spirit, took after a funeral, which also connects to the site's burial aspects.

A third leyline runs south from Arbor Low, a stone circle and henge in the north of England, through the immense megalithic complex of Avebury and down to Stonehenge. Another runs due west from the monument to the town of Glastonbury and directly along the axis of its now-ruined Abbey, intersecting there with the famous Saint Michael leyline that courses the length of the country.

Followers of earth-based religions, from the builders of Stonehenge through to the early druids, who shared many beliefs about the natural world with them, and modern-day pagans and geomancers, recognise the unique swirling vortex of energy formed when two leylines intersect. The ancients established sacred ritual spaces, initiation centres and healing temples at these points to utilise the amplified energy and boost healing and spirituality, and it is these qualities that people today are seeking when they visit sacred sites.

This quality also ties in with a new archaeological suggestion, based on findings related to recently unearthed skeletons that were buried around the monument, that Stonehenge may have at some time been a healing centre, an ancient Lourdes, where people flocked from all over Europe to touch the powerful stones, drink water charged with their energy and be treated by the priests of the day.

The concept of healing has long been associated with the circle. In the earliest writings about it, the stones were described as having great curative powers for everything from wounds to serious illnesses. In the 1100s Geoffrey of Monmouth claimed that the giants who had constructed Stonehenge poured water over the stones then ran it into baths in which they immersed their sick. "There is not a single stone among them which hasn't some medicinal value. In these stones is a mystery, and a virtue against many ailments," he wrote.

A century later English poet, historian and priest Layamon recorded that it had magical healing powers, and: "Men that are sick fare to that stone and they wash that stone, and with that water bathe away their sickness." The tradition continued into the 18th century, when James Brome, a clergyman and travel writer, published a book that included a local belief: "If the stones be rubbed, or scraped, and water thrown upon the scrapings, they will heal any green wound or old sore."

It was assumed that the stones charged the water that fell on them with their innate healing power, like crystals do, so people gathered the water that sat in the gullies and fissures of the fallen stones to both drink and bathe in. When there wasn't enough in the natural pools, fresh water was poured over the monoliths and collected. Others placed their hands on the stones to absorb their healing energy, while some lay full length on the Altar Stone hoping for a miracle.

Today people still pray for healing within the circle or lie on the fallen central stone in the hope it will trigger wellness. This monolith, known by some as the Goddess Stone, was long believed to have particularly powerful healing properties, as well as the ability to help women conceive, a common motif in goddess worshipping cultures. Others charge a crystal or a bottle of water with the power of the stones, so they can continue drawing on it when they're back home.

The leylines boost the natural power of all the stones. And the bluestones also have additional, unique healing properties – they're said to be useful in boosting immunity and fertility, treating inflamed bone and joint conditions, increasing memory and clarity of thought and assisting during childbirth, as well as in general healing. Emotionally they balance male and female energies, enhance past life recall, meditation and dreaming, and can help centre and ground you.

Bluestones are native to Carn Meini in the Preseli Hills in Wales, a beautiful, rugged and peaceful mountainous area dotted with healing springs. Archaeologists believe that, thousands of years ago, it was a place of pilgrimage for people seeking physical cures. The springs all had sacred altars and shrines made from the bluestone rocks set up around them, and were surrounded by Neolithic earthworks.

It's now being speculated that the builders of Stonehenge may have decided to make their own pilgrimage site to attract people to their area – as well as a local hospital – by creating a monument from these healing stones, which would explain why they dragged the bluestones so far across the country at such incredible effort.

In the Preseli Hills there's an ancient stone circle, Gors Fawr, made from the same famous bluestones as Stonehenge, but so tiny in comparison that I was surprised at the power it emits. Set in a lonely field, it's comprised of sixteen stones, with two outer ones creating a solstice alignment. One of these is known as the dreaming stone, and has an intense magnetism that you can physically feel. This circle has a very gentle, feminine quality to it, which may have been a consideration when the stones were being selected for Stonehenge.

"Summer solstice commemorated the consummation of the gods when the world was created. The intention is yearly fertilisation during a visual re-enactment of this marriage which everyone could witness. The sun's rays penetrate the Earth Mother's womb – the stone circle – to arrive at the misnamed Altar Stone."
Terence Meaden, English archaeologist and author

At different times Stonehenge has contained within it solar and lunar alignments, making it a temple to both the sun and the moon, and an alchemical melding of masculine and feminine. This has resulted in many fascinating goddess connotations, which is not surprising given that at the time Stonehenge was erected people all over the world believed in and worshipped the Great Mother goddess, particularly through nature, and built fertility shrines and other ritual places throughout the landscape in her honour.

An important ceremony – which is still performed by pagans today – was the Great Rite or Sacred Marriage, that symbolised the union of god and goddess. Re-enacting this moment, which they believed created the universe, reassured people that life would go on. It also united the two forces of masculine and feminine and the elements of yin and yang that were so central to nature-based religions.

The ritual could be performed literally by priest and priestess, or through the rays of the sun piercing the earth or a specially built structure, such as the megalithic tomb of Newgrange in Ireland, where the rays of the solstice sunrise enter the womb-like mound and illuminate the inner chamber. At other places, including Stonehenge and Avebury, a phallic shadow created by the sun rising behind a rock pillar would creep over a feminine-shaped stone, symbolising the sacred union of god and goddess in a different way.

There are a few such alignments at Stonehenge, some of them involving the central monolith known as the Altar or Goddess Stone. This unique green-tinged slab of sandstone once stood in the centre of the monument, sparkling more brightly than any other in the complex. Some believe the arrangement of trilithons and bluestones surrounding it represented the womb of the goddess, which was inseminated by the light of the sun to symbolically recreate the Sacred Marriage.

It's claimed that on the morning of the summer solstice the shadow of the phallic-shaped Heel Stone reached out and touched the centre of the Goddess Stone. This would have been a powerful ritual to ancient people, who saw in this sacred re-enactment on this sacred day the continuation of life and the ongoing union of the goddess and god, and suggests that at one time Stonehenge was a temple of the goddess.

It's now known however that the Heel Stone was not a lone monolith but actually one of a pair, and that the rays of the sun rose between the two, not over one, so the Heel Stone could not have been the earthly manifestation of the god. Yet at one point there were another three pillars, including the Slaughter Stone, positioned in the entranceway of the henge, so it's possible that the sunlight crept between the Heel Stone and its partner and cast a shadow from the middle of the next three stones onto the central Goddess Stone.

Other significant masculine-feminine pairings existed even earlier, between the four Station Stones. Two were "male" stones, taller and more pillar-like, and two were "female", with grooves naturally occurring in the faces of the rocks. At sunrise on the summer solstice, one of the male Station Stones created a shadow that touched one of the rounder female stones. At sunset on the winter solstice, the other male stone cast a shadow that penetrated the groove of the other female stone. And the two equinox sunrises were indicated by an alignment between a Station Stone and another that stood in the Avenue.

It wasn't just the solstices and equinoxes that were revealed by these alignments. The cross-quarter day of Beltane, which falls in early May in the northern hemisphere, was also an important day in Ancient Britain – the major fertility festival, of both the land and the people, and the first day of summer. On Beltane Eve, while standing in the centre of Stonehenge's circle, the sun set over the western female stone, indicating that the next day was the festival. This same alignment also occurred at Lughnasadh, which was the first day of autumn, while the other female stone marked the Samhain and Imbolc sunrises and the first day of winter and spring respectively.

However these cross-quarter alignments no longer existed when the sarsens were erected, because the hulking trilithons blocked the sight lines – one of the dangers of archaeoastronomical theories that don't take account of the dates of construction of the different phases.

The angles of the rectangle formed by the Station Stones are believed to have indicated the two northern and two southern extremes of moon rise and moon set over each 18.6 year cycle, and continued to do so after the monument was complete – although whether later people still used this knowledge is uncertain.

Astronomers have noted that the alignments of the Station Stones wouldn't have been the same at any other latitude. At this location the lines between the four stones create a perfect rectangle, whereas if it had been located further north or south the alignments would have made a parallelogram, which wouldn't have fitted within the circular bank and ditch of the henge. Salisbury Plain is one of the few places these rising and setting points occur at right angles to each other.

In all our searching to uncover the purpose of Stonehenge however, we must remember that our own preconceptions colour our understanding. We're misled when we try to imagine its meaning because we apply modern ideas and perceptions to it – which is unavoidable as we can never truly think the way ancient man did.

The builders of Stonehenge lived in a time before the scientific breakthroughs we take for granted, when people believed the sun was a god that ruled their lives from the heavens, which we can't comprehend because we know it's simply a star the earth revolves around, independent of our actions, and not a deity who must be appeased.

So while we can calculate the dates of eclipses past and future with computer technology, and now understand what creates them and when they'll recur, this doesn't mean the ancients would have wanted to predict them, known how to or even realised that they could. These people regarded eclipses and other planetary events as omens and signs from the gods, anomalies sent to warn them of impending famine, disaster or war, rather than regular, normal celestial events that could be predicted and charted.

Our modern wording also takes us away from the truth. Describing the trilithon arrangement and its inner bluestone setting as horseshoes is incorrect in one sense, as there were no horses in Britain then, and distracts us from the original purpose. It's more likely that the placement of the stones was intended to be crescent-shaped like the moon, indicating a lunar purpose, or womb-like, symbolising the ovaries of the goddess and creating an inner sanctum echoed in the burial mounds of the period, which would reveal it was a place of goddess worship. Even the word calendar limits our perception, because we're enslaved to the concept of time and dates in a way the ancients were not.

We also have to remember, in trying to uncover the intention of the builders, that the monument was constructed over a period spanning fifteen centuries, so its use would have changed over time. The first phases of Stonehenge, including the henge earthwork and Aubrey Holes, probably were utilised to mark the cycles of the moon, as ancient peoples were aware of its movement and lived by its phases, which were easily observed in the night sky. The first calendars were lunar, with Cro-Magnon people credited with inventing one around 32,000BCE, using the moon's phases to mark the passing of time. Stonehenge may also have been a lunar temple back then, reflecting the worldwide trend to revere the silvery orb as a goddess.

Later, sun worship became more important to all cultures, and at some point the monument became a solar temple and an observatory. It marked the movement of the sun, with the summer solstice sunrise alignment a major focus for a long time – and the one that endures to this day. During another period the winter solstice sunset became more of a focus, as the purpose shifted according to the changing religious and spiritual beliefs of the local people and their needs.

At some point the purpose changed again, to a commemoration of the dead, with the holes once used to hold astronomical marker stones now utilised to bury cremated remains. This doesn't mean the seasonal rituals and sun worship necessarily ceased – they may have carried on in varying forms while the structure was also used as a crematorium – and new evidence shows it may always have been a burial place.

Burnt human bones have been found at many stone circles, leading to speculation that they were constructed as community or even family graves, or ritual sites to celebrate the eternal circle of life, death and rebirth. This reveals a people with a reverence for death and ancestor worship, which was reflected in the purpose of Stonehenge.

At various times it has also been a place of deep ritual magic and ceremonies to symbolise the marriage of masculine and feminine, as well as a temple of healing. It's possible too that the druids used it as a classroom, court of law or gathering place, or adapted it for their own celestial observations. And others, in their own time, may have used it for their purposes, such as the Romans in the pre-Christian days. In the same way a castle or manor house was taken over to become an army barracks or hospital as people's needs changed, Stonehenge was many things to many people over its long life, and remains so today.

"Modern Stonehenge has become an archaeological site, a tourist attraction, a marketing opportunity. But prehistoric Stonehenge was never this – it was a sacred place of uncomprehended power on a mysterious earth. Most important today is the enduring attitude to the place that alternative beliefs offer, not as an artefact tamed by our own age but as a sacred place. Here there is a resonance with the truth of an ancient Stonehenge."
Christopher Chippindale, British archaeologist and author

Like a modern church, Stonehenge had many uses. After all, why would people invest more than thirty million man hours over fifteen hundred years just to mark two days of the year that could have been calculated in a far simpler way? A church hosts religious services, weddings, christenings, funerals and Easter and Christmas celebrations, and Stonehenge too was a multi-purpose site. Many of the uses may have occurred simultaneously – a solar temple where the sun was worshipped, a calendar that marked the seasons, a monument to the dead and site of religious observances, a gathering place for ceremony and special occasions in the community, even an amphitheatre for performances, given new studies regarding the acoustics of the stones.

The continuing investigations and the changing ideas about the meaning of Stonehenge are fascinating, and I'm almost more intrigued at how dramatically the way humanity thinks has changed, than the actual purpose itself. Not that long ago it was inconceivable that humans could have existed earlier than the time of the Romans, and for a while the possibility that Neolithic man had lived as far back as 4000BCE was considered as dangerous an idea as Darwin's theory of evolution. And even as it was finally accepted that people had lived then, no one believed primitive man was capable of building the monument, so it was assumed to have been giants or Merlin's magic.

But those who dreamed up Stonehenge aren't that different to us. In evolutionary terms we're pretty similar to the people of five thousand years ago, who were capable of political thought, religious construction, societal and family ties and moral judgement, just like us.

And yet today some people still feel that aliens must have built the monument, because they can't work out exactly how it was done. It's all relative though – I don't understand how someone designed an airplane or invented a cure for cancer, yet I know they did. So why is it so hard for us to imagine that someone like us raised a circle of stones to worship within and mark the passing of time?

While we may never know the original purpose of Stonehenge, in the end it doesn't really matter why it was built, it just matters how it influences and affects us now. While it wasn't actually constructed by druids, it was clearly the work of a people attuned to the cycles of the seasons and aligned with the power of the earth, and in modern times it was the druids who revived the monument, imbuing it with their essence and giving it a new purpose, so in a way it is a druid temple.

Today it remains a place of worship, an outdoor shrine and sacred site that helps people remember their own sacred purpose. Visiting now, connecting to its energies and feeling the emotions that come from standing within the circle or even on the perimeter, gives an incredible sense of perspective on life. In its unchanging grandeur and eternal wisdom it shows us how unimportant and short-lived we are in the grand scheme of things – yet by its continued existence this glory built by man, which has stood for thousands of years, also demonstrates the meaning we can create if we choose to.

Ultimately we give Stonehenge meaning. As mysterious as it feels and as ancient as it is, the important thing is not why it was built or for what purpose – it attracts people today because it moves us now. It has a sacredness to it that is of this moment. While it was erected by long-ago people as part of their spiritual beliefs, it's used today to celebrate the seasons and connect to the earth – and ourselves – in a blend of spirituality that is ancient yet thoroughly modern.

In the same way, we give our own lives meaning. It doesn't matter what someone else wants for you, or expects of you, or even what you're doing right now. You can create your own meaning, your own purpose, and live the life you dream of. Standing in the shadow of this famous structure, touching the ancient stones, I realised *we* must give our life meaning, rather than just assuming it has one. Whether you call it life purpose, destiny or simply the dream you've chosen to pursue, it's your responsibility to create meaning and take charge of what you want to be, what you want to do and what you want to leave as your legacy.

You can create your own monument to live on through time, be it a physical construction, a work of art, a foundation in your name that raises money for an issue close to your heart or simply a kind deed that changes someone's life and lives on through them long after you're gone. And while the meaning of your legacy or purpose may be different to everyone else, the important thing is how it affects and moves you.

The psychic connection

Tips to immerse yourself in the energy of Stonehenge

1. Get your very own piece of Stonehenge. Bluestones, which make up half of the monument, are used for physical and emotional healing, and are a powerful aid for grounding, centring, meditation and psychic work. You can buy a small piece, sourced from the same Preseli Hills outcrop Stonehenge's were brought from, as a small chunk, carved trilithon, piece of jewellery or pendulum, and attune yourself to its energies by wearing it, holding it or sleeping with it under your pillow.

2. Sit under a tree in the park and watch the shadows move as the sun passes across the sky. Following the movement of the sun, moon and stars through the uprights of Stonehenge is a magical, mystical experience, but you can be aware of the same sensations wherever you are. From a hill near your home, or just from your window, take note of where the sun rises and sets in the middle of summer, and watch how this changes as the seasons progress, getting furthest away at midwinter, before slowly returning to the same point. Attuning yourself to the movement of the planets and the passing of time calms you down, centres you and gives you a greater appreciation of life.

3. Create your own stone circle, with pebbles, rocks, crystals or clay. A shape without beginning or end, a circle symbolises eternity and the continuing cycle of life. Magical rituals take place within them as they mark the boundary between the worlds and create a protective barrier that contains the energy raised and keeps out negativity. Size isn't important – you could create one big enough to sit within, or a tiny one to keep on an altar or bench to charge crystals. You can also create a sacred protective circle with white candles or salt.

4. Practise psychometry, a form of divination that uses the sense of touch to gain mental impressions from an object. Psychics use it to connect to the person they are reading, tune in to them and pick up messages, because everything has an energy imprint, from a piece of jewellery or a book to a person or a house (think of how easy it is to pick up on negativity or anger when you walk into a room). Touching the stones of Stonehenge triggers floods of images in many people, as the wisdom stored within them is accessed, and you can also do this with other rocks, or any object you want to gain information from.

5. Celebrate the summer solstice. Watch the sun rise, pondering the symbolism of the Sacred Marriage of the sun god with the earth mother as the first rays light up the horizon and bathe you in light. Breathe in this active energy, and vow to take action to manifest one of your goals into reality. As the longest day of the year, you have the most time to start creating whatever it is you want to leave of yourself to the world.

The armchair traveller's way to visit

"Witches recognise the importance of flowing with nature's rhythms, seeing in our own nature the reflection of the moon's orbit around the earth. Knowing that the moon rules the tides, and being ourselves made up of a high content of water, we can maximise the energy of our lives by understanding this lunar influence."
Titania Hardie, Australian-born English-based witch and author

While the solar association with Stonehenge is openly celebrated, the lunar connections have long been obscured, much like the gentle, feminine goddess elements of life are today overshadowed by the more aggressive, masculine god aspects. But you can connect to the energy of this ancient stone circle and the philosophy of balance inherent in its builders by learning about the phases of the moon.

This beautiful silvery orb still exerts power over us, particularly on women, who are physically attuned to its cycle. It's long been regarded as magical, and has been worshipped as a goddess throughout time and across cultures. To the Ancient Celts, and magical practitioners before and after, the phases of the moon symbolised the phases of a human life – birth, adolescence, adulthood, death and rebirth – and were associated with the Triple Goddess, the Great Mother deity that included the aspects of maiden, mother and crone within her.

These were represented by Rhiannon, the young maiden goddess of inspiration and the new and waxing moon, Arianrhod, the mother goddess of fertility and the full moon, and Ceridwen, the crone goddess of death, rebirth and the waning moon. In Ancient Egypt Isis was the mistress of the moon, in Rome Diana was the lunar deity, and in Greece it was Selene and Artemis. Many other goddesses of different cultures are also associated with lunar energies, feminine mystery and psychic ability, so work with whichever one you feel most drawn to in order to increase your intuition and your connection to the moon.

Invoke them in a ritual, write to them, channel a message or meditate on or draw their image. Or create a garden filled with plants that flower at night, like moonflower, angels trumpet, evening primrose and jasmine, to create a sacred space where you can communicate with them.

Spending time outside in the moonlight gives a different perspective on life, showering you with mystical light and casting a silvery glow on the world. It connects you to the feminine energy of the universe, which has nothing to do with gender but is simply a sense of gentleness and intuition you can tap in to. Psychic powers and divination have long been tied to the moon, and basking in its light can increase your intuitive abilities and help you get in touch with your inner self.

Another way to absorb the energy of the moon is by leaving a glass of water outside under the full moon then drinking it the next morning, feeling yourself energised and re-attuned. Or work with moonstone, an iridescent, milky crystal that looks like a piece of the moon illuminated with rainbows, which increases psychic visions, enhances intuition and sensitivity and boosts dream awareness and spiritual awakening.

The phases of the moon are determined by its position in relation to the earth and sun, as it orbits our planet roughly every 29.5 days, the basis of the original month. The moon has no light of its own – instead it's illuminated by the light of the sun reflecting off its surface, with its phases created by the amount of the illuminated side we can see.

You can picture these phases by imagining a clock. The earth sits in the centre of the clock face, with the sun above the direction of 12 o'clock. The moon is at the end of the minute hand, circling around the clock face – and the earth – in an anticlockwise direction. It begins its cycle at 12, directly between the sun and the earth, which makes the moon invisible to us because the side that reflects the light of the sun is facing away from the earth, towards the sun. This is the dark moon.

A day or two later, as the moon moves towards 11 o'clock, a tiny sliver of the illuminated side can be seen, which appears as a thin crescent. This is the new moon. In the southern hemisphere it looks like a C, while in the northern hemisphere it's reversed, appearing as a backward C, and at the equator it's horizontal rather than vertical.

The crescent continues to increase as the moon moves from between the earth and the sun, and the angle between them allows us to see more of the moon's reflected light. By the time it gets to nine o'clock, which takes about a week, it's at right angles to the earth in relation to the sun, and we see a half circle. This is the first quarter moon.

When the moon gets to six o'clock, it's on the other side of the earth from the sun, with the earth in between. The whole of the side we see is reflecting back sunlight, so we see a round moon in all its shining, silvery glory. This is the full moon. The size of the moon hasn't changed, it's just that we're seeing the fully illuminated side.

After that it appears to decrease as it progresses back to the dark moon. When it gets to three o'clock we again see a half moon in the sky, although this time it's facing the other direction, a C in the northern hemisphere and a reverse C in the south. This is the last quarter moon. From there the moon continues back towards 12 o'clock, with the crescent getting smaller each night until it finally returns to the beginning, where it's invisible again, and the cycle starts over.

As well as lunar calculations published in newspapers, almanacs and online, you can determine the phase of the moon by its shape, as well as the time it rises. This occurs about fifty minutes later each day, although it varies slightly depending on the season. It can be remembered by the old adage: "The new moon rises at sunrise, and the first quarter at noon. The full moon rises at sunset, and the last quarter at midnight." So if you see a half moon in the afternoon it's the waxing first quarter, which rose around midday and will set around midnight, but if you see it in the morning it's the waning third quarter moon.

As the moon goes from dark to full it's the waxing or growing period, a time of new beginnings, growing vitality and increasing energy. As it goes from full back to dark it's the waning period, a time of lowering energy and introspection. Magical practitioners use the cycles of the moon to increase the power of spellworking, harnessing the universal energies inherent in each phase. So do fishermen, who understand the incredible pull the moon has on the tides of the ocean.

Gardening also operates to the rhythms of the moon, as its phase can enhance or hinder plants. To boost growth, sow crops that produce above the ground in the period between new moon and full, as the light and energy increases, and plant crops that produce below the ground, such as root vegetables and bulbs, between full moon and dark.

Hair growth too is influenced by the moon. If you want your hair to grow faster, trim the ends between the new moon and the first quarter. If you want it to grow thicker and fuller, trim it during the full moon phase. And if you really like the style and want to maintain it, have it cut around the third quarter, so it grows out more slowly.

The moon affects tides, plants, animals and even the behaviour of people. Some can't sleep during the full moon, others feel more emotional or have strange dreams. It's common to feel more energy during the waxing phases, and more tired when it's waning. There are also many tales of accidents and psychic breakdowns increasing at the full moon.

The moon's effect on us today is no doubt much less intense than it was back in the time that Stonehenge was erected, when people were far more aware of its phases and could clearly see it rise and set. Today its journey across the sky is obscured by buildings and we've lost touch with nature – even women's cycles, which used to be intimately connected to the moon, are now controlled by chemicals.

But the moon does still affect our energy and emotions, and has been used since ancient times to influence the outcome and power of rituals, spells and ceremonies, and empower any project you want to complete. Here's how to take advantage of the phases of the moon.

New moon: The day the tiny new crescent moon is first sighted, and a day or two afterwards, is a period of heightened energy and new beginnings, and is a good time to start new projects, make resolutions and vows you want to stick to, take a new direction or look for a different job. Chinese New Year always begins at the new moon, bringing energy and vitality to the coming year. It's the time to plant seeds, both literally and metaphorically, be it in the garden or in your life, where you sow ideas, dreams and hopes. A simple yet powerful new moon ritual is to write down your wish for the coming month at this time, and keep it somewhere you can see it as you harness the power of the subsequent moon phases to make it come true.

The waxing moon: From new moon to full the energy is strong and positive, so concentrate on attracting and drawing things to you. It's the optimum time for magical workings to bring love, abundance and new career opportunities, and for learning new things, expanding your outlook, increasing spirituality and boosting fertility. If you need to release something while the moon is waxing, reverse the intent so it still fits with the moon's energies. So rather than giving up smoking by releasing your addiction, create a ceremony to attract willpower to you. If you're doing healing work, draw good health to you when the moon is waxing, and release illness when it's waning.

The waxing crescent moon, spanning the week after the new moon, is the sprouting phase, when you nurture the seeds you planted at the new moon. It brings energy and new growth to projects, and helps you manifest them into reality. The waxing half moon, the first quarter, halfway between new and full, is the growth phase, although the energy can be a little challenging, pushing you towards achieving your goals and working to finish a project. And the waxing gibbous moon, spanning the week that it is moving towards full, is conducive to expressing yourself, being in touch with your feelings and taking action.

Full moon: The three days of the full moon – the day of, the day before and the day after – can be used to boost any intention or project. This phase represents achievement, culmination and abundance. The world is filled with energy and potential, and it's a great time for healing work and manifestation. Magical practitioners have long celebrated the magical power of the full moon, performing rituals to draw down its energy and embrace the divine inspiration contained within its light. Stand beneath the shining moon and give thanks for what you've achieved so far, and breathe in the energy and power and harness it for self-expression and inner strength. It's also a great time to charge crystals and amulets with new energy, and psychic abilities are at their strongest, so practise any divination methods you are drawn to.

The waning moon: From full moon to dark the energy is slowing down. It's a time for banishing and release work, for letting go of things that no longer serve you, such as past relationships, a bad habit, a characteristic like procrastination or any material things weighing you down and blocking your progress. It's the perfect time to do releasement rituals to banish things, people and situations from your life. If you need to attract something while the moon is waning, reverse the intent to make use of the different energies – so rather than doing a spell to draw new love to you, cast one to banish loneliness.

The disseminating gibbous moon, in the first few days after full, is a phase of introspection and self-assessment. In the garden this energy promotes root development, and in life it's a time to stand strong within your own self and find your inner power. The waning half moon, the third quarter, brings a reflective energy, and is the time to focus on what you've achieved and what you still need to do. And the waning crescent moon is the letting go phase, a time to release things so you can prepare again for the new beginnings of the new moon.

Dark moon: While some magical practitioners take a day off at the dark moon, others use it to go within, using the introspective energies to examine their feelings and thoughts and delve deep within their psyche. While the moon is hidden it's also a powerful time to scry and perform any kind of divination that will uncover your truths, and for getting in touch with your inner wisdom and approaching the mysteries.

Eclipses: Lunar and solar eclipses, while fairly rare, also affect the energies of the universe – and our emotions – and were connected to Stonehenge from its earliest phase. An eclipse occurs when one celestial body obscures another, either partially or fully. Because of the angle of their orbits, the sun, moon and earth rarely align precisely, which is necessary for an eclipse. But when the moon is directly between the other two, which can only happen at the dark moon, it blocks the sun's light from the earth, creating a solar eclipse that makes the sun seem either totally or partially invisible. When the earth is directly between the sun and the moon, which can only happen at the full moon, the earth blocks the sun's light from reaching the moon, producing a lunar eclipse that dims or even totally obscures the moon for a brief time.

Energetically, eclipses create opportunities for change. They push you, forcing you to move forward and continue on your path. To some they're a wake-up call, nudging you on and making sure you don't lose sight of your dream. A solar eclipse puts you in touch with your intuition, and is a time to take stock of where you're at and examine your inner self, while a lunar eclipse gives you the strength to be honest about who you are and move forward without fear of judgement.

"Druidry is a spiritual path rooted in the green earth. It means learning from archaic traditions, three centuries of modern druid scholarship and the always changing lessons of the living earth. It means embracing an experiential approach to religious questions, abandoning rigid belief systems in favour of inner development, and individual contact with the realms of nature and spirit."
John Michael Greer, American druid and author

Learning about the path of druidry and incorporating some of its spiritual principles into your life is another way to connect with Stonehenge. The druids have long been associated with the sacred circle, adopting it as their own, and today they remain closely linked to it, carrying out seasonal rites and initiations there. They are also guardians of sorts, campaigning to protect the monument from overcommercialisation and making submissions and suggestions about the proposed highway scheme and other issues that affect it.

Modern druidry is a beautiful nature-based spiritual path with strong roots in the Celtic past, and a fierce environmental consciousness in the present. Then as now the druids held the earth as sacred and revered all of nature, including the land, the sea, the sky, the stones, the trees, the rivers, the creatures, the sun, the moon and the stars. They were connected to the rhythms and cycles of the universe, and had an intimate knowledge of plant lore, animal spirits, trance-induced journeying, seasonal shifts and healing.

While the roots of druidry, like other shamanic religions, stretch back twenty-five thousand years, significant periods of development began when the megalithic builders constructed their incredible monuments across Europe. These people aren't identified as druids, but their philosophy is closely linked, and they displayed an astronomical knowledge and engineering prowess we can barely grasp today.

Later, the Celtic druids who settled in Britain during the Iron Age were documented by first century BCE Roman emperor Julius Caesar. In his tome *The Gallic Wars* he wrote: "The druids were in charge of religion, judges and arbitrators in disputes, and teachers and keepers of knowledge. They look after public and private sacrifice and hold long discussions about the heavenly bodies and their movements, about the size of the universe and the earth, about the nature of the physical world, and about the power of the immortal gods."

The druids were the priests, scholars, healers and philosophers, and this remains true today of those who follow this gentle spiritual path. Traditionally there were three branches – bards, ovates and druids – although modern adherents usually learn all aspects of the craft, whether they glean a brief overview of the principles or study the subject in depth for many years as an ongoing religious practice.

Bards were the storytellers, musicians, artists and keepers of wisdom, who studied for twelve years or more to learn the poems, stories, philosophies, history and music of the land. They performed these at festivals and ceremonies, and also created new tales to record important current events and encapsulate the spiritual power of the day, finding inspiration and creativity in nature and their deities.

Ovates were the healers and seers who communicated with the gods, divined the future and healed physical and emotional illness with herbs, magic and spiritual methods. They were the community's medicine man or woman, the midwife, the one who helped people face death, communed with the ancestors and oversaw healing ceremonies. Modern witchcraft traces its lineage from this aspect of druidry.

Druids were the wise elders, scientists and judges who advised kings and individual communities, directed rituals, interpreted the law and passed judgement. They oversaw education, teaching a wide range of topics both magical and mundane, and were also metalworkers, alchemists, astronomers, engineers and mathematicians. They spent their entire life studying and imparting their knowledge, hence the image of them as white-haired old men like the wizard Merlin.

With the infiltration throughout Great Britain of Christianity, which was the dominant religion by the sixth century, this nature-based path went underground. Some druids converted to the new ways, melding their wisdom with it, while others practised divination and the healing arts in secret. Some of the teachings were preserved by the monks and priests, and other parts were hidden in myths and legends.

It wasn't until the 16th century, with a revival of interest in ancient Greek and Latin writers, that scholars began studying the old knowledge, and a druidry revival began which painted this form of spirituality in a less primitive new light. A romantic image began to emerge, encouraged by William Stukeley, and by the 19th century groups such as the Theosophical Society and the Order of the Golden Dawn began teaching the magical principles that underpin druidry.

In the 20th century, George Watson MacGregor Reid started a group, later known as the Ancient Druid Order, which was inspired by old literary works, folklore and druidic research combined with various mystery traditions and their own observations of nature. They offered health care to members, campaigned on social issues and performed ceremonies at Stonehenge. In the 1950s two members, Gerald Gardner and Ross Nichols, branched out and developed new traditions. The former recreated the neopagan religion of Wicca, which incorporates the magical arts, and the latter reinterpreted druidry, focusing on Celtic lore, mythology, the sacredness of the natural world and the seasons.

Druidry blossomed during the peace and love hippie era of the 60s and 70s. Folk band Jethro Tull peppered their albums with references to nature, standing stones and the gods, and John Lennon wrote about druidic rituals in his song *Mind Games*. Since then it has slowly become more widely known, and is now recognised as a serious spiritual practice that welcomes people of all religious traditions.

Once druidry was limited to the sacred groves of the British Isles, but today people all around the world study the path, and you can learn about it through individual apprenticeship, books, workshops and online courses. OBOD, the Order of Bards, Ovates and Druids in the UK, offers in-depth training, but while it can be approached in an almost scholarly manner, with different levels of knowledge to be attained, you can also simply adhere to the basic spiritual principles.

Druids are connected to nature and hold it as sacred. They celebrate the eight sabbats of the Wheel of the Year, becoming attuned to the changing seasons which they regard as a metaphor for life. Many are vegetarian because their reverence for the natural world extends to the animal kingdom, and environmental principles guide their life, with many being vocal activists in issues ranging from forest preservation to anti-war rallies. Most worship the god and the goddess, as single deities or a pantheon of nature-based aspects of the divine spirit, but some are Christians and others are atheists, believing that it is within nature and the earth that all truth, sustenance and life lies.

They believe in a realm beyond the natural world, an Otherworld where spirits, animal guides and wisdom reside. This is the place they think they will go to when they die, but they can also access it in life through dreams and visions, in meditation and through shamanic journeying and trance states. They perform divination, including psychometry with stones and other things of nature, and understand the movement of the planets and the pattern of the night skies.

For some druidry is a religion, for others it's a spiritual path, and there are those who see it simply as a way of living in harmony with the planet, a philosophy of life and way of being that steps gently on the earth. It's a form of spirituality that can be followed anywhere, and learning its wisdom can connect you to the earth energy and power of Stonehenge and the people who lived and worshipped in its shadow.

"Trees in particular were mysterious, and seemed to me direct embodiments of the incomprehensible meaning of life. For that reason, the woods were the place where I felt closest to its deepest meaning and to its awe-inspiring workings."
Carl Jung, Swiss psychiatrist and founder of analytical psychology

Trees were very important to the druids, a gift from the goddess that both sustained physical life and symbolised the eternity of existence. They provided food, shelter, warmth, flowers and medicine, as well as spiritual lessons and deep healing. Druids worshipped within groves of sacred trees, rather than indoors, so they could be connected to nature and nurtured by the ancient strength of these majestic plants. The word druid is believed to have come from the ancient Celtic word for oak, dru, and truth, druidh, or from drus, the Greek word for oak, combined with the root word wid, which means to know, so druid meant wise person of the oak.

They used trees in magic and for protection and healing, and you can tap in to druidic energy by growing one of their sacred trees, creating a wand from a fallen branch, using the leaves in herbal preparations or simply sitting beneath a tree and connecting with its spirit. Many druids are also involved in tree planting and reforestation projects, another great way to show your love for the earth.

The following are some of the traditional sacred trees of the druids, but all trees and plants have healing power, magic and something to teach. Connect with these trees, or find your own favourite and attune to it, learning all you can from its characteristics, spirit and healing qualities. Each country has a variety of beautiful trees, and you may feel more drawn to one that's native to your land.

Apple: This tree represented innocence, youth, peace and joy, and the wood was popularly used to make wands. The apple was also the mystical fruit of the Otherworld, associated with the goddess and used in fertility rituals and love spells as well as to increase abundance. It symbolised wisdom and hidden knowledge, which was revealed in the five-pointed star found when an apple was cut crossways.

Ash: One of the most sacred of all the trees, the wood of the ash was used to make druid wands specific to healing and solar magic, while the leaves were placed under the pillow at night to stimulate visions and prophetic dreams. The tree represented the element of air but was also associated with fire, and was thus connected to resurrection and renewal. Its deep roots indicated grounding and protection.

Birch: Revered by the druids, this tree represented new life and new beginnings, and symbolised the goddess. The bark was used in love potions, and a sprig of the leaves was worn for luck and love. It was also connected to purification and protection, and for this reason witches chose birch twigs to fashion their brooms, which were used to energetically cleanse and purify both their home and ritual area.

Elder: The queen of the trees, elder held the wisdom of the crone and had powerful feminine energy. It represented renewal and regeneration, aided transformation and deepened visions and visualisation rituals.

The wood was used for protective wands, and was associated with the summer solstice and the sun. It was used for magic involving nature and the spirits of the earth, and had powerful healing properties.

Hawthorn: A contradictory tree, with beautiful white blossoms but large thorns, hawthorn represented duality and balance, a melding of masculine and feminine as well as life and death. It was associated with Beltane. The wood was popular for wands, and was used for love spells and in marriage rituals, as well as for protection and healing.

Hazel: This tree represents knowledge and inspiration, as well as forgiveness. The wood was used to make wands for healing and ceremonial work, and forked twigs of hazel were used to divine the location of water and energy leys. It was associated with the sun, so it was used in solar magic, as well as when working with faeries, and it helped people understand the traits of humans and animals.

Ivy: This beautiful twining vine symbolised endurance and survival through all situations and conditions, as it clung on through the harshness of winter. The five-pointed leaves were used as an amulet of protection, it was woven into headpieces to symbolise clarity and knowledge, and was a powerful healing tool. Because it grew in a spiral pattern it also held the qualities of rebirth and interconnection.

Mistletoe: Associated with the winter solstice, this evergreen bush was considered a gift of the gods, representing the sacred marriage of heaven and earth. The berries were used in love spells and incenses – a connotation they retain today in the ritual of kissing under the mistletoe – and the leaves were hung around the home to protect against negativity. It often grew around oaks, a magical combination.

Oak: Considered the king of the forest, the oak is sacred in all cultures. Druids revered it for its size and great age, and it was a tree of courage, strength and endurance, connecting people to the wisdom of the earth. The wood was used for divination and to make wands, the roots were used to make magical tools, and the acorns were a nutritious food as well as being used in fertility and protection spells.

Pine: A tree of purification, pine was known as the sweetest of woods, and was burned to cleanse an area physically and psychically, while a branch was used to sweep a place of old energy. The tree encouraged strength and courage, and had revitalising and re-energising powers. Pine cones were used in fertility spells and carried as charms, and pine needle ritual baths were taken to stimulate and cleanse emotionally.

Rowan: Sacred to the druids, rowan was used for protection and to guard against enchantment. The wood of the tree was used to make wands for psychic work and wisdom, as well as druid staffs, divination tools such as runes and rods for divining water and energy, similar to what a dowser uses today. The flowers symbolised cleansing and blessings, and the berries were regarded as the food of the gods.

Willow: Druids would sit within willow groves to receive divine messages and communicate with the dead, and artists would go there for inspiration. The willow was associated with water and the moon, and as such was a powerful ally in developing intuition and divination powers. Wands made from its slender, flexible branches were used in lunar magic, and it had qualities of flexibility and adaptability.

Yew: Representing rebirth and regeneration, yew was sacred to druids and Christians, who both regarded it as a symbol of eternal life. It was used in funeral rites, connected with the ancestors and the Otherworld, and to increase divination powers. The wood was used to make bows and the handles of athames, the magical ritual knives.

"Merlin represents the great old sage-wizard archetype. He's known as a powerful magician, a spiritual teacher and a psychic visionary. Merlin comes to those who have a sincere desire to learn the spiritual secrets of alchemy, divine magic and manifestation skills; his knowledge is his prized possession, and he shares it willingly with those whose hearts are loving and pure."
Doreen Virtue, American author and angel therapist

The magician Merlin can be invoked if you want to increase your psychic skills and your ability to prophesy. He is the mythical character so famous in the King Arthur stories, the wise old wizard who ensured Arthur's birth through magic and enchantments, and who served as the chief advisor to several kings. Merlin has long been associated with Stonehenge and its construction, and he remains a powerful archetype of learning and wisdom.

There are beautiful legends throughout the British Isles, as well as from Brittany in France, of Merlin's love for Vivienne, also known as Nimue, the pretty priestess he taught all his secrets to, of the sword he placed in the stone for his protege Arthur to remove and thus claim the crown, his creation of the magical Round Table, his building of Camelot and his amazingly accurate visions of the future.

The ultimate druid, it's believed that the Merlin we know of is based on the legends of Myrddin Wyllt, a sixth century Welsh bard who was so traumatised by war that he fled civilisation and remained in the woods as a hermit, living with the animals, surviving on plants and working with herbs. He was a sage and elder with strong prophetic powers and magical abilities, and is represented in paganism as the Green Man or Horned God, the primary male deity and nature god.

The Merlin also came to be the title of the chief druid of the land, in the same way that the Lady of the Lake referred to the highest priestess. This man was wise beyond reckoning, filled with the power of nature and able to harness the elements of earth, air, fire and water to perform magic, an enchanter who worked with herbs to create spells and healing potions. He handed down the sacred druidic lore, teaching his apprentices all he knew, and could shapeshift into different animals.

Whatever you believe him to be and however you picture him, Merlin is an archetypal energy that can be called on to aid you in developing, controlling and increasing your own divination skills and psychic abilities. You can also invoke him for protection spells, advice and counsel, and to connect with the old gods and the old wisdom.

Many people work with Merlin in the physical realms to protect the land and achieve environmental goals, for he is the champion of nature and the earth. Ask him for inspiration and advice on the best method to help the planet and maintain its sacredness, then watch for signs of the most effective ways for you to make a difference. He is also patron of herbcraft and healing, so you can connect with him by learning about herbal medicine or studying a healing technique – attuning to his vibration will increase your abilities and understanding. And he is an expert in astronomy, so seek a message from him in the stars too.

One simple way to call on him is by visiting one of his sacred standing stones, which can be found all over the world, and placing your hands on it, tuning in to the wisdom held within. You can also go to a sacred grove of trees and meditate within it, or sit with your back against the trunk of a single tree. Listen to the wind whispering in the leaves above you, and try to discern any messages or feelings Merlin, the spirit of the tree or your higher self is trying to impart to you.

Another way to invoke Merlin is by drawing pictures of the wise old wizard, which can be as simple or as complex as you like, and connecting with his aura and energy. Or write a letter to him asking for advice – you may be moved to scrawl down his reply, for automatic writing can be a very effective form of divination. The night of Samhain – in early May in the southern hemisphere and early November in the northern – is a particularly powerful time to communicate with him.

You can also ask him to come to you in a dream. Drink peppermint or rosehip tea before bed and put ash leaves or calendula flowers under your pillow, drawing on the magic of herbal lore to open up your consciousness, then enjoy the wisdom and answers Merlin – or the inner wizard of your own self – imparts to you in your sleep.

Postcard from Stonehenge

Cassandra Eason is a British psychic researcher, clairvoyant, reiki healer and tarot reader. She's had her own TV series in the UK, appeared on many shows and been the dream analyst on *Big Brother*. She is also the author of more than fifty books, including *A Year and a Day in Magick*, *The Modern Day Druidess*, *Pendulum Dowsing*, *Becoming Clairvoyant* and *Pagan in the City*.

She originally trained in teaching and psychology, but became fascinated by the spiritual world in her late thirties when her young son Jack, namesake of his mystical grandfather, told her his father was falling off his motorbike as it was happening fifty kilometres away. Cassandra teaches inspiring magical courses in Europe and runs an extensive website with articles, original research and online classes. Visit www.cassandraeason.com.

I first visited Stonehenge as a little girl when we went on a coach trip from my home in the industrial Midlands – one of those "seven wonders of England in a day and be back home for tea" adventures. My father Jack told me we were going to see the enormous magic stones created by Merlin the magician, who had waved his wand and turned to stone some wicked giants who'd made a circle around King Arthur and were trying to kill him. Although my father was a factory worker, he loved all things mystical and wondrous and filled my head with fantasies.

When I first saw the circle of stone giants looming out of the mist it was like entering a faerytale, and I drove everyone mad asking where Merlin was and why he wasn't guarding the giants. We didn't stay long, but I left my magic wand from my Christmas faery set under the biggest stone for Merlin. Years later I still love my father's version of the building of the stones, even though archaeology suggests he was a few thousand years ahead with his dates.

As I became an adult, long before I worked as a spiritual practitioner, the stones were a place I'd go to feel permanence and stability in what seemed a frantic life that I could barely control.

Now, as a solitary druidess, my beautiful stones are enclosed and even Merlin must pay a fee and book a time to enter. I prefer to circle the perimeter after the solstice crowds have gone home. As I do, the sturdy little Midland child I once was dances eagerly beside me with her magic wand and darts in and out of the stones, while my now long departed mother organises a picnic and scolds my father for turning a sensible teacher-in-the-making into a wild pseudo-Celtic renegade.

As a spiritual teacher I don't see the physical barriers now protecting the stones, but can weave my way following the earth spirals on that flat, windswept plain. I can walk with the pilgrims of long ago to a site fabulous in tangible tourist terms but a thousand times more glorious on those times when moon and sun vie for sky space and the car park is deserted, when the stars claim centre stage above the unmoving silent stone witnesses of the turning centuries.

Once I saw Merlin at Stonehenge when, distressed and alone, I'd driven a hundred miles only to find the site closed. I walked in the mist and the mud with the little girl anxiously holding my hand and my mother offering her cold tea and awkward sympathy. In a sudden flash of sunlight through the clouds Merlin appeared above the stones, large as the giants he conquered, glorious with his wand of swirling stars, and for a moment all the giants circling me in my life were turned to stone. Then he was gone and the world still turned and I went home.

You can't avoid the leyline energies at Stonehenge. Walk anywhere around the plain and your feet are drawn, burning, through the earth, following and linking spontaneously with the feet of the mysterious builders of the stones, the druids who later reclaimed a spiritual heritage, and those through the millennia who have come in their coach and caravan loads to stare or walked solemnly in procession. All have been silenced by the same unchanging earth rhythms – older than religion, defiant of analysis and measurement and indifferent to the need to justify religions, science or scepticism.

Stonehenge is. It exists independently of the curious with their cameras, the myriad spiritual groups drawn by the sun and those in the thundering traffic who stop, stunned by the sanctity of the place.

Increasingly, as the modern world fails to answer questions of who we are, where we come from, where we belong and where we return to, the stones offer tangible proof of a world that endures as empires rise and fall. They are sacred symbols beyond words of a vision we still can scarcely understand, constructed by simple farming people with primitive tools as an accurate observatory of the stars, moon and sun, in a pattern echoed albeit less magnificently throughout Europe.

With modern technology, people around the world can now watch the most perfect summer solstice sunrise at Stonehenge from their computer, and can create in their own gardens and backyards mini marker stones, personal Stonehenges that follow the same sun, the same cosmic forces and, like the giant stones on Salisbury Plain, rest their roots in Mother Earth.

For Stonehenge is not just a monument in one place, it's an icon of how far we've come and how far we still have to travel spiritually so we can see Merlin turning his evil giants to stone, or whatever story for us expresses the wonder we pass down the millennia to future generations.

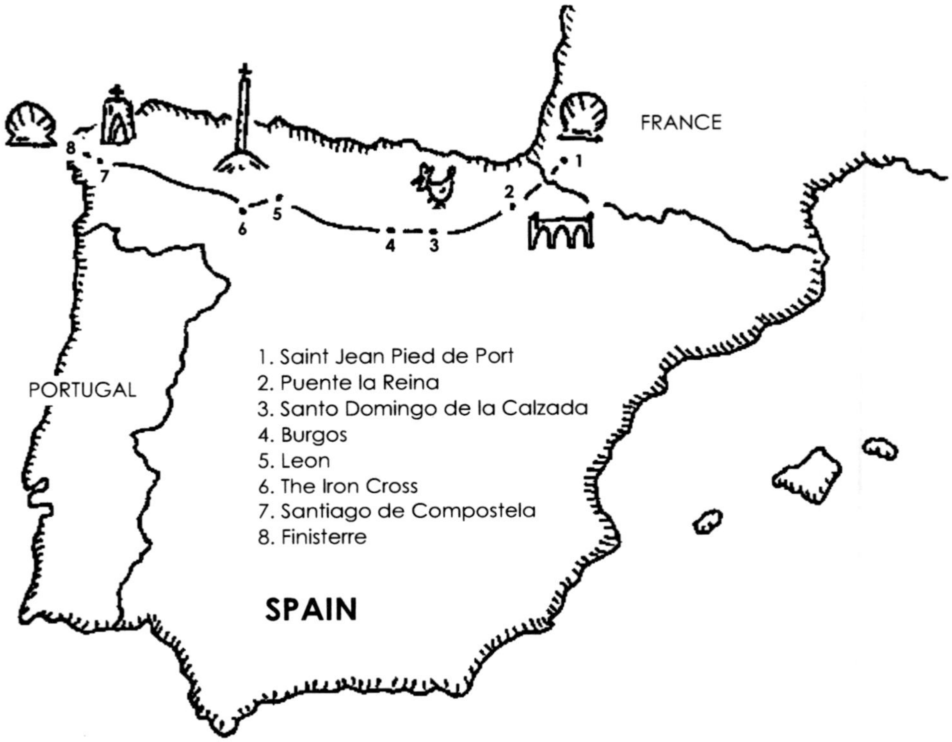

FRANCE

8

7

5

6

1

2

4 3

PORTUGAL

1. Saint Jean Pied de Port
2. Puente la Reina
3. Santo Domingo de la Calzada
4. Burgos
5. Leon
6. The Iron Cross
7. Santiago de Compostela
8. Finisterre

SPAIN

UK

FRANCE

SPAIN

*Make a pilgrimage
to your inner self*

The Camino
Northern Spain

Leave your ordinary life behind as you set out on
an ancient pilgrimage to find your true self, letting
the energies of the earth open your heart and transform
your soul as you go on a journey both inward and
outward, which will unlock the enlightenment
and wisdom you already hold deep within.

The place

"The pebbles are smoothed from the feet of the pilgrims.
The stones were changed – and so were the travellers."
Paulo Coelho, inspirational Brazilian author of The Alchemist

The Camino de Santiago – the Way of Saint James – is an ancient pilgrimage path that people of many different cultures and beliefs have been following for thousands of years. They walk it to seek the religious glory imparted by touching the relics of Saint James, which are believed to be located at the cathedral in Santiago de Compostela, or the spiritual enlightenment that's promised in reaching the edge of the world at the town of Finisterre, at the end of the route.

Stretching eight hundred kilometres westward across the north of Spain, the Camino travels up steep mountains, down lush valleys and across flat, desert-hot plains. It winds past vineyards, rolling hills and fields of fruit and flowers, along tiny dirt tracks and massive freeways, and through small villages, huge cities and old towns rich in architectural wonders, art and historically significant monasteries and cathedrals.

Pilgrims wish each other well as they pass, butterflies dance around the path, the scent of morning dew, sunbaked cobblestones, ripening apples and exotic flowers assault the senses, and a series of yellow arrows painted on rocks, road signs and the bare earth show the way forward, a way worn smooth by countless feet over the centuries.

The purpose of the pilgrimage has changed and evolved over time, and today it means different things to different people. Christians walk it to do penance, be absolved of their sins and feel closer to their deity, pagans follow it to communicate with the gods and goddesses of old and absorb the powerful earth energies, and other spiritual seekers make the trek in their quest for solitude, enlightenment and inner wisdom.

Some people connect with past lives as they walk along the route, others examine their present situation, and there are those who get glimpses of their future. Over the years the journey has been undertaken by kings and queens, saints and sinners, peasants, priests, politicians and pop stars, actors taking time out from Hollywood and even criminals sentenced to walk it as punishment.

The pilgrimage can take anywhere between four weeks and a few months to complete on foot, as people find their own pace and begin their corresponding journey within. Some ride a bicycle along the path, and others drive. Some have done it in a wheelchair, and in the Middle Ages it was often completed on horseback.

Yet the overwhelming majority of pilgrims set out with a bottle of water, a stick and a good pair of shoes and walk the full distance, determined to appreciate every stunning view, every tiny wooded track, every meeting with a local or a fellow walker, every ache and pain and every tiny step they take towards their goal.

While the destination – midday mass at the cathedral in Santiago de Compostela in northwest Spain or sunset on the beach at Finisterre on the Atlantic coast – is important, the journey itself is the real point.

Absorbing the energy of the earth and of those who have walked it before. Staying in refuges, the hostel-like accommodation provided exclusively for pilgrims, and experiencing the hardship and simplicity of another way of life. Visiting the plazas, museums and ancient cathedrals of the beautiful towns along the way – according to UNESCO there are almost two thousand buildings of historic interest on the route. Meeting strangers and sharing stories, advice and inspiration. And walking alone and learning to be at peace with yourself.

One of the first recorded pilgrimages took place more than a thousand years ago, and people have been writing about their experiences of the trek ever since. Best-selling international author Paulo Coelho walked the Camino as a religious test on his path to higher knowledge, and uncovered an inner world of magic and ritual that was detailed in his first novel *O Diario de um Mago* (The Diary of a Magus), which was published in English as *The Pilgrimage*.

For Oscar-winning actor and spiritual searcher Shirley MacLaine, journeying along this physical and etheric pathway activated deep past life memories and visions of new insight within her, which led to personal healing and her book *The Camino: A Spiritual Journey*.

Many modern-day pilgrims lace on their hiking boots and head west along the ancient path in an attempt to heal their grief at the loss of a loved one, deal with the pain of a divorce, seek spiritual healing for an issue that is holding them back from fulfilling their potential, or find answers when faced with a life-changing decision.

For the gruelling trek is a journey inward as well as outward – a physical challenge that leaves the body battered and bruised yet ultimately fitter than ever, as well as an emotional journey that can transform the soul and leave a person seeing the world, and their self, with new eyes.

The Camino follows a major leyline, a path of energy and power connected to changes in the earth's magnetic fields, and it is from this that the pilgrimage is thought to attain much of its spiritual impact. Walking along this sacred ground and interacting with these energies activates personal growth and allows your thoughts to become deeper and clearer, triggering change and incredible realisations, expanding your consciousness and opening you up to the power you hold within.

While a few people undertake it as a test of endurance or simply to enjoy the countryside, architecture, history and culture of northern Spain, the Camino is primarily done with the intention of finding your deepest spiritual meaning, be that traditionally religious or otherwise. Walking for ten hours a day for a month or more is a healing, liberating experience that creates purpose and clarity. Physically you will be filled with a sense of accomplishment and a new respect for your body and all it is capable of, while emotionally you will be empowered with a new understanding of your deeper self and your individual place in the world.

Whatever your intent in setting off on this pilgrimage, by completing the journey you will be changed by the natural miracles of inner transformation that unfold along the way.

The present

"Keep walking, though there's no place to get to. Don't try to see through the distances. That's not for human beings. Move within, but don't move the way fear makes you move."
Rumi, 13th century Persian poet and theologian

Most pilgrims set out on their Camino adventure from Saint Jean Pied de Port or Roncesvalles, two pretty, distinctive villages in the Pyrenees Mountains that mark the beginning of the Camino Frances, the most popular route to Santiago de Compostela.

Saint Jean Pied de Port, nestled in the hills on the French side of the border with Spain, is incredibly beautiful – tiny, colourful, medieval and full of character. It's an old town, where the weight of history, wisdom and tradition can be felt. The winding cobbled streets, white houses with red trimmings, stone archways and bridges over the gently flowing river transport you to another time, and another mindset. Looking out at the mist-shrouded mountains and listening to the church bells ring out to prepare walkers for their journey sinks you deeper into the magic of this ancient place and pilgrimage route.

Roncesvalles, just across the Spanish border from France, is famous as the setting of the medieval poem *The Song of Roland*, which details one of Roman emperor Charlemagne's famous eighth century battles against the Moors, the people who came from northern Africa to inhabit the Iberian Peninsula that includes modern Spain. Echoes of this history, and other legends, still abound in this pretty town.

Its monastery was once the most important in the area, documented as a refuge for those walking the Camino since the early 1100s. The village also features a cemetery for pilgrims, a museum of religious art and sculpture, royal tombs and a beautiful Gothic church where a 12th century pilgrim blessing is still read each night after mass.

I spent a few days in Saint Jean Pied de Port, exploring the old streets and absorbing the tangible culture, before I tackled the start of the Camino. That morning I woke up in the dark, struggled out of bed and into my clothes and crept quietly outside, where I followed a woman with a massive backpack towards the Spanish Gate, part of the medieval wall that still surrounds the town. The huge stone pillars were lit up with tiny faery lights that reflected the stars shining overhead, and were a fitting tribute to those setting out on their journey.

The path began with a steep but stunning walk through beautiful forests of beech, hazel and hawthorn, up quiet mountain paths, through quaint villages and across tiny wooden bridges over gurgling streams. Walking beneath the black sky sparkling with morning stars was an unforgettable experience, and my heart expanded with joy and wonder as moonlight flooded the track before giving way to the flush of pre-dawn colour that slowly illuminated the wild roses, nettle and blackberry bushes winding along the side of the road, and the fields of swaying crops and grape vines stretching off into the distance.

The mountain peaks were covered in a thick white mist that rolled slowly across the green hills. At times I walked into it, and it was wet and cold but not like rain. I breathed deeply, filling my lungs with the crisp mountain air, the scent of flowers assailing my senses and the sound of cowbells tinkling on the edge of my consciousness. It felt really dream-like and surreal, as though I was in a Swiss picture book and Heidi was about to walk around a bend in the road with her goats.

The morning was freezing cold, yet it wasn't long before I had to peel off my gloves and jumper as my body warmed up, my breath started to catch from the exertion and I could feel a slight ache in my calves. But I could sense the energy of those who had walked this way before me, and it encouraged me to push on.

Centuries of penance and adoration, forgiveness and release, pain and healing have soaked into the land. Hope, faith, prayers, visions – all the energy of all the people who've followed this path, who've struggled with it and overcome the physical obstacles to achieve their goal, still lingers. I could sense their intent and the echo of their rituals and beliefs, and I felt connected to something greater than myself as I walked. Millions of people have made this pilgrimage throughout history, following the sun westward to Santiago de Compostela, and I could feel their shadow and their spirit encouraging me onwards.

Mostly though I was impressed by the stillness and the immense quiet. I felt totally enveloped by the world, alone in the sacredness of each perfect moment. It seemed like I was floating on a cloud, all on my own, wrapped up in myself and my own stuff, independent and apart. For me, my days walking the Camino were a time out of normal life, time to be alone and silent and go deep within. Walking alone, with no complications, no one to deal with, nothing to do but walk. No one to talk to, just pure time to myself. Precious days. And it was the beauty of the solitary countryside, rather than the pretty towns along the route, that inspired and moved me the most.

The first quarter of the Camino, covering roughly two hundred kilometres, winds through the regions of Navarra and La Rioja, passing beautiful old churches and monasteries, some still in operation, others abandoned, and pre-Roman and medieval ruins. The path goes through old villages with red-shuttered farmhouses and woods of oak and pine, along stretches of two-thousand-year-old stone paved

Roman road and past huge crosses dedicated to Saint James – and cemeteries dedicated to the pilgrims who didn't make it to the end. On the other side of the mountains the countryside transforms into fields of olives, grapes and wheat, stands of poplar trees, cypress and willows, vividly coloured flowers and strongly scented herbs.

Notable towns include Pamplona, famous for the annual Running of the Bulls; charming Puente la Reina, with its 11th century bridge and life-size pilgrim statue that marks the convergence of the Arles route with the Camino Frances; beautiful Estella with its old palace and churches; and historic Logrono, the capital of the La Rioja region.

On top of one mountain is Fuente Reniega, the Renouncement Fountain. According to legend the devil tried to tempt a thirsty pilgrim to give up his faith in return for water. When he refused, Saint James appeared and showed him a nearby spring. All along the Camino there are freshwater fountains that provide clean, cold water for sweaty pilgrims, making the walk possible. And it's amazing how excited I became at the sight of them – and how my needs were narrowed down to such simple things as water and shade. Many times when I found a fountain I'd fill my bottle, drink, refill, drink, then splash around in the cascading water, running my arms and swollen fingers through it, splashing my face and laughing with such utter, pure joy. It wasn't just relief, it was child-like fun and excitement too.

A few days further ahead is Fuente del Vino, the wine fountain, which flows with free wine provided by a local vineyard for pilgrims passing by. It's situated below the 12th century Cistercian monastery of Irache, and is a highlight for many – thirsty pilgrims consume 35,000 litres a year. It's the site of many funny moments as dedicated walkers take a moment to relax from their gruelling schedule and let their hair down, but in the 40°C heat I was more interested in water!

The sun in Spain has been described as "without mercy", and setting out early each morning is recommended both to ensure a bed at the next town and to beat the heat. I suffered the consequences of a late start when I walked from Puente la Reina, with its gorgeous cobbled streets, wrought iron balconies and huge pots of flowers, to Estella. It was a beautiful journey, across the old bridge spanning the Rio Argas and along tiny dusty paths, through wide open paddocks and sleepy little towns, but the afternoon sun nearly defeated me.

Crossing field after unshaded field as the sun's rays beat down, there were times I thought I'd pass out. I greeted each rounded hay bale with excitement, pressing myself against it in the desperate hope of a little shade – a big ask when the sun is directly overhead. I must have been quite a sight, chasing haystacks and pools of shade, although many people hallucinate and imagine these mounds of hay are castles or cathedrals, and at least I didn't try to walk inside any of them.

But my whole existence and thought process was reduced to how long it would take to cross a field, how far until the next water fountain, how many more steps I could take before I really had to sit down, the degree of difficulty of getting up again if I did sit, how quickly I could cover the five kilometres to the next town, and the possibility of it having shade and a shop that sold cold drinks.

This stretch was hot, harsh and arid, yet stunning. The earth was red and cracked, but fields of green crops stretched out in the distance, a river flowed through the dusty valley and occasional vineyards provided an oasis of colour. A heat haze shimmered over everything, and the contrast from the first day's mountain-cool walk was extreme. I was excited when I reached the tiny village of Cirauqui – the viper's nest – an ancient hamlet atop a steep hill, as it was filled with medieval streets like a maze and cool stone arches to walk beneath.

Further along, as the afternoon heat peaked, a stretch of Roman road flanked by cypress trees provided a little shade, and later the path wound through olive groves and alongside a stream. In medieval times the latter was famous for its poisoned water, which killed any horse that drank it – a fact locals exploited, sitting on the river bank with a knife waiting for a hapless pilgrim to come by, then skinning their horse once it had drunk and died, and selling the hide.

"Give me the clear blue sky above my head, and the green turf beneath my feet, a winding road before me, and a three-hour march to dinner – and then to thinking!"
William Hazlitt, 19th century English writer

During the next two hundred kilometre section, the path meanders through the regions of La Rioja and Castilla y Leon, with more medieval hilltop villages, fields of cereal crops and fruit, rustic houses and storks' nests waving in the breeze atop church towers. There are long stretches of desolate, shadeless tablelands known as the meseta, interspersed with deep valleys, cliffs with caves that were once home to religious hermits, and countless shrines dedicated to local saints.

Significant towns in this stretch include Santo Domingo de la Calzada, named for its own saint, Dominic; San Juan de Ortega, founded by Dominic's disciple John, who was later sainted for his construction of roads along the Camino and a monastery that still houses and feeds pilgrims; the enchanting city of Burgos, home to the Gothic cathedral considered Spain's most stunning; and Villalcazar de Sirga, a former stronghold of the Knights Templar that boasts a magnificent church with a chapel dedicated to Saint James.

There are several famous miracles related to the Camino, and many ordinary men were transformed into saints for their work along this pilgrimage route. Some intervened when pilgrims were threatened, and others helped by building refuges for shelter or bridges and roads to make the going easier. It's fascinating to visit the sites of these miracles, even if you don't believe in them literally.

In Santo Domingo de la Calzada, legend recounts that a pilgrim walking the Camino with his parents was set up by a barmaid who, angry that he'd rejected her advances, slipped some silver in his backpack then told the innkeeper he'd stolen it. He was hanged the next morning for his crime, and his devastated parents continued onwards to Santiago de Compostela, praying for a miracle.

When they returned to the town on their journey back home they were astounded to find their son alive, albeit still hanging from the gallows with his feet supported by Saint James. They raced to the local magistrate to proclaim their son's innocence, but he was so annoyed at them interrupting his dinner that he dismissed them, saying that if their story was true the roast chicken he was eating would rise from his plate and crow – which it did. In honour of this miracle (or perhaps simply to lure in more tourists), two white chickens are always kept in a coop in the local cathedral.

It was in this historic little town that I lashed out and stayed in the luxurious Parador hotel, which was originally constructed as a pilgrim shelter by the 11th century hermit monk Dominic. He also built a church, as well as bridges and more than a hundred kilometres of roadway through the once-inhospitable forests surrounding the community. Calzada means road or causeway, so he became Saint Dominic of the Roads, and the town was named after him.

Saint Francis of Assisi stayed in this refuge during his own Camino, as did thousands of other pilgrims throughout the years, but the old shelter has now been converted into a hotel and the refuge has moved down the street. Standing in its lobby, I stared up at the beautiful high ceilings with their thousand-year-old wooden beams and heard the whispers of earlier pilgrims and the echo of their feet across the centuries. The hot bath was also a near-religious experience!

A little further west is the village of San Juan de Ortega, named after Dominic's disciple John, who founded a monastery 50 kilometres from his master's dwelling place to assist pilgrims further along their journey. This Romanesque monastery still receives pilgrims today. John, who was a priest in the local province of Burgos before becoming a hermit, was also sainted for his services. As the ortega in his name refers to nettles, it's believed that he was also a practitioner of herbal remedies, as many monks back then were.

The next two hundred kilometre section continues through the flat, baking hot meseta and wheat fields of Castilla y Leon, passing along empty, desolate plains with a bleak, unchanging horizon. It's this section that has reputedly broken some people – it seems that it should be relatively easy to pass through because it's so flat, but the monotonous tableland and intense heat have driven many a pilgrim crazy. Between Carrion and Sahagun is a 45 kilometre stretch bereft of towns, services or even water, so walkers have to stock up on food and carry water with them across this arid, seemingly interminable plain.

Fortunately the desert-like meseta finally gives way to verdant groves of poplars and oaks, fields of vegetables, cherries, grapes and cereals, and sweetly scented patches of wild herbs such as thyme, sage and lavender. The way becomes more fertile as it progresses westward, and passes several cute little villages built into the hillsides. With the more interesting mountain pathways however come hugely steep and difficult climbs, but each section of the Camino has its positives and negatives, its beauty and its hardship.

Interesting stops in this section include the old Roman garrison town of Leon, formerly the centre of the Order of Santiago and impressive for its ancient monuments and beautiful old churches; Astorga, which once boasted twenty-one refuges and is home to architect Antoni Gaudi's acclaimed bishop's palace, as well as the remains of a Roman villa and shops and stalls overflowing with mantecadas, the region's famous sweet pastries; and Foncebadon, the tiny abandoned village where a 12th century hermit ran a shelter for pilgrims, but which has since become home to several wild dogs.

The way also passes Cruz de Ferro, the Iron Cross, one of the most iconic symbols of the Camino; the town of Ponferrada, which features the imposing ruins of a Knights Templar castle; and Villafranca del Bierzo and its Puerta del Perdon, the Door of Forgiveness. In times gone by the church declared that pilgrims who were too sick or injured to continue their journey all the way to Santiago de Compostela could pass through this door and receive the same dispensation for their sins as if they'd completed the whole trek.

This is an intriguing part of the route for its history, legends and strange encounters. I was nervous as I approached the ghost town of Foncebadon, which is a sad, desolate place to pass through. The ruins of the church and hospice built by the hermit monk Gaucelmo almost a thousand years ago loom alongside several fallen down, long abandoned houses, but there is a small bar that serves hot tea and tasty sweet treats to fortify pilgrims for their walk past the wild dogs.

This town has been mentioned in many Camino accounts for the ferocity of its dogs and their propensity to attack pilgrims. Shirley MacLaine sent them love when she was faced with a growling pack, and Paulo Coelho got down on his knees and barked back at his challengers. My heart beat faster as two large canines approached me on the outskirts of the village, barking and snarling aggressively, but I spoke as soothingly as I could as I hurried by, trying to ignore them while also being very much aware of exactly where they were. Finally, with much relief, I got past them, and continued up the mountain to the Iron Cross, the symbol of the pilgrimage's power to help you release the past.

"Think about any attachments that are depleting your emotional reserves. Consider letting them go. We can't become what we need to be by remaining what we are. Turn your wounds into wisdom. Breathe. Let go."
Oprah Winfrey, American TV host and publisher

Situated on the summit of Monte Irago, the Iron Cross marks the highest point of the Camino, at 1504 metres, and has long been used as a landmark to help pilgrims get their bearings in the mountains of this region. The cross was left there by the Romans in the time before Christ, and was a homage to Mercury, their deity of walkers, travel and trade, and a messenger of the gods.

The small metal cross itself extends from a 10 metre wooden pole that has all sorts of things tied, taped and attached to it – scallop shells, flowers, ribbons, prayer flags, photos, messages for other pilgrims, even an old boot. Around the base of this is a milladoiro, a huge cairn of stones, which was known to the Romans as the Mount of Mercury.

It's now a Camino tradition that pilgrims bring a stone or a pebble from home, or find one along the way, and pour their troubles into it as they walk. Then when they get to the Iron Cross they leave it on the pile, symbolically leaving behind their burdens, their past or their sins.

It has become a powerful releasement ritual that helps people let go of the emotions they've been carrying for so long and lay down the baggage from the past, opening the way for healing and allowing them to move forward with more energy, strength and power. Some pilgrims consider that they're leaving their sins behind, while others give over a belief that's been holding them back, a physical illness, guilt, grief or emotional pain, or a relationship that no longer serves them.

You can put whatever is weighing you down emotionally into the stone. To do this you can simply hold the stone and use the power of intention to transfer your emotions into it, or you can employ a shamanic technique and physically blow the pain into the stone. Another way is to sleep with the stone under your pillow or keep it in your backpack as you walk, allowing it to absorb everything you want to let go of. Some people call the pebble they leave at the Iron Cross a sorrow stone, and fill it with years of pain so they can release it all and open up their heart to more love, confidence and inner fire.

Despite all this misery though, it feels surprisingly happy and light at the site. Fortunately the sadness doesn't linger in the air or the earth, but is transmuted by the intent of the pilgrims, the power of this ancient ritual and the purity of the sunshine and mountain air.

This is a ceremony that goes beyond any system of faith. Spiritual seekers of today use such rites to release illness, negativity, relationships and grief. The ancient pagans and the Romans did it, and it's also developed into a powerful Christian symbol. Adding a stone to the pile makes you part of a tradition stretching back more than two millennia and crossing cultural boundaries – Spaniards, Germans, Australians, Americans and pilgrims of many other nationalities all take part in the ritual, and it's become widely known around the world.

A little way further on from the Iron Cross is the abandoned village of Manjarin, famous for the tiny rustic refuge that is run by modern-day hermit Tomas, who has devoted his life to helping pilgrims in much the same way that the saints of the past did. He provides food, shelter, information and Gregorian chants, and assists anyone caught in the bad weather common in the mountains.

The narrow winding path down through the mountains from Manjarin to the pretty little town of Molinaseca is beautiful but incredibly steep. Descending was much more difficult than I'd expected – harder than going up sometimes, especially when the ground is shaley, which is why so many pilgrims use a walking stick or hiking pole. The trail passes through tunnels of tree branches, chestnuts and roses, alongside a stream and through fields of broom that I had to push my way through, like an enchanted walkway.

There are tiny traditional villages perched on the slopes, which each have a Saint James statue, a church and a few sweet wooden houses with slate roofs, overhanging balconies and external staircases, all interspersed with pine-scented forests, wildflowers and colourful birds and butterflies. I paused to rest for a while and have a snack in a little sacred grove, surrounded by vivid blooms and shade and pools of filtered sunlight, and was overwhelmed by the beauty of the place and the incredible sense of peace that descended on me as I sat there.

The last two hundred kilometre section of the Camino, through the region of Galicia, is one of the most challenging for hikers, but also the most beautiful, with spectacular views, a lush Celtic beauty and an unspoiled countryside dotted with vivid purple heather and bright, bobbing sunflowers. Much of the path winds up and down mountains or along rolling hills, passing through forests of chestnuts, oaks, pines and eucalypts, along cobbled lanes and into tiny hamlets that still retain their medieval character. And every five hundred metres there's a sign counting down the distance left to Santiago de Compostela.

It's a mystical, mist-shrouded and magical region, and the weather is often more like Ireland's than the sunny days usually associated with Spain. Gentle rain, the reason for the rich green beauty of the area, is likely, and downpours are not uncommon. Galicia was once inhabited by the same Celtic tribes who swept through the British Isles, and because of this the people of the region share many ties with Ireland and Brittany, from their musical styles and dress to their political views, food, lifestyle and culture.

Memorable places in this section include the village of Cebreiro, which sits atop the mountain of the same name and is famous for its tiny round pallozas, the old straw-roofed Celtic dwellings, and the church that housed its miracle; the sixth century town of Samos, with its impressive art-filled Benedictine monastery, which still provides accommodation and services for pilgrims; Portomarin, whose church was moved stone by stone to higher ground when the old town was submerged to build a dam; and Melide, which boasts a fascinating museum charting the history of Galicia and one of the oldest churches and religious crosses on the route.

Towards the end is the village of Lavacolla, whose name means "washing one's loins", which was the place that pilgrims in the Middle Ages bathed in preparation for entering the Holy City of Santiago de Compostela and taking part in the mass; and Monte de Gozo, the Mount of Joy, where modern pilgrims catch their first glimpse of the spires of the Catedral de Santiago, which is just five kilometres further on.

In the village of Cebreiro, legend states that a 14th century priest who'd stopped believing in what he preached was shocked and disdainful when a pious farmer climbed the mountain through a raging snowstorm to attend mass. He was resentful because the man displayed more faith than him, and angry at his lot. To honour the farmer's devotion and shock the priest back onto his path, it's said that during the consecration the bread turned into the flesh of Christ and the wine transformed to blood, renewing the priest's faith. Today the paten that allegedly held the flesh and the chalice that held the blood still sit in the chapel to be revered by the faithful.

The Camino path becomes more crowded from this point onwards, and the refuges fill more quickly, because people short of time – or the endurance to travel the whole route – begin their pilgrimage in this section. Walkers only have to trek the last hundred kilometres to receive the official certificate of completion from the church (and a guarantee of a place in heaven), so there are many people trudging along this section of the track who are just starting to get blisters. Some of the serious pilgrims, who've already walked seven hundred kilometres and been suffering for weeks by this stage, look down on the new arrivals, particularly if they can't get a bed because of them.

But all the frustrations fall away when the end is reached and the pilgrims finally stand in the shadow of the grand cathedral in the town of Saint James – the focus, for some, of the entire pilgrimage.

It's a beautiful building, so large, ornate and intricate against the deep blue sky and the warmth of the sunshine that illuminates it in an almost divine fashion. It has a grandeur that impresses people of all spiritual and religious beliefs, with its triple nave and radiating chapels, imposing Romanesque structure and sweeping spires and turrets. It was begun in the ninth century, destroyed by the Moors in the 10th and rebuilt with even more splendour in the 11th, with additions continuing until recent times.

As exhausted pilgrims climb the steps they feel an overwhelming sense of achievement, relief and completion – and sometimes also a feeling of loss that it is over. But there are several rituals to mark the end of the journey. Most lay their hands on the pillar inside the doorway, which has resulted in a groove being worn in the stone, then hug the large 13th century statue of Saint James above the elaborate altar, kiss the gold scallop shell and finally pay their respects at the crypt where a silver casket houses what are said to be his remains.

At noon each day there's a Pilgrim Mass, during which the country of origin and Camino starting point of successful pilgrims are read out. In Holy Years, when Saint James's feast day of July 25 falls on a Sunday, the massive botafumeiro, an incense burner, is swung from the ceiling. Traditionally this was done to hide the stench of those who had walked so far in such basic conditions, although today it's more symbolic.

The cathedral is on one side of the Praza do Obradoiro, the main plaza of the town's Old Quarter. Next to it is the pilgrim hospital built in the late 1400s by Queen Isabella and King Ferdinand after they completed their Camino, which has been converted into a luxury hotel, the Hostal Dos Reis Catolicos. This grand building still boasts the original chapel and its artwork, and continues the tradition of serving pilgrims, giving away thirty free meals a day to the first to arrive.

On the other side is the 12th century bishop's palace, which adds to the atmosphere and history of the square, and the magnificent Pazo de Raxoi, a more recent palace that was built for seminarians but which now houses the mayor's office, city council and the Galician Culture Council. The surrounding streets are closed to traffic, and walking through this old section is amazing. Santiago de Compostela is a beautiful, peaceful town, with winding cobbled streets and medieval stone buildings contrasting with the bustling, colourful markets, street entertainment, thriving university culture, art, theatre, restaurants and fascinating Galician customs and food.

"You cannot travel the path until you have become the path itself. No one saves us but ourselves. No one can and no one may. We ourselves must walk the path."
Buddha Siddhartha Gautama, fifth century BCE founder of Buddhism

While it's possible to complete the walk in a month, and many guidebooks split the route into thirty individual days with accommodation options based on that, this is a really full-on schedule that requires up to ten hours of walking and a minimum of 20 or 30 kilometres every single day. Six weeks allows a more relaxed program, and there are usually refuges every 10 to 15 kilometres, and sometimes even more frequently, so your schedule can be adapted depending on how you feel physically and emotionally each day.

If you can take an even longer break it will give you the freedom to have the occasional rest day, provide you with the luxury of getting lost for a day and not really minding, recover if you're unwell or injured, and allow time to explore some of the beautiful cities, towns and villages the route passes through, so you can see and feel the land and its people and culture rather than simply rushing through.

Not everyone can take a month or two out of their "real" life to go on such an adventure, but the magic of the Camino can still be experienced even during a short break. Many people work out how long they have for their pilgrimage and count backwards, beginning their journey at some point part of the way along the pathway. A popular starting place is Leon, just over three hundred kilometres before Santiago de Compostela. It can be comfortably walked in two weeks, fulfils all the requirements for a certificate of completion, and takes in pretty medieval towns, stunning mountains, the Iron Cross, quaint churches, castle ruins and historical monuments.

If they just have a week to walk, many people start near Cebreiro, 160 kilometres shy of the end, and make their way through the beautiful Galician region. Others just walk the first week of the Camino, through the Navarra and La Rioja regions to somewhere like Logrono, or any other section that captures the imagination. And some choose the individual days that most appeal to them, set out in many travel guides, and walk that day's route, then get a bus to the start of the next section that they like the sound of – although public transport can be a bit tricky to co-ordinate, especially in the smaller towns.

Many Europeans do the pilgrimage as a long-term project, completing a week or two each summer, then returning the following year to take up where they left off. There are also many tours offered with guides and drivers, where participants walk for a few hours each day along the prettiest parts of the route, then are driven the rest.

The Camino is a very personal experience, and how you do it, how far you walk and how long you take is up to you. While more than ninety per cent of pilgrims follow the Camino Frances from Saint Jean Pied de Port or Roncesvalles to Santiago de Compostela, there are several other recognised pathways too. The Camino del Norte crosses the French border into Spain near Irun and follows a coastal route, past pretty little fishing ports and across dramatic rivers, until it rejoins the main Camino in Galicia. The slightly longer but more peaceful Camino Mozarabe, or Via de la Plata, route begins in Seville, the cultural centre of southern Spain, and winds its way northward through beautiful landscapes and gorgeous historic towns until it meets the primary Camino at Astorga.

There are also two shorter paths that pass through the neighbouring country of Portugal on their way to Santiago de Compostela, one along the Atlantic coast and the other via an inland route. These also feature numerous wayside crosses dedicated to Saint James, stories of a pilgrim miracle or two and important churches and shrines.

However long your journey lasts and whichever path it takes, the significance of the famous yellow arrows that lead ever onwards can't be overlooked. They point the way forward, through busy city streets, down narrow country lanes and across fields, mountains and forests.

Some are simply painted on surfaces, while others are specially made ceramic tiles embedded in city buildings. Some are vivid blue metal signs with a stylised golden arrow in the shape of a scallop shell, the symbol of Saint James and the Camino, and others are faded markers painted on rocks and fences that still show the way years after they were first wrought. Some are part of street signs or etched on the road itself, while others are scratched on walls and lamp posts or carved in the paving. Some are brightly emblazoned or intricately sculpted, while others are haphazardly marked but no less appreciated.

It would be almost impossible to do the Camino without these pointers, and the relief when I came across one just as I was wondering if I was going the right way was amazing. There were times I nearly cried in gratitude when I stumbled on an arrow at the perfect moment, and every time I saw one I blessed the person who put it there.

Centuries ago people had to navigate their way along the route using the sun, moon, stars and even the Milky Way, the constellation synonymous with the pilgrimage. The Romans called the Camino the Via Lactea, the Road of Milk, believing that the path flowed beneath the constellation and that those who walked it absorbed the energy of its stars. Getting lost, stopping until the skies cleared then asking for directions was all part of the journey. But today the trail is clearly marked and the arrows point the way boldly forward, so there's little chance of getting lost – at least not for too long.

The accompanying scallop shell, native to Galicia, is also a significant symbol. A thousand years ago Christian pilgrims would pick up a shell after they reached Santiago de Compostela and take it home as proof of the successful completion of their journey. It was also used for more practical purposes, such as gathering water and eating food out of. And while it later came to be associated with Saint

James, in pre-Christian times it was a fertility symbol that also represented the setting sun towards which pilgrims were heading.

Today most people carry a scallop shell with them throughout their pilgrimage, as a kind of talisman, and to identify themselves with the spirit of the way. Some carry a large shell tied to their backpack, some embroider one on their cap, and others wear silver jewellery scallops.

Also graffitied alongside some of the arrows, and shouted from the windows of cars going by, is the word Ultreya, which means "moving forward with courage". It's become a symbol of encouragement and camaraderie to dusty, sweaty pilgrims as they march ever westward, and can lift the spirits at crucial moments.

In addition there are many inspiring statues of pilgrims in the towns along the route, dressed in the traditional three-cornered hat and cape, with a scallop shell and a staff in hand. Some are fashioned on anonymous pilgrims, carved as tributes to the millions of people across the centuries who have walked the Camino, but others are of Saint James in his aspect as a pilgrim.

Even as saints go James is a complex hero. On the one hand he's depicted as Matamoros the Moor-Slayer, the brutal warrior on a white horse with defeated soldiers lying at his feet, as displayed in sculptures and graphic paintings in many churches across Spain. Yet he's also portrayed as the patron saint of pilgrims, as a pilgrim himself, and as a miracle healer of the sick. It seems odd that he'd be a pilgrim making a pilgrimage to himself, until you consider that the very definition of pilgrimage is to go within and discover yourself and your true essence.

To acknowledge your own pilgrimage you can apply for a Compostela, the certificate of completion, which is an official church document written in Latin. There's also a different certificate for those who've completed the Camino for spiritual rather than religious reasons, as the church doesn't want to give free passes to heaven to those it doesn't deem worthy. To qualify for either you must have walked at least the last hundred kilometres or ridden the final two hundred kilometres by bicycle. They are dispensed by the Pilgrims Office near the cathedral to those who can show their completed Credencial del Peregrino, the Pilgrim's Passport.

This passport is a record of your Camino, and also gives access to the pilgrim-only refuges along the way, as well as cheap meals and entry to cathedrals and other historical sites. It's stamped once each day at a refuge, church, monastery, town hall, cafe or bar to verify your progress, and twice a day over the final hundred kilometres. They can be arranged through a pilgrim association before you set out, from the pilgrim office in Saint Jean Pied de Port or Roncesvalles, or from some of the refuges, churches, police stations, tourist bureaus or council offices along the walk.

"Staying in a refugio is part of the Camino experience. The purpose of the refugios is to provide a place to sleep and bathe; it is a place of refuge. Because they are simple and cover only the basic human needs, they put you in touch with the fact that all you really need in this world is you."

Shirley MacLaine, American actor and spiritual writer

The refuges, also known as refugios or albergues, are much like backpacker hostels, with dorms filled with bunk beds and shared bathrooms, and varying levels of facilities and cleanliness. Many are just a few euros a night or by donation, and most walkers stay exclusively in them as part of their pilgrimage. Some are run by the local parish, some by the council, others by former pilgrims or pilgrim associations, and a few by monks in monasteries.

They are basic but usually adequate, and the often-cold showers, smelly bodies, loud snoring and crowded dorms are considered an essential part of the Camino experience – although some people do choose to stay in hostels, B&Bs or even hotels along the way, putting a good night of sleep above tradition, suffering or saving money.

Some refuges maintain the spirit of ages past, when they were created and supported by the church, nobles or royalty to accommodate the weary pilgrims risking their lives to make it to Santiago de Compostela. The beds of straw have been replaced with bunks, although some are surprisingly old, poorly maintained and lacking in hot water, electricity and food. Others are wonderful, run by warm-hearted former pilgrims who offer care, encouragement and shelter along with hot soup and assistance for minor ailments. Many are staffed by volunteers, as they were in medieval times, others by the government, private associations or the local church.

Pilgrims can only stay a single night in each one, unless they have a doctor's certificate stating that they need a day off from walking, and most must be vacated by 8am (which isn't really a problem as it's not a sleeping-in kind of adventure!). Most towns and villages have at least one refuge, and often more, but they can fill quickly in the busy summer months, and walkers sometimes have to keep going to the next town. Many spend the odd night out under the stars rather than struggling on to the next refuge (and some prefer that), or take a room in a hotel.

Walking the Camino is incredibly rewarding and fulfilling, but it's also a major challenge both physically and mentally. By the end you'll be sunburned and blistered, aching in every muscle and bone of your body, dehydrated, exhausted, smelly and most likely bordering on temporary insanity. Most people experience at least a day or two of sickness along the way, a sprained ankle, bad bruises from a fall or bites from strange insects. Others need more serious medical treatment and can be stuck in a town for days or weeks, and occasionally pilgrims have had to give up and return home to recuperate fully.

For while it's relatively easy to walk 20 kilometres on a flat road in cool weather, many of the days are through treacherous mountains or along desert plains in extremes of temperature. Some days the sun beats down mercilessly as you struggle up hills and down valleys that challenge your sense of balance and make every muscle in your body scream in agony. Other days it snows, pours with rain or throws a lightning storm your way, and you have to trudge through ankle deep mud and fight your way forward against gale force winds.

Yet at other times it's a gentle path. Some days the road meanders through cool, prettily scented forests, alongside gurgling streams and across sweet meadows surrounded by stands of ancient oaks providing shade. The beginning and end are mountainous, but the middle is so flat in parts that some people find it boring. (There's no pleasing some!) And it's said that the energy from the earth and particularly the leylines along the route give you strength and help you along the way.

The Camino has been walked by people of all ages, fitness levels and experience, from the very young to the elderly. Many have never walked around the block let alone hiked across an entire country, and did no training before they set out. Shirley MacLaine was in her mid sixties when she tackled it, and while she's a trained dancer and very fit – and made it to Santiago de Compostela in a month – she was certainly not the oldest to make the trek. Because you can take it at your own pace, it's possible for anyone to do it. One woman in her seventies spent eight weeks on the path, beginning with just 10 kilometres a day and working up to twice that by the halfway point.

There are buses joining the towns along the route, if you ever get into difficulty, and people along the way who've made it their life's work to help pilgrims. Many who've walked the Camino return to set up a refuge, massage people's feet or offer their services in some way, in an effort to give back for the life-changing benefits they received.

The Spanish government also protects those who walk the path, and despite the language barrier most locals have a great deal of respect for anyone doing the pilgrimage. Farmers, shopkeepers and others offer food, cups of tea, minor medical assistance and words of encouragement to weary pilgrims in an effort to keep their enthusiasm up and help them carry on. The Red Cross and some medical facilities also offer free or reduced price treatment to walkers.

In medieval times many on the Camino died from illness or the effects of the elements or were murdered by bandits, but these days it's very safe. There have been a few deaths though – on the roads, in the snow or from a heart attack – and touching memorials have been constructed to honour their memory. Just outside Navarette a plaque commemorates a Belgian pilgrim who died en route, and on the outskirts of Rabanal is a memorial to a Swiss pilgrim. After El Acebo there's a sculpture of a bicycle to mark the death of a German cyclist, and further on is a pair of bronze shoes that mark where an elderly pilgrim died of natural causes just a day before the end of his Camino.

In 2007 a pilgrim froze to death between Saint Jean Pied de Port and Roncesvalles when he continued walking into the night, against the advice of locals, and got caught in a snowstorm. Two others died a few years earlier when they ignored instructions to avoid the higher path in the snow. While death is rare, you need to be aware – flying down a steep winding road on a bike or walking along a busy highway without paying attention to the traffic can be dangerous in any country, as can being exposed to the elements in any mountains during winter.

The best times to walk are in spring and autumn, which avoids the intense sunshine and crowds of summer and the icy cold of winter, and ensures the flowers and trees are at their most beautiful, but it can be done at any time. Many pilgrims endure the summer heat to arrive in Santiago de Compostela by July 25, the feast day of Saint James, which is a major festival with entertainment, fireworks and celebrations. Others go when they have time to spare, regardless of the weather.

The main advice is to take as little as possible, because you'll be lugging everything with you up mountains and through blinding heat, like a little snail with your whole world on your back. The road is littered with clothes, shoes, books and all manner of things discarded as pilgrims stagger westwards, and it's a great opportunity to work out what you really need and realise how little you actually require to survive. It's recommended that you carry no more than ten per cent of your body weight in your pack – any more and you'll struggle on a flat road, let alone a mountain, and add immense pressure to your knees.

A good pair of hiking boots, walking shoes or sandals is essential, and they should be broken in, not bought new for the journey. And while some people do set out at a moment's notice with no training at all, it helps to have done at least some walking sessions before you begin.

Most importantly, try to let go of your expectations and any determination to complete the journey in a set time. Listen to your body. If you have to cut your walk short one day, do. The Camino is challenging, but it shouldn't be all about suffering, and pushing yourself too far too soon could put an early end to your pilgrimage.

Progress along the route is both physical and spiritual, as the pilgrimage is an intertwined journey both inward and outward. Delays, injuries, frustration and disappointments are all part of the process, so try to accept them gracefully. Rather than keeping you from your spiritual goal they're an integral part of it, a reflection of life and a mirror to show your reactions and patterns and help you learn and grow.

The past

The Christian history

"We see in these swift and skilful travellers a symbol of our life, which seeks to be a pilgrimage and a passage on this earth for the way of heaven."
Pope Paul VI, sovereign of the Vatican from 1963 to 1978

To many people the Camino is a Christian pilgrimage, and it is in reaching the tomb of Saint James in Santiago de Compostela's cathedral and touching his remains that the purpose of the journey is achieved. In medieval times it was believed that a person became closer to God through being close to the relics or remains of a saint, so church authorities strongly encouraged pilgrimages to such sites in order for people to prove their faith and devotion. The discovery of holy relics was big business back then, and could make or break a country's wealth as well as its religious influence.

According to legend, Saint James – Santiago in Spanish – was once one of the twelve apostles of Jesus, and was referred to as James the Great to distinguish him from other religiously significant Jameses. He was a fisherman, the son of Zebedee and Salome, and the brother of John. He was considered by some to be one of Jesus's closest friends, while others claimed they were cousins. It's been written that he was talking with Jesus on the Mount of Olives, and was present at the Transfiguration as well as at appearances after the resurrection.

After the Crucifixion James is thought to have gone to the Iberian Peninsula, as Spain and Portugal were then known, to preach the gospels and encourage Christianity. Later he returned to Jerusalem, where he was beheaded in 44CE by King Herod Agrippa and martyred. The stories of the Camino recount that two of his disciples took his body and sailed west, docking on the coast of Galicia in northwest Spain then walking inland to bury him. One of the miracles of the pilgrimage must be James's very existence there, as it's said that the disciples travelled in a stone boat, and that their journey from the Holy Land took only a week, another miracle assumed to imply angelic assistance.

Nothing was heard of James for several centuries after that, until in 813CE a religious hermit called Pelayo followed a falling star, heard a heavenly choir and found the long-forgotten tomb. A town was built on the site, which was named Santiago de Compostela – Santiago for the saint and Compostela for *campus stellae*, the field of stars.

Despite the lack of communication back then word soon got around, and the local bishop, the Spanish king and then the Pope all confirmed that the bones were the saint's. This immediately set the town up as a place of religious pilgrimage and brought immense wealth to the area.

More importantly, the discovery of the holy relics was regarded as an answer from God to the prayers of the Christians for assistance against the invading Muslims. For a hundred years they'd been battling the Moors, tribes of people from northern Africa who wanted to convert the peninsula to Islam, and who brought their exotic culture and customs to the land. After the bones of Saint James were found, there were many reports of him miraculously appearing to lead the Christian troops to victory against the foreigners, which is how he got the name Matamoros, the Moor-Slayer, and was declared Spain's patron saint.

The devoutly Christian emperor Charlemagne, who ruled over the Roman Empire that covered most of Europe in the ninth century and spent much of his life fighting the Moors, is said to have had a vision of the saint, who told him to make a pilgrimage to his tomb, liberating the road so others could follow in his footsteps. Legend has it that this was the first Camino undertaken in honour of Saint James – although it wasn't the first time the path had been walked with reverence.

Nobles, soldiers and peasants quickly began trekking westward in the hope of improving their chances of salvation, because the church offered indulgences to any of the faithful who made the journey, cancelling out the sins committed in this lifetime and ensuring a safe passage to heaven. They also believed some of the holiness of the saint would rub off on them if they stood in the presence of his relics.

In addition, the pilgrimage was tied to the concept of penance, and the idea that physical suffering and sacrifice was the way to God. Setting out with no possessions and throwing yourself on the mercy of strangers for food, shelter and protection was believed to increase a person's piety and humility. Many criminals were also ordered to walk the route as part of their sentence.

Whether you believe the story of Saint James or not – and many scholars today dispute his presence in Spain at all, let alone that his bones were buried there – they did back then, and he became the centre of a huge commercial operation. For the first hundred years after the discovery of the relics it was mostly Spanish pilgrims making the journey, but slowly people started coming from neighbouring France and Portugal, and then from further afield. When pilgrimages to the Holy Land became dangerous after Jerusalem and the Holy Sepulchre (the tomb of Jesus) were seized, the Camino became the most popular Christian pilgrimage in the world. During the 11th and 12th centuries it was walked by millions of pilgrims, with the monastery in Roncesvalles alone recording that it fed a hundred thousand people a year.

This led to a thriving community of monasteries and pilgrim refuges along the way, many of them still in use today, as well as new settlement in an area that had long been wild and unpopulated. The Camino became the lifeblood of northern Spain, and today the path winds through many towns that grew up along it. Ecclesiastical architecture also adapted to cope with the increased crowds, and the route permanently changed the face of the regions it passed through.

In the early 1100s French priest Aymeric Picaud wrote five books about his pilgrimage, detailing safe places to sleep, dangerous areas to avoid and holy sites, monuments and relics to visit. They were published as *The Codex Calixtinus* and credited to Pope Calixtus II, a common practice back then. The publication raised the Camino's profile even higher, and the Pope granted the pilgrimage Holy Year status.

This meant that from then on anyone who undertook the journey in a year when Saint James's feast day of July 25 fell on a Sunday would receive a plenary indulgence, which wiped out a whole lifetime of sin, as opposed to doing it in a normal year, which only atoned for half of a person's sins. Once people learned that a few months of gruelling physical endurance gave them the chance to ascend so easily to heaven, the pilgrimage's popularity increased even further.

Most pilgrims walked the path to prove their faith and as a sacred obligation, some did it as a petition to God to save their village from disaster or plague, and wealthy people often paid someone else to walk for them – buying their stairway to heaven. Today it's hard to comprehend just how significant it once was to be in the presence of the relics of a saint, and how acceptable it was to just down tools and walk off in search of salvation. With no cars or planes, people walked from wherever they lived to Santiago de Compostela, then turned around and walked back home, often travelling for six months or more in total. Imagine explaining that to a modern-day boss, landlord or spouse!

"The pilgrim route is a very good thing. It takes one away from succulent foods, makes voracious obesity disappear, restrains voluptuousness, contains the appetites of the flesh which attack the fortress of the soul, purifies the spirit, invites man to the contemplative life, humbles the haughty, raises up the humble, loves poverty. It rewards the austere who do good works, and it does not snatch the miserly and sinful from the talons of sin."
Aymeric Picaud, 12th century French priest, in The Codex Calixtinus

The desire of the devout to do the pilgrimage was fuelled by the church's recommendation as well as the high-profile people who completed it. Renowned Spanish political leader El Cid and the Bishop of Lille famously walked the path in the 11th century, English king Henry II and French monarch Louis VII did it in the 12th, Francis of Assisi made the journey in the early 13th century, and British poet Geoffrey Chaucer walked it in the 14th. Queen Isabella and King Ferdinand II, who were determined to unite all of Spain under Catholicism, made the pilgrimage in the 15th century, and later built shelters to help others follow in their footsteps.

Some years half a million people made their way to Santiago de Compostela, and there were many reports of pilgrims receiving miraculous healings attributed to Saint James – although some say the fresh air, exercise and simple foods along the route were the reason for those. Successive popes praised the Camino for the Christian charity that sprang up along the path, the monasteries that took pilgrims in and the encouragement and sharing of faith that occurred when people from different countries met along the way and walked together.

It was the religious orders that built hospitals and refuges for the pilgrims and provided meals, medical aid and religious services as well as protection. In the Middle Ages it was dangerous to travel the countryside alone, especially through the untamed regions of northern Spain. Wild animals, thieves, invading Moors, the weather, sickness, plague and the distance to medical assistance if you were injured made it a risky adventure, and pilgrims travelled together for safety. There were no hotels or B&Bs, so the priests and monks opened their monasteries to walkers where they could. Orders of soldier monks also formed to offer protection against robbery and violence.

The Knights Templar were one of the main branches, initially created to protect the pilgrims walking to Jerusalem. The ruins of their castle on the hill above Ponferrada are worth a visit as you pass by, to picture how it looked hundreds of years ago and absorb the energy of protection and religious charity it still exudes. The Templars formed in the early 1100s, and were renowned for protecting pilgrims, providing shelter and acquiring knowledge and treasures. They answered to the Pope, and were well regarded as a religious order.

They are credited with instituting the modern banking system, as they were entrusted with a pilgrim's wealth when he set out, and gave him documents that allowed him to draw the money out at various locations along the route. The Templars built up vast wealth through their shrewd business dealings and management of land, farms, vineyards, manufacturing businesses and ships. They also constructed churches, which added to their good reputation and influence. However they also attracted enemies in high places, and King Philip IV of France decided that not only could he not afford to repay his loans to them, but he wanted all their riches to continue his battle with England.

On Friday October 13, 1307 – the origin of the Black Friday tradition – he had the Templars arrested, falsely accused of heresy and tortured until they "confessed", which gave him an excuse to seize their wealth. He also pressured the Pope into disbanding the order. Many of the members who escaped being burned at the stake joined similar orders, or set up shop in countries not controlled by Rome. Spain welcomed many of the fleeing knights, who continued their work protecting pilgrims under the name the Order of Santiago.

The popularity of the Camino slumped in the late 16th century, partly due to the Protestant Reformation, which refuted the authority of the Pope and the significance of the relics of saints. Even more damaging was the fact that James's remains were misplaced. When La Coruna, just north of Santiago de Compostela, was raided during the Spanish-English War, the archbishop, terrified the soldiers would march south and steal the relics, opened James's tomb and moved them to a safer place – so safe they weren't found for three hundred years.

This revelation led to a sharp decline in the number of people making the pilgrimage. It wasn't until the late 1800s that the relics were rediscovered, "authenticated" by the Pope and reinterred under the high altar, where they remain to this day. Yet while the purpose of the pilgrimage had been reinstated, the lengthy absence of the bones had a profound effect. Religious beliefs had also changed, and the Camino had disappeared from people's consciousness. Even the most faithful were unaware of the ancient route. The 1900s were also marred by Spanish civil war and two World Wars, and such travel was unsafe and unappealing. It seemed to be a thing of the past.

In the Holy Year of 1948 however, an international publicity blitz took place. Books about the Camino were published, postage stamps were released, and Pope Pius XII declared the pilgrimage a powerful and holy proof of faith. People started walking the old route again, an even more difficult journey then than it is today. The yellow arrows and many refuges now taken for granted didn't exist back then. Directions were hard to follow, and the infrastructure of old had crumbled. Pilgrims relied on the kindness of strangers, of farmers offering a hayloft for the night or monks willing to share their cells.

The path slowly came back to life. In 1982 a Galician priest, the author of a small guidebook, walked from the Pyrenees to Santiago de Compostela with a tin of yellow paint, marking the way forward for future pilgrims. His arrows, emblazoned on trees, road signs, fences, buildings, rocks and the earth itself, are now closely associated with the Camino, and have been maintained and embellished to this day.

He lobbied local councils to reclaim the ancient path – which had been planted over by agriculture and built on by growing towns – preserve the old churches and buildings and provide shelter. He also instigated a network of pilgrim associations, and today there are many such groups and websites set up to help people walking the Camino.

Also in 1982, Pope John Paul II, who had hiked the Camino as a young priest and recognised its potential as the "new evangelisation" of Europe, visited Santiago de Compostela – the first pontiff to do so – and publicly encouraged Catholics to make the pilgrimage. And it was he who decided that only the last hundred kilometres had to be walked for someone to qualify as a genuine pilgrim, making it much easier.

In 1987 the Camino was declared the first European Cultural Route by the Council of Europe, and six years later UNESCO proclaimed it a World Heritage Site, noting that it aided cultural exchanges between European nations during the Middle Ages, and is today a testimony to the power of the Christian faith among people of all social classes.

Since then, as more and more people search for spiritual meaning in their lives, pilgrim numbers have continued to grow. According to the local archbishop, just 2500 people walked the Camino in 1986, 23,500 a decade later and 90,000 in 2005. There's a huge jump in Holy Years – in 1993 there were 100,000 pilgrims, in 1999 there were 150,000, in 2004 there were 180,000, and in 2010 around 200,000. The next Holy Year, in 2021, will surely exceed this number again.

And these figures only record those who have requested the official religious certificate at the end – many more people these days are going on the journey for their own spiritual purposes and aren't included in church records, adding to the increasing swell of people setting out to make their individual pilgrimage along the ancient path.

The magical history

"There's a science to pilgrimage that concerns the earth and its landscape, akin to the human body with its etheric energy structure of meridians, acupuncture points, chakras and kundalini flows. Pilgrimage involves a calling to reach a goal that is sacred in a profound way. The spirit embodied in the earth calls us to it."
Peter Dawkins, *English author and sacred geomancer*

Emperor Charlemagne may have been the first to walk the Camino in Saint James's name, but people had been walking the same pathway in search of spiritual meaning for several thousand years. Long before the coming of Christianity to the area or the discovery of the saint's relics, Stone Age people followed the same route in their quest for self-reflection and self-realisation, and megalithic monuments dated to 4000BCE are a testament to their presence in the region.

Later the Celts and their druids made the journey, struggling across mountains and desert plains and battling wild animals and harsh weather as a spiritual exercise to find meaning and purpose – the same reason many do the Camino today. They walked it in celebration of life and nature, and to follow the path of the sun that they worshipped for its life-giving warmth and light. Their pilgrimage began from wherever in Europe they lived, wound through the Pyrenees and across the top of Spain – the same as the route recognised today – and continued 80 kilometres further west of Santiago de Compostela to Finisterre, a tiny town perched on the edge of the Atlantic Ocean.

This town, named from finis terrae, which means "end of the earth", is on a rocky peninsula that juts into the sea, and was long considered the most westerly point of the continent and the end of the known world. To the druids it was the threshold to the great beyond, the Celtic Otherworld they envisaged as an island just beyond the waves where spirits went after death. By walking the Camino they believed they were following the path the soul would take when it left the earthly realm.

This wild and rugged region has a decidedly pagan air, with its storm-ravaged cliffs and treacherous seas, its mist, green forests, sacred stones and ancient gods. The whole of Galicia retains a rich Celtic folklore, with tales of myth, magic and legend, and of witches known as bruxa or meiga who were recognised as healers rather than the forces of evil that they were regarded as in other parts of Spain.

The sacred standing stones of the area also play an important role in the history of Galicia, attributed with healing powers and associated with ancient fertility rituals that are still performed today. Some of them are now part of legend, such as the carved serpent stone that is either a druidic one relating to wisdom or a Christian one depicting a priest casting out the pagans, depending on your viewpoint. There is also the famous stone chair, and the tomb of Orcabella, a weathered stone monument said to have an old woman trapped within it.

Chief amongst the standing stones, dolmens and burial tombs scattered throughout the countryside is the Ara Solis, an ancient stone altar dedicated to the sun god. It's located high on Monte Facho, a mountain topped by a lighthouse that looks out over the ocean and the town of Finisterre, and is surrounded by other sacred stones that are carved or inscribed. Some claim that together they served a similar purpose to Stonehenge, tracking the sun, marking the seasons and being a part of the rituals and magic of the ancients.

Long ago the Camino was also a fertility pilgrimage walked by couples who had difficulty conceiving, in the hope of being blessed with a child. When they reached Finisterre they would lie on this sacred stone altar to increase their fertility, and there are people today who still practise this ritual in the hope of falling pregnant.

The long climb up Monte Facho to the Ara Solis reveals a place of stunning sunsets, enchanting views and dramatic coastline, which inspires awe and an almost religious fervour in those who witness its beauty. And while the ancient stones aren't exactly as they were – Queen Lupa ordered the destruction of the sun altar when she converted to Christianity after encountering Saint James's disciples as they brought his remains to the area – visitors claim they still hold great power, and are able to connect people to the earth and nature like many of the stone circles that still stand throughout Europe.

In the second century BCE the Romans began a lengthy occupation of the Iberian Peninsula, and the Camino, so long a druidic pilgrimage path, also became a Roman trade route. There are still bridges along the way that were constructed two thousand years ago by sandal-clad legionnaires, which gives some perspective to time and existence.

Like the Celts before them, the Romans believed Finisterre was the end of the world and the transition point between life and death, and that the realm where the souls of the dead resided lay out to the west in the place where the sun dipped below the ocean each night. They also continued the earlier solar worship that had taken place there, using the ancient stone altar to give thanks to their sun god Sol.

The Romans integrated the previous druidic fertility rituals with their own as well. The scallop shell that had been used by the druids, and is still a symbol of the walk today, has also been attributed to the Romans and their worship of Venus, the goddess of love, beauty and sexual healing. While the Christians later claimed the shell as the symbol of Saint James and his pilgrims, to the followers of Venus it represented fertility, rejuvenation and spiritual renewal, the cycle of life, death and rebirth, and was considered a talisman against evil.

Surprisingly, the Christians also believed in the fertility-boosting power of the stones at Finisterre, although they claimed it was Saint Guillermo, a hermit monk who lived in a cave near the site of the sun altar, who had the power to help women conceive. They rechristened the stones pedras santas, holy stones, and claimed the stone altar had been the saint's bed. Fertility rites continued to take place there in his name, with any successes attributed to his intervention.

Nearby there's a hermitage dedicated to Guillermo, as well as a church of the Virgin Mary, which houses another Camino miracle – the statue known as the Santo Cristo da Barba Dourada, Christ of the Golden Beard, which has a beard that allegedly grew after it was placed in the church, and is also said to sweat.

These miracles ensured that many religious pilgrims continued on to the coast after they honoured Saint James's remains in Santiago de Compostela, to throw themselves before the statue and be close to the relics of Saint Guillermo. A refuge was built for them to stay at, and a few others have since sprung up between Santiago de Compostela and the coast, but the church no longer encourages this extra leg, as the cathedral is now the sole point of the religious pilgrimage.

The Christians built churches on sites sacred to the pagans and adapted their rituals in order to convert them, and in the same way they transformed the old pagan Camino into their own, declaring it to be in honour of Saint James rather than the sun god or the goddess Venus.

But it's no wonder it became a religious pilgrimage of some kind, because walking through the incredible landscape of northern Spain can't help but bring you closer to your concept of god. It gives you time and space to understand your spiritual heart, whether you believe the divine is an entity outside of yourself or a state of grace within, and whether you worship the Christian deity, an ancient pagan goddess or simply the universal energy and power innate in all people.

To me, and many other pilgrims, the sacredness of the Camino lies less in the old churches, carved crosses and pilgrim statues in each town, and more in the absolute beauty and grandeur of nature. Inhaling the scent of herbs as you walk through a wooded area, catching your breath as you look out over fields of sunflowers stretching towards the vivid blue horizon, marvelling at the sunsets that paint fingers of colour across a vast sky, being enchanted by the mystical prettiness of each region – all these things stir your soul, filling you with a sense of wonder and communion with the whole world.

In pre-Christian times the route was dedicated to the goddess and the divine feminine within each person who made the journey, both males and females, and even today it's considered feminine. The path activates the caring, loving part of everyone who walks it, opening you up to the feminine energy of your own soul so you can nurture yourself as well as the world around you. Being in balance – embracing both masculine and feminine energies, and understanding the yin and yang of life – helps you be all that you can be and achieve everything you dream of, and walking the Camino is a good way to find this balance.

Today, as the Old Ways experience a resurgence and people seek a sense of reconnection and spiritual awakening, some pilgrims continue their journey to Finisterre, a further three or four days past Santiago de Compostela. Standing on a rock overlooking the Atlantic and gazing out across the ocean to where the sun sets at the end of the world gives a sense of closure and a magical end to your new connection with nature. Especially for those who feel no affinity with Saint James and place little significance on the cathedral, walking to where the land meets the ocean, to the place where you can literally go no further, gives a far more meaningful sense of completion and fulfilment.

Many perform a solemn ritual of burning their sweaty, dusty clothes then diving into the ocean, which represents a discarding and releasement of all you have been holding on to, and a cleansing transition to a new way of thinking, living and being as you incorporate the lessons of your Camino into your heart, your mind and your life.

The purpose

"The spiritual journey does not consist in arriving at a new destination where a person gains what he did not have, or becomes what he is not. It consists in the dissipation of one's own ignorance concerning one's self and life, and the gradual growth of that understanding which begins the spiritual awakening."
Aldous Huxley, English author, humanist and mystic

A pilgrimage is an adventure of outward as well as inward discovery, a journey along a physical path as well as within your own heart, from which you return changed by everything you've seen and experienced along the way. The word comes from the Latin peregrinus, meaning travelling, and from peregrine, which refers to coming from another region or country. From the same word comes peregrination, meaning a journey or voyage, and in Spanish a pilgrim is a peregrino.

Pilgrimages have been made and written about for as long as history has been recorded, and probably long before. They are sacred journeys and rites of passage common to all peoples, cultures and religions, designed to prove your faith, help you commune with your gods and give you time out of your real life to get to know your true self.

The pharaohs of Egypt travelled to Karnak and other temples from 3000BCE onwards. In 1000BCE Assyrian king Shalmaneser went to a religious shrine in Babylon. In Ancient Greece pilgrims journeyed to the Temple of Zeus at Olympus, which continues to this day, and the Oracle of Delphi. From the time of Buddha's death in the fifth century BCE, his followers have visited his birthplace in Nepal, the site in India where he found enlightenment and the town where he died.

Christians have always made pilgrimages to sites related to the life and death of Christ, including the Holy Sepulchre in Jerusalem and the tombs of Peter and Paul in Rome. The famed Crusades of the 11th to 13th centuries were armed pilgrimages to the Holy Land. And today peasants still climb the stairs on their knees at the shrine of Our Lady of Guadalupe in Mexico, Catholics stagger up rocky Croagh Patrick mountain with bare feet in blinding mist and driving rain in Ireland, and since 1858, when a fourteen-year-old peasant girl claimed several visions of the Virgin Mary, the tiny French town of Lourdes has been a place of pilgrimage that attracts five million people a year.

And wherever pilgrims journeyed, inns and refuges were built to cater for them and towns swelled to accommodate them, marking the rudimentary beginnings of the tourist trade.

Traditionally a pilgrim was defined as someone who travels to a holy place for religious reasons, but today it has developed to mean anyone who makes a special journey along a spiritual path. Catholics still visit Rome and the Vatican, Jews travel to Jerusalem's Western Wall, Muslims are required to make their hajj to Mecca and Hindus bathe in the holy water of the Ganges – but others seek out ancient wisdom in the places of the priestesses of old, visiting sacred isles and dancing within stone circles, and some explore the ancient ruins of the Mayan or Aztec civilisations or make their way to the home of a modern-day guru promising spiritual enlightenment.

Not every journey is a pilgrimage. I've walked the streets of the Garden District in New Orleans, where Anne Rice and her vampires lived and loved, and drunk coffee in the cafes where Lestat warmed his hands, which imbued her magical books with added layers of meaning and connection. In Brazil I spent a week in Ilheus, author Jorge Amado's town, and ate each night in the same bar his characters dined in, wandered down the roads he had walked and stood in the house he grew up in. I learned about him, but not about myself.

Elvis Presley fans tour Graceland, get married in a Las Vegas chapel and worship at the casino shrine. Sports addicts spend years saving up to travel to Europe for soccer's World Cup, Australia for cricket's Ashes tour or America for the famous Superbowl. Dracula devotees follow the shadow of the iconic vampire through the mist-laden Carpathian Mountains of Romania to the birthplace of Vlad Tepes, the prince who inspired the legend. Movie lovers fly to the bright lights of Hollywood to stare at the famous sign, the mansions of celebrities and the glittering pavement stars of acting legends, and classical music buffs pay their respects in Vienna, the resting place of countless composers and musicians who continue to fascinate people today.

Some go to pay tribute to athletes or entertainers who have moved them, or to try to tap in to whatever it was that led someone to pen a story or compose an opera that has lasted centuries. But while beneath the postcards, souvenirs and team colours there's a yearning for new experiences or to be connected to something greater, and these trips can be fun, educational and inspiring, they lack the true meaning of pilgrimage, which is to learn about yourself, listen to your own heart and acquire a deeper understanding of what it is you've done, are doing and want to be in this life.

Often it's the intent with which it's undertaken that turns an ordinary trip into a sacred journey. Walking the Camino in the footsteps of the druids or in honour of Saint James is a way to commune with the divine, either within or without – but it can also be completed as a fast-paced physical challenge bereft of spiritual insight. Scaling a mountain like Everest simply to get to the top is, while an incredible experience, a very different journey to climbing a sacred peak with the intent of bowing before the gods.

A true pilgrimage is spiritually significant and provides an opportunity for personal growth. It involves separation from your life, your work, your friends and family and your everyday existence. It throws you into a different reality, where everything is changed, and you are changed as a result. There are those who go on a pilgrimage as an act of penance or to commune with their god, asking for forgiveness or guidance or giving thanks in the traditions of old, but increasingly people are making these journeys in a spiritual rather than religious context, as a way to connect with their own divine guidance and inner self, or to soak up the magic at a place where the earth energies activate a change of consciousness.

The Camino is all these things. Christians do it as an example of their complete surrender to God, but today just as many people set out in an attempt to surrender to themselves, to learn what makes their heart sing and how to give their life meaning. They go to make a decision, or to mark the end of one thing and the beginning of another.

They walk to let go of grief and pain and to heal after a loss, a death, a divorce. The separation from all that's familiar, plus the obvious physical hardship, gives great clarity to any situation. Some people aren't even sure exactly why they're doing it, they just feel compelled for some reason they can't explain, drawn by the tales of other travellers or a stirring in their heart when they hear about it.

Whatever the reason, the Camino always marks a turning point, whether it's done to deal with a major crisis or for a subtler quest. It's a journey of personal reflection and healing, during which you can uncover the knowledge you already have within you but are afraid to follow, and unlock the secrets to your own emotional fulfilment. It's different for everyone, but each pilgrim undergoes a kind of rebirth. You'll find what you need, even if you didn't know it was lacking.

The Camino is whatever you require it to be. It's a religious route recommended by the Pope as a show of faith. It's an ancient path walked by Celtic druids and Roman goddess worshippers to find spiritual meaning. It follows the earth's leylines, which activate consciousness and open the heart. And it provides a long period of silence in which to contemplate life and the things that create your deeper purpose.

"Solitude is a fount of healing which makes my life worth living. Talking is often a torment for me, and I need many days of silence to recover from the futility of words. What you think of as a few days of spiritual communion would be unendurable for me with anyone, even with my closest friends. The rest is silence!"
Carl Jung, Swiss psychiatrist and founder of analytical psychology

I was drawn to the Camino by the idea of being alone, and for many people the constant solitude is the most appealing aspect. It's an indulgence that gives you time to yourself to think, to wonder, to reflect. To ponder life, the world, your job, your friendships and your true self.

You can learn a hundred spiritual practices, read all the healing books ever written and do all the self-development courses you like, but it's hard to maintain your sense of inner peace when you live in the city, work crazy hours, share a house with several people and have no time to yourself. My days on the Camino were my gift to myself, a time out from my hectic life to go within, to remember my priorities and to affirm what is most important to me.

There is a power in silence and solitude, because you come to know yourself. The most inspiring political leaders – Nelson Mandela, Mahatma Gandhi – spent years in jail as prisoners of conscience, emerging as stronger, more powerful people, with new depths of purpose and priority, because they knew themselves and had resolved any insecurities and personal issues they suffered from.

Being wrapped in silence and solitude and so separate from the so-called real world gives you an important new perspective on your life. English poet John Keats said: "The only journey worth taking is the journey within," the Dalai Lama advised: "Spend some time alone every day," and American poet May Sarton wrote: "Loneliness is the poverty of self; solitude is the richness of self." Today we don't place enough value on time out, time alone, time in silence, and we don't give ourselves the luxury of experiencing it. But walking alone along this sacred path gives you the time and space to get back in touch with your inner self and reconnect to your deepest soul.

With nothing else to do but walk and think, you're able to review your life, your loves, your family, your work, your friendships, your exes, your achievements, your regrets. And you start to understand your thought processes, your personality, your actions, your relationship patterns, your motivations and your passions.

Far away from normal life, where you're defined by your relationship with others – as a child, spouse, parent, friend, teacher, student, worker – you begin to discover who you truly are, as opposed to who people think you are. Often when we return to our childhood home as an adult we revert to old patterns and behaviours, acting as our parents see us and not as who we are now. But in the wilds of Spain, alone for days on end, you can let go of what others think of you and become more truly who you are. The real you, the inner you.

As you progress along the path you lose your fear of pleasing others and start doing what you want to do, learn to please yourself and come to understand the things that are important to you – which are all immensely valuable realisations. And even though you may return to your usual roles when you finish your pilgrimage and go back home, you'll always be able to hold the real you within your heart.

This self-knowledge is a valuable tool for transformation, and will help you resolve inner conflicts and be at peace with yourself. Self-knowledge leads to self-acceptance and self-love – and the ability to accept and love others. You need to understand yourself and your motives in order to have healthy, loving relationships, which is probably why so many people are drawn to walk the Camino when they've just ended a marriage, are contemplating beginning one, or are unsure of how to proceed in a romantic relationship.

Understanding yourself is also crucial to interacting with people in a compassionate way, because your reactions to other people and events are determined by your past – by old relationships, by your experiences, both good and bad, by your upbringing, beliefs and viewpoint. When you argue with a partner or friend, you're not just fighting with them, but with everything that's ever happened to you – and to them. And because the other person is reacting from their life experiences and past issues too, misunderstandings can quickly spiral out of control. Often you're not even arguing about the same thing, because you each go off on your own tangent, becoming defensive at perceived slights and spinning a web of self-protection to safeguard your heart from what it fears is an attack – but usually isn't.

As I walked I thought a lot about a friend I'd had a falling out with, and saw how I'd misconstrued her intent, and she mine, and that a series of misunderstandings had left us both needlessly hurt. I decided that if I ever feel like I'm being attacked or insulted again, I'll ask exactly what the person means, because as my feet pounded along the hot ground and my mind soared above, I realised that it's usually not the conclusion I've jumped to. And I vowed to be clearer when I'm trying to explain something, so there's less chance of misinterpretation. Words have such power, yet they mean something different to every person. Understanding the things that trigger your defensive patterns and why you react to things the way you do makes it much easier to avoid offence, heal conflict and even prevent it in the first place.

The perspective you gain by being alone also makes you more empathetic to others and helps you realise that you shouldn't take things personally. If a friend doesn't call for a few days it's more likely that they're snowed under at work, sick in bed or away for the weekend than that they suddenly don't want to speak to you. And if someone is angry or bitter it usually has more to do with them than you, so try to understand where they're coming from, rather than getting angry in response and escalating the situation out of control.

Everyone acts and reacts from their own perspective, not yours. They don't understand what motivates you, what hurts you, what matters to you, because they only know their own heart. A comment that would devastate you because it touches a raw nerve might not upset your friend in the least, so it's not vindictiveness if they say it but simply this gap in knowing how you feel that can lead to so much pain. It's rare that anyone will actively do something to hurt another person – usually they're just oblivious to how their actions affect others.

One of my realisations on the Camino was to get over myself. Other people aren't judging my every word, dwelling on my mistakes, waiting for me to ask for help or trying to hurt me – they're too busy living their own life and worrying about their own insecurities.

Knowing who you are and what you want and need is a valuable lesson, and a gift of the Camino. People are often disappointed in a relationship because they don't feel they're getting what they need from the other person – but often we don't even know what we want, let alone tell the other person, so how can they fulfil us? Being able to view a relationship problem, family issue or work conflict from a distance also empowers you to see it in a new way, understand your place in it and be able to work out the best way to improve the situation.

As wonderful as the solitude is though, it can get intense. You can go for hours, even days, without speaking to anyone, cut off from communication from home and enveloped in a bubble of isolation, especially in the regions where they speak a local dialect. Some pilgrims find this, and the emotional processing that results, even harder to deal with than the physical pain, because there's nowhere to hide, nothing to distract you from your thinking, from your own head and from the deep inner work that results whether you like it or not.

The silence and lack of contact can be challenging – and after so long alone you can feel that your sanity has deserted you too. I had moments of hysterical laughter, of sudden depression or anxiety, of talking to myself, of being convinced I'd lost my grip on reality. Although what is reality anyway? If life is what we create, then at that moment I had created the solitude I crave, outside in the nature I love, walking towards my own future that I was inventing as I went.

"In the end what matters most is: How well did you live? How well did you love? How well did you learn to let go?"
Buddhist proverb

Walking the Camino helps you realise what you want to keep in your life and what you can let go of, both physically and emotionally. The path and the refuges are strewn with things people have cast off as they figured out how few physical objects are actually necessary in life. After her pilgrimage Shirley MacLaine declared that all you need is a good pair of shoes, a stick and some water, and most people have similar epiphanies along the trail, returning home to declutter their house and their life, and placing less importance on material goods. This is a vital lesson today, in a time when the environment is in such bad shape and we all need to be much more aware of what we have, what we consume and what – and how – we dispose of things.

As you walk westward, discarding the physical things you don't need, you'll also start to let go of the emotional baggage you no longer require. Walking the Camino prepares you to let go of physical objects as well as emotional burdens – to find the courage to release old patterns, beliefs and habits, give up bitterness and anger about the past, and to access your inner wisdom to decide what's necessary and what is not. The pilgrimage gives you the strength as well as the tools to let go, and the ability to identify what you really need.

You'll also develop a deeper appreciation of what you do have – friends, family, health, your body and its sacredness. Every day I walked I whispered a prayer of thanks to my legs, my feet, my muscles and my heart, so grateful for their strength, their stubbornness, their ability to carry me forward. The body is an amazing thing, not just a temple for your spirit or soul, but an incredible vehicle that propels you through life and helps you achieve your dreams in the physical.

The path tests you, and there will be days when you'll think you're going mad, or you can't walk another step, or all you can focus on is the pain in your left ankle or the blister on your right foot, which is all part of it. Allowing yourself to just be with the sensations is a type of meditation which teaches that all things pass. As the symbolic and literal meld, you'll start to understand that just as physical pain heals, so too does emotional pain, freeing you to wallow in any sense of loss or grief, knowing it will eventually pass and leave you stronger.

A major part of the experience and the healing is the physical challenge of the walk and the endurance required. There's something very powerful about pushing your body beyond its limits and transcending the pain, which frees your mind to expand and allows your heart and your soul to soar above, see within, look ahead. As you concentrate on walking, breathing, sleeping and surviving, as you focus on the pain in your legs and the physical sensations in every muscle, everything else falls by the wayside. Little things no longer matter.

So far from the drama of your life, with your whole existence narrowed to the road ahead and the energy-sapping heat or mud-inducing rain, your worries about work, friends and relationships seem almost pointless. And you realise that the pain you felt at a friend's betrayal no longer hurts so deeply, the guilt you suffered over something you did no longer seems so terrible, the career crisis that plagued you no longer feels so life or death. With distance, only the big things matter – the people you love, the health you're blessed with.

It gives you a new perspective, and petty squabbles, office politics and family disagreements suddenly seem less important. Much like when people are faced with a life-threatening illness that throws everything else into perspective, getting away from your daily life and focusing only on your physical survival allows you to reprioritise.

Walking the Camino gives you time to really think about what you want to do in your life, what you've always dreamed of and what your heart truly desires. As your feet pound out a rhythm on the earth, your mind and heart are free to soar, to recall the ideas and ambitions that used to make you burn with enthusiasm and inspiration.

In the day-to-day routine of life, when your time is filled with work, habit and exhaustion, it's easy to forget what you really want out of life, or to dismiss your dreams as childish or impossible. When you're sweating over a deadline, working overtime again or squashed on the train in a crush of tired and frustrated commuters, it's harder to visualise that your dreams really can be fulfilled.

This pilgrimage is a time out of real life and a way to get back in touch with your dreams, with your soul, with the inner part of you that is waiting to reawaken. You'll start recalling your passions, be it while walking or as you lie exhausted in a tiny bunk in a refuge at night. And each day you can work out a different aspect of achieving them. Your mind will throw up all sorts of excuses and reasons why you can't reach your goal – it's not practical, you're too old, it's too late, it won't pay enough – but a few miles later you'll get flashes of inspiration of ways you can make it happen, and reasons why you should.

Achieving things along the Camino also builds confidence – reaching the top of a mountain you were scared you wouldn't be able to scale, becoming stronger and able to cover more ground each day. All the physical goals you tick off reassure you that you can also achieve your life goals. If the road is a metaphor for life, then each small goal or town you reach along the route represents a step towards the fulfilment of your life's purpose and your own happiness and contentment.

"Finish each day and be done with it. You've done what you could. Some blunders and absurdities have crept in – forget them as soon as you can. Tomorrow is a new day. You shall begin it serenely and with too high a spirit to be encumbered with your old nonsense."
Ralph Waldo Emerson, 19th century US writer and transcendentalist

Every day the world is born anew – both on the Camino and back at home – and you can be too. You can let go of anything that saddened you about the previous day, or the previous year, and begin again with a clean slate. Shrug off your grief, your shyness, your past, anything you regret, and be reborn. Everyone deserves this fresh start, including you. The Camino helps you to let go of the past, of the so-called mistakes you've made, the "bad" choices you followed and the regrets you have. It gives you the chance to start over, and encourages you to be who you are now, not who you were before.

It's also an incredibly liberating experience. Each morning there's a decision to make – when to start, how far to walk, which towns to visit, where to eat, whether to talk to someone or press on alone – and you get to choose. You're in control of every moment. You do what you want to do and get to be truly yourself, free of the weight of expectation. As a result you'll begin to view each day as a new start, a fresh adventure, and see yourself and the world with new eyes.

This sense of independence and competence is a powerful feeling. I had to rely on myself, because there was no one to help me – often no one even knew where I was – and I liked that. I realised I'm more capable than I gave myself credit for. Stronger. There is power in being so vulnerable and alone, being totally responsible for yourself, and coping.

I learned I can survive anywhere, on my own, and that I don't need anybody. I don't even really need a language. There's freedom in not being able to communicate, in being stripped bare and going back to the most basic primal needs. I tapped in to a sense of intuition I had somehow turned off, and communicated with people on a deeply instinctual level. And realising I didn't need anyone made me confident that when I did choose to be with someone I'd know it was totally by choice, because I wanted to be with them, and not because I needed them to help me get through life or fill a void in my heart.

I absolutely loved the solitude of the Camino, and many people say the only way to walk it is alone and in silence, but there are benefits no matter which way you do it. Couples make the trek to uncover the things that bind them together. Mothers and daughters travel the path to redefine and nurture their relationship. Groups of friends do it as a fun, bonding adventure. Sick people and their carers undergo the arduous journey in the hope of a cure or as a way to make peace with themselves, their life and their thoughts on what happens after death.

There are many different combinations of people walking, and not all of them finish the way they started. Some set off alone but end up sharing the experience with others and making life-long friends. Others walk in solitude then catch up with people they've met along the way at the end of each day to swap stories. Some begin in a group then splinter off and walk alone as people set their own pace. It's a personal choice. There's no right or wrong method. Everyone's experience is their own, and unfolds the way it's meant to.

It's said that the way you walk the Camino is the way you live your life, and that how you do it will reveal a lot about you and your approach to the world, giving valuable insight into your personality and attitude. Some people take life as it comes, and make their pilgrimage in the same way, stopping when they're drawn to, soaking up each experience, each town, each person they meet, relaxed and in touch with themselves and their world. Some progress through life, and along the path, with their head down, staring at the ground, focused on the minute details but oblivious to the bigger picture.

Others plan their lives – and their walking schedule – down to the last second, with no room to move or be spontaneous, and get stressed if anything out of the ordinary happens that requires them to be flexible. And there are those who are goal orientated in life and desperate to achieve as highly as they can, who are so busy looking at the horizon that they trip over the things on their path, and so focused on the end point that they don't bother to enjoy the process, missing the joy of their surroundings, of sunsets and flowers and friends and love.

There are no prizes for completing your Camino in record time, and if you see it as a physical challenge to be endured, and rush from town to town in a competition with yourself to get to the end, you could miss out on a lot of the realisations the pilgrimage will present for you, not to mention the beauty of the places you'll pass through.

For some people this is the primary lesson of their walk – to let go of their concept of success, achievement, direction and goals and be present in every moment, wherever they are, enjoying the journey and not thinking each day away or worrying about where they're headed.

My realisation was about my "real" life. While I took in every stunning vista as I walked and was absorbed by the magic of every experience, I recognised that sometimes I forget to do that back home. Sometimes it takes being away to remind me of the beauty of the world and how amazing every moment is. I shouldn't have to travel to appreciate the warmth of the sun, an hour alone, the kindness of strangers, a grand realisation. I have to remember to enjoy and appreciate every day, no matter where I am or what I'm doing, and to allow myself time alone to breathe in this wonder.

It was so nice to simply walk, with no responsibility, no deadline, no pressure. To just sit and think and do nothing. To stare at the sky, the sunshine and the trees. To sip iced coffee in a cobblestone plaza and daydream. At home if I wasn't doing anything I'd feel agitated, but on this pilgrimage it's okay. There's no pressure to be doing something all the time – in fact that's the point, to slow down and remove yourself from the world and the things that stress you.

The power of nature is also an important part of the Camino. For me, being out in the countryside was a huge source of energy, revitalising me physically and filling me with such a feeling of joy and bliss. Living in the city, being cut off from nature, can drain you, but being out in the elements recharges you and brings you back to what is most important. It's humbling to stand in a thunderstorm, clamber through mud, watch flowers opening up or leaves changing colour, to breathe in the energy of a sunrise as it paints the whole world golden.

Being outside in nature also helps you re-attune to the rhythm of the earth, to the cycles of the seasons and the turning of the planet, which creates a sense of balance. Walking through sun-dappled forests or past fields of bright sunflowers made me so happy. Standing on a mountaintop admiring the view filled me with peace and tranquillity. Splashing in fountains or bubbling streams refreshed me, both body and soul. Sitting in a grassy meadow flooded me with elation, as energy surged through me from the ground beneath me and the sky overhead.

The Camino follows the earth's leylines, and you can definitely feel this energy in a very physical sense as you wander the path. The ancients walked it barefoot to better absorb this energy, and while today a good pair of supportive, worn-in shoes is recommended, you'll still be absorbing the wisdom and power. Walking along leylines and interacting with them for so long and in such concentrated bursts as you do on this journey physically increases your own energy and vibration. It also activates emotional realisations, unlocks past memories and instigates personal revelations that can change your life.

Leylines stimulate awareness and psychic ability, unlock intuition and allow your heart and mind to work together, increasing spiritual consciousness. They amplify emotions and energy, including anything in your life that's unresolved, forcing you to deal with it. This can be emotionally draining and difficult to process, especially as you struggle physically to keep moving forward, but it's ultimately very healing.

The meaning and purpose of the Camino has changed over the centuries, yet it still has the power to transform the lives and hearts of all those who walk it. The power of the rituals performed along the way are profound and lasting, be they attending pilgrim mass in Roncesvalles, leaving your sorrow behind in a stone at the Iron Cross, hugging the statue of Saint James in the cathedral in Santiago de Compostela or diving into the ocean at Finisterre to mark your spiritual rebirth.

The lessons and the realisations you come to as you journey both inward and outward are life changing and permanent, and they don't end in the cathedral. This point is more truly the beginning, for it is only when you return home and start incorporating your experiences into your life that the magic of all you endured starts to unfold.

Centuries ago people risked life and limb to touch the relics of a saint in the hope that the holiness would rub off on them, or went on long voyages across the seas to discover new lands. Today we hoist on our backpack and hiking boots and set out on a pilgrimage with the intention of exploring new parts of ourselves, and being transformed physically, emotionally and spiritually.

The psychic connection

Quick tips to integrate the wisdom of the Camino

1. Meditate on the direction of west. The Camino path heads ever westward, towards the ocean and the setting sun. In nature-based religions, west symbolises endings, emotions, introspection, strength and the courage to face your deepest feelings. The four directions are each aligned with an element, west commonly being water, which is associated with healing and purification. If you have an altar, light a candle in the west and meditate on what part of your life or heart needs healing. If you can, watch the sun set over the ocean and consider the things in your life that have ended or which you'd like to end, then work out how to transform them into new beginnings.

2. Get up a bit earlier each morning and go for a walk. It will clear your head, focus your mind on the day ahead, give you space to reflect on yourself and your life, and unleash your creativity. The physicality of it will boost your health, as walking is one of the most effective forms of exercise, and it's also the basis of a form of meditation which will help you attune your physical, emotional and spiritual bodies.

3. The symbol of the Camino is the scallop shell, so find an actual shell, get a metal or plastic one, or draw a picture. For pilgrims the spokes of the shell represent the various routes of the Camino that all come together at Santiago de Compostela, and in a broader sense they portray all the possible paths to reach your destiny. Consider all the different ways you can achieve your goals, and know that even if one seems to be a dead end, there are other routes to your destination. Scallop shells also represent rebirth, travel and movement, as well as the ocean, which makes them a reminder of nature and its power.

4. If you feel drawn to the religious aspect of the pilgrimage, ponder the life of Saint James. There's some information in *The Bible* and a little in Catholic tomes and online, as well as portraits that were painted of him. He is the patron saint of Spain and pilgrims, and also of arthritis sufferers, labourers, blacksmiths, pharmacists and equestrians. If you're more intrigued by the Roman history of the path, learn about Venus, the goddess of love depicted in Botticelli's famous painting *The Birth of Venus*, in which she rises from the sea on a scallop shell. Invoke her in a ritual and ask for her blessings and guidance.

5. Absorb the Camino's transformative power by immersing yourself in the images, art and reflections of those who have walked it. For centuries people have painted the landscapes, sculpted artworks and written about their experiences – and more recently constructed online blogs with photos – in an attempt to impart the magic of the route to others. US pilgrim Melissa West displays her striking Camino-inspired artwork at www.mswest.com, Benedictine monk Father Jerome Tupa's colourful, surreal paintings can be viewed at www.jerometupa.com, and several other artists feature at www.sacredstepsinspain.com.

The armchair traveller's way to visit

"I haven't got any special religion. My god is the God of Walkers. If you walk hard enough, you probably don't need any other god."
Bruce Chatwin, English novelist and travel writer

If hiking across an entire country sounds too hard, don't despair. You can capture the essence of the Camino without leaving home, because at its core it's a journey to your inner self. The trek forces you to look within your own heart, to examine your thoughts and motives, remember your hopes and dreams and figure out what's most important to you – which you can do anywhere, if you allow yourself the time.

Walking the Camino gives you distance and perspective on your life and makes it easier to let go of pain, loss or guilt and see problems in a new light – after all, what else can you do when you're walking ten hours a day except think of yourself? But the very act of walking is a great way to look inward, and you can do that wherever you are, and no matter how busy you feel. Even the shortest walk can give you clarity and space, a time out from the world. A healer once suggested I walk for ten minutes every night after work so I could process all my thoughts, emotions and stresses rather than letting them build up in my head and give me migraines. I was sceptical about the benefits of such a short time, but it does help. And if ten minutes a day can make a difference, think how much more powerful a longer stroll would be.

I've had incredible insights while walking in the park across the road from my city apartment. There's something about the rhythmic pattern of walking that connects you to your own heartbeat, and to the energy of the earth and the wisdom of nature. Plus it's great exercise, and a strong body creates a strong mind.

Whenever I got stuck while writing this book I'd put on my sneakers and go walking in my park. Climbing the hills, striding around the lake, watching the clouds in the sky, feeling the breeze on my face and inhaling the colours of sunrise or sunset allowed my mind to roam and communicate with my heart and my soul. Answers came – a new idea, a better way to write a section, an element that was missing.

There's something about walking that assists the integration of your physical, emotional and spiritual selves, so it's no accident that so many faiths suggest walking as a form of meditation. One method is to drop your pace and walk so slowly that you're barely moving forward, concentrating solely on the placement of your feet and the awareness of your body in space. It can be frustrating at first, but it's a powerful exercise that really focuses your mind.

Spending a day hiking in a national park or along a beach or river will also lull you into a trance-like meditative state, and allow you to access deeper layers of consciousness and encourage issues, problems, past events and solutions to surface and begin to be processed.

In this case nature and the energy of the earth play an important part, as they do on the Camino. Whether you're consciously aware of it or not, you'll be breathing in the sunlight and absorbing power from the ground that will help you go within. The beauty of your surroundings will also have a soothing, hypnotic effect, visually as well as aurally. It's hard to be anything but peaceful and reflective as you walk along the seashore hearing the rushing of the waves, or wander through a forest and listen to the sounds of the breeze through the trees.

A power walk is also a good way to integrate wisdom, because when the endorphins kick in and you feel the wind brush against your face and see the world passing by, you experience a sense of elation and perceive your life and any problems you're having in a lighter, more positive way. Walking can spark moments of intense clarity, solutions to problems and insight into things that are worrying you, with a new perspective on issues and simple answers popping into your head.

"Meditation is the art of learning how to be present with your self. The best way in our fast paced world to learn this is to just go out in nature, because nature vibrates on that level. We need to take time to relax, get quiet and get present with ourselves and with nature – it's a way of replenishing ourselves."
Shakti Gawain, US author and environmentalist

Moving meditations such as yoga, qigong and tai chi also help you access your inner self by aligning your physical and emotional bodies and getting you in touch with your psyche. Seated meditation is another way to allow these processes. It requires practise, dedication and application – some people find walking the Camino easier than meditating for an hour a day – but the benefits can be immense.

Meditation enriches the soul, helping to still the mind, focus your attention inward and develop insight and wisdom. It encourages contemplation and spiritual growth, taking you beneath your patterns to your inner self, and is considered by many to be the road to enlightenment. It also has physical benefits, controlling anxiety and stress, decreasing blood pressure, boosting concentration, combatting the effects of ageing and improving breathing and sleep quality.

One of the simplest ways to start meditating is to listen to a tape or CD of a guided meditation. There are dozens of different kinds, from Buddhist, shamanic and pagan chants to spoken visualisations and musical pieces, so find the one that's most effective for you. Some people prefer a male voice, some a female. Some like American or British accents, some don't. Some want constant instruction, and others prefer a basic guideline and then to be left to their own devices.

Another method is to focus on physical sensation, narrowing your awareness to your breath, the tip of your nose, the breeze brushing your skin or even the various sensations in your body, from the itch on your arm to the pulse in your neck and the pins and needles in your foot. You can also sit by a river, close your eyes and lose yourself in the sound of the water rushing over rocks and gurgling downstream.

Others prefer to stare into a candle flame, restricting their focus to that single jet of light, which is known as trataka, steady gaze. A state of meditation can also be achieved by staring at the full moon, the horizon or any other object, concentrating on a prayer bracelet or rosary, or repeating a mantra over and over again. And there are many meditation courses, from two-hour weekly classes to weekend or week-long retreats, that cover a variety of different styles and faiths.

You can also recreate the silence of the Camino, which gives you time and space to discover so much about your self and your world. Quiet time is an indulgence that will help you look within, whether you spend just a few minutes a day or go on a course such as Vipassana, a ten-day silent meditation retreat. It's a powerful tool that takes you deep within your psyche, uncovering and exposing the layers of learned behaviour, guilt and fear you've held on to, and the defences you've built around your heart in a lifetime of human interaction.

Most people in the 21st century are frantically busy with work, commuting, family commitments, study, socialising and all the millions of things we try to fit in our modern lives, and sadly we usually put ourselves and our own physical and emotional health last. But everyone needs time to relax and recharge, to focus on their own life, look within and understand their inner self. Whether you sign up for regular yoga, meditation or even boxing classes, schedule time to paint, draw or play music, or just take a bath or sit with a cup of tea and daydream, it's essential to give yourself the luxury of time to think and process where you are, what you're doing and if you're truly happy with the life you're currently living and the person that you are.

Keeping a journal is another great way to get inside your head and unveil the patterns of your actions and reactions. Writing about your thoughts, emotions, motivations, heartbreaks and successes helps you understand your life and make sense of the world, providing insight, freeing your spirit and connecting you to your heart and soul.

Through writing you become more self-aware, as well as more aware of others, and are able to look back at events with more clarity, perspective and truth. It gives you a chance to be totally yourself, in the way travelling does, without the weight of other people's expectations. You don't have to edit yourself or limit your thoughts, you can simply express your inner self, unafraid of judgement or consequence. You can spill your biggest dreams, darkest secrets and harshest opinions, and work through them in your own time.

Journalling can help you integrate the lessons you've learned and stop repeating mistakes. Seeing things in black and white and noticing your patterns is a powerful tool. You can write about any hard times and darkness you've been through, purging your heart of sadness and providing distance and perspective on events. It provides order to chaos, helps you make sense of a situation, and is more productive than constantly worrying over an issue. Just as importantly, recording events reminds you of the good things you've experienced, which many people overlook when they're considering their life.

Writing can also assist you in manifesting your dreams, because putting your thoughts on paper is the first step to creating an outcome. It takes the energy of your idea out of the etheric and into the physical, requiring you to articulate the end result and reminding you of the goal, your actions, the steps you need to take and all the little successes along the way. And it allows you to pause and reflect, to understand who you are and what you really want, and how to go about getting it.

Another way to connect with the inner truths of your life is to sit quietly and write a question about a situation or problem you're facing with the hand you write with, then start answering it with your other hand. When you can finally decipher the scrawl, you'll discover some incredible pieces of wisdom which were within you all along. It's all about unlocking the energy, power and knowledge you already possess, and going deep within to learn what you already know.

You can also absorb the energy of the Camino by training for it. Whether or not you ever actually do it, you can prepare physically and mentally. Walk at least five days a week, starting with short distances if you prefer then building up to longer ones. Vary your path, adding hills when you can, walking through forests or along sandy beaches if you're able to. You might even fall in love with hiking as a result, graduating to marathons or events like Oxfam's annual Walk Against Want, which raises funds for the world's poor.

"Most of the luxuries, and many of the so-called comforts of life, are not only not indispensable, but are positive hindrances to the elevation of mankind. With respect to luxuries and comforts, the wisest have lived a more simple and meagre life than the poor."
Henry David Thoreau, 19th century American philosopher and author

Once your fitness starts increasing, think about what you'd take in your backpack if you were to walk the Camino – then extend that to your life. A big lesson of the pilgrimage route is simplification, and that can be worked on at any time. Consider what you really need and what is simply collecting dust and taking up space – space that could be filled with new energy, people, experiences or things.

The ancient science of feng shui, which balances the energy of your environment to enhance your life and promote health, wealth and happiness, states that possessions you no longer need, use or want weigh you down and literally drain you of energy and motivation. One of the most common yet easy to fix feng shui issues is clutter, which is metaphorical congestion. A room filled with junk has very low energy, which will make your life stilted, chaotic and stagnant – just stand in a messy room and note what happens to your mood and energy levels. In clearing clutter you're inviting transformation to occur, and opening the way for positive new opportunities to enter your life.

Do a massive spring clean and clear out your wardrobe, home office, kitchen, lounge room and garage. Go through the house and consider each item and the value it has to you. Anything that you love, that is used often or which holds happy memories attracts positive energy, but any object you don't like, never use or have negative emotions about – guilt at buying it, sadness because of who gave it to you – will drain you, block new experiences and unbalance your life.

Give the things you don't need to charity or have a market stall, then marvel at the energy that flows in when you make space for it. You'll be flooded with new ideas and opportunities, meet new people and feel more energised and positive about everything in your life.

Consider your consumption too. Discuss with your friends giving each other things you need for birthdays and Christmas, rather than buying something that will clutter the home, take up space and drain energy. You could exchange experiences rather than gifts – a hot air balloon ride, high tea at a posh hotel, a French lesson, tickets to a concert – or do something worthy in their name, like buying a goat for a family in Africa or contributing to a homeless shelter in their area.

A big realisation of the Camino is how important the simple things – food, water, shelter – are in life, and how lucky most of us are, so helping someone in need will attune you to the old energy of the walk, when pilgrims were dependent on others for survival.

You can also channel the feeling of the Camino by exploring the cuisine of northern Spain, which is renowned throughout the world. (A few pilgrims even set out with their primary goal being to sample the local food!) Each region has unique recipes, flavours and produce, but one of the most enduring pilgrim meals is the garlic soup, Sopa de Ajo, found in most of the refuges, cafes and restaurants along the route.

Heat 1 tablespoon of olive oil in a frypan and saute 8 whole garlic cloves until lightly browned and soft. Remove from pan. Add 1 tablespoon of olive oil and fry 4 slices of bread, then set aside. Add another tablespoon of olive oil to the pan and stir in half a teaspoon of cumin and 1 tablespoon of smoked paprika. When hot and fragrant, add a pinch of saffron and 6 cups of water and bring to the boil. Chop or crush the roasted garlic cloves and add to the broth. Simmer for 10 minutes, adding salt to taste. Add the bread to the soup and serve. Traditionally Galicians broke 4 eggs into the pot and baked it for 4 minutes in the oven so each person had a poached egg in their soup. Today some people use stock instead of water, but it can overpower the other ingredients and ruin the delicate flavour.

In Navarra, near the beginning of the pilgrimage, fresh salmon, trout, quail and rabbit are popular. The region is also famous for its peppers, Pimientos del Piquillo, and asparagus, which pilgrims would recognise from walking past so many fields of them. La Rioja is best known for its wines, boasting some of the most beautiful wineries in Europe, but they're also gastronomically accomplished, acclaimed for their vegies and with favourite dishes including snails and potatoes with chorizo.

A staple ingredient of the region of Castilla y Leon is chickpeas, and the most common dish is stew. While there are many variations, it's usually based around chickpeas, meat and cabbage. The area is also famous for its fresh bread, crisp apples and high quality meats such as ham, chorizo and lamb. The region of Asturias is reportedly the best place in Spain to eat clams. It has a range of impressive homemade cheeses, a practical winter special called fabada, a stew made from haricot beans and chorizo, and instead of wine they make cider.

In Galicia, fresh seafood is a staple because of the coastal location. Favourites include Pulpo Gallego, a Galician-style octopus dish, caldeiradas, a type of bouillabaisse, and succulent vieiras, the scallops famous along the route. A popular recipe is Grilled Pilgrim Scallops.

Fry 1 chopped onion and 1 crushed garlic clove in olive oil until brown, then add 100 millilitres of white wine. Bring to the boil then reduce to a simmer. Stir in 50 grams of butter, 1 tablespoon of chopped parsley and 4 tablespoons of breadcrumbs. Cover 12 scallops, in their shells, with the breadcrumb mixture, and bake in a hot oven for 15 minutes, or grill to make extra crispy. Serve with fresh lemon juice.

Another distinctive pilgrim recipe, which will link you to those walking the Camino, is Tarta de Santiago, Saint James Cake, an almond cake sold along the route to celebrate the pilgrimage.

Coarsely grind 2 cups of blanched almonds in a food processor and set aside. In a bowl cream 200 grams of butter, 1 cup of sugar and a splash of vanilla, then stir in 4 beaten eggs. Add 2 cups of self-raising flour, the ground almonds and the juice and zest of one lemon, and mix well. Pour into a cake pan and bake in a moderate oven for 35-45 minutes. Allow to cool, then sprinkle powdered icing sugar on top.

In Santiago de Compostela these cakes have a small cross pattern on top – simply cut out a paper cross and place it on top of the cake before sprinkling with icing sugar, then remove the paper to leave the shape.

"Learn a new language and get a new soul."
                                    Czech proverb

A great way to attune yourself to – and prepare for – the pilgrimage is to learn Spanish. While in the bigger towns and cities many people know English and you can get by with a phrase book, in a lot of the small villages they speak only Spanish, or a regional dialect. Learning the language not only helps you, but connects you to the locals, enriches your experience and demonstrates your respect for the country.

Learning any language expands your mind, opens you up to another culture and teaches you about the world and ultimately yourself. Being able to speak Spanish will deepen your understanding of the country and the pilgrimage, giving you access to more of the information and history of the route. You'll be able to read books in their original form and immerse yourself in the music, films and poetry of the region, which will provide further insight into the people.

Language influences culture, so learning another can help you unlock the essence of a country, which will in turn increase your appreciation for your own and help you understand how others think. To understand the soul of a nation you need to communicate in their language. It's so much a part of how we express ourselves and even how we see ourselves – all our thought processes are limited by our grasp of words, and can be expanded if we learn more than our own tongue.

For many foreign pilgrims, the language is a barrier as well as a freedom. At times I felt happily isolated and loved the sense of liberation at not being able to communicate with people. I felt cut off from the world, which enhanced the effects of the solitude I loved. Yet it also made things really hard. Despite my phrasebook and a short language course before I set out, I had difficulty ordering food – particularly being vegetarian and allergic to tomatoes – and was frustrated when trying to find my way around. While I had a moment of pride when I managed to ask how to get to a church in Spanish, and most importantly understood the answer, there were also occasional tears when the sheer effort of trying to communicate over the simplest things broke me.

A basic knowledge of a foreign language will help you get by when you travel, but mastering it will enable you to have real conversations, to get to the heart of the history of the place, the political and religious beliefs and the things that are important. Even if locals speak English, as their second language it will be harder for them to express their deepest feelings, so understanding them will benefit you immensely.

Spanish is the third most widely used language in the world, after Chinese and English, and the most common in the west. It's the official language of twenty-five nations, including Mexico and most of South and Central America, and the second language of many others. It's one of the six official UN languages, and has similarities with other Romance languages – the ones that descend from Latin – which makes it possible to communicate with French, Portuguese, Romanian and Italian speakers. When I was in Romania I was amazed (and grateful) that the friend I was travelling with could understand and be understood by speaking Spanish, because of its similarities to Romanian.

Learning a language has been found to improve your studies in other subjects, because of the brain muscle it builds, and has been credited with delaying the onset of dementia because it keeps the brain active. Research discovered bilingual people have a wider intellectual ability than those who speak only their mother tongue. Mastering a second language also improves your grasp of your own and helps you express yourself better, as well as offering greater opportunities for work.

On a more fundamental level, I'm always embarrassed when I travel to a place where I don't know the language. It's such a western view that everyone else should learn English – many western airports only print information in English, while other countries, from Indonesia to Finland, have signs in several languages. Part of the purpose of the Camino has always been the convergence of so many different cultures and belief systems among the pilgrims walking the route, and the exchange of ideas and customs, and this is increased dramatically – on the path and in life – if you understand their language.

Ultimately though, all of our answers lie within, and the pilgrimage we most need to take is an internal one. Walking the Camino helps you facilitate this, mirroring your inner journey in the physical world, but it's not the only way to discover your inner self. Spiritual revelations can be experienced anywhere, if you're open to it and ready to learn and grow and move forward with joy and passion. A pilgrimage will always change your life, whether you go halfway around the world to make it, or set out on an emotional journey in your own backyard.

Postcard from the Camino

Shirley MacLaine is a Hollywood actor and author who has inspired millions with her own spiritual search. Books such as *Out On a Limb* and *Dancing in the Light* were ground-breaking explorations of her discoveries of other dimensions of herself and the world. In her mid sixties she was guided to walk the Camino, and a few years later she had processed her experiences enough to write *The Camino: A Spiritual Journey*, which is as much about personal growth and inner wisdom as it is about her gruelling trek.

Shirley was one of the first to bring New Age themes to the mainstream, and has been challenging, educating and opening people's minds about spirituality and alternative health for four decades. She has created a website that is a portal to spiritual information and transformation, which includes interviews, articles, environmental news and enviro-friendly products, chat rooms, a weekly radio show plus personal messages and guided meditations from Shirley. Visit www.shirleymaclaine.com.

The Camino is a walk through your self. You are basically alone, moving. You have to think about your family and your work and your fears and your pleasures and your love life and your children and all the things that you think about when you walk a long time alone. Then you start getting into who you are, basically, and who you were. That's when it all happens.

When you walk for more than ten hours a day for thirty days, you begin to realise some of the spiritual aspects inside you that you didn't know were there. And you will discover that you are much more than you thought you were when you began.

I got in touch with a lot of past life experiences as I walked. And I learned why I was particularly drawn to this pilgrimage – I had lived there before. I realised I had once been a Moorish girl who was tending to the sick on the Camino path – I had been there. And then as I pursued it, as time progressed, I went even deeper, and back into time further. It was overwhelming. I was overwhelmed for a year or two after the walk in relation to what I had been through.

All these things came up for me because the energy of the Camino still exists. The route follows the leylines that reflect the energy from the star systems above it. Just as our human body has chi, or life force, running through it, so does the earth. Leylines are the spiritual life force that activates the earth itself into a living being.

This earth energy can't be seen or tasted, and it doesn't have an odour, but the effects can be experienced. It isn't loud, but it can be heard. It can't be touched, but it can definitely be felt.

There are many sacred pilgrimages, but the energy on the Camino is so much stronger than any I'd walked before. I've experienced the spirituality of nature on other walks, but it wasn't as activated as this one. The ground and the rocks and the land absolutely speak, and I had a communication with all of nature.

I did the pilgrimage for the spiritual aspect, but some people treat it as a tourist hike with friends, or they want to experience the fine restaurants, because northern Spain has wonderful restaurants. Others were very serious about doing it alone, which is what one really ought to do. Some people go on the Camino because their husbands or wives left them and they just need to cool their head. Others simply want to experience the countryside.

But you won't go through the total cleansing if you go as a tourist. You really should experience what the pilgrims were doing it for, which was walking alone. You should go and beg for food. I did that to some extent, and sometimes only ate the food that was in the shelters.

It's such an arduous physical journey, walking forty kilometres a day. Being a dancer, I thought I knew about pain, but I didn't until I'd done this. You have to experience what happens if you trip and sprain an ankle, or break a leg. A lot of people have to stay in a shelter for a few weeks because they can't walk after falling down a mountainside.

I felt safe as a woman walking alone. The Spanish government protects pilgrims. You can go right to the slammer if you interfere with a pilgrim in Spain, and everyone knows that. And a woman walking alone like I did – and it's very essential to walk predominantly alone – you make friends with people along the way. It's really hard to extricate yourself from these new friendships, because you want to commiserate, you want to discuss what's happening to you and so forth. But while there were a lot of people – millions go every year – you can go for long spaces of walking where you don't see anybody.

If I did it again I would give myself forty days instead of thirty. And I recommend travelling light, because you will find that you don't need all the things you think you need. When I came back, I really pared down my life and made it simpler. I think we become addicted to material things. And it is not that I don't appreciate beautiful things, but I haven't bought much of anything since I got back.

The most important thing travelling taught me is that wherever I would go, it was a journey into myself. You're splashed up against a foreign culture, something that's not familiar, and when you do that you learn who you are. Because the journey within is the only journey worth taking, it really is.

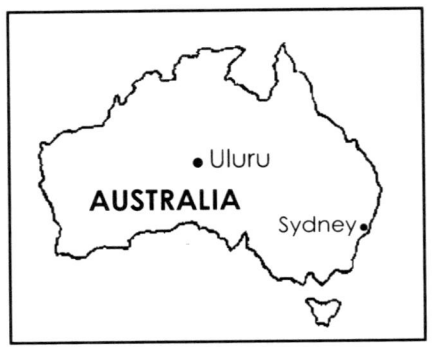

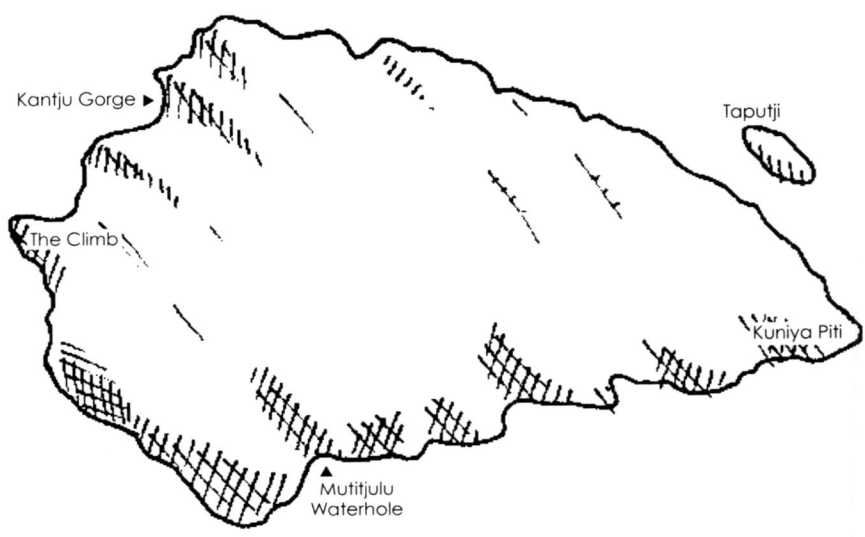

Kantju Gorge ▶

Taputji

The Climb

Kuniya Piti

▲ Mutitjulu
Waterhole

Reconnect to the heartbeat
of this sacred earth

Uluru and the Red Centre
Northern Territory, Australia

Absorb the unique energy of this ancient monolith
and the powerful vibrations of the desert landscape
that surrounds it, finding a spirit of place and a sense
of environmental consciousness as you open your
self up to the lessons of the people who have lived
in its shadow for tens of thousands of years.

The place

"Around the base of Uluru there are twenty-eight important sites of sacred significance. In a very real sense these monoliths are cathedrals where the members of the congregation are the Anangu people who camp near its base."
Burnum Burnum, Aboriginal activist and author

Uluru, the massive monolith in the desert of Australia's Red Centre, is the spiritual heart of the great southern land. As iconic as the Sydney Harbour Bridge, it is a geological wonder, a huge rock rising almost 350 metres above the desert plain. Yet it is also a cultural marvel, a sacred place to the Anangu, the local Aboriginal people, who have lived in the region for thousands of years and whose spiritual beliefs charge them with the responsibility of looking after the Rock and its surroundings, protecting the environment and the secrets held within this giant stone.

Scientists describe Uluru as a large magnetic mound. It has quartz crystals within it, the substance that powers watches, compasses, computers and lab equipment. It's located on a major planetary leyline and grid point, like the Great Pyramid of Giza, and some consider it the solar plexus chakra of the earth. Others claim there is a light source within it. There is definitely a warmth that emanates from the Rock, even in the chill of a desert dawn – the warmth of the heart of this vast, mysterious and beautiful country which Uluru anchors energetically.

Nearby are the thirty-six rock domes of Kata Tjuta, which is also a profoundly spiritual location, full of vibrational power and rare natural beauty. It is a place of men's sacred sites though, and only initiated Anangu males know the stories of its creation and the special meaning it has. But even without understanding its significance, a sense of the sacred can be felt when wandering through the gorges and valleys and while contemplating the immensity of this isolated but rich desert landscape.

Up to half a million people visit the Red Centre every year to see Uluru, formerly referred to as Ayers Rock, and Kata Tjuta, which is also known as The Olgas. Less than a third of them are Australian, because like many sacred places this area is far more popular with overseas visitors than locals – which is ironic, given that to international travellers it is the country's most distinctive, and most intriguing, tourist site.

The region, in the southwestern corner of the Northern Territory, is stunning and more varied than anyone could imagine. It's a desert, but trees grow, grasses flourish and wildlife is abundant. Waterfalls cascade down the sides of Uluru after rain, filling the waterholes, forming gullies and bringing the arid landscape to life.

The colour of the Rock changes dramatically depending on the time of day and the mood of the countryside – deep orange in the midday heat, transforming to electric purple in a thunderstorm and graduating through several different hues from blood red to pink, lavender, grey and blue at sunrise and sunset. Its unearthly appearance, and the contrast with the smooth desert sands, adds to the stark beauty of the landscape.

Another surprise is the shape of Uluru. On postcards, stamps and book covers it looks like a smooth-sided, rectangular structure, yet from the air and walking around its base it is revealed as almost heart-shaped in form, with jagged points where gullies and gorges cut into its sides. Each section has its own unique feel and look – some sides are smooth, while others are honeycombed with caves or ribbed with sedimentary layers. In some places the path around the base crosses the hot sands, then at other spots it passes beneath tall, shady trees or alongside cooling waterholes.

Visually, the flatness of the surroundings and the desolation of the landscape make Uluru even more impressive. It can be seen from miles away, its instantly recognisable shape looming up from the desert floor. And it is cloaked in a silence that aids reflection, and a sense of isolation that fills those who contemplate it with bigger questions and creates the space to dream the answers into being. There is something unknowable and unexplainable about the ancient monolith, and it has a mystery and power that is deeply moving.

For many people Uluru was first impressed on their consciousness in 1980 with the Lindy Chamberlain case, which made headlines around the world when a mother claimed her baby had been taken by a dingo while the family camped at the base of the Rock. Her story – and the Red Centre – was later immortalised in the Meryl Streep film *Evil Angels*, which was released internationally as *A Cry in the Dark*.

Uluru was also the centrepiece of the country's national airline advertising campaign, and the location of the final triumphant scene in *Priscilla: Queen of the Desert*, the award-winning Australian movie starring Guy Pearce, Hugo Weaving and Terence Stamp (although it was actually filmed at nearby Kings Canyon in the Watarrka National Park, so as not to cause offence by exposing sacred sites).

Most importantly, the Rock is a symbol of land rights and the struggle for reconciliation between indigenous and non-indigenous Australians, and today it also represents the first land management collaboration between the Aboriginal community and the federal government. It is the heart of Australia – both literally, at the centre of the country, and metaphorically.

No matter how many photos you've seen of this natural wonder, you will be stunned when you view it up close, and awestruck as you touch its weathered sides and feel the hum of energy that lies within.

Visiting Uluru is a completely humbling experience, partly due to the Rock itself, and partly because of the beautiful people who have lived harmoniously around its weathered sides for so long, who have performed ceremonies in its shadow and merged their heartbeat with the very earth. You can feel their reverence for the country and see their care for the natural world in every curve of the Rock, every tree that stands near it, each waterhole so lovingly preserved.

Uluru affects and changes visitors because of the vibrations of the earth around it and the hum of the Rock itself. By its side you really do feel in tune with nature, with the planet, with the seasons, with life itself. At this sacred place you can feel the spirit that moves through all of us and links each one of us to the land and to creation.

The present

"Uluru is incredibly beautiful, completely mesmerising in a way I'd never expected. There is something which is literally captivating, as if it has some special cosmic significance. Somewhere in the deep sediment of your being some long-dormant fragment of primordial memory, some little severed tail of DNA, has twitched or stirred. Uluru has an importance at the species level."

Bill Bryson, American travel writer and author

The Red Centre of Australia is one of the most breathtaking, stark and incredible places to visit in the world. Flying in from the east, the plane passes over salt lakes that stretch silvery grey into the distance like the surface of the moon, contrasting greatly with the harsh red land around Uluru that is more evocative of Mars. As you approach it seems an alien place, yet up close the desert is gentle, peaceful and teeming with life. Spinifex grasses hold the dunes in place, desert oaks stretch skyward and tiny colourful wildflowers dance on fragile stalks, adding a surprising vibrancy and vividness to the arid landscape.

At the base of Uluru are more trees – mulgas, bloodwoods, acacias and ghost gums – tumbleweed, spinifex and introduced grasses, plus bush tomatoes, wild figs and a host of wildlife. There is a whole kitchen larder – and medicine cabinet – in the shadow of the Rock, which has ensured the survival of the local people for thousands of years.

There are not just plants that can be eaten, but also those that provide an antidote to snakebite, leaves that cure coughs, headaches and other physical ills, a tree whose bark contains a substance that protects from sunburn, a grass that keeps away insects when burned, and another that relaxes muscles and relieves pain during childbirth.

The ancient landscape of the Red Centre holds countless secrets, which the Anangu people have learned and passed on for millennia. They are deeply connected to the earth, and its geological features play a part in their survival as well as their stories of creation. A series of incredibly powerful sacred sites stretch out in the distance, the most significant of which is Uluru, the manifestation of their spiritual beliefs and a symbol of protection and nurturing.

Many claim it's the largest monolith on earth, although that distinction actually goes to Western Australia's Burringurrah, also known as Mount Augustus, which is more than twice the height. But the sheer size of Uluru when you first see it is impressive and awe-inspiring – even from a distance I couldn't fit it all in my camera.

As you get closer though, the stunning beauty and stark contrasts of the iconic Rock and its surrounds have even more impact than its size.

One of the best ways to experience the diversity of the area is on foot. The circuit around the base of Uluru is one of the oldest walking tracks on the planet, a nine and a half kilometre trek that twists and turns through the gullies, gorges and crevices carved into the side of the Rock. It's a beautiful journey, with the track meandering along shady paths lined with trees, through pretty wooded sections, by tranquil waterholes and past scrubby areas of more typically desert plants, with the humming of Uluru always at your side. The trail is flat and easy to follow, and can be walked independently or as part of a guided tour.

I went on the fascinating Uluru Walk, a five-hour experience offered by Discovery Ecotours which highlights the cultural and natural significance of the place. It circumambulates the Rock, and includes a wealth of knowledge about the different areas the path winds through, and both the geological history and the Aboriginal lore of the area.

There were lots of stops so the guide could point out meaningful formations and share their scientific explanation as well as the stories of their creation that have been handed down by the Pitjantjatjara and Yankunytjatjara people, known as the Anangu, who are the traditional owners of this land and have lived around the Rock for thousands of years. The place where the ancestral being Kuniya the Woma Python slithered along the base, creating a tunnel, the cave of the willy wagtail and the paths of the ancients were identified, along with many other locations instrumental in the creation legends of Uluru.

Yet some of these traditional stories are secret, and a few sections of the Rock are individual sacred sites with restrictions attached, which the Anangu ask that visitors do not go within or photograph. There are hefty fines for violating this request – up to $5000 – and the rangers remove film if they see anyone taking pictures of these places.

One is the spot where Anangu women used to give birth, which is covered with a type of grass that relaxes muscles and relieves pain when it is burned. Another is a site where the grandmothers taught the young girls how to gather food and prepare natural remedies, and educated them in the ways of their lore. Other places are sacred to men, and their stories are known only to the initiated males of the area. Within Anangu culture this gender restriction is taken very seriously. Depending on whether it is a male or female sacred site, it is taboo for the opposite sex to go there or even look at it. These places are well signposted, with polite requests not to enter them or take photos.

There are additional restrictions on publication, and some of the pictures I was allowed to take for my personal photo album were not permitted to be printed in this book (www.SereneConneeley.com/gallery.html) or online. Ignoring this causes deep pain to the traditional owners. One way was literal – a young Anangu man googled Uluru and saw images of a women's sacred site on a traveller's blog. Because he had seen it, albeit through no fault of his own, he was punished by being speared in the leg, which is tragic given that it was a tourist's ignorance that caused the situation.

Many visitors also ignore the Anangu warning to drink a litre of water for every hour spent walking in the sun and to wear a hat and sunscreen at all times. It is a sunburned red land, and strangers will fry if they don't respect the heat and conditions. Survival in this harsh environment depends on understanding the weather and climate, and being able to interpret the heartbeat of the earth.

The Uluru Walk begins before sunrise to take advantage of the cooler temperatures and the golden pre-dawn light, followed by an incredible wash of colour as the sun rises, painting the Rock from dark brown to lavender to burnt orange and all shades in between. At times the trail moved directly into the path of the sun, which dazzled with its streaming light, energising power and the gentle warmth of the early morning.

As the day progressed and the sun climbed higher, the shade of the trees and the coolness by the waterholes at the base of Uluru became even more welcome. The heat in the Red Centre is intense year-round, and all the tours centre on dawn or dusk to ensure people can be in a cafe, an airconditioned hotel room or the swimming pool by noon, when the sky pales from the heat haze and the sun is merciless. In this stark environment people are forced by the harsh climate to be aware of and in tune with nature, the need to be out of the blistering midday sun and the natural rhythms of day and night.

This also ensures that Uluru is viewed at sunrise and sunset, when it is at its most spectacular. It's at these transitional times of day and night that the Rock's striking moods are most evident, and watching the sun rise or set over this ancient place truly is a spiritual experience. The wide expanse of the desert sky is incredible, vast and open, and unmarred by buildings or any other obstruction as it transforms from blue through all the colours of these enchanted times.

The rising or setting sun also paints Uluru with a thousand shades of red-pink-grey-violet. The shadows lengthen and move on its sides, illuminating different geological features, and in that instant you can believe, as the Anangu do, that ancestor beings shaped the monolith and are even now living and breathing within it.

The spiritual nature of the place lies in the land, and there is an eeriness and power that emanates from the Rock which moves people deeply. It's humbling to sit and watch the colours change and contemplate the size and timelessness of the monolith. Its immensity and spiritual grandeur make you question your place in creation and yearn to be connected to this beautiful, inspiring landscape.

Most visitors to the Red Centre get up in the cool pre-dawn darkness to watch the sun rise over Uluru, opening up their chakras, opening up to the day, to the energy and power of the sun and the earth, and the life force of the planet. They jostle for position, steaming cups of tea in hand, as the sky slowly lightens, the sun explodes over the horizon and the whole world is bathed in golden light.

At the end of the day they watch the sun set over the Rock, closing their chakras for the night, falling into the rhythm of nature and feeling the peace and emotional stirring of this incredibly moving live art show. The sunset viewing is a wildly different but equally spectacular experience compared to the sunrise. The red-orange earth remains stark against the deepening sky, there are lavender-coloured mountain ranges in the distance, and Uluru darkens to a deep purple in the encroaching twilight. In the other direction the sun sets over Kata Tjuta, making the tiny red domes blaze vividly in the last of the light.

"Finally I had come home to claim my ngura – my land, my place of birth – to revive my deep connection to my country. When I see Uluru I feel as though I'm home, and that home is a comfortable, secure, relaxed feeling – mentally, spiritually, physically as well as psychically. Uluru is my home and I belong here."
Bob Randall, Yankunytjatjara elder and traditional owner of Uluru

The best way to understand Uluru and its cultural and spiritual context is from the traditional owners of the land. To share this wisdom they have formed Anangu Tours, which offers guided walks that begin with the sunrise or end with the sunset. The tours are led by an Anangu elder and an interpreter, who together explain the stories of creation that make up the Tjukurpa, commonly known as the Dreamtime. It's touching to watch the beautiful relationships that have been forged between the elders and their white Australian friends, and see their light-hearted, heartfelt and respectful interactions.

The elders speak in their own dialects, Pitjantjatjara or Yankunytjatjara, two of the Western Desert languages. While many of them also speak English, conversing in their own tongue is an important aspect that keeps their culture alive, empowering them and strengthening their connection to the land and their history. That the interpreters have learned the Anangu languages and cultural inflections is a beautiful step forward, because in the past the government and the church tried to wipe out the links of all indigenous Australians to their identity and culture, including their language.

Their Liru Walk began with a sunrise viewing of the Rock in all its splendour, followed by breakfast at the fascinating Uluru-Kata Tjuta Cultural Centre. From there the two kilometre walk meandered back across the desert sands to the base of Uluru, retracing the path of the Liru ancestors. The beautiful, gentle and wise elder told some of the stories about the creation beings Liru the Poisonous Snake and Lungkata the Blue Tongued Lizard, whose body they believe still lies at the base of the Rock and can be seen in its geographical features.

Along the way he stopped to share ancient bush skills, such as how to start a fire without matches, make kiti, a type of bush glue, from the resin of the spinifex plant, carve wooden tools with a rock, and make and throw a spear. Only men and boys can learn this crucial hunting technique, and my husband found it fascinating to try his hand at it. Yet it's also interesting just to watch, to listen to the description of how to do it and hear traditional stories about life in the desert and how these incredible people adapted to the harsh conditions of the landscape and created a loving and spiritual society.

The elder also explained about the wildlife that's linked to their creation stories – reptiles, birds and animals – and its place in sustaining the Anangu with food and shelter. Their ingenuity ensured there was no waste, and nothing was thrown away. Every part of a plant or animal had its place, so when they caught a kangaroo they used it all, including the meat for food, the skin for shelter, and the sinews of the leg, which were stretched out to bind spear points to their shaft.

Some people shuddered as he spoke of hunting – sanitised to the reality of just how a cow goes from a green field to a Big Mac to provide their meals – but the Anangu only ever killed what they needed for food, and they did it with great respect and reverence for the animal that was giving them life. They've lived their lives in a state of grace and gratitude, and there is so much we could learn from their beautiful spirituality and ingrained sense of conservation.

It's an involving, intriguing tour, and I was moved by the interpreter's obvious love and respect for the elder. He deferred to his partner, respected him, sought permission for photos, protected him from video cameras and helped share his stories with warmth and empathy.

The company also offers the Kuniya Sunset Tour, which incorporates the gorgeous Mutitjulu Walk. This one began at the Cultural Centre, where the Anangu guide and his translator explained the history of the region and the stories of Kuniya the Woma Python and Liru the Poisonous Snake, two of the central ancestral creation beings of the area. Their long-ago battle can still be seen in the features of the southern section of Uluru, such as the wavy lines where Kuniya moved in to attack, the crack where she hit Liru over the head and the blood stains on the Rock from the fatal blow.

Then, after a short drive to the base of Uluru, they led us on a 1500 metre walk that passed by these unique features on the way to beautiful Mutitjulu Waterhole, known to some as Maggie Springs, which has been a life-giving source of water for thousands of years and is one of the few permanent waterholes in the area. Along the path are the sacred caves where the ancestors once sheltered and where local people lived until quite recently, which is why the Anangu named their nearby modern community Mutitjulu.

The smaller of the caves is covered in paintings that have been fashioned in time-worn ochre, charcoal and white clay on the rock walls. This artwork is only a few centuries old, as the older paintings have faded away, thanks partly to tour operators of the 1950s who threw water on the walls to illuminate the patterns for black and white photography. These paintings continue the traditions of the Anangu people, who used art – as well as singing, storytelling and sacred ceremonies – to pass down their wisdom to their children. This makes these outdoor art galleries classrooms of sorts, and the paintings that do remain are a vibrant link to the rich history of the area.

In a small clearing further along the tree-lined path, the elder taught our group about local bush foods and customs, pointing out the urtjanpa, the spearwood bush they make their hunting tools from, passing around different types of fruit – tiny bush plums, quandongs, figs, berries and peaches – as well as roots, herbs and spices, showing how to prepare grass seed flour and explaining where and how to find and catch food such as kangaroos, emus, reptiles and witchetty grubs.

It's hard to get your head around just how extensive the Anangu people's knowledge of their surroundings has always been. They knew which plants were medicinal and what conditions each one helped with, and what they needed to eat to obtain all the required nutrients – things scientists and nutritionists have only recently discovered. They had medicine men and women who used plants, animals and energy medicine to heal their community, much like the shamans of other earth-based indigenous cultures, and those who could work with the elements and the seasons to ensure a tribe's survival.

The elder also displayed some of the traditional gathering implements, such as the small bowls known as wira and the larger ones called piti, which are made from mulga wood and are used to carry water, food or belongings. They have designs based on the landscape and stories of creation burned into them, and are traditionally carried on the head atop a handspun ring called a mungari, made of grasses and bird feathers and bound with human hair, which balances the bowl.

And he explained the Anangu use of tobacco, which they mixed with ash and chewed to release the nicotine, avoiding the lung damage of smoking, as well as the physiological differences that mean Aboriginal people can't metabolise sugar – which has made the introduction of alcohol, soft drinks and processed foods by westerners so devastating to their health and culture.

Afterwards the tour moved to the sunset viewing area so we could watch the sky colour and Uluru change dramatically as the light slowly faded. This is the iconic image emblazoned on postcards, stamps and guidebooks, smooth and symmetrical, but after being up close to the monolith and seeing the crevices and gullies in its sides and hearing the enchanting stories of its creation, the subtleties and vague patterns on its face were now easily discernible, even from a distance, and it came alive in a truly magical way.

Another tour is the pretty Mala Walk, along the northwest side of the Rock. An elder shared the legends of the Mala, the Rufous Hare-Wallaby People, as we followed the gentle, shady 1500 metre path to Kantju Gorge, a sacred waterhole at the base of Uluru. It passed some of the sites where the ancestral Mala Men prepared for their ceremonies, the place the women gathered food, their painted caves and the route of the vengeance that was wreaked on them by another tribe.

All of these walks can also be done independently or with a park ranger, and there are evocative, descriptive guidebooks at the Cultural Centre that help identify the features of the creation beings on Uluru's face. Anangu Tours also offers dot painting workshops run by local artists, which teach painting techniques and discuss Aboriginal art and its important place in indigenous society. For thousands of years the arts have been a crucial part of their culture, used to pass down knowledge, preserve wisdom and express the heart and soul of their beliefs, and today it also provides a source of income as well as identity to the many artists in the region.

In addition there are camel treks across the sands to Uluru from the camel farm near the tourist resort, which arrive at the Rock in time for sunrise or sunset. Camels played an integral role in the white man's history of Central Australia, being crucial to exploratory expeditions, early settlement and the development of the Overland Telegraph Line that opened up communication in the heart of the country.

These animals were introduced in the mid 19th century, primarily from India and the Middle East, and were the main mode of transport and supply carriage in the Outback until roads and railways were established. They were an essential part of most expeditions – the first Europeans to see Uluru were riding camels – and were also instrumental in the creation of the transcontinental Central Australian Railroad that linked the country from north to south, which was named the Ghan after the incorrect assumption that all the cameleers were from Afghanistan.

By the 1920s, with the introduction of cars and trucks, camels became largely unnecessary, and many were left to fend for themselves in the desert. Today there are close to a million feral camels in the Outback – the largest population in the world – and they have become pests, competing for food and water with local animals and munching their way through valuable vegetation. Live camels are now being exported overseas, and at the camel farm you can feast on their meat along with homemade beer bread, wattle seed dip and bush fruits.

There's also a fascinating stargazing event, the Night Sky Show, held most evenings at the Ayers Rock Observatory near the resort. The stars and planets shine with unusual brilliance in the desert, lighting up the velvety darkness and providing an unforgettable experience.

An astronomer took us on a journey through the constellations, explaining stars, planets and other astral bodies as we watched through the massive onsite telescope. He explained the significance of each in terms of ancient mythology, modern astronomy and astrology as well as the Aboriginal stories of creation, offering insight and wisdom and an open-minded approach that dipped from science to the zodiac and the Tjukurpa with equal enthusiasm.

Constellations such as the Pleiades, also known as the Seven Sisters, are part of the legends of many different cultures from around the world, including the Anangu. The story of the Seven Sisters is part of a creation songline that crosses Australia from the east coast to the west. At Uluru, the sisters were seen by the hunter Wati Nehru, also known as Orion, who pursued them across the country – and after their death he continues to chase them across the sky each night.

We also saw Jupiter, with three of its moons orbiting around it, as well as pretty, shimmering constellations, a star made up of a blue one and a yellow one, and our own moon, which was massive and absolutely mind-blowing brought into such close focus, with its many depressions and patterns on the surface and its incredible silver glow.

The astronomer also pointed out the Southern Cross, which is used to find true south in the southern hemisphere, Venus, the Morning Star, which was important to Aboriginal women as they prepared for their hunting and gathering, the sparkling stream of the Milky Way and the Large Magellanic Cloud, which contains around ten thousand million stars – a tenth of our galaxy's stellar population – and lies about a hundred and sixty thousand light years from earth.

It was an awesome experience, especially because (very) early that morning, in a black sky dazzling with twinkling diamonds, I'd seen a shooting star in the pre-dawn darkness. To astronomers this is simply a piece of rock or dust burning up as it enters the earth's atmosphere, but to many people it's a sign of happiness and luck, and seemed a fitting omen in this magical land.

An astronomy talk is also part of the famous Sounds of Silence Dinner, where guests are driven out into the desert around Uluru to drink champagne as the sun sets over the Rock, then enjoy a star-lit three-course meal under the twinkling night sky. For another way to experience the iconic Rock, there are Harley Davidson motorbike tours of the Red Centre as well as helicopter rides that give a bird's eye view of the striking landscape from the skies.

"By not climbing Uluru, we pay homage to an ancient spirit – call it awe, call it worship, call it faith in something that, unknowable, gives shape and sense to life – that infuses and connects all the peoples of the world. These rites and beliefs comprise the spiritual foundation of Uluru. In honouring them, we honour and sustain the sanctity of the site."
Don George, American author and former* Lonely Planet *travel editor

With all these fascinating activities, there's no reason to climb Uluru, and the traditional owners respectfully ask that people don't because it follows one of their sacred ancestral paths, and treading it disturbs the energy of the place. In Anangu culture, only initiated men walk this track on the western face of the Rock, and only during important ceremonies. This is an important part of their spiritual and religious lore, and climbing against their wishes is sacrilegious and deeply offensive. In addition, the treading of millions of feet over the years is wearing away the surface of the Rock and damaging this iconic structure, both physically and spiritually.

The Anangu are also concerned for people's safety. It's a very steep and dangerous climb, reportedly much harder than it looks, and requires a huge level of fitness. Many tourists foolishly attempt it in blazing heat without a hat, sunscreen or water. More than forty people have died while climbing, from falling off or collapsing from a heart attack, and one man was decapitated as he fell. Many more have died back in their hotel room afterwards – at least eighty related deaths have been recorded, while a lot more go unreported – and others have died from the exertion after returning to their country. It's been estimated that one person dies every month as a result of the climb.

This causes great pain to the local Anangu people, as they feel a great responsibility to protect visitors to their lands. They are devastated when someone dies, even though the death was caused by something they asked the person not to do. They feel deep sorrow that each death means a family will never see their loved one again.

They have a strong belief that a person should die where they were born so that their spirit can be at peace and still connected to their ancestors. And it also disturbs the energy at the Rock if someone from another place dies at Uluru, with restless spirits in the ether.

To some it sounds harsh that people are asked not to climb, but no one questions being told not to leap up on a Catholic altar or walk all over a mosque, and that's what Uluru is – it's the Anangu's sacred place, their temple. It saddens me that people are so callous about their sacred law, because other religions demand – and receive – a much higher level of respect even if people don't follow their beliefs.

The Anangu haven't banned climbing, because they know that for some people scaling mountains is a spiritual experience, and they respect that, but if something is so contrary to someone else's religion, can it be considered spiritual? There are also many people who do it simply because they can, because they think they have the right to do whatever they want, even if it is hurting someone else. A girl I know of climbed the Rock despite the Anangu plea that she didn't – when asked why she just shrugged and said: "Well, they don't stop you."

Unfortunately the traditional owners can't legally stop people, no matter how much it means to them and how deeply it offends them. When the government finally returned Uluru to the Anangu, one of the conditions was that visitors still be able to climb. The only time the path to the top can be closed is during the period of mourning that follows the death of a local elder – and even then there are complaints from some tourists and government officials, although others welcome the restriction and the thought-provoking issues it raises. The climb is also closed when weather conditions make it more dangerous than usual – in extreme heat, high winds and pouring rain.

The Anangu call tourists minga, black ants, from the steady progression of tiny black figures scuttling up the climbing path, clinging desperately to the chain hammered into the Rock. It's a striking image – although photos of it aren't allowed to be published.

The sides are almost sheer, with an angle of eighty degrees for the most part, and the climbing path only slightly less steep. Many climbers stop at a small outcrop about a hundred metres up, too terrified to continue and also scared about the difficult path back down. It's known as Chicken Rock, because it's where so many people chicken out, and where many have had to be rescued from.

Tour operators estimate that half of the five hundred thousand visitors each year climb Uluru, despite signs everywhere asking that you don't, information in every hotel room and on every tour, and more requests and details about why you shouldn't at the Cultural Centre. It astounds me that so many still climb when it is so clearly and sincerely asked that you don't, especially as there are so many beautiful walks around the Rock, which open your heart and your soul to the magic of this ancient land and the healing vibrations of this sacred place.

People have also been taking away pieces of Uluru for decades, sneakily chipping bits off or picking things up from the ground, despite instructions not to. Many later post them back to Park Management – who have received items ranging from tiny pebbles or bits of sand to a 35 kilogram rock – begging them to return them to their original resting place in order to halt their bad luck, as they've come to believe the pieces are cursed. Others, on learning more about the culture and beliefs of the people of Uluru, return their piece with an apology.

The government, which took the whole Rock, finally apologised for its treatment of the Aboriginal people of the country and their dispossession from their land on February 13, 2008. With the election of a new government, which includes indigenous rights activist, environmentalist and former Midnight Oil singer Peter Garrett, Australia at last took the first positive steps on the road to reconciliation, starting with the "sorry" that former prime ministers had refused to say.

The whole nation stopped to watch this immensely moving and historic moment, applauding the symbolic power of a gesture that will hopefully form the basis of a new spirit of healing between indigenous and non-indigenous Australians, and the foundation of practical actions the government has planned to close the gap in health care, life expectancy and employment opportunities. Bob Randall, a traditional owner of Uluru and member of the Stolen Generation, sat in parliament with quiet dignity as the thoughts, prayers and tears of millions of people focused on Prime Minister Kevin Rudd's heartfelt apology and celebrated a new beginning across the country.

The Cultural Centre near the base of the Rock is a great place to learn more about the history and customs of Uluru and its traditional owners. It's a wealth of information and inspiration, and features fascinating exhibits and constantly screening videos of ancient ceremonies, hunting methods and wisdom teachings that provide a glimpse into Anangu culture and explain some of their beautiful creation stories, traditions, beliefs and lore.

There are photo collages, interactive language learning displays and artefacts, as well as art and craft demonstrations, bush tucker sessions, plant walks and cultural presentations that give an introduction to the Tjukurpa and the Anangu way of life, both traditional and current. It provides insight into the history of the area and its people, the languages spoken in the region, information on the local wildlife and a peek at the way the park is run and managed.

The Cultural Centre was built in 1995 to mark the 10th anniversary of the handover of Uluru to its traditional owners, and is shaped like the two ancestral snakes Kuniya and Liru. It includes a cafe, a shop that sells local paintings, books and souvenirs, and two thriving art centres.

At Maruku Arts, visitors can watch local artists at work painting, weaving, sculpting, wood carving and making jewellery, and buy beautiful original creations. The centre features pieces from Aboriginal communities throughout the Western Desert region, and is owned and run by the Anangu, offering support, promotion and sales assistance to hundreds of indigenous artists.

The Walkatjara Art Centre is also owned and operated by local artists from the nearby Mutitjulu Community, and boasts unique ceramic pieces, crafts, tools and paintings based on the surrounding desert landscape and the ancient stories of the Tjukurpa. Artists are often at work here, and the gallery also sells works by other communities under the umbrella of Desart, the Association of Central Australian Aboriginal Art and Craft Centres.

"Outback Australia is in the middle of a tourist boom. Thousands of people visit the Central Desert region each year, yearning to connect with Aboriginal culture, with our land and its immense spiritual power. Many non-Aboriginal people are fascinated by the deep spiritual relationship we have for our country. It's the fourth dimension of our identity."
Bob Randall, Yankunytjatjara elder and traditional owner of Uluru

Uluru is part of the Uluru-Kata Tjuta National Park, and there is a small entry fee – $25 for a three-day multi-entry pass, maps and guide booklet – which goes towards upkeep and maintenance of the park and its sacred sites as well as the training of Anangu park rangers. There is no accommodation inside the park, and no camping is allowed within its boundaries. All visitors must either drive a fair distance or stay at the tourist town of Yulara, also known as Ayers Rock Resort, which was built in 1983 just outside the park and far enough from Uluru to ease the environmental pressures of so many tourists.

This service town features a camping ground, backpacker hostel and five different hotels, varying from cabins to five-star suites, plus restaurants, souvenir shops, a supermarket, post office and bank, as well as an information centre, tour booking service, car hire and the Mulgara Art Gallery. There is also a free shuttle that drives around the town circuit for those who don't feel like walking the short distances between all the amenities.

Yulara is 19 kilometres from the Rock, but all the tours pick up passengers from the door of their hotel or campsite. There is also a shuttle between Yulara and Uluru for those who want to go exploring on their own, although the wide variety of guided tours is recommended so people can learn about the place from the Anangu perspective. I'm not usually a fan of guided tours, but these ones impart so much extra information and insight that can't be found in guidebooks.

Nearby Connellan Airport has flights from Sydney, Melbourne, Perth, Cairns and Alice Springs, and there are also buses from most capital cities and regular coaches from the regional centre of Alice Springs. Many visitors plan their trip to Uluru based out of the latter, unaware that this desert town is more than 450 kilometres – and at least a five-hour drive each way – from the Rock, and that a direct flight is the most convenient way to get there for those with little time.

If you have a more relaxed schedule, a Red Centre pilgrimage can include time at some of the other incredible sacred sites in the region. Kata Tjuta is about 50 kilometres west of Uluru and is just as spectacular, especially at the magical times of sunrise and sunset. It's made up of thirty-six massive rock domes – the highest, Mount Olga, is 546 metres tall – and their silhouette has been described as "splitting the horizon like the temples of an ancient city".

The domes vary in size and shape, and there are stunning valleys between them filled with a surprising array of plants, from shrubs and spinifex to gum trees, wattles, lilies and daisies. Birds congregate at the waterholes, filling the air with their happy sounds, and the areas of shade and cool winds provide sweet comfort in the heat of the desert.

Kata Tjuta means many heads, and is named for its many startling rock formations. It's an important ceremonial site, a place of initiation for Anangu men, and visitors are strongly urged not to climb it. Like Uluru, the walks around the base and between the boulders are fascinating, so there's no need to clamber over the sacred stones.

The Valley of the Winds Walk is a strenuous three- or four-hour trek through the most picturesque of the site's valleys, surrounded by dramatic gorges and the surreal domes, and providing an excellent view of the desert landscape from the higher points. The Walpa Gorge Walk is a shorter but no less mystical and beautiful hike, with knowledgeable guides explaining the formation of the rocks over millions of years, the diversity of the flora and fauna, and how the surrounding desert developed and sustained Anangu life.

While it's believed Kata Tjuta was originally part of the same mountain range as Uluru, it's vastly different in size, structure and impact, with the domes each having different shades, shapes and angles. On the way there from Yulara there's a viewing platform in the sand dunes, which provides a stunning panoramic vista that puts the domes in perspective, because up close the massive rocks are way too large to take in together. Sunrise and sunset viewing precedes or follows the tours, and the walks can also be taken independently.

Atila, also known as Mount Conner, is another grand formation, about 90 kilometres east of Uluru. It is aligned with Uluru and Kata Tjuta on an east-west axis, and there are songlines and creation stories that pass through all three. Many people mistake Atila for Uluru as they pass by on the drive from Alice Springs, although it appears longer and flatter than its more famous neighbour.

It has a horseshoe shape, with a narrow, flat ridge on top that flares out to a wider base. It rises 300 metres above the desert sands, and is surrounded by vast salt lakes that remain from the period when an inland ocean covered the area. Atila has long been a sacred place to the Anangu, but today it's on private property, part of the Curtin Springs cattle station, so it can only be visited as part of an official tour or by organising it through the owner. Tours can be booked at Yulara or Alice Springs, and inquiries can be made at the Curtin Springs Road House on the highway between Alice and Uluru.

Watarrka, also known as Kings Canyon, is an area of natural beauty and spectacular landscapes three hundred kilometres northeast of Uluru, which features sandstone walls that soar skyward, palm tree and fern-filled crevices, gorges and permanent waterholes. The walking trails pass through beautiful areas such as the Garden of Eden and the Lost City, and past surprisingly lush areas of vegetation. And there are more than six hundred species of flora and fauna in this amazing desert oasis, making it an important environmental area.

The six kilometre Kings Canyon Rim Walk takes in the most spectacular areas and offers incredible views, while the shorter, flatter Kings Creek Walk meanders into the centre of the canyon for those with less energy. The area covered by the Watarrka National Park has been home to the Luritja people for more than twenty thousand years, and the canyon contains many sacred places as well as gorgeous scenery.

The best times to visit the Red Centre are during spring and autumn, although it is stunning at all times of the year and dramatically different as the seasons change. Although winter days are mild and you can work up a sweat in the middle of the day, nights can get very cold, often falling below freezing. And in summer temperatures soar higher than 45°C, with the harsh desert sands and lack of shade making the heat even more extreme.

In January, the height of Australia's summer, there are occasional dramatic lightning storms and flash floods that turn Uluru a deep purple and cause water to career down the sides, waterholes to fill and vegetation to spring back to life. In winter many of the reptiles go into hibernation, but by August the temperatures start rising again, plants begin to flower and fruit, the snakes and lizards come back out and animals begin breeding, marking the return of spring. Wildflowers bloom, but different species flower at different times of year, so there is always a profusion of vegetation no matter what the season.

In summer the sun rises at around 5.30am, which means tours begin at 4.30am, while in winter it doesn't rise until 7.30am. Sunset similarly varies, occurring at around 7.30pm in the warmer months and 6pm during winter. But the early wake-ups are not an issue, because while there are nice restaurants and cafes at Yulara and live entertainment in some of the bars, the reason people travel all the way to Uluru is not to sample the nightlife but to experience the power of nature and the many moods, feels and colours of the Rock.

The past

The white history

"Standing out there in the stark desert, its weather scarred walls rising sheer and bare, the Rock seemed to dwarf the mind by its presence. Yet drop your eyes from it you cannot. You feel as a little thing and of no account. It looks like some deliberate trick of nature, dropped there to guard and sentinel forever the great western deserts that lie beyond."
Alan Breaden, 19th century European pastoralist

European settlement of Australia began on January 26, 1788, but for more than forty thousand years – and possibly as long as a hundred thousand – the indigenous people of the country had lived a semi-nomadic existence in harmony with the land, moving around their area of the countryside as the seasons changed to take advantage of the available plants and animals and ensure no location was exhausted.

This was not random, as has been suggested by some, but cleverly plotted to maximise their hunting and gathering skills. They understood the environment, the climate and the patterns of animal migration and plant growth, and cared for and protected the land, performing ceremonies to enrich the earth and passing on their knowledge of nature and their spiritual belief system of Tjukurpa to their children.

They lived in close-knit communities with strong family ties, but their peace was shattered when the British came and declared the continent "terra nullius" – land of no one or empty land – and claimed the country as the property of the faraway king. Two hundred years later, on January 26, 1988, activist Burnum Burnum sparked awareness of this gross injustice by planting the Aboriginal flag on the cliffs of Dover to claim England for his people, as Captain James Cook had done to his country on behalf of the British.

The Burnum Burnum Declaration is a heartbreaking statement about what was done to indigenous Australians from the time of white settlement. Some of the lowest points include the slaughter of entire tribes, the taking of Aboriginal children from their mothers and fathers, the sterilisation of women and the stealing of their land.

Initially white settlement was restricted to the southeast of the country, which still remains the most heavily populated region due to the fertile soil, (relatively) plentiful water supply and temperate climate. Not coincidentally, few of the Aboriginal languages and cultures from this area remain, as the original inhabitants were chased off their lands, driven to find shelter in less hospitable places and murdered if they tried to stay.

For almost a century Uluru and its surroundings were protected from the invaders by the isolation as well as the harsh climate and the vast distances from the early settlements, and the traditional owners remained there in peace, living as they always had. But as a generation of explorers started making inroads across the mountains from the coastal towns, into the hinterland and west across the middle of the country, the Anangu of Central Australia were also forcibly relocated from their home.

In 1872 English explorer Ernest Giles entered the region while trying to find a route westward from Alice Springs to Perth, the west coast capital that had been settled in 1829. He spotted Kata Tjuta, which he named Mount Ferdinand after his beneficiary Baron Ferdinand von Mueller, but he couldn't make it to the red domes, being forced to turn back by a large lake. He was also denied naming rights – the baron insisted the highest dome be called Mount Olga, after the Russian-born German queen who had bestowed his rank on him, and that the whole stone complex be known as The Olgas.

A year later Ernest returned on another expedition, this time sighting Uluru, which he called "the remarkable pebble". But English explorer and surveyor William Gosse was travelling a similar path and beat him to it, and on July 19, 1873 he became the first white man to climb Uluru, accompanied by an Afghan camel driver named Khamran. William described it as "the most wonderful natural feature I've ever seen", and named the intriguing monolith Ayers Rock after his boss Sir Henry Ayers, the premier of South Australia, the state which at that time controlled the lands now defined as the Northern Territory.

Most 19th century exploratory expeditions concluded that Central Australia was unsuitable for settlement, which delayed large scale European movement into the area, but by the 1920s farmers were starting to take up large pastoral leases to run their cattle, and were determined to control the land and the people who had lived on it for so long. The government forced Aboriginal people onto reservations – large tracts of land deemed unsuitable for cultivation – while the farmers fenced off the more fertile ground.

With no commercial interest in Ayers Rock or The Olgas, the sacred sites were "given" to the Anangu as part of the Petermann Aboriginal Reserve, and they were able to continue taking care of the land, performing ceremonies to ensure its (and their) spiritual survival and passing on the stories of its creation, knowledge of the local animals and plants and the traditions that ensured protection of the fragile ecosystem and the maintenance of their community.

For another twenty years the only people interested in the area around Uluru were gold miners, animal trappers and anthropologists – and the government officials and church missionaries who took generations of Aboriginal children from their parents and sent them to institutions, a horrifying practice that continued from the early 1900s to 1970. It's now recognised that more than fifty thousand children – known as the Stolen Generations – were taken from their families and their land in an attempt to Anglicise them.

They were denied any knowledge of their own traditions and spirituality, and were forced to adapt to a culture totally foreign to them. The rest of Australian society is only just beginning to understand the deep connection the Anangu have to their land – it is a source of strength and purpose to them – and that ripping children from their parents and extended family, as well as from their country, destroyed the soul and spirit of all those who were stolen away and stolen from, and caused a breakdown in their culture that has still not healed.

Adding to the physical and emotional destruction of the people, European farming methods were destroying their environment. The introduced cattle and sheep polluted the waterholes that had sustained both them and the wildlife they'd hunted for food, and devoured the plants they'd used for food and medicine. Yet if an indigenous person took a farm animal to feed a family that was starving because their own food supplies had been wiped out, it was punishable by death.

I can't even comprehend how humans could do this to each other, but farmers were allowed to kill any Aboriginals on "their" land, as well as assault the women, and the police tracked and shot many indigenous men on the flimsiest pretext. There was no law against it – they had no rights in their own country, no wage equality, no access to education, and were treated as second-class citizens in every area.

Aboriginal people in Australia were not granted the right to vote in federal elections until 1962, and were not counted in the census until five years later, when more than ninety per cent of the population voted that they be granted citizenship rights in their own country. Today the standard of health in Aboriginal communities and the gap between the life expectancy of indigenous and non-indigenous Australians remain a horrifying indictment on the damage inflicted on the original inhabitants of the land by white settlement.

The first sightseers visited Uluru in 1936. Although initially there were only a few each year who braved the Outback heat and lack of facilities to make the journey, which took several days from Alice Springs back then, the increasing interest of tourists was the death knell to the Anangu's physical connection to their sacred place.

In 1940 the Petermann Reserve was cut in size, with the land taken back to allow gold surveying. And in 1958 the government excised Uluru, Kata Tjuta and the surrounding area from the reserve, declaring it the Ayers Rock-Mount Olga National Park.

A year later an airstrip was built near the Rock and motel leases were signed. Tourism operators flocked to the area with groups of sightseers, and banded together to campaign the government to "move on" the Anangu who were living at the base of Uluru, so that the tourists could better enjoy the area. The traditional owners were again chased from their land, away from their source of water, food and spiritual nourishment, which had a devastating effect on their physical health and wellbeing as well as their spirituality and sense of self.

By 1975 the ecological impact of badly planned tourism at the Rock was increasing, and the government approved a small area of land north of Uluru, outside the boundary of the national park, on which to develop the tourist village of Yulara. Until then visitors had stayed at the base of the Rock or camped on top of it, dirtying the waterholes, desecrating it with litter, tramping through sacred sites and disturbing the energy of the place. They didn't mean to cause offence, but there was no infrastructure and no facilities to support the ever-increasing tourist trade, and few Anangu were allowed in to the area to share their information on how to care for it.

Thankfully all the campgrounds and motels closer to Uluru were gradually closed down and tourists were restricted to Yulara, which was built to help protect and maintain the sacredness and energy of Uluru, and thus increase its appeal to visitors. The Anangu still had little, if any, access to their lands, coming to Uluru to sell their paintings but discouraged from living in the area.

But a groundswell of support and activism was sweeping the country, and Uluru became the centre of the long fight for land rights and the reversal of the erroneous "terra nullius" declaration that had destroyed the Aboriginal way of life since white settlement.

"We are different, you and me. We say the earth is our mother – we cannot own her, she owns us. This rock and all these rocks are alive with her spirit. They protect us, all of us. They are her temple. How does one repay such gifts? By protecting the land."
Oodgeroo Noonuccal (Kath Walker), author and Noonuccal elder

The land rights struggle has long been misunderstood – Aboriginal people don't believe in land ownership in the way that westerners do. Their relationship with their country is not about possessing it in a material sense, it is about custodianship, about the right to care for the land and continue their interaction with the country that is so much a part of their life and lore. When settlers moved in around Uluru, the Anangu were concerned about the effects of farming, mining and tourism on the natural environment, and the damage these activities were doing to their sacred sites.

They have a special relationship with the environment and particularly with the land where they were born. Their spiritual beliefs charge them with responsibility for the care and protection of that part of the country and the ongoing reverence of the ancestral beings they believe live within the landscape. They still perform the ancient ceremonies to sing the land and its features into continued existence, strengthening and renewing the energy of the earth with their own energy and in turn receiving strength and power from the land.

While the Aboriginal Land Rights Act was passed in 1976 and Prime Minister Bob Hawke acknowledged Aboriginal title to Uluru in 1983, it wasn't until October 26, 1985 that the Rock was returned to the traditional owners, with freehold title of the area given to the Uluru-Kata Tjuta Aboriginal Land Trust.

It was a powerful, symbolic moment, acknowledging the traditional ownership of Uluru and the park that surrounds it, and was the culmination of a decade of campaigning. But one of the conditions of the handover was that the park had to be leased back to the government, through Parks Australia, for ninety-nine years, and tourists had to be allowed to climb the Rock – which reneged on an earlier promise that climbing would be prohibited.

In return the Anangu receive rent and a quarter of park entrance fees, which has enabled them to build their own community, Mutitjulu, in the shadow of Uluru, allowing them to resume their caretaking role of the area that has been so significant to them for so many millennia.

The people who run Anangu Tours, the elders who are guides, the artists who sell their paintings at the Cultural Centre – and in galleries around the world – and other traditional owners of Uluru live at Mutitjulu. They control access to their community, and have been able to develop a place where they can maintain aspects of their traditional lifestyle while generating income from tourism and their acclaimed artwork, as well as contributing to the protection of the land and the environment by their joint management of the national park.

This joint management began after the handover, and since then a unique relationship has grown and developed between Anangu and non-Anangu Australians. The aim is to maintain Anangu culture and heritage, conserve and protect the integrity of the ecological systems within the park, and provide enjoyment and learning opportunities for visitors – all guided by the traditional laws of Tjukurpa and the wisdom of the local community.

Anangu are being trained as park rangers and tour operators, enabling them to be employed on their land. And in turn they are delivering cross-cultural training to park staff, local residents and visitors, teaching scientists how best to care for the land, and sharing their methods for protecting the fragile desert ecosystems.

A recent initiative was the reintroduction of the mala, the tiny rufous hare-wallaby, to the park. Malas were once common in this area, and were an important part of the Tjukurpa – as explained on the Mala Walk tour – but introduced cats and foxes wiped them out. They have been extinct in the region since the mid 20th century, but park management has constructed a safe enclosure and reintroduced twenty-five malas that they hope will adapt to the local conditions and start to breed, so they can be released back into the wild.

The Anangu have also finally been acknowledged for their wisdom in controlling and shaping their environment and the landscape around them. For thousands of years they have influenced the growth of native plants and animals, protected threatened species and performed a method of controlled burning, known as firestick farming, which prevented wild bushfires, controlled plant growth and assisted with hunting. After years of ignoring their special knowledge, westerners have finally begun to learn from them.

Today, a visitor's experience of Uluru can't be separated from the Anangu people who live there and protect and empower the landscape. They are interwoven with the earth, and the Rock breathes with their spiritual power. As a reflection of the growing recognition of this special connection to the land, the name of the park was finally changed to Uluru-Kata Tjuta National Park in 1993.

This symbiotic relationship was also acknowledged by UNESCO. In 1987 they awarded the national park and its sacred sites World Heritage Site status for the breathtaking geological features, rare ecosystem and exceptional beauty. In 1994 they acclaimed its cultural significance, declaring it only the second place in the world, after New Zealand's Tongariro National Park, to be listed due to its living cultural landscape. Just twenty-seven of the more than nine hundred World Heritage Sites are noted for both their natural and cultural values, including Kakadu National Park north of Uluru and Machu Picchu in Peru.

This new rating recognises that Uluru and Kata Tjuta have cultural and religious significance to the Anangu, symbolising the spiritual link between these people and their environment and forming part of the belief system of one of the oldest human societies in the world.

It also reinforces the place of Tjukurpa as a spiritual philosophy and way of life that links the Anangu to the land, and recognises the importance of their culture as a part of the landscape, and the landscape as a part of their life and culture. And it acknowledges that their Tjukurpa-influenced land management methods have sustained and protected the delicate ecosystem of their desert home since long before recorded white history began.

The Tjukurpa

**"We have no books, our history was not written with pen and paper.
It is in the land. The footprints of our creation ancestors are on
the rocks, hills and creek beds they created as they travelled. We
learned from our grandparents as they showed us these sacred
sites, told us the stories, sang and danced with us the Tjukurpa.
We remember it all in our minds, our bodies and our feet as we
dance the stories. We continually recreate the Tjukurpa."**
Nganyinytja, Anangu elder of the Pitjantjatjara lands

There are two different explanations for the formation of Uluru – the
scientific, geological development of the monolith over millions of years,
and the creation by the ancestral beings that is part of the Tjukurpa.

Tjukurpa is the foundation of Anangu existence, a complex belief
system that encompasses their ancient law and lore. It continues to
shape their culture, guide their morals and provide a code of behaviour,
and also teaches them how to care for the land and be environmentally
aware. It is a system of spirituality and philosophy that explains the
relationship between people, their families and society, as well as
their connection to the land, animals and plants.

It also incorporates the period during which they believe the world
was created by the ancestral beings, whose actions influence the
Anangu way of life and rules and restrictions even today. Tjukurpa
was translated as the Dreamtime by some early scholars, but it more
accurately means ancestral times or the time of creation. Although
Tjukurpa is past, present and future at once, a kind of all at once
time, it has no basis in dreams. To the Anangu it is very real, and they
consider their creation stories to be not myths or symbolic parables
but literal recountings of how their world began.

The Anangu believe that before the ancestral beings there was
nothing. The earth was flat and featureless – no hills, trees, rocks,
animals or people. Then the creator beings, known as Tjukaritjas,
appeared. They took the form of humans, animals and even plants,
and their adventures as they travelled created the landscape. Mountains,
caves, waterholes, valleys and other features formed in the places they
stopped to eat, sleep, do ceremony, love, fight, have children or teach.

Any place where a significant event occurred became a sacred
site, and the Tjukaritja's energy and some of its spirit was left in the
ground there. The Anangu can access this energy for their own
wellbeing, and they also maintain and renew the spirit of the
ancestors with their ceremonies. Like leylines, these sacred sites
have a high magnetic intensity which increases the vitality, perception
and health of anyone who spends time there. Aboriginal people are

so deeply connected to the land that they sense these sites and feel the energy of the earth flowing in their veins.

The creation ancestors were supernatural beings, what some cultures would call gods. Like the Egyptian deities they could change from human to animal form, embodying the characteristics of each. As a result they are the ancestors of both animals and people, so the Mala Tjukaritja is the forefather of a tribe of people as well as a species of wallaby. According to the laws of Tjukurpa, no tribe can eat their totemic ancestor, so it is taboo for Mala Men and Women to eat the mala wallaby, a conservation measure that ensured its survival in that area.

When the ancestral beings were done creating, they went into the earth, their bodies being transformed into part of the landscape – thus you can see the head of the python Kuniya in one of the folds of Uluru and the patterns of the lizard Lungkata's skin on the Rock face. In this way Uluru is a temple to the Anangu. Each crevice, cave and waterhole reveals further strands of their beliefs and their creation stories. They don't need a church because the spirits of the ancestral beings are within the Rock and the rest of nature, worshipped through their ceremonies and reverence. This makes the land and all its features sacred, and keeps the ancestors alive and part of their daily life, allowing the Anangu to interact with them and continue to learn from them.

Part of Tjukurpa describes the way the Anangu care for each other and the land, and they see the landscape as evidence that the ancestral beings still exist. To them, Uluru is a manifestation of the Tjukurpa. The curves and crevices in its sides are the marks left by the creation beings as they lived, loved and died in this area. Each feature in the Rock, each cave, crack and curve, has its own meaning.

As you walk around the base of Uluru the creation stories leap to life – it's easy to identify the profile of the Mala Wati Man, a sacred site whose image cannot be reproduced, the paw prints of Kurpany the evil dingo creature, and Malaku Wilytja, the cave of the Mala Women. Some of the ancestors associated with the Rock are listed below, although visitors are only entrusted with a very basic outline of the stories.

The Rainbow Serpent: Different Aboriginal groups have different ancestors and different Tjukurpa stories, depending on which part of the country is their home, but the Rainbow Serpent is a constant, described as the mother of life. She is said to have come out of the earth at Uluru. Some stories recount that she pushed the Rock up from within the ground to the surface – where it fell over on its side, matching the scientific explanation – and made her way into the light, where she gave birth to the animals and people who became the creator ancestors. Others recount that she came south across the water with all the people and animals who would inhabit Australia on her back – which coincides with the scientific belief that the ancestors of the Aboriginal people arrived via land bridges and short sea crossings from Asia.

The Rainbow Serpent has many different names, and is variously depicted as either male or female. Its movement is thought to correspond to the earth's leylines, geomagnetic strands of energy that cross the planet and manifest the etheric into the physical. Cultures throughout the world have a serpent in their creation stories, and it is seen as the foundation of consciousness and of life, a unifying cosmic energy. According to the Anangu, the Rainbow Serpent now lives in the waterholes of Uluru, nourishing its people and guarding the area.

Kuniya, the Woma Python: This ancestral being was from Uluru, but had moved away. However as she prepared to give birth she wanted to return to the Rock so her offspring could be born in her homeland, an example of the importance of place to the Anangu. When she arrived with her eggs, she learned that her nephew had just been speared to death there by a group of the Liru, the Poisonous Snake Men. Not knowing that it was as punishment because he had broken their law, a devastated Kuniya battled the Liru in revenge, and the blows they traded can still be seen on the face of Uluru.

The Kuniya story begins to the east of Uluru at Erldunda, a three-hour drive from the Rock. The songline of this story is known by many different communities throughout the desert, and each one has responsibility for remembering, sharing and protecting the section of the tale that crosses their land. At Uluru, most of these events can be seen on the Kuniya Walk, which takes in Taputji, where she rested, Kuniya Piti, where she camped, and the section near Mutitjulu Waterhole where her body created an indentation along Uluru's base.

Her head is visible above one of the caves, curled back on itself, and at the place where she hit a Liru Man with her digging stick there's a huge crack in the rock with a red trickle spilling down, a strange phenomenon as all the other streaky lines are black. When her rage subsided she took her nephew's body to Mutitjulu Waterhole, where they were transformed into Wanampi, rainbow snakes, which still live there today, protecting the waterhole for the Anangu.

Mala, the Rufous Hare-Wallaby: The Mala connection to Uluru began when the Mala People travelled from the north and west to perform a sacred ceremony, an inma, at the Rock. They separated into different groups – young men, male elders, young women and children, female elders – to begin preparing for the ritual, and their individual campsites can still be recognised now. Some of the men climbed the sacred path to the summit, the same route that tourists climb today, and planted a ceremonial pole to mark the beginning of the ceremony.

Then the Mulga Seed Men arrived and invited them to join their ritual, but as the Mala had already begun their own and couldn't stop until it was finished, they had to decline. Their refusal angered the Mulga, who conjured up Kurpany, an evil dingo-like creature, to wreak revenge. The dingo raced first at the women, where they were preparing food, but they were warned by the cry of Lunpa, the Kingfisher Woman, and fled. Some of the men were killed by Kurpany, while the rest ran south, pursued by the malevolent creature.

The story of the Mala People runs across the northwest side of Uluru, from the base of the climb to Kantju Gorge. Some of Kurpany's paw prints can be seen on the face of the Rock, as can the fallen bodies of some of the Mala Men, the food the women were preparing and even Lunpa, who was turned to stone as punishment for her warning and can be seen near the waterhole. The songline of this story continues down into South Australia, where the Mala People sought safety and were rescued by the Emu Men.

Lungkata, the Blue Tongued Lizard: Some of the other Rock features are part of the Tjukurpa story of Lungkata, who taught the Anangu how and when to burn the spinifex grass to prevent bushfires and maintain the balance of the ecosystem. But he was sometimes lazy, and one day when he saw an emu staggering towards him with a spear sticking out of its body, he caught it and took it to his camp, even though he knew the bird was someone else's dinner.

Two Bellbird Men came looking for their emu, but Lungkata yelled to them that he hadn't seen it and pointed them in the opposite direction, then grabbed all the meat he'd chopped up and dragged it to a better hiding spot. He dropped some of the pieces on the way though, and the Bellbird Men soon discovered his deceit and demanded the return of their food. They chased him into his cave high up in the side of Uluru, and when he refused to give back the meat they lit a fire at the base to smoke him out. Today you can see the pattern of his skin on the Rock face where he tumbled down the side, his body at the base and an emu leg with a spear in it.

There is also a legend about two young boys who formed Uluru when they were playing in the Kantju Waterhole. They created a huge pile of mud, which hardened into the Rock, then sat on top of it, running their fingers through it as they slid down the steep slopes, thus giving it the ribbed effect much of Uluru displays now.

There are many stories about the creation of Uluru and the surrounding sacred sites, and of the events and ancestral beings that shaped them, although only a few can be revealed to outsiders or uninitiated Anangu. Even then we are given just the barest glimpse into the magic of the entire story and the lessons contained within it. All of the knowledge of the Tjukurpa – of the creation time, law, medicine workings and relationships of people and nature – is imparted through a system of apprenticeship, starting when the children are very young and developing throughout their lifetime.

Visitors are only told the kindergarten versions of the complex lore, so any retelling of the Kuniya or Mala legends is very basic, just the merest outline of the complex layers of the real body of wisdom contained within the whole story. It's a mistake to assume their belief system is simplistic – it's just that outsiders are only entrusted with the knowledge the Anangu impart to the youngest of their children.

Each year these kids learn a little more of the deeper meanings, of the history and wisdom, the medicine traditions and the magic. Knowledge is imparted based on merit and maturity, not simply age, and it is a life-long education. As the young people learn and grow and are able to handle the responsibility of more information, they are initiated further into this complex and beautiful web of spirituality, geology, environmentalism, history and medicine ways.

Their study of spiritual and religious knowledge is marked with teaching, tests and initiations. All people within traditional Anangu society are valued and all contribute. They nurture and encourage individual talents and skills, and observe their children so they can educate them in the areas they show an interest in. Someone who seems connected to plants will be taken to the medicine person to learn the healing arts. Others might be taught to hunt, or how to pass down the lore through storytelling, song or art.

Some knowledge is reserved for men and some for women, depending on its cultural significance, but none is more – or less – important. Some outsiders have assumed that Anangu society is sexist because they have sites that are sacred to either men or women, and some lore is restricted to one gender. Yet their traditional culture and beliefs are respectful of all people. Men and women each have their roles to play, and both genders are equally important and equally honoured.

Both can learn about healing and bush medicine, and both are teachers of the young. Individual differences are respected, and people are encouraged to be all that they truly are, not try to be something or someone else. In honouring male and female, they honour the concept of balance – of night and day, sun and moon, drought and flood – the contrasts that make up the world and make up completion.

The Tjukurpa is an immensely complex spiritual and philosophical system which governs Anangu lives, actions, relationships and ceremonies. Tjukurpa is the Pitjantjatjara term for it, but each tribal group has its own word, including Wapar to the Yankunytjatjara people and Alcheringa to the Arrernte people around Alice Springs.

In a similar way the Pitjantjatjara use the term Anangu, which means people in their language, to describe themselves, just as indigenous Australians from other areas of the country use their word for people, such as Koori, Yolngu, Noongar, Nungar and Murri.

The meaning of the Tjukurpa and its equivalent is slightly different in different communities. There was never a single religion or belief system amongst the Aboriginal peoples of Australia – there were more than five hundred tribal groups or clans, and each had its own language and developed its own philosophy and beliefs based on their unique relationship to the land and their creation ancestors.

While there are similarities between them, there are also striking cultural differences. For one, the people of Central Australia don't play didgeridoos, as the tree they are made from and the wood-eating termite that hollows out the centre to create these instruments only exist in Arnhem Land, further north, where they are used. One of our guides was bemused yet also a little frustrated as he recounted the story of a tourist who sat on top of Uluru playing a didgeridoo in order to feel connected to the Rock and its lands – using an instrument unrelated to the culture and oblivious to the offence he'd caused by climbing. And boomerangs weren't used for hunting by people in Central Australia – instead they were a musical instrument played in sacred ceremonies.

The Tjukurpa is not taken lightly. It provides guidance and instruction, charging the Anangu with responsibility for the land of their birth and ensuring that they'll always provide for family, friends and people in need. They have strict rules, codes of conduct and expectations. Far from being the savage people they were depicted as by early white settlers, they have a strong ethical base, which stems from the Tjukurpa and is grounded in a sense of personal responsibility combined with their belief in looking after each other and the land.

In their ignorance westerners call them unsophisticated, yet it is common for the Anangu to speak three languages. Their environmental awareness, social conscience and spirituality are highly developed, and those who live on the land can survive in conditions most people would die in. In the past they often helped stranded white settlers and explorers find food and shelter, and their forgiving nature continues today.

The scientific history

"The evolution of the landscape of this part of Central Australia is a story of unimaginable continental upheavals, active and extensive erosion, formation of inland seas, deposition of sediments and remnants of some early forms of life."

Dr Anne Kerle, Australian biologist

The geological explanation of the creation of Uluru is also fascinating. Scientists now know that it evolved over hundreds of millions of years into the shapes and patterns it displays today. Considering how hard we find it to comprehend a time before the Egyptian pharaohs ruled – a mere five thousand years ago – it's almost impossible to grasp how long it took for the Rock to form.

Uluru is comprised of arkose, a coarse-grained type of sandstone that is rich in the minerals feldspar and quartz, which formed from the hardening of the sandy sediment that had eroded from nearby mountains. It's situated to the south of the Amadeus Basin, which developed nine hundred million years ago as a depression in the crust of the earth. Over millions of years this basin slowly filled with layer upon layer of sediment, raising the ground level of the region.

Around five hundred and fifty million years ago the floor of the basin buckled, creating the immense Petermann Range to the west of Uluru. There was no vegetation or animal life back then, let alone people – algae and bacteria were the only life forms – so rain and rivers easily eroded the massive range, as it had no plants to hold the soil in place. The sand and rock that washed away down the slopes built up into sections of sediment called alluvial fans at the base of the range. One was primarily sand, and this marked the beginning of Uluru, while another was made up of pebbles and rocks, which later formed the conglomerate domes of Kata Tjuta.

About five hundred million years ago the whole area was submerged under an inland sea – which explains the salt lakes of the region – and the alluvial fans were gradually covered with more sand, sediment and even some ancient marine creatures, which compressed together on the sea floor, under the weight of the ocean, to form hard rock.

After a hundred million years or so the sea receded, and the earth that was left was subjected to new geological forces that exerted massive pressure. Landmasses collided, faults ran through the earth, the ground buckled and folded, and the whole of Central Australia rose above sea level, significantly changing the surface of the land.

New mountain ranges formed to the north, and the alluvial fan that would eventually become Uluru rose further and then tilted almost ninety degrees, so that it was standing on end. The layers of sandstone which were once horizontal became vertical, which explains the flowing vertical patterns and folds in the Rock today.

Back then Uluru was much taller, and the ground around it was far lower, but about sixty-five million years ago, in a period of high rainfall, river sands, dirt and coal filled in the area between Uluru and Kata Tjuta, raising the ground level between the two and burying much of their mass. Uluru today is just the tip of the iceberg, so to speak, the top of a massive slab that once stood several kilometres tall, but now extends deep down into the earth's core because most of it has gradually been surrounded by sediment.

The part that remained exposed, which we know as Uluru, has suffered much erosion over time, and the Rock's face is marked with holes, gashes, pits, gullies, caves and rib-like surfaces. Rain water contributed to this, especially on the southern side where the valleys and waterholes formed. Some of the softer rocks and sediment that were part of the formation washed away, leaving raised ridges. More recently (in earth if not human terms!), the desert climate developed – it was only half a million years ago that this part of the country became dry – and sand erosion began to add to the effects of the water.

The many unique caves in Uluru's sides are believed to have been formed by tiny pools of water gathering on the surface of the Rock and weathering away, over millions of years, backwards and upwards, eating in to the sandstone slab. The honeycomb caves higher up were created by a combination of this weathering and the flaking off of pieces of the arkose rock, which occurs when the minerals within the monolith decay from being exposed to water and air.

Interestingly, Uluru is actually grey – it simply has a red coating on the outside. The stone is grey, but on the surface the iron in the arkose oxidises, or rusts, giving it its distinctive red hue. Deep within some of the caves you can see this grey colour in the parts where oxidation has not yet occurred. The desert sands in the region are also stained red, rather than the usual yellow, from the iron oxide content.

Scientists say that all the features of Uluru were caused by erosion, from the face of the Mala Wati Man to the tracks of Kuniya and the cave made by Itjaritjari the Marsupial Mole. Yet one of the guides on the Uluru Walk circuit tour, a geologist by trade, told us that although she knows the scientific explanations, she prefers the Anangu stories of how the Rock came into existence.

Out in the desert there's a hole geologists explain was caused by a meteorite crash, while the Anangu say it was made when a bowl was dropped by one of their ancestors while she was in the Milky Way. The black marks on Uluru are either the blackened algae that blossoms during high rains then dies, staining the Rock in the dry season, or the stripes left by Kuniya's patterned body as she slithered along the base to meet her nephew's attackers. The sedimentary layers running vertically instead of horizontally were either formed when the arkose slab tilted over on its side four hundred million years ago, or because the boys who constructed Uluru from a pile of mud raked their fingers through it as they slid down its steep sides.

To give some perspective on the time it's taken for all these changes to occur, the first Aboriginal people to come to this area, estimated to have been at least forty thousand years ago, would have encountered a landscape very much like the one there today. Uluru was in its current form by then, and even the sand dunes were as they are now. No human was around to see the cataclysmic earth changes – or ancestral beings – that created and shaped Uluru, not even the Anangu, who are recognised as the oldest culture on the planet.

Despite the difference in their creation stories, today science and tradition are joining together to protect this incredible environment. The Uluru-Kata Tjuta National Park is not just home to the two sacred sites, but also incorporates the fragile ecosystems of the area. The desert region has low rainfall and exceedingly high temperatures, but the rocks and mountains, including Uluru, contribute to the diverse array of flora and fauna through their waterholes and the shelter and shade they provide with their caves, overhangs and crevices.

There are hundreds of different species of vegetation in the park, with the waterholes at the base of Uluru providing habitats for a number of rare, unique plants. Many others have adapted to survive the frequent drought-like conditions of the desert by modifying their leaves, which are commonly tiny, waxy or needle-like to avoid water evaporation, and their root systems, which descend deep into the earth to find the water that sits in layers far below the surface.

Other plants have become drought avoiders, evolving so their seeds can sit on the desert sands for years then germinate as soon as the rains come, growing rapidly to produce new seeds before withering and dying when the drought returns. The animals have also adapted to the climate, becoming nocturnal so they can hunt at night and rest in the shade of caves, burrows and trees during the day. Others hibernate for long periods when it gets too cold or too hot and dry to survive.

There are more than a hundred and fifty species of birds and twenty-four rare native mammals in the park, as well as seventy-two different reptiles – the greatest number in the world, which includes many lizards, such as the rare giant desert skink and Australia's largest, the perentie, which grows more than two metres long. There are also hundreds of insects, including honey ants, which have long provided a sweet treat for the Anangu, as well as countless flies and strange creepy crawlies that piled up outside our hotel room door at night.

The plants and wildlife of the Red Centre are protected by the rangers who maintain and care for the area, enforcing the rules of the park which ban off-road access and camping within the boundaries. Work is also being done to deal with the problem of introduced foxes, camels and cats, which disturb the delicate balance of the ecosystem and compete with the local wildlife for vegetation for food. The Anangu and the scientists are working together to restore the balance, combining supposedly contradictory and opposing strands of wisdom to maintain and protect this sacred place.

The purpose

"At Uluru you walk out into that landscape and there's no sign of man. It's a big sky and big landscape that suits big emotions. You can find God and the spirit of the land and see yourself as a pretty insignificant dot in the universe. It was very much the cure for my depression at the time."

Shane Howard, Australian musician and
environmental and indigenous rights activist

Spending time at Uluru will reconnect you to the land, to your own country, and to your self. For Australians it is a literal connection to the ground we walk on, but regardless of where you are from, this awe-inspiring sacred monolith, the rawness and energy of the desert landscape that surrounds it and the power of the elements will stir your spirit and make you feel the heartbeat of the earth.

Being out in nature, feeling the soft caress of the wind, the warmth of the sun and the strength of the Rock, is soothing to the soul, a balm to the stresses of life. Uluru epitomises the wildness and purity of nature. Standing in its shadow you experience yourself as a child of the universe, connected to the land, the sky, the stars, the animals, the rhythm of life and nature. There is something so nurturing, invigorating and energising about being so close to the earth, a power that puts things in perspective and reminds you of your priorities.

In the desert, time slows down, expands, fills you. You become attuned to the earth, to the rising of the sun and the shining of the stars. Everything is unhurried, relaxed and laid back, and the unchanging nature of the landscape has a powerful, trance-inducing effect. This Rock, these sand dunes, these vast vivid skies have all been gazed upon and venerated for millennia.

In contrast the tiny details of life no longer seem so important, swept away by the size and impact of Uluru and its spiritual presence. Nothing else matters out here, yet in a strange way this realisation fills you with energy and the ambition to achieve everything you want to achieve and be all that you can be.

It is both humbling, because its grandeur makes you feel so insignificant, yet at the same time deeply inspiring, as it makes you seem a part of something ancient, unchanging and eternal.

There is something primal about the Red Centre. Far from the technological advances of the city, these ancient sands strip you of the veneer of progress and return you to a more basic state. You are who you are, not what you do, what you have or who you know. The hot winds that blow across Uluru and disperse the wisdom of this sacred centre whisper to your true self.

Out here, far from anywhere, there is no judgement, and nowhere to hide your true nature. The ancient echo of this place recalls hidden memories, forgotten parts of your own soul, and allows you to catch glimpses of what it is you yearn for. You realise, in the mirror of this desolate and wild desertscape, that you are already enough. Complete. You don't have to learn new processes, read more books, study another subject. The wisdom of the earth – and of your own self – can be accessed by opening your heart to it, and at Uluru simply breathing in the energy of the land will connect you to this universal truth.

The vibration of the Rock also affects you physically. Walking beside it, touching your hand to its weathered sides, you feel the deep hum of it, sense the energy that emanates from deep within. It alters you a little, draws you to it and holds you close. It has an undeniable presence, a power that takes your breath away. Timeless, enigmatic and heartbreakingly beautiful, it evokes a sense of wonder and awe, and a questioning of your own mystery. A wave of emotion will sweep over you when you first see it, and you'll feel a physical sensation within as you approach it and stand in its shelter, connecting to it with body and soul. Its very essence touches the heart.

The huge skies, openness and isolation of the desert also have a deep impact. It is the perfect place to think, ponder and reflect on your life. You can be totally alone, exposed to the elements and free to breathe in the life force that is so strong out in the centre of this vast land. There are no distractions, no phones ringing or people clamouring for your time. Meditation comes easy, and it is the perfect spot to try to get in touch with your inner thoughts and focus your mind. You can't help but connect to the universe at this place where the energy lines of the earth intersect. It's easy to understand why Aboriginal culture identifies Uluru as the centre of creation.

"The Aborigines are the true magical leaders of Australia. Having come to this continent forty thousand years ago, they are profoundly connected to the spirits of this land, and as such their religious beliefs and practices, their methods of healing and divination, are the real witchcraft of Australia. Their Dreamtime is one of the most advanced spiritual concepts of any culture."
Fiona Horne, Australian singer, author and witch

The spirit of the people who live in the Red Centre also has a huge impact on visitors. Uluru and the secrets it holds within it symbolise indigenous wisdom and the immense value of Anangu beliefs. These people give meaning to the land, and it gives meaning to them. They interact with it in such a way that you can't separate the two. They maintain the landscape with ritual and ceremony, and they gain strength and a sense of purpose from the earth.

Initiated elders have as much knowledge about the land, the world and the spirit as shamans of other nature-based cultures. They would conduct healing, communicate with the ancestral beings, care for the land, pass on lore and law, solve disputes, dispense punishment, encourage forgiveness, teach how people should live, who they should marry, the moral code of behaviour – yet their philosophy has been dismissed by outsiders because they don't understand or value it.

As I listened to the elders sharing their stories of living on the land and of how their world was created, I felt humbled and awed and full of love. This is a society full of spirituality and deep bonds of caring, a culture that celebrates knowledge, wisdom and experience. The elders of the community are revered and respected in a way that is beautiful and heart-warming. People, and things, are appreciated rather than being deemed disposable.

Being in Central Australia and seeing this beautiful relationship with the land inspires a connection to nature – and a heightened ecological awareness – in visitors. The Anangu walk lightly on the earth, in harmony with the natural world, with each other and with themselves. Their environmental knowledge and message of conservation is so important and so necessary right now, and it is inspiring that this wisdom is being used by park management, and that there is such huge potential for more widespread sharing of it.

The traditional owners of Uluru care for and respect the planet and their environment. Within their Tjukurpa are methods to protect the land, conserve water supplies, plants and animals and find sustainable resources. Their semi-nomadic lifestyle, which involved moving around their tribal lands in order to find food and water, meant they didn't damage or seriously alter the landscape. And while today most live in modern communities, they still share this gentle earth consciousness.

Some people believe that an energy has been lost in some areas of Australia because the indigenous people have been taken from their land, and haven't been able to perform the ceremonies or pass them on. In some places there are no initiated elders left, in others there are no children to learn the Old Ways and pass the local stories and knowledge on to. When these people lose their connection with the land they risk losing their way, and the land also loses something.

The Anangu have been at Uluru for tens of thousands of years, which gives it some of its spiritual power. In times of drought they travelled further afield to find water and food, and in the last century they were chased off their land by the government, but they have always come back, always been present to sing the land awake, protect it and conserve it. Now more have returned, after being stolen as children, and have relearned the sacred ways of the Tjukurpa and of the earth.

They are reclaiming their connection to the land, the wisdom of the ancestors and their sacred duty to protect their country. They've established a community at the base of Uluru, and after a period when their culture was banned in favour of assimilation policies, children are being taught again and the knowledge of the elders is being passed on, not just to their own young family members, but also to people of other nationalities who respect their ways and want to learn.

This, the oldest living culture on earth, is finally starting to be respected and valued. An increasing number of tourists visit Uluru not to climb the Rock but to absorb the spiritual power of the place and learn from its traditional owners, to experience its sacred nature through the eyes of those who have revered it for so long.

There is also a new awareness within the Anangu themselves of the sacred, precious nature of their culture. The traditional owners of Uluru created Anangu Tours to provide insight into the mighty monolith and the surrounding land, and to share their stories and customs and the places that are so sacred to them. The company has also created employment opportunities and self-empowerment for their community. They welcome those who want to learn, and are open and generous in passing on some of their cultural traditions.

Another inspiring Anangu-owned company, Desert Tracks, provides three- and five-day cultural immersion experiences, known as Bush College, which allow visitors to camp on Pitjantjatjara lands with the Anangu elders and learn some of the stories and ceremonies of the Tjukurpa. Participants dig for, hunt and cook bush foods, create traditional artefacts and sit around the campfire at night and talk with the Anangu hosts. The elders created this experience, in consultation with their people, to teach visitors the sacred significance of their Tjukurpa and keep their culture and country alive.

Increasingly indigenous Australians are preserving and recording their culture in books, films, art and music, and sharing parts of it. They hope to instil pride within their own community, and understanding and a realisation of its importance and immense beauty in others. In the past anthropologists desecrated Aboriginal sites and dug up sacred objects, taking them away to museums because they thought the culture was dying out and needed to be preserved for posterity. Now people are realising that this culture is still strong and vibrant, and it will endure for as long as the people can remain close to their land.

The Anangu value things some people consider simple, yet a lot can be learned from them. They place importance on family, spirituality, education, the elders, the connection between all things, the sustainability of the earth, and the long-term survival of plants, animals and people. Their philosophy covers the four strands of kanyini – beliefs, spirituality, land and family. White settlement destroyed these things by taking children from their families and their land, and forcing them to replace their own nature-based spiritual beliefs with Christianity, but today a new spirit of respect and understanding is beginning to infiltrate across cultures.

Part of the Anangu belief system includes not holding a grudge. Our guide explained that when a man commits a serious crime he might be speared in the leg by the person he offended, but then that person will nurse him back to health, finding food for him and looking after him until he heals. Whatever happened is forgiven, and they both move on with their lives, learning from the experience yet not dwelling on it or making the person pay over and over for what he did.

After their suffering at the hands of white people the Anangu still offered their hand in friendship, struggling to understand this foreign culture and ways while not having the same courtesy returned. The two elders I met were filled with a quiet dignity. Watching their peaceful walk, their understated talk, their gentle beauty, was humbling. I felt my heart open to them, filled with compassion for all they have been through and the way they have handled it. Their incredible generosity in sharing their land and their culture is moving and inspiring.

"Indigenous people believe that the blood of the gods, the subtle magnetic, celestial flow, circulates in the veins of the earth. This concept underlies the extensive occult science of geomancy, the study of leylines. Scientists have found that the Aborigines possess an acute sensitivity to magnetic and vital force flows emanating from the earth, which they refer to as songlines."
Robert Lawlor, American anthropologist and author

Their connection to nature and the environment is also something to aspire to. The Anangu are attuned to the earth in a way others have forgotten. There have long been claims by westerners who spend time with Aboriginal people that they possess telepathic abilities, being able to communicate with family and friends over vast distances, or access the wisdom of the Tjukurpa beings through trance states and meditation. Scientists have also found that those who still live on the land have an acute sensitivity to the magnetic energy of the earth, which explains their incredible ability to find their way over vast desert landscapes without discernible landmarks or maps.

Some believe that people like the Anangu, who've lived at one with the land for thousands of years, may have evolved highly developed instincts akin to the migratory senses of birds, who can navigate over large bodies of water in a way that is hard for us to comprehend. Research into the power of magnetic force on the human sense of direction seems to indicate that those who live in harmony with the land are more closely connected to the leylines that flow through the earth. Being so attuned to this energy and able to sense these magnetic flows increases intuition and activates a sense of spiritual connection.

Uluru sits on a vortex of such energy lines, which many sense as a subtle hum in the ground, a vibration they can feel, a wash of emotion that affects them viscerally. Others experience a change in their breathing or physical sensations in the body as they absorb the energies, which open people up and give them a heightened awareness of the world around them as well as the inner world of their own being.

Today dowsers, those who detect underground water supplies or minerals, attune themselves to this energy with divining rods or pendulums, but when people live so close to the land, observing its cycles, its patterns and its seasons, they are naturally connected to it.

The Anangu instinctively sensed the magnetic fields of the earth, the energy of where they believe the creation beings once walked and the sites where their spirit was absorbed into the ground. During the Tjukurpa these ancestors sang the earth into being, and each landscape feature has an ancient song, a chant and a ceremony attached to it, which are still being performed to keep the land alive.

These paths the ancestral beings made as they travelled the country, which link the sacred sites, are known as iwara, songlines, and they still reverberate with the energy of the creator beings and their passing. Songlines are maps made in song that follow the energy lines of the earth. They record the landscape and are a direction finder and navigational tool – the Anangu can traverse the country by following their path through the song cycles they've learned.

According to Central Australian guide Brett Graham: "The best way to describe songlines is to imagine a travel book. But instead of reading the chapters, you visit the chapter places and hear the stories being told and sung. Each traditional owner in each location has their own chapter – their own part of the songline story."

The songs, dances and rituals for each sacred site have been handed down by the elders to the younger generations for thousands of years, and provide not only a spiritual link to the past, but also a means of travel and social connection in the present. The song cycle of each site is remembered, retold and taught regularly to keep the story – and the physical location where it took place – alive. These ceremonies are believed to increase the life force not only of the land but of the ancestral being associated with the site, while also increasing the people's connection to the planet. It's a beautiful circle – the Anangu protect and renew the earth, and it protects and renews them.

Within the narratives of the songlines the Anangu learned how to find water and food in any area, when and where to hunt, whether a species needed protection, and even the correct way to behave. The Ngintaka Songline, which runs for three hundred kilometres through the Pitjantjatjara lands south of Uluru, records the story of Ngintaka, the Perentie Lizard Man, and his creation of the landscape. It identifies places of food and water as well as teaching the law and ethics that still govern Anangu society – in this case about the uselessness of possessions and the morals of stealing.

The Seven Sisters Songline crosses the whole continent, and teaches of passion, betrayal and the benefits of sisterhood. A significant part of it passes through the Cave Hill area south of Uluru, where the traditional owners maintain the sacred places – including the cave paintings that comprise one of the most significant ancient art sites in the country – with singing and ceremony.

Each community was responsible for the sections of the songlines that ran through their land, and a part of each of their creation stories. Many run for hundreds of kilometres, with some stretching right across the country, so there were often several communities with responsibility for an individual songline and knowledge of its ceremonies. At Uluru there are twenty-eight sites of sacred significance, which figure in different songlines that spread out across the country in various directions. So while the Rock is the home of the Pitjantjatjara and Yankunytjatjara people, it also has significance to many other indigenous groups who live on land that the songlines of Uluru extend through.

The Anangu made pilgrimages, following the songlines of Uluru and singing the relevant songs, performing the dances and conducting the ceremonies at each location to ensure the landscape stayed alive and was imbued with sacred energy. During the dances their bodies were painted with beautiful symbols that represented the stories of creation and the location of special places and events. In this way they became part of the landscape, and the geography of the land was a sacred thing, with the features of the earth a part of their identity.

"Spirit of place! It is for this that we travel, to surprise its subtlety. And where it is a strong and dominant angel, that place, seen once, abides entire in the memory with all its own accidents, its habits, its breath, its name."
Alice Meynell, 19th century British poet and essayist

Visiting Uluru won't suddenly make you conscious of the earth and its energy in such a profound manner, or enable you to find your way across the country with the skill of the Anangu, but it will fill you with a sense of the sacred power of nature, and sweep you up in the magic of the universe. It can also help you find a sense of your own identity, because the Anangu encapsulate the spirit of place that so many people yearn for.

When I was overseas, visiting other sacred places, I was often asked if I'd been to Uluru. I was embarrassed that I hadn't, yet its stark desertscape seemed more foreign to me than the lush jungles of Peru or the green hills of the British Isles that I longed to see. Many of the American women who asked me had never visited the sacred places of their homeland either, despite travelling internationally. In Ireland too I met lots of people who admitted that I'd seen more of their country than they had, and I have friends in London who have never been to Stonehenge, although they've travelled all over the world.

Often we're so keen to travel outside of our home, and outside of ourselves, that we overlook what is right nearby, and right within us. Uluru reminds us that we already have all we need, and inspires people from other places to explore their own land, and their own selves.

For years I was more interested in faraway shores, but eventually I felt a strong yearning to visit this ancient place in the heart of my own country. I wasn't sure what I would feel when I finally got there, or if it would affect me as deeply as other sacred sites have, but it did. I was moved by the whole experience. There were places around the Rock that seemed incredibly familiar. I felt my eyes welling with tears as I stood there, haunted by a memory, a connection, something old and primal, and I felt part of an ancient power and beauty.

Being at Uluru and walking the paths of those who've lived there for thousands of years also made me question my identity, and made me very conscious of the land and of where I'm from. I am Australian, and being overseas made me more fiercely aware of that than ever, but while I was born in this country – as were my parents and grandparents before me – I've never felt wholly of it. There is a group of people who are truly part of this land and its long history, and I was always vaguely aware of being an intruder.

But being at Uluru gave me a sense of connection to my country, and allowed me to feel as though I belong. In its unchanging grandeur and power, the Rock permits all people to feel a part of it. It is a portal to a connection to the whole planet, and a reminder that we are all one people. Uluru provides a sense of belonging to the earth, no matter what your cultural background, and will inspire you to find a connection to your own homeland too.

At Uluru I finally understood the power and spirit of place, and now it is something I can conjure and hold on to wherever I am in the world, because it is a part of me. I know now that I am connected to the earth, to its people, to the universe, and I thank the Rock and its custodians for this gift.

The psychic connection

Quick tips to absorb the power of Uluru

1. Watch the movie *Kanyini* and read the book *Nyuntu Ninti*, both collaborations between Anangu elder Bob Randall and white Australian filmmaker Melanie Hogan. The documentary film explains the philosophy and spirituality of Bob's people, their concept of kanyini – the interconnectedness of humanity and the land – the bitter history of black and white Australia and, perhaps most importantly, the hope that exists for the future. The beautiful book adds further to the spiritual wisdom that underpins it all.

2. Uluru is a silent, majestic force sitting alone on a desert plain. While hundreds of people clamber around its base, it has a sense of solitary strength that is inspiring. Find a quiet place and some time to yourself and meditate on this isolation. Like the Rock, you have a stillness and strength within you that you can access, but you need to consciously take yourself away from the hustle and bustle of life to reconnect to it, access your inner core and find your deepest truths.

3. Take Fire Essence. The White Light Essences range incorporates the qualities of the four elements – water, air, earth and fire – plus higher self, devic and angelic. Made at sacred sites around the world, they're a form of vibrational medicine, altering the vibrations of your body and aura to create physical and emotional healing. Fire Essence was created at Kata Tjuta, overlooking Uluru, and incorporates the fiery nature of the region. It holds the ancient healing qualities of the Red Centre, and encompasses the passion and energy of fire, helping to burn off the physical and spiritual impurities in your life, inspiring you to follow your life path and giving you a feisty sense of purpose.

4. Music has always been important to the people who live around Uluru, a way to connect to the land, their history and their culture. Inspiring indigenous artists include Archie Roach, Kev Carmody, Ruby Hunter, Christine Anu, Tiddas, Jimmy Little and rock bands Yothu Yindi and No Fixed Address. White Australian artists who brought the landscape of Central Australia and the displacement of Aboriginal peoples to prominence include Shane Howard's group Goanna, who wrote the anthem *Solid Rock*, singer/songwriter Neil Murray, and Midnight Oil, whose album *Diesel and Dust* (amongst others), captures the emotion of the Red Centre. The songs on it were inspired by their Outback tour with cross-cultural act The Warumpi Band, who were the first to record a rock song in an Aboriginal language. Singer Paul Kelly has also written songs about indigenous issues, worked with indigenous performers and championed their causes and their talents.

5. Uluru can't be separated from the people who live at its base and hold it as sacred. It is their energy and love that has protected the land, yet they also need our energy to reconnect to their inner wisdom and strength after years of disadvantage. The Indigenous Community Volunteers organisation, www.icv.com.au, brings together volunteers who teach specialised skills in Aboriginal communities, rather than completing a project for them, so that people learn new skills and gain control of their own lives. These projects lead to career opportunities, self-employment and community development for the indigenous participants, as well as new knowledge and wisdom for the volunteer.

The armchair traveller's way to visit

"Take me to the places on the earth that teach you how to dance, the places where you can risk letting the world break your heart. And I will take you to the places where the earth beneath my feet and the stars overhead make my heart whole again and again."
Oriah Mountain Dreamer, Canadian poet and author

Uluru represents a profound connection to the earth and the environment, and even if you live in a place that's far removed from nature, this is something you can create for yourself. The earth hums with vibrational energy, and although it may not be as obvious in the city as it is when you place your hands on the side of the Rock or walk through a rainforest, you can learn to hear and feel it.

It's always there, a subtle breath that vibrates beneath the sound of traffic and sirens and people and phones. And you can become aware of it at any time, in the simplest ways – by losing yourself in the beauty of a flower, the stillness in the shade of a tree, the feel of the wind on your face or the peace of the ocean waves.

Find a site out in nature where you can connect with the spirit of place. It might be a large rock, a small stream, a sand dune, an old tree or simply a tiny park in the midst of a sprawling city. Spend time there tuning in to nature's vibrations. Breathe in the clearer air, feel the sun on your skin and listen to the sound of the birds, the water or the wind. Many people today have lost their connection to the earth, but it can be regained through focus and intent.

Communing with nature provides a sense of peace and calm. It lowers stress, eases depression and puts you back in touch with yourself. Diving into the ocean, walking around the harbour, pottering in your garden – even if it's just nurturing a pot plant on your balcony – sitting in the sunshine or playing a CD of forest sounds can transport you to another state of being and transform your mood. Even just looking at pictures of nature or imagining yourself there has been proven to lower stress levels and induce a feeling of tranquillity.

The natural world lifts the spirits, calms the mind, soothes the soul and gives perspective on anything that is worrying you. Drama fades, and your attitude and outlook become more balanced. Even at my saddest, seeing a butterfly dance, a thunderstorm rage or a flower bloom takes me outside of myself and makes me smile. Life can be draining and discouraging, it can break you down and tear you apart, but outside in the wildness and beauty of nature I feel the tiny pieces of me take shape again. I feel lighter, whole again. Complete.

You can also experience the humbling grandeur of the world by staring up at the night sky. The stars may not be as bright elsewhere as they are above Uluru, but they are there, and their tiny twinkling lights have a magical quality. Learning about the stars and planets in your sky and being able to identify the constellations, be it the Southern Cross above Australia or the North Star Polaris in the northern hemisphere, connects you to your country. Some cities have amazing observatories where you can look through powerful telescopes and hear stories and lessons about the night skies, but even if you're not near one you can gaze up at the heavens and feel the energy of these sparkling jewels strewn across the velvet blackness.

The moon as it sails across the sky is also an awe-inspiring sight, whispering of magic and peace and a timeless rhythm, and affecting emotions. The phases of the moon were the basis of the first calendars, and becoming conscious of the waxing and waning of this silver orb will make you more aware of time, in a way unrelated to achievement and busyness and more about the natural turning of the earth.

Once people lived in tune with these cycles – they rose with the sun and slept when it set, ate the vegetables that grew in their gardens and local produce when it was in season, and conserved their energy in the winter months when the earth too was sluggish. Today western society has lost its instinctive connection to nature partly because people no longer need to know when plants flower or fruit, or whether animals are calving or hibernating or migrating. Today "hunting" is done at the supermarket, where out-of-season food is flown in from faraway climes, frozen, or forced to grow with chemical assistance.

Many organic farmers and environmentalists suggest that we should only eat the produce available in our region, not only because of the physical health benefits of consuming fresh seasonal food, but also because it results in a renewed connection to and awareness of the land. Additionally it lowers the price and the emissions of transporting food around the globe, reducing greenhouse gas production and cost.

Feeling part of nature also leads to a greater sense of environmental consciousness, because you stop seeing yourself as separate from the earth and its creatures and instead become part of a greater whole. You realise we are all connected, dependent on each other, and that we have a responsibility to do something to halt the destruction of the planet and its plants and animals.

"Preserving what we love has never been a greater challenge. Listening to native people and learning from them has never been more crucial. They have preserved the ancient wisdom that we are part of nature, and that what happens to nature happens to us. Indigenous communities nurture the values that can sustain us in the future and help keep the earth alive."
Christopher McLeod, filmmaker and environmentalist

You can also connect with the energy of Uluru by emulating the inspiring conservation efforts of the Anangu of Central Australia. For tens of thousands of years they lived in harmony with the seasons, the climate, the environment and the flora and fauna, protecting species and caring for the land. In the two hundred years since white settlement, twenty-two Australian mammals have become extinct – the worst record in the world. In addition, more than a thousand native plants and animals are now endangered, including the mala wallaby that is so central to the traditions of Uluru, and three thousand fragile ecosystems also face extinction. The figures are similar all over the planet.

You can get involved in conservation and environmental activism in many ways, from simple things such as making a small donation to a cause or lobbying politicians to create change, to more committed and complex methods such as taking part in the physical labour of healing the land or starting your own group to work on an area close to your heart. There are many organisations that conserve the world's precious natural resources, and myriad ways you can make a difference.

Conservation Volunteers Australia, www.conservationvolunteers. com.au, organises practical projects all over the country, with similar groups operating overseas. Even if you don't have much time to spare, there's a range of wildly different activities you can take part in at locations throughout Australia, from Sydney Harbour to the Red Centre and countless beaches, national parks and small towns across the continent. Some projects take just a few hours, while others involve a week or two at the site and may include camping or staying nearby.

There are international equivalents for those who want to make a difference in other countries, from Ireland and the US to the Galapagos Islands and Africa. Do an online search for "conservation volunteers" to find your local centre, or visit www.i-to-i.com for exotic inspiration.

Activities vary from protecting endangered animals such as sea turtles and working alongside scientists and rangers to monitor sites for pests that are decimating the local wildlife, to planting trees and native flora and stabilising sand dunes, collecting seeds and recording growth in national parks, taking part in wildlife surveys to check on threatened species and constructing pathways and fencing.

Australian Wildlife Conservancy, www.australianwildlife.org.au, does its bit to save threatened wildlife by buying large tracts of land to establish conservation reserves. Through public donations and fundraising the group now owns twenty-one sanctuaries covering more than six million acres, which protect more than half of the nation's bird and mammal species, and three hundred ecosystems.

Australia is home to more biodiversity than any other developed nation on earth – but much of it is under threat, with the country facing an extinction crisis. Many other regions, from Hawaii to the Amazon, have similar issues and similar groups, which raise money to buy land to ensure the preservation of the plants and animals that live there.

The Australian Conservation Foundation, www.acfonline.org.au, and sister organisations around the globe, promotes a wide range of environmental issues, including protecting areas, land management, climate change, nuclear threats, forests, oceans, environmental law reform, water preservation and ecologically sustainable development. It focuses on advocacy, policy research and community education rather than hands-on projects, protecting, restoring and sustaining the environment by educating people to make individual changes.

You can read up on all manner of topics, support the foundation's work financially or use the website to educate yourself and make a difference in the world. It has an EarthKids section that encourages children to become involved in saving the planet, with information, practical solutions and fun activities, and you can sign up for the Green Home Challenge and learn how to tread more lightly on the earth.

Wildlife Warriors, www.wildlifewarriors.org, is an international group that was started by passionate Aussie environmentalist and *Crocodile Hunter* TV star Steve Irwin and his American wife Terri, which works around the world to protect injured and endangered wildlife, enhance the natural environment, undertake research and raise awareness of environmental and conservation issues. It also co-operates with other like-minded groups to bring about change.

Since Steve's death in 2006 Terri and their young daughter Bindi have continued the organisation's important conservation work, boosted by public donations given in Steve's honour. The family's Australia Zoo on Queensland's Sunshine Coast covers administration costs, so money raised is used wholly to fund conservation projects around the world, such as buying land to protect habitats, and running the Australian Wildlife Hospital, which treats sick, injured and orphaned native creatures then releases them back into the wild.

"The starting point is to recognise that the problem starts with us non-Aboriginal Australians. It begins with the act of recognition, that it was we who did the dispossessing. We took the traditional lands and smashed the traditional way of life. We brought the disasters. We committed the murders. We took the children from their mothers. We practised discrimination and exclusion. But ever so gradually we're learning to see Australia through Aboriginal eyes, beginning to recognise the wisdom contained in their epic story. We are beginning to see how much we owe the indigenous Australians and how much we have lost by living so apart."
Paul Keating, Australia's then-prime minister, 1992's Redfern speech

Another way to connect to the spirit of Uluru is to learn the history of your own region. Many nations have been built on invasion and the dispossession of the indigenous people – sadly this is the history of humanity from when time began – and often a country's true past isn't taught in schools because history is written by the conquerors, couched in their language and cultural perceptions.

As a child I learned about the brave early settlers and their amazing feats in colonising the land. It was only later, listening to artists like Midnight Oil and Paul Kelly as a teenager, that I discovered the stories of dispossession and human rights abuses, and realised the true heroes were indigenous Australians like Yami Lester, a Yankunytjatjara activist who fought for recognition of the effects of the Maralinga atomic tests that blinded him, Vincent Lingiari, a Gurindji man who fought for equal pay for equal work, and Truganini, a Palawah woman who became a symbol of the horrifying massacre of Tasmanian Aboriginals. And it was through musician Archie Roach's touching autobiographical song *Took the Children Away* that I realised the deeply shameful reality of the Stolen Generations.

We can't change what happened, but we can change how we live now. We can learn the truth, acknowledge the wrongs done and the incredible hurts inflicted on indigenous people the world over, and make a start on the journey of reconciliation, which requires a change in the psyche of the nation as much as a governmental apology.

If you have kids, you could ask at their school for a more balanced view to be presented, or investigate your country's history with them yourself. There are many fascinating books and documentaries, educational resources and organisations that provide information.

In Australia there is also an increasing number of Aboriginal Cultural Centres across the country, and many diverse tours and retreats led by indigenous people keen to share their knowledge. In Sydney there's an amazing Aboriginal Cultural Cruise that takes people on a journey around the harbour to learn the stories of the original inhabitants who lived in the area before white settlement.

It includes a visit to an island, a welcome ceremony, singing, dancing and a sharing of native culture. Traditional fishing and food gathering techniques are described, and historical figures are brought to life, from Bennelong, an Aboriginal warrior imprisoned by the British, who once lived where the famous Opera House now stands, to governor's wife Elizabeth Macquarie, who fought her husband over indigenous land rights and nursed Aboriginal people suffering from introduced diseases. It's run by the Tribal Warrior Association (www.tribalwarrior.org), which also provides training and employment to indigenous youth in an attempt to share and revitalise Aboriginal culture.

In other parts of the world you can connect with this ancient earth energy through tracing your own country's chequered history, and finding the significant places and wisdom teachers of the indigenous people who lived there long ago.

"The art means to carry on our stories, so non-indigenous people can know about us in the future, how we fought to keep our culture strong for the sake of our children's future. The art is about who you belong to, about what country you belong to, it's about the only way you can know and others will know too."
Valerie Napaljarri Martin, artist and former chairperson of Desart

You can also absorb the energy of Uluru through the incredible artwork of the region. Painting and other art forms have long been a way for Aboriginal people to pass on their knowledge of the Tjukurpa and educate their children, and is an important way to express their connection to the earth, their cultural identity and their history.

Traditionally art was created for cultural and ceremonial purposes, and much of it was only able to be made, and viewed, by those who'd been initiated to a certain level. Now though, while this kind of art is still made and remains important, other works are being created for public viewing, allowing people an insight into their beliefs. Art, as well as traditional music and the dances now being performed for outsiders, is a bridge that is strengthening understanding around the world.

The first Aboriginal artist to receive international acclaim was Albert Namatjira, a Western Arrernte man from the Hermannsburg community between Uluru and Alice Springs. His beautiful watercolour paintings of the Outback inspired the Hermannsburg art movement, which included many talented artists. Other Central Australian painters embraced a more traditional style, including the brightly coloured dot paintings that are so widely known.

Around Uluru and in the Western Desert region are many incredible artists creating unique works in a variety of mediums, from acrylic on canvas to leaf and bark painting, wood carving, sculpture, tools and weaponry, headdresses, engraved or painted musical instruments and ceremonial clothing. At Mutitjulu Community, in the shadow of Uluru, the artists are recognised for their traditional wood carvings and other crafts, as well as vivid dot paintings that often incorporate Kuniya and the other ancestral beings of the area.

It's no wonder there are so many artists emerging from Central Australia, because the desertscape is so stunningly beautiful, starkly contrasted and unexpectedly full of colour, vibrancy and life. There is a special quality to the light too, and a tangible spiritual presence in the air that inspires and motivates everyone who visits.

Symbols of the Tjukurpa are hidden within the artwork, further preserving and passing on Anangu culture. Paintings are believed to hold the spirit of the ancestral being, so they are much more than something pretty to put on the wall – they are a way to recreate the events of the Tjukurpa, communicate with the spirit world and ensure a continuing relationship with the ancestors. To the Anangu, art is a form of worship and expression and an important cultural process.

Geographical features and ancestral events are woven into the patterns. A wavy line can represent lightning, running water, a serpent or a rope, while a series of circles may mean a cave, a rock hole, a campfire or a mountain. Layers of meaning are present in each piece, so that one viewer might simply see a waterhole, while an initiated person will see an entire ancestral story unfolding.

In recent years Aboriginal art has become internationally sought after, with artists commanding much respect and earning high prices for their beautiful works, and critic Robert Hughes describing it as the last great art movement of the 20th century. There are an increasing number of galleries around the world that carry authentic pieces, and also many online galleries that make indigenous art and craft available to purchase no matter where you live.

Maruku Arts brings together the work of hundreds of artists from communities in the Western Desert region. As well as paintings they sell traditionally crafted tools, carved wooden sculptures, boomerangs, woven grass baskets and jewellery. Anangu owned, it supports indigenous artists by co-ordinating the marketing, promotion and sale of their work, providing advice and working with them to further the profile and understanding of indigenous art. It has a retail outlet at the Cultural Centre at the base of the Rock, where artists and craftspeople can be watched as they work, a warehouse within Mutitjulu Community and an online gallery (www.maruku.com.au) so anyone, anywhere, can own a little piece of the spirit of Uluru.

Desart, the Association of Central Australian Aboriginal Art and Craft Centres, is based in Alice Springs and represents several Aboriginal-owned art centres and galleries across the country. It supports indigenous artists from the area, protecting them from exploitation, obtaining fair prices for their work, advocating on their behalf and providing training and employment opportunities. Their website (www.desart.com.au) has information about indigenous art as well as contact details for major indigenous art galleries and organisations, which you can visit or buy from online.

Aboriginal Art is another company that links Aboriginal-owned and operated art centres in Central and Northern Australia. Their website (www.aboriginalart.org) provides maps of the region and lists of the many diverse art centres, with information on the artists and their unique styles, from bark painting and fibre craft to glass work, memorial poles, screen prints and didgeridoos from Arnhem Land.

Birrung Gallery is an initiative of World Vision, and represents more than three hundred indigenous artists from twenty-five remote communities, providing them with a forum to sell their work around the world. It holds exhibitions at its Sydney gallery as well as selling pieces online (www.worldvision.com.au/birrung), and also raises money to fund indigenous community developments, provides scholarships and training, supports preventative health programs in rural and remote Australia and advocates for the artists.

Learning about indigenous art, supporting the artists and appreciating the beauty of their work is a nice way to connect with the spirit of Uluru and absorb the energy of this amazing country. You can also try painting your own pictures, and your own history, drawing on the colours and symbols of the place where you live, or using the colours of the Red Centre to fire up your creativity and passion.

"Call it a clan, call it a network, call it a tribe, call it a family. Whatever you call it, whoever you are, you need one."
Jane Howard, American author and journalist

On a personal level, you can experience some of the power of Uluru by learning the lessons of the people who live there, so close to the land, so in tune with the needs of the earth, and so in touch with the importance of family and spirituality. A beautiful teaching of Uluru and its people is to respect the elders in your life. Hug your grandmother.

Listen to your grandfather. Spend time with your family, and get to know your history and your relatives. Give thanks to them, and to anyone else who has touched your life and helped you to grow.

The concept of elders is universal in earth-based and eastern cultures, although it seems to have been lost in modern society. They are those who provide wisdom, unconditional love and acceptance, mentors who inspire and encourage people to fulfil their dreams, who pass on their own lessons and share the insight they've accrued throughout their lives. It might be a tribal elder, a grandparent or a school teacher, a village wise woman or a businessman long retired.

They are respected and revered for their knowledge and wisdom, but today there is less patience with the elderly and less respect for their hard-won lessons. There also seems to be a lot less time available, and people are far more insular, less inclined to know their neighbours or be part of community groups, so this wisdom is being lost.

The indigenous people of Uluru – and all of Australia – have a deep respect for their elders and an appreciation for awareness gained through life experience and study. They share deep kinship ties and a level of caring for each other that goes far beyond the love and loyalty westerners imagine. Their caring nature and sharing of everything they have shows another level of co-existence and being. They never put work ahead of their family, which can cause problems for them in white society, but which is something those struggling to balance the work-life dilemma could open up to.

Listening to the elders at Uluru share their wisdom, and learning of how the grandparents pass on the teachings of life and love to their grandchildren, I was overwhelmed with sadness that my grandparents have all passed on. I felt a deep sense of loss, which came partly from regret at the knowledge that I no longer have access to, and partly from knowing my sense of connection to the past is gone.

Yet my grandparents remain part of me. Their morals and beliefs helped shape me, and while my outlook is quite different to theirs, their blood runs in my veins and their life whispers within me. Their choices, through their upbringing of my parents, helped shape what I believe, where I live and how I think.

Their memory also connects me to the web of life, to the continual cycles of life, death and rebirth. As they became more frail, their great-granddaughters, my sister's children, became stronger. And so the cycle of life goes on. On some level all we need to know can be learned from the patterns of nature – the rising and setting of the sun, the turning of the seasons, the cycles of man. My nieces won't know their great-grandparents, yet their blood runs in their veins too. It's a sad thought, yet there is also happiness in the knowledge that in this way we continue, we live on. It is the way of the earth, and the people of it.

Postcard from Uluru

Jude Currivan is a British scientist, healer, author and educator. She has a PhD in archaeology and a masters in physics, specialising in cosmology and quantum physics, and a few years ago quit the corporate world to help people understand the sacredness of the earth and reach their own inner potential.

Jude has worked with the elders of many spiritual traditions, and is the author of *The 8th Chakra*, *The 13th Step* and co-author of *CosMos*. She also leads spiritual journeys, appears on TV and radio, gives talks and teaches workshops around the world. She has spent time at Uluru and the Red Centre of Australia, and was transformed by the beauty of the landscape, the energy of the earth and the wisdom of the people who have lived there for thousands of years. Visit www.judecurrivan.com.

Central Australia, the country's Red Heart, resonates with the primordial heartbeat of Mother Earth. Aboriginal people have walked this land for tens of thousands of years, their continuing presence gifting us the most ancient living lineage in the world. In their continuous co-creation of the Tjukurpa, land, animals, Dreamtime beings and living people co-create an indivisible matrix of consciousness.

I was privileged to visit the Red Heart and the great monolith of Uluru with a small group in 2002. We all fell in love with its vibrant beauty, the amazing play of light and shadow throughout the day and the glory of the clear sky awash with stars at night.

For the first few days we stayed on the land with an Aboriginal family who generously shared their wisdom with us. Already enamoured with the landscape and the contours of the rocks, and amazed by how much water and life there is despite its apparent aridity, we learned from them how to see the land with new eyes, hear it with new ears and feel it with new hearts. Their mythic reality allowed us to see beyond the surface appearance to glimpse the spiritual depths of the Tjukurpa, which gives fundamental meaning and purpose to their lives and harmonises them within their landscape and the wider cosmos.

With these insights, our journey on to Uluru gained a deeper resonance. The entire land is sacred, but as we visited the sites around the Rock deemed especially significant we were able to experience them more profoundly and sense their energies more powerfully. For we too, with those brief but joyous days with our Aboriginal friends, were now a conscious part of the Tjukurpa!

At Uluru we met members of the Anangu people and heard some of the specific Tjukurpa stories that relate to it – although many of these stories can't be shared. For a crucial part of this ancient knowledge is that it's only passed on as people become ready to take on the responsibility that accompanies such initiation. Many of the sites around Uluru are thus only accessible to initiates, and unauthorised entry is perceived as desecrating their sanctity.

One part of Uluru where this is the case is its summit. While there is a rope that marks the route, visitors are discouraged from attempting the arduous climb. Typical of the many indigenous peoples I've been privileged to meet, the Anangu generally don't ban something. Instead they state and explain their view, allowing the other person to make their choice and take responsibility for its consequences.

However no Aboriginal person – from the smallest and most inquisitive child, as we'd learned when staying with our new friends – would ever consider going against such a tribal taboo, recognising that to do so would affect the harmony of the Tjukurpa relationship between the entire tribe and the land.

The aim of our visit was to experience not only Uluru but also a second vast landform, Kata Tjuta. Sensitised now to the earth energies of the area, I felt powerfully the male essence of Uluru and the gentler yet equally powerful female essence of Kata Tjuta. On then learning that Uluru is suffused with initiatory sites for Anangu women and Kata Tjuta with such sites for Anangu men, I was deeply touched that this wisdom, from time immemorial, has enabled tribal women to become more attuned to male energies and vice versa.

A fundamental aspect of our group's growing awareness was recognition of the universal expression of not only male, outgoing or yang energies and female, incoming or yin energies, both within us and permeating the earth, but a third type of energy. In many spiritual traditions this third, neutral, child energy forms an integral co-creative element in a cosmic trinity. As we connected more deeply with the landscape, we perceived that the primacy of the male energies at Uluru strengthened and complemented the archetypal feminine energies of Kata Tjuta. Yet we sensed something was incomplete.

On our last day my husband Tony called me over and showed me a postcard. Taken from the air, it showed Kata Tjuta huge in the foreground, Uluru further away and, hardly visible on the horizon and perfectly aligned with both of them, a third monolith.

Called Atila by the Anangu, this was our third geomantic point, and the embodiment of the child energy in the landscape. These three vast landforms rising hundreds of metres above the surrounding desert together embody the archetypal balance, harmony and health of the Red Heart of Australia.

Information and inspiration

Here are a few of the books, websites, organisations, people and things that may help you find the magic on your own adventure.

Machu Picchu and the Amazon, Peru

There are many books on shamanism and its different aspects, and many people offering spiritual courses as well as tours of the sacred sites of Peru. Find out as much as you can about any teachers you plan to work with, no matter what the tradition, ask lots of questions and trust your intuition.

Shirley MacLaine's books *Out On a Limb* and *It's All In the Playing* include her adventures in Peru, from spiritual encounters and alien tales to past life experiences, being stranded without transport and getting sick. All her books are inspiring and thought-provoking, combining travel and the insights it triggered with her own exploration and investigation. She was the first to openly talk about her spiritual searching – it's hard to imagine now, with New Age shelves in every bookstore, that in the 70s and 80s it was a huge risk to talk about leylines and trance channelling, and that she was advised not to publish her books for fear of public ridicule. She opened the way, and people's minds, with her fearless questing, and continues to do so today.

To sponsor a child in Peru, or another developing nation, there are many agencies to choose from – I've been doing it through Plan International for more than twenty-five years. Plan helps children in more than sixty countries, working with mostly local staff to best identify need and implement change. It's amazing to see the difference that can be made in a child's life, and to be a tiny part of it. In Australia: www.plan.org.au, in the United States: www.planusa.org, for other countries: www.plan-international.org.

UNICEF, the United Nations Children's Fund, also does incredible work for kids in Peru (and all over the world), providing long-term humanitarian and developmental assistance to children and mothers. It works to alleviate poverty, increase child health and education and reduce the maternal mortality rate, operating on the basis of need without discrimination, and having no political, racial or religious affiliations: www.unicef.org.

A billion people worldwide suffer from hunger and malnutrition – to add to the millions of cups of food already distributed: thehungersite.com. To help protect the precious Amazon jungle: therainforestsite.com. To boost funding for child health preventatives and treatments: thechildhealthsite.com.

You can also help people in Peru (and elsewhere) through Kiva, which makes loans to people in developing nations so they can start their own business – a food stall, an internet cafe, a taxi, sewing or farming business – and become self sufficient, breaking the cycle of aid dependence and empowering them to take control of their own lives. I've made nine so far: kiva.org.

Glastonbury, England

One of the most enchanting places in Glastonbury is the Chalice Well Gardens. You can visit the sanctuary for a few hours or all day, stay in the cottage in the grounds with 24-hour access to the gardens, and become a Companion and support their work. Their site features information, workshop details, links, an events list and beautiful photos: www.chalicewell.org.uk.

The first time I was in Glastonbury there was a cafe in the building over the White Spring, opposite Chalice Well Gardens, with the sacred water running across the floor beneath your feet. It closed down, but recently a group began work to conserve the spring and its surrounds: www.whitespring.org.uk.

For articles, information, photos, links, inspiration and a uniquely local perspective on the town, visit the Isle of Avalon: www.isleofavalon.co.uk.

Glastonbury Tourist Information Centre: www.glastonburytic.co.uk.

For a huge range of accommodation options, from B&Bs and self-catering cottages to the local hostel: www.glastonbury.co.uk/accommodation.

Visit the Glastonbury Oracle to find out what's on in the town right now, and several months in advance: www.glastonburyoracle.co.uk.

Journey to the Glastonbury Goddess Temple: www.goddesstemple.co.uk.

For tours of the sacred places of the town, and brilliant local books that you can order from anywhere in the world: www.gothicimagetours.co.uk.

Glastonbury Conservation Society is involved in projects such as tree planting and improving pathways to prevent erosion of the Tor, and volunteers are always welcome. Find out more: web.ukonline.co.uk/jim.nagel/ap/consoc.

Great books: *The Mists of Avalon* by Marion Zimmer Bradley is about the priestesses of Avalon and the deep connection to nature that continues to be experienced by those who visit the place today. *In the Nature of Avalon* by modern priestess and teacher Kathy Jones (www.kathyjones.co.uk) outlines pilgrimage paths around the town that weave between its beautiful sacred places. *Glastonbury: Maker of Myths* by Frances Howard-Gordon, *The Isle of Avalon* by Nicholas Mann, *King Arthur's Avalon* by Geoffrey Ashe and *The Avalonians* by Patrick Benham will also deepen your insight into the area.

Great art: I have a print of John Shannon's beautiful Lady Avalon on my wall, and it enchants me with the magic of the priestesses each time I gaze at it: www.jeshannon.com. I also have some of Jessica Galbreth's goddess paintings in my office, which lift my heart, help unlock the wisdom within and inspire me to connect to my own self and write my truths: www.enchanted-art.com.

Ancient Egypt's pyramids and temples, Africa

More has been written about Egypt and its history, rituals and deities than any other country, and there are also heaps of films and documentaries so you can work out which of its sacred places call to you. A good starting point is www.touregypt.net, which has travel tips, maps, news stories, history, photos, tour information, weather, consulates and much more.

As in Peru, there are many spiritual tours of Egypt, led by shamans, healers and authors. Lynn Andrews (www.lynnandrews.com), Nancy Joy Hefron (www.heartlights.net) and Elisabeth Jensen (www.isismysteryschool.com) are a few who lead tours that incorporate healing, ritual and ceremony.

The Fellowship of Isis, led by Olivia Robertson, was founded at Clonegal Castle in Ireland in 1976, with the priest/esshood derived from a hereditary Egyptian line. There's a beautiful temple to Isis set up in the castle, which is open to the public, and the group provides information, articles, books, international centres, spiritual practices and events, as well as a College of Isis that confers degrees and initiations: www.fellowshipofisis.com.

For a modern twist on an ancient land, the famous Sound and Light shows play at the Pyramids of Giza and the temples of Karnak, Philae and Abu Simbel, which are all World Heritage sites. Lighting, laser and projection technologies bring the pharaohs and deities to life to tell their stories and help you visualise the mysteries of old: www.soundandlight.com.eg.

The islands of Hawaii

Great books: The most beautiful book I read about Hawaii was *Voices of Wisdom: Hawaiian Elders Speak*. Compiled by journalist MJ Harden, it includes interviews with twenty-four Hawaiian elders, explaining their culture, history and beliefs in their own words, on topics such as spirituality, healing, nature, craft, preservation, entertainment, genealogy and activism. Rima Morrell's *The Sacred Power of Huna* is also a moving book, which explains the spirituality and shamanism of Hawaii from a modern slant. And Dan Millman's *Sacred Journey of the Peaceful Warrior* blends fact and fiction into an adventure through the jungles of Hawaii with Mama Chia, a mysterious kahuna who teaches him the principles of ancient huna wisdom.

The Big Island's tourism, activity and attractions website has volcano updates, adventure activities, music, eco tourism, travel stories, festivals, accommodation, weather, museums and more: www.bigisland.org.

For all the details on Hawaii Volcanoes National Park, from volcano and weather updates to plant and animal information: www.nps.gov/havo.

The Hawaiian Volcano Observatory, on the edge of Kilauea Caldera, furthers scientific study, researches all the volcanoes of Hawaii and works with emergency response officials to protect visitors to the park. For updates on the lava flow, photos of new land being created, a weekly newsletter and scientific information: volcano.wr.usgs.gov/kilaueastatus.php.

Check out the Onizuka Center for International Astronomy Visitor Information Station: www.ifa.hawaii.edu/info/vis/. Mauna Kea Summit Adventures takes people to the top of massive Mauna Kea on eight-hour adventures that teach about the geography, geology, history and culture of the legendary volcanic mountain, as well as offering amazing sunset views then a night of stargazing: www.maunakea.com.

To experience the little-visited Forbidden Isle of Niihau, you can go on a limited half-day tour as guests of the island's owners: www.niihau.us.

Nature Conservancy Hawaii preserves the plants and animals of the islands. They've bought two hundred thousand acres of land to provide vital habitat for threatened native species, and organise field trips through the areas they protect: www.nature.org/wherewework/northamerica/states/hawaii.

To swim with dolphins: www.sunlightonwater.com, www.joanocean.com, dolphinjourneys.com, dolphinessence.com; whale watching: ilovewhales.com.

Stonehenge, England

English Heritage protects and promotes England's spectacular historic environment, from Stonehenge and Avebury to ancient monuments, abbeys and castles, and even the house where Jimi Hendrix lived in the 1960s. The website has lots of information on Stonehenge – and you can also organise private inner circle access: www.english-heritage.org.uk.

The National Trust is a charity that preserves and protects the countryside, coastline and buildings of Britain, in particular caring for the mysterious ceremonial landscape of ancient burial mounds, processional walkways and enclosures that surround Stonehenge: www.nationaltrust.org.uk.

Great books: *Stonehenge Complete* by archaeologist Christopher Chippindale is a fascinating scientifically based book that also includes the more magical theories. *Stonehenge in its Landscape: Twentieth Century Excavations* is a drier archaeological report commissioned by English Heritage. *Ancestors of Avalon* by Marion Zimmer Bradley and Diana L Paxon presents a fictional imagining of the way Stonehenge was constructed. And *The Sun and the Serpent* by the wonderful Hamish Miller (www.hamishmiller.co.uk), while not about Stonehenge, discusses leylines and the energy of the earth.

For special inner circle access tours: www.salisburyguidedtours.com and www.stonehengetours.com, plus for weekend archaeological excursions: www.andantetravels.co.uk, and for longer tours: www.sacredbritain.com.

For information and displays of historical artefacts related to the monument, Devizes Wiltshire Heritage Museum: www.wiltshireheritage.org.uk and Salisbury and South Wiltshire Museum: www.salisburymuseum.org.uk.

To find out how you can help protect the circle: www.heritageaction.org and www.sacredsites.org.uk. To buy a piece of the same bluestone as Stonehenge or bluestone jewellery: www.loststones.co.uk, www.rhiannon.co.uk, www.celtworld.co.uk and www.stonehengestones.com.

The Order of Bards, Ovates and Druids: www.druidry.org, which has links to international member groups. The Druid Network: www.druidnetwork.org. In Australia, Pagan Awareness Network: www.paganawareness.net.au.

The Camino, northern Spain

There are fantastic online resources including blogs, guidebooks with suggested itineraries, and many countries have their own pilgrim association to provide guidance. Good sites include: www.xacobeo.es, www.jacobeo.net, www.caminodesantiago.me.uk and www.caminosantiagocompostela.com.

The official site of the destination city, www.santiagodecompostela.org, has lots of information, as does the cathedral's site: www.catedraldesantiago.es.

The Confraternity of Saint James, www.csj.org.uk, has detailed information about the route, as well as providing credencials and having a great online store for Camino books and guides. Their laminated A5 booklets are brilliant, focusing on essential details such as refuges, bed numbers, the distances to the next shelter, food info and prices of necessities along specific routes. Their Australian page, www.csj.org.uk/australia.htm, has local contacts.

In USA: American Pilgrims on the Camino, www.americanpilgrims.com. In Canada: The Little Company of Pilgrims, www.santiago.ca. In Ireland: Irish Society of the Friends of Saint James, www.stjamesirl.com.

To get a credencial, write to or visit Accueil Saint Jacques, 39 rue de la Citadelle, 64220 Saint Jean Pied de Port, or the Oficina del Peregrino, Rua do Vilar 1, Santiago de Compostela, or an abbey or refuge along the way.

Great books: Lonely Planet's *Walking In Spain* has a chapter on the Camino, with basic information and a thirty-day schedule with directions, refuges and where to eat. *The Camino* by Shirley MacLaine and *The Pilgrimage* by Paulo Coelho have few practical details but are inspiring and entertaining.

Uluru, the Red Centre of Australia

To stay close to Uluru, you're limited to Yulara, the Ayers Rock Resort, which has five hotels and a campground plus shops and amenities. They can also book any of sixty-five tours and activities: www.ayersrockresort.com.au.

Anangu Tours is an Aboriginal-owned company providing tours for visitors who want to learn about this sacred place from the local perspective. Discover the meaning and history of Uluru as passed down from the ancestors. Anangu guides lead all tours, speaking in their own language with a skilled interpreter translating into English: www.ananguwaai.com.au.

Discovery Ecotours also offers informative and fascinating tours, including the Uluru Walk around the base of the Rock, which explain the creation stories and the geological development of the area: www.ecotours.com.au.

Pitjantjatjara tours and Bush College: www.deserttracks.com.au.

The Uluru-Kata Tjuta National Park site includes activities, opening hours, maps, accommodation information, park history, geological insight, permits for photo use and much more: www.environment.gov.au/parks/uluru.

Art: www.desart.com.au, www.maruku.com.au, www.walkatjara.com.au, www.aboriginalart.org, www.worldvision.com.au/birrung.

Great books: A beautiful story is *Songman* by Bob Randall, an Anangu elder and traditional owner of Uluru. He shares his life, the history of the Rock and the spiritual teachings and sense of connection indigenous people have with the land. He's also the subject of the film *Kanyini*, made with Melanie Hogan, and the two collaborated on a book, *Nyuntu Ninti*, which encompasses natural wisdom, spirituality and beautiful photos. Visit: www.kanyini.com.

Close the Gap is Australia's largest campaign to improve indigenous health across the country: www.closethegap.org.au and www.oxfam.org.au/campaigns/indigenous-health. You can also add your name to the Sea of Hands and join others in calling for reconciliation: www.antar.org.au.

White Light Essences: www.ausflowers.com.au.

The guidebook *Australia Walkabout* lists hundreds of indigenous tourism adventures across Australia, from cultural centres, cruises, walks, fishing trips, 4WD desert tours, hunting safaris and mountain treks to art galleries and performances: www.contactguides.com. Aboriginal Tourism Australia also lists many great experiences: www.aboriginaltourism.com.au.

International information

UNESCO, the United Nations Educational, Scientific and Cultural Organisation, created the World Heritage Convention in response to people causing damage to natural areas, in an effort to conserve and protect the world's cultural heritage for future generations. Its World Heritage Listing aims to preserve threatened sites and endangered species. The website has information on all the listed places around the globe, with descriptions, photos and the reasons for their inclusion on the list: whc.unesco.org.

Air travel does impact on the environment, although recent studies claim it contributes less than two per cent of global greenhouse emissions compared to fourteen per cent from land transport such as cars. Most airlines now offer carbon emission offsets – you pay a small tax (a return flight from Sydney to London via Singapore emits 3.858 tonnes of carbon per passenger, with an offset of $46.30), which goes towards greenhouse gas abatement projects such as tree planting, energy efficiency measures and renewable energy: qantas.com/flycarbonneutral, www.virginblue.com.au/carbonoffset/, www.britishairways.com. Or you can plant trees yourself, donate to a group buying land to protect our rainforests (such as www.worldlandtrust.org, supported by David Attenborough) or choose your own method of offsetting.

To boost awareness of the world's sacred places and preserve them for the future, a campaign was launched to find the New Seven Wonders of the World. Voted by a hundred million people worldwide, they are: Machu Picchu in Peru, the Great Wall of China, Petra in Jordan, Mexico's Chichen Itza pyramid, Brazil's Christ the Redeemer statue, the Colosseum in Rome and India's Taj Mahal. (The Seven Wonders of the Ancient World were the Great Pyramid of Giza, the Hanging Gardens of Babylon, the Statue of Zeus at Olympia, the Temple of Artemis at Ephesus, the Colossus of Rhodes, the Mausoleum of Maussollos at Halicarnassus and the Lighthouse of Alexandria.)

Voting is now underway to determine the best natural site in the New Seven Wonders of Nature list, which runs until 11/11/11. Finalists include Australia's Uluru and Great Barrier Reef, America's Grand Canyon, Ireland's Cliffs of Moher, Germany's Black Forest, South America's Amazon rainforest and Iguassu Falls, the Dead Sea between Jordan and Israel, Mount Vesuvius in Italy and the Galapagos Islands: www.new7wonders.com.

About the Author

Serene Conneeley is an Australian author with a fascination for history, travel, ritual and the myth and magic of ancient places and cultures. She has written for magazines about news, travel, health, spirituality, social and environmental issues and entertainment, and has contributed to international books on witchcraft, psychic development and personal transformation, as well as the best-selling history compilation *Dateline*.

She loves yoga, hiking, reading, rainbows, drinking tea with her friends and celebrating the energy of the moon and the magic of the earth. Her heart blossomed as she climbed mountains, sat in stone circles, walked a pilgrimage, performed rituals with shamans in South America and priestesses in Avalon, wandered through ancient cathedrals and stood in the shadow of the pyramids, and she's also learned the magic of finding true happiness and peace at home.

Serene is a reconnective healing practitioner, and has studied magical and medicinal herbalism, angel therapy, reiki and many other healing modalities, as well as politics and journalism. She is the editor of the preschool magazines *Little Friends* and *Playhouse Disney*, and has worked for publications such as *Cosmopolitan*, *Dolly*, *Woman's Day*, *The Daily News* and *The West Australian* newspapers, *Hot Metal*, *Spellcraft* and *Your Destiny*.

She is the author of *Seven Sacred Sites: Magical Journeys That Will Change Your Life* and *A Magical Journey: Your Diary of Inspiration, Adventure and Transformation*, and creator of the CD *Sacred Journey: A Meditation To Connect You To the Magic of the Earth*, which includes seven meditations that take you on an inner journey, connecting you with the power of the elements and balancing the masculine and feminine energies of your heart and soul to reawaken the divine spark within you. She is also the co-author, with Lucy Cavendish, of *The Book of Faery Magic* and *The Book of Mermaid Magic*.

www.SereneConneeley.com.

"The real voyage of discovery consists
not in seeking new landscapes,
but in having new eyes."

Marcel Proust,
20th century French writer and intellectual

CPSIA information can be obtained at www.ICGtesting.com
Printed in the USA
BVOW01s0350260215

389420BV00001B/47/P